Subversive Legal History

Provocative, audacious and challenging, this book rejuvenates not only the historical study of law but also the role of Law Schools by asking which stories we tell and which stories we forget.

It argues that a historical approach to law should be at the beating heart of the Law School curriculum. Far from being archaic, elitist and dull, historical perspectives on law are and should be subversive. Comparison with the past underscores: how the law and legal institutions are not fixed but are constructed; that every line drawn in the law and everything the law holds as sacred is actually arbitrary; and how the environment into which law students are socialised is a historical construct. A subversive approach is needed to highlight, question, de-construct and re-construct the authored nature of the law, revealing that legal change on a larger scale is possible. Far from being archaic, this recasts legal history as being anarchic.

Subversive Legal History is not a type of Legal History but is its defining characteristic if it is to be central part of Law School life. It describes a legal method that should not be the preserve only of specialist legal historians but rather should be part of the toolkit of all law students, teachers and researchers.

This book will be essential reading for all who work and study in Law Schools, proposing a radical new approach not only to the historical study of law but also to the content, purpose and ambition of legal education. A subversive approach can revolutionise Law Schools providing a more ambitious legal education which is grounded in the socio-legal reality, helping to ensure that today's law students are better equipped to be the professionals and citizens of tomorrow.

Russell Sandberg is Professor of Law at Cardiff University. His research interrogates the interaction between law and the humanities with particular expertise in Law and Religion and Legal History. He co-edited the multi-volume *Law and History – Critical Concepts* (Routledge, 2017) and is co-editor of Routledge's *Transforming Legal Histories* series, which this book launches.

Transforming Legal Histories

Series Editors: Lydia Hayes, Katie Richards, Russell Sandberg, and Sharon Thompson

This series provides a home for scholarship that uses historical methods to question, analyse, challenge and therefore transform understandings of law. Books in this series are aimed at a general legal readership and include work which may not fall under a conventional understanding of legal history. They use historical methods to develop a critical understanding of legal and social change and to encourage law students and scholars to rethink their assumptions about law.

The *Transforming Legal Histories* series publishes monographs (both long and short form) and edited collections. The reach of the series is not limited in time or space, producing books that cover a wide range of jurisdictions and periods. It includes work that disturbs conventional legal narratives by paying greater attention to gender, sexuality, age, class and disability inequalities and the roles of individuals in terms of campaigning for reform and also in using law strategically. The objective is to collate world class scholarship that provides innovative and challenging ways of using history to de-construct and re-construct our understandings of law.

Titles in this series:

Subversive Legal History
A Manifesto for the Future of Legal Education
Russell Sandberg

For more information about this series, please visit: https://www.routledge.com/Transforming-Legal-Histories/book-series/LAWHISTORY

Subversive Legal History

A Manifesto for the Future of Legal Education

Russell Sandberg

Routledge
Taylor & Francis Group
LONDON AND NEW YORK

First published 2021
by Routledge
2 Park Square, Milton Park, Abingdon, Oxon OX14 4RN

and by Routledge
605 Third Avenue, New York, NY 10158

Routledge is an imprint of the Taylor & Francis Group, an informa business

British Library Cataloguing-in-Publication Data
A catalogue record for this book is available from the British Library

Library of Congress Cataloging-in-Publication Data
A catalog record has been requested for this book

ISBN: 978-0-367-19129-0 (hbk)
ISBN: 978-1-032-04441-5 (pbk)
ISBN: 978-0-429-20061-8 (ebk)

Typeset in Galliard
by codeMantra

To Emma, with love.

Contents

1 The Trouble with Law Schools

Everything law students think they know is a lie.

Law Schools are strange places.

From day one of their degrees, law students in England and Wales have a different experience compared to other students. The sources and materials they draw upon are unique. Authority is unquestionably attributed to primary legal materials: legislation and the reported decisions of senior courts. These materials are alien to outsiders. As William Twining noted of the Law Library, 'there is probably no branch of the humanities and social sciences that at first sight seems less user-friendly to the non-specialist'.[1] Moreover, the way in which law students use their materials is distinctive: their quest is not to read books from cover to cover but to consult them, more like a detective than a scholar. As Twining put it, law is 'a participant-orientated discipline': law students are constantly reminded of the practical impact of their subject and are forced to make decisions.[2]

Law Schools are dangerous places.

Throughout their degrees, law students are socialised into thinking differently. It is often asserted that law students do not study methodology, but this is nonsense. First year law modules induct students into legal method: how to interpret and use legal doctrine. The study of doctrine quickly becomes a form of indoctrination. Law students learn not only how to use but also how to respect authority and how to operate within the world of law. Students are trained that their role is to systematically present and apply the law. Their role is also to critique the law but, crucially, this is only within law's own terms. As Lord Goff noted extra-judicially:

> The prime task of the jurist is to take the cases and statutes which provide the raw material of the law on any particular topic and by a critical re-appraisal of that raw material, to build up a systematic statement of the law on the relevant topic in a coherent form, often combined with proposals of how the law can be beneficially developed in the future.[3]

1 William Twining, *Blackstone's Tower: The English Law School* (Sweet & Maxwell, 1994) 195.

2 Ibid 130.

3 Lord Goff of Chieveley, 'Judge, Jurist and Legislature' (1987) 2(1) *Denning Law Journal* 79, 92.

Law students are taught to 'think like lawyers' and employ reasoning and interpretative skills that are different from elsewhere in the academy. This does not mean that these are less demanding skills. Systematising the law involves sophisticated interpretative tools and critical techniques employed to evaluate the coherence of legal discourse and proposed legal change.[4] Yet, as Anthony Bradney has argued, doctrinal legal study (defined as 'attempt to explain law solely through the internal evidence' provided by primary legal sources) leads law students not only to 'assimilate' but also to 'accept the values of the community that they are studying'.[5] At first, these ways of seeing are 'at odds with what law students have previously experienced and continue to experience outside their studies'. However, throughout the law degree what was once odd becomes normalised. And certain questions and ways of looking become excluded from the law student's gaze. As Bradney put it:

> doctrinal study explicitly identifies questions outside the doctrinal range as being something not relevant for the doctrinal student. It implicitly devalues such questions and treats them as not being worthy of consideration within the precise, objective word of the law school.

As the US scholar Robin L West pointed out, the argument 'is not that law schools instil an overly acquiescent attitude toward existing law – far from it'.[6] Rather, the argument is that 'law students and lawyers are trained to identify certain kinds of problems'. They are taught to spot gaps in the law rather than looking at the issue 'on a systematic or structural basis'. Law students are not 'taught to think in a proactive way about problems of social justice and whether law might be part of their solution'.[7] West noted that 'legalism', 'the moral way of being into which students are accultured while in law school', led 'to the common complaint that law school renders law graduates amoral'.[8] Bradney has gone as far as to say that in order to 'become a law student the student must forget who he or she is'.[9]

4 Douglas W Vick, 'Interdisciplinarity and the Discipline of Law' (2004) 31(2) *Journal of Law and Society* 163, 179.
5 Anthony Bradney, 'Law as a Parasitic Discipline' (1998) 25(1) *Journal of Law and Society* 71, 79, 73, 76.
6 Robin L West, *Teaching Law: Justice, Politics and the Demands of Professionalism* (Cambridge University Press, 2014) 114.
7 Ibid 115.
8 Ibid 64. For a classic statement (also in a US context) see Duncan Kennedy's pamphlet 'Legal Education and the Reproduction of Hierarchy: A Polemic against the System', first self-published in 1983 but republished with critical commentaries: Duncan Kennedy, *Legal Education and the Reproduction of Hierarchy: A Polemic against the System* (New York University Press, 2004).
9 Anthony Bradney, 'Law as a Parasitic Discipline' (1998) 25(1) *Journal of Law and Society* 71, 77.

The content of a law degree is more consistent between universities than the content of other humanities or social science degrees.[10] The main modules studied are invariably uniform: the core modules present the common law, focusing on the law of obligations, property and public law; there are then a number of optional but now well established modules that have much more specific focuses, dealing with areas that are perhaps more recognisable to the non-lawyer or in practice such as family law, employment law and commercial law; and finally there are the more idiosyncratic modules, which take a variety of forms – some theoretical, some comparative, some with non-legal components, some with a clinical or legal practice focus – and which, although they are far more common than they once were, nevertheless remain exceptional. A law degree without tort, trusts or contract is unheard of. And even the content of such modules is remarkably similar, thanks to the tyranny of the textbook tradition.

For each of the main modules (core and optional) on a law degree there are shelves after shelves full of textbooks, all with similar if not identical contents. These justify and perpetuate the content of the law degree. The focus is typically on the doctrinal exposition of legal rules.[11] As Rosemary Auchmuty has noted, 'most of us are content if, by the end of the module, our students can apply the correct law to the facts of a problem question and give competent advice'.[12] And this doctrinal exposition of rules is more often than not presented as an objective fact. It is forgotten that it is actually an interpretation. The law degree as a whole and the modules that make it up provide a story of the law: a story about the role, nature and place of law. The textbook tradition conceals this. This means that the law student does not ask what or whose story is being told. The assumptions, presumptions and biases in the story are not acknowledged, let alone questioned. It is not appreciated that law's story is authored, subjective and contestable. The stories of law are presented in a linear and straightforward manner. The textbooks are full of progress narratives whereby the law has come to the rescue, has rationalised itself and has found the answer. The story is invariably how the law, though not perfect, has improved and that further improvements along the same course are desirable.

The authors of the story of the common law are invariably white, male, conservative and middle class. They systematise the law from that vantage point, with their own expectations and own values. These set the standards, the criteria

10 For a historical discussion see Susanna Menis, 'The Liberal, the Vocational and Legal Education: A Legal History Review – From Blackstone to a Law Degree (1972)' (2019) 54(2) *The Law Teacher* 285.

11 There are exceptions, most notably the Law in Context series published by Cambridge University Press. However, these are mostly used as a supplement to the doctrinal texts and vary to the extent to which they include non-doctrinal perspectives. They typically adopt a socio-legal approach rather than a historical one but for a notable exception see Alan Norrie, *Crime, Reason and History: A Critical Introduction to Criminal Law* (3rd ed, Cambridge University Press, 2014).

12 Rosemary Auchmuty, 'Land Law and Equity and Trusts' in Caroline Hunter (ed) *Integrating Socio-Legal Studies into the Law Curriculum* (Palgrave, 2012) 69.

against which the progress of law is measured. More so than most other academic disciplines, law is shaped by the culture and expectations of practice and of a legal profession that predominately shares certain cultural values.[13] Although most Law Schools can be found geographically within university campuses, the cultural and political influence of the legal profession is significant. Many law students apply to Law School with the intention of entering the legal profession, though far fewer actually do so. The requirements of regulatory bodies shape not only the content of the law degree but also how it is taught.[14] While it is true that Higher Education in general does not serve as an apprenticeship for becoming an academic, it is arguable that law students are taught to think more like lawyers than like scholars as shown, for example, by the significance attached to problem questions in assessments.

Law Schools continue to be torn between being vocational and academic.[15] Their location within the University has meant that Law Schools have been subjected to the same expectations as other parts of the University. Increasing general pressures facing universities have pushed Law Schools in a number of competing, often contradictory, directions.[16] Escalating tuition fees have led to Higher Education being seen as a market with students as consumers with expectations of individual consumption of content on demand.[17] At the same time the scholarly pursuit of knowledge has been reduced to the need to show evidence of quantifiable outputs and results with overriding emphasis being placed upon the impact of research as the manifestation of its worth. However, the Research Excellence Framework and its predecessors, for all their bureaucratic and other ills, have led to an increased focus on and sophistication of research in Law Schools.[18] Research has become more central to Law Schools

13 See Fiona Westwood and Karen Barton (eds) *The Calling of Law: The Pivotal Role of Vocational Legal Education* (Ashgate, 2014).

14 For a discussion of the influence of other regulatory bodies besides the legal professions see Anthony Bradney, 'Who Controls University Legal Education? The Case of England and Wales' in Ben Golder, Marina Nehme, Alex Steel and Prue Vines (eds) *Imperatives for Legal Education Research: Then, Now and Tomorrow* (Routledge, 2020) 143.

15 See, generally, Anthony Bradney, *Conversation, Choices and Chances: The Liberal Law School in the Twenty-First Century* (Hart, 2003). Though it is also worth noting that universities have generally moved towards being more vocational: Margaret Thornton, 'The Demise of Diversity in Legal Education: Globalisation and the New Knowledge Economy' (2001) 8 *International Journal of the Legal Profession* 37, 43.

16 There is a significant literature on the nature and place of Law Schools, most notably in the pages of *The Law Teacher* and in the Lord Upjohn Lectures (on which see the essays in Chris Ashford, Nigel Duncan and Jessica Guth (eds) *Perspectives on Legal Education: Contemporary Responses to the Lord Upjohn Lectures* (Routledge, 2016)). A pivotal publication was Peter Birks (ed) *Pressing Problems in the Law, Volume 2: What Are Law Schools For?* (Oxford University Press, 1996).

17 William Twining has conceded that the acceleration of the pace of change in terms of legal services and technology has been underestimated: William Twining, 'Rethinking Legal Education' (2018) 52 *The Law Teacher* 241, 250.

18 On how Law Schools have become more like corporations, see: Richard Collier, 'The Liberal Law School, the Restructured University and the Paradox of Socio-Legal Studies' (2005) 68 *Modern Law Review* 475.

in the twenty-first century. Law academics are now more likely to possess a PhD than to come from a career in practice.

This has stoked further the tension at the heart of Law Schools in England and Wales.[19] While the doctrinal mindset largely prevails in Law School teaching, the same is perhaps no longer true in relation to legal research.[20] In 1998, Bradney asserted that in research terms the doctrinal project that has historically dominated Law Schools was 'entering its final death throes' and that 'few serious scholars of law under forty [were] now attempting such work on any significant scale except as a student exercise for a doctoral dissertation'.[21] There has been a significant increase in the use of insights, theories and methods from other disciplines. Bradney provocatively alleged that this 'new spirit' has meant that Law should be seen as a 'parasitic discipline': law is no longer a unique and self-contained discipline but rather 'parasitic in large part on work started elsewhere in the university'.[22] However, it is worth noting that for Bradney, this change is not a *volte face* but rather a new stage in an evolutionary process of Law Schools.[23] Legal academics have realised that the doctrinal approach alone is not sufficient. Even in trying to understand the narrowest of legal rules, doctrinal lawyers have constantly felt it necessary to ask questions which could not be answered by their own methodology. While in the past the doctrinal lawyer sought to deal with these questions by 'mere anecdote, hearsay, and assertion', it is now recognised that it is unacceptable to deal with any material or any question with anything less than full attention. It is likely that Bradney has overstated the extent of this change, but he was correct about the general direction. As Fiona Cownie's empirical research showed, insights from other disciplines are being used alongside (rather than instead of) doctrinal analysis. Only half of her respondents described themselves as taking solely a socio-legal or Critical Legal Studies approach.[24] Indeed, 'several of the respondents stressed that in order to

19 The situation in England and Wales differs from other jurisdictions. Markus D Dubber noted that 'the US trend is all about the rediscovery of law as the subject of legal scholarship and of [doctrinal work] as a respectable, even important way of going about the academic study of law' given the 'now decades-long interdisciplinary orthodoxy'. By contrast, 'in the civil law world, the move has been away from legal doctrine, not towards it. Interdisciplinary is the name of the game': Markus D Dubber, 'Legal History as Legal Scholarship: Doctrinalism, Interdisciplinary and Critical Analysis of Law' in Markus D Dubber and Christopher Tomlins (eds) *The Oxford Handbook of Legal History* (Oxford University Press, 2018) 99, 100. Given these marked differences, this book focuses upon the situation in England and Wales.

20 See the 25th Lord Upjohn Lecture in 1996, now published as Dawn Oliver QC, 'The Integration of Teaching and Research in the Law Department' in Chris Ashford, Nigel Duncan and Jessica Guth (eds) *Perspectives on Legal Education: Contemporary Responses to the Lord Upjohn Lectures* (Routledge, 2016) 228 and the response Jessica Gath, 'Fostering Curiosity: The Importance of Research and Teaching in Law Schools' in ibid 240.

21 Anthony Bradney, 'Law as a Parasitic Discipline' (1998) 25(1) *Journal of Law and Society* 71.

22 Ibid 73.

23 Ibid 72.

24 Fiona Cownie, *Legal Academics: Culture and Identities* (Hart, 2004) 54.

be a good socio-legal lawyer, it is imperative to have a good grasp of the law'.[25] In legal research, doctrinal work is now often infused with rather than replaced by other techniques.

Yet, this infusion has not been felt throughout the Law School's activities. The use of non-doctrinal methodologies is mostly visible in relation to research and to a lesser extent in terms of some forms of teaching, such as at postgraduate level and to an extent through optional undergraduate modules.[26] Yet, overall, the Law School continues to be torn in two directions. This can lead to tension. Doctrinal legal scholarship has been criticised as being inconsequential and 'not true scholarship'.[27] Perhaps the strongest critique came from Pierre Schlag who asserted that legal scholarship was 'dead' on the basis that it was 'just not the sort of thing that requires or permits the display of great intellectual prowess' and was 'fundamentally uninteresting', having 'no great texts, no sophisticated methodologies, no great questions, and nothing else of any fundamental intellectual value'.[28] Doctrinal legal scholarship has been criticised for being 'nothing but sycophancy – academics pleading for nods of approval from father-figure judges'.[29] And, on the other hand, interdisciplinary work in Law Schools has been criticised either for not being sufficiently grounded in the other disciplinary approach that it claims to follow or for losing its connection to law: 'although it might be scholarship, it is not *legal* scholarship'.[30] This tension is felt by individual legal scholars. The increasingly interdisciplinary research conducted by law academics sits uncomfortably with their perceived teaching role in preparing their students for legal practice. The dominant approach in Law School teaching is anti-interdisciplinary at heart. As Rosemary Auchmuty noted, the textbook is 'the authority in many of our classrooms' and the textbook tradition focuses on the doctrinal 'exposition of current principles and authorities' which furthers the assumption that 'law, as a discipline, has traditionally recognized no sources but its own'.[31] Law Schools are increasingly characterised by a plurality of approaches, presumptions and values which at first glimpse often appear to be contradictory.

25 Ibid 55.

26 This is particularly true of clinical work and classroom activities encourage law students to analyse at both micro and macro levels, scrutinising real world texts within their real world context. On which see the essays in Linden Thomas, Steven Vaughan, Bharat Malkani and Theresa Lynch (eds) *Reimagining Clinical Legal Education* (Hart, 2018).

27 Robin L West, *Teaching Law: Justice, Politics and the Demands of Professionalism* (Cambridge University Press, 2014) 194.

28 Pierre Schlag, 'Spam Jurisprudence, Air Law, and the Rank Anxiety of Nothing Happening (A Report on the State of the Art)' (2009) 97 *Georgetown Law Journal* 803, 804, 809, 807, 812. He noted that 'even interdisciplinary scholarship typically submits to this legalist form': ibid 813.

29 Robin L West, *Teaching Law: Justice, Politics and the Demands of Professionalism* (Cambridge University Press, 2014) 194.

30 Ibid 195. To put it another way, such scholarship is 'law-lite': Russell Sandberg, *Religion, Law and Society* (Cambridge University Press, 2014) 257.

31 Rosemary Auchmuty, 'Land Law and Equity and Trusts' in Caroline Hunter (ed) *Integrating Socio-Legal Studies into the Law Curriculum* (Palgrave, 2012) 69, 77, 74, 75.

This is all complicated further by the sheer number of disciplinary perspectives that can be applied to law. The number of potential bedfellows can feel overwhelming. As Mathias Siems and Daithí Mac Síthigh have argued, legal scholars in the UK are faced by a choice as to 'whether to "go American" in moving closer to social sciences, or "go German" in remaining closer to the humanities'.[32] The continued existence of these two options is reflected by the way in which funding for legal research projects is available from both the Arts & Humanities Research Council (AHRC) and the Economic and Social Research Council (ESRC). However, although work is done in both directions (with a burgeoning focus on Law and Literature and the textual analysis of law in the humanities camp), it is social science research which has been the most prevalent. Talk of interdisciplinary research in law or use of the terms 'law in context' or 'socio-legal'[33] is usually synonymous with the employment of ideas and methods employed in the social sciences.[34]

Yet, the purpose of this book is to argue the need for and the benefits of a different disciplinary approach: history. However, it will be contended that this requires a different approach to Legal History than that which has been previously prevalent in Law Schools in England and Wales. A historical approach to law can and must be subversive. A historical approach can highlight and correct the indoctrination that doctrinal legal study perpetuates. It can question the story of law that law students are socialised into. A subversive historical approach can reveal the authors, assumptions and values of the common law and the role that orthodox legal education currently plays in indoctrinating law students in a way that limits their questioning powers. This book will argue that a subversive historical approach needs to be at the beating heart of Law School activity, not just in research but also embedded in teaching. A subversive approach can revolutionise Law Schools, providing a more ambitious legal education which is grounded in the socio-legal reality, helping to ensure that today's law students are better equipped to be the professionals and citizens of tomorrow.

The remainder of this introductory chapter will fall into three sections. The first will explore the paradoxical place of history in Law Schools. The second will

32 Mathias M Siems and Daithí Mac Síthigh, 'Mapping Legal Research' [2012] *Cambridge Law Journal* 651, 673.

33 The distinction drawn by CM Campbell and Paul Wiles between socio-legal studies as the empirical study of the 'actual operation of law and its effects upon people' and the sociology of law as a theoretical 'understanding of the nature of social order through a study of law' no longer holds weight (C M Campbell and Paul Wiles, 'The Study of Law in Society in Britain' (1976) 10 *Law and Society Review* 553). See: RezaBanakar, *Merging Law and Sociology: Beyond the Dichotomies in Socio-Legal Research* (Galda Wilch 2003) 14–15.

34 The Nuffield Inquiry on Empirical Legal Research (*Law in the Real World, Improving Our Understanding of How Law Works* (Nuffield, 2006) pointed to the dearth of empirical and indeed non-doctrinal methods in Law Schools. See also the essays in Caroline Hunter (ed) *Integrating Socio-Legal Studies into the Law Curriculum* (Palgrave, 2012), Dermot Feenan (ed) *Exploring the 'Socio' of Socio-Legal Studies* (Palgrave, 2013) and as means of response, David Cowan and Daniel Wincott (eds) *Exploring the 'Legal' in Socio-Legal Studies* (Palgrave, 2016).

propose seven reasons why a historical approach to law is necessary and desirable. The third and final section will introduce the chapters that follow which will make the argument for a 'Subversive Legal History'.

The End of Legal History

In English and Welsh Law Schools, Legal History is paradoxically both everywhere and nowhere.

On the one hand, Legal History is everywhere. The study of the past is unavoidable in a common law system based on precedent. Doctrinal legal study is always a historical study. Every law lecture which reviews a case law is an exercise in historical analysis looking at how law has changed over time. It is rare that a legal development is genuinely new and even where it is, a historical perspective will show how it became considered to be necessary for that gap in the law to be filled.

Yet, Legal History is also nowhere. In the vast majority of lecture halls and tutorial classrooms cases are presented as authorities that exist in a historical vacuum. They are presented chronologically but without any attempt to understand the case within its time. The purpose is to understand what the law is today. Historical method and context are both overlooked. While placing law into its social and political context has become more commonplace within Law Schools, history is often conspicuous by its absence.[35] Modules devoted to particular areas of law tend to include little or no historical material.[36] They do not explain the historical trajectory of areas of law or key legal ideas but rather focus on the law as it currently stands, looking at materials from the past only in so far as they are part of the modern law and without placing such provisions within their historical context. Rosemary Auchmuty has noted that even where law textbooks do include history it 'is confined to an early chapter and largely ignored thereafter'.[37] Moreover, such accounts are 'for the most part, antiquated, self-justifying, uncritical and partial'.[38] As Robert W Gordon has written:

35 Even in the early 1990s it was noted that 'history is becoming less and less significant in accounts of the legal system': Raymond Cocks, 'History in Eclipse? The Role of the Past in Books on the English Legal System' in Peter Birks (ed) *The Life of the Law* (Hambledon Press, 1993) 257.

36 As Philip Handler has noted, 'those trained as lawyers … may have had only a limited exposure to the study of legal history. The subject does not occupy a central place in the English Law school curriculum': Philip Handler, 'Legal History' in Dawn Watkins and Mandy Burton (eds) *Research Methods in Law* (2nd ed, Routledge, 2018) 103.

37 She noted that where a historical background is provided, 'the version we have in most textbooks – the history of ruling-class men without controversy, nuance, or anything after the late nineteenth century hardly fits the bill': Rosemary Auchmuty, 'Land Law and Equity and Trusts' in Caroline Hunter (ed) *Integrating Socio-Legal Studies into the Law Curriculum* (Palgrave, 2012) 69, 74, 75.

38 Rosemary Auchmuty and Erika Rackley, 'Feminist Legal Biography: A Model for *All* Legal Life Stories' (2020) 41(2) *Journal of Legal History* 186, 192.

> Lawyers and historians have always cohabited in a relationship of intimate antagonism. Lawyers have always needed history, appealed to it for authority, and made significant contributions to writing it. They have also persistently been accused … of abusing history, distorting the past, and making demands upon it to carry burdens of current relevance that it cannot possibly sustain.[39]

Moreover, as Gordon noted, history is usually invoked 'for conservative rather than reactionary purposes': 'The legal enterprise is usually committed to stabilizing present advantages and expectations – or at most to encouraging incremental reforms – rather than to rolling back to the past in a way that would require radical undoings of the present dispensation'.[40] In short, the type of history that is ubiquitous in Law Schools is not really history at all.[41] It is 'bad history'.[42]

History in its fuller sense is therefore largely absent from the Law School curriculum. The experience of most law students studying modules on constitutional law, contract law, land law and so on can be described by using a novel analogy. The law student's experience is like that of a reader who is reading in isolation a chapter somewhere towards the end of a novel. By focusing on that one chapter, the reader has little if no grasp of the story so far, the extent to which the current chapter moves that story on or what is likely to come next. The same experience is true of students studying most law modules. They become experts on a very small part of the story and have little insight as to how the story has previously developed and its future likely trajectory. Indeed, they are unlikely to appreciate that it is a story, that the current system came from somewhere, that there was a time when things were done differently. Reading previous chapters would not necessarily show a linear movement towards progress. When read in detail, chapters in the historical development of areas of law (like chapters in a novel) often do not advance the plot directly but rather complicate or reverse plot points. Indeed, this is why starting with the later chapter and then looking back often leads to bad history. The benefit of hindsight colours the interpretation and makes a journey which was complicated and unintended look

39 Robert W Gordon, 'The Past as Authority and as Social Critic: Stabilizing and Destabilizing Functions of History in Legal Argument' in Terrence J McDonald (ed) *The Historic Turn in the Human Sciences* (University of Michigan Press, 1996) 339.

40 ibid 340.

41 This is the form of history described by Robert W Gordon as being 'not of the work of professional legal historians but of the background assumptions about law-in-history that are present in mainstream legal scholarship generally': Robert W Gordon, *Taming the Past: Essays on Law in History and History in Law* (Cambridge University Press, 2017) 223.

42 The label 'historicism' is sometimes used to refer to this common but often shallow popular misuse of history. However, this label will not be used in this book because the term is used in a number of divergent ways: Raymond Williams, *Keywords: A Vocabulary of Culture and Society* (revised edition, Fontana Press, 1983) 147.

straightforward and deliberate. But focusing solely upon a later chapter without even glancing backwards is worse still: it gives the reader no understanding of the chapters yet to come and of earlier plot points that may become significant once more. It limits the frame of analysis.

It is true, of course, that there remain bespoke modules in Law Schools on Legal History or the historical development of particular areas of law.[43] However, these modules typically exist only as an optional module on law degrees if at all and such modules are less common than they once were.[44] They also perpetuate the idea that historical study is something separate, the preserve of experts and not part of legal education generally. Moreover, not only are such modules declining but they are themselves getting increasingly specialised. Historical modules in Law Schools increasingly focus on particular parts of the story. The 'traditional' study of the history of the common law is out of fashion in twenty-first century Law Schools. It is true that there remains a rich body of Legal History scholarship with specialist journals and societies and a number of prolific figures. However, Legal History has become inaccessible to newcomers. Though much continues to be published in the field through specialist monographs and journals, little is aimed at a non-specialist readership or designed to be student-friendly.

There is also a feeling that Legal History has become rather stale as a field of study. The field has become a ghetto: works are largely written for other legal historians rather than experts, let alone students in particular areas of law who are interested in the historical development of their particular specialism. The ghost of Frederic W Maitland – the leading nineteenth century legal historian who is often regarded as the founder of modern Legal History – continues to rule the discipline: his 'lifetime's worth of seemingly miraculous writing' has resulted in a 'superhuman myth engulfing him',[45] and the perpetuation of a tradition

43 There is a comparatively large literature on the history of international law, for instance. See, for example, the essays in Bardo Fassbender and Anne Peters (eds) *The Oxford Handbook of the History of International Law* (Oxford University Press, 2012) and the articles published in the *Journal of the History of International Law*.

44 This is not true of other jurisdictions. For instance, the wealth and variety of Legal History in the US is shown by the essays in Robert M Jarvis (ed) *Teaching Legal History: Comparative Perspectives* (Wildy, Simmonds and Hill, 2014) in which the members of the American academy of legal historians reflect upon their teaching.

45 S F C Milsom, 'Maitland' (2001) 60(2) *Cambridge Law Journal* 265. This was underlined by S F C Milsom's introduction to the reissued second edition of the legendary 'Pollock and Maitland' which began by noting that Maitland 'would have been saddened by this re-issue of his book, and not only by the inadequacy of an introductory essay that is the sole addition of what last left his hands just seventy years ago. He felt sorry for those whose work became classical: it meant that vitality had been lost from the enterprise they had loved'. The introduction similarly concluded: 'Maitland himself would probably wish his work to be superseded. There is little sign that this will happen soon': S F C Milsom, 'Introduction' in Frederick Pollock and Frederic W Maitland, *The History of English Law* (2nd ed, Cambridge University Press, 1968) xxiii, lxxiii.

of doctrinal Legal History scholarship.[46] Historians of the common law still begin their study through the eyes of Maitland: 'Their questions still take the form: was Maitland right?'[47] The student texts on English Legal History remain those first written fifty years ago by Cambridge dons in Maitland's shadow.[48] Although such works are, of course, outstanding and deserve to be read by successive generations, it may be questioned where the new works are; critiquing and developing old orthodoxies, revisiting old debates and introducing the field to new readerships. It is true that a significant amount of historical research on law is done,[49] but much of this is either done outside Law Schools, or by legal academics who would not identify themselves as legal historians. Legal History has an image and reputation problem. It is difficult to disagree with Daniel Siemens' assessment that 'one gets the impression that legal history is slowly and inevitably dying—or that it has been in a coma for the last 30 years, at least'.[50]

The Importance of Legal History

The comatose state of Legal History in England and Wales is to be regretted.

The study of Legal History is not simply the study of out of date law that law students are usually advised to avoid. It is, rather, the study of the complex trajectory of law, the elucidation and questioning of the story of the common law. Aside from the benefits and pleasures of historical study for its own sake, what Frederic Maitland referred to as the subject's 'thrilling interest',[51] there are seven (overlapping) reasons why the study of Legal History is important.

First, as the novel analogy discussed above suggests, a historical approach is needed to understand today's substantive law in its context. Robin L West lists Legal History courses as one of 'a range of interdisciplinary offerings [which]

46 David Sugarman, 'Promoting Dialogue between History and Socio-Legal Studies: The Contribution of Christopher W Brooks and the "Legal Turn" in Early Modern English History' (2017) 41(S1) *Journal of Law and Society* S37, S38.

47 S F C Milsom, 'Introduction' in Frederick Pollock and Frederic W Maitland, *The History of English Law* (2nd ed, Volume 1, Cambridge University Press, 1968) xxiii, ixxi, xxiv.

48 Milsom's *Historical Foundations of the Common Law* was first published in 1969. The most recent edition is S F C Milsom, *Historical Foundations of the Common Law* (2nd ed, Butterworths, 1981). Baker's overly modestly titled *An Introduction to English Legal History* was first published in 1971. The most recent edition is John H Baker, *An Introduction to English Legal History* (5th ed, Butterworths, 2019). More recent scholarship has, however, explored modern Legal History: see William Cornish *et al.*, *Law and Society in England 1750–1950* (2nd ed, Hart 2019) and Ian Ward, *English Legal Histories* (Hart 2020).

49 A significant amount of work on legal topics is being done in History Departments and Legal History is flourishing in other jurisdictions. This is true, for instance, of Scottish Law Schools.

50 Daniel Siemens, 'Towards a New Cultural History of Law' (2012) 2 *InterDisciplines* 18, 19.

51 FW Maitland, 'Maitland to AV Dicey, c. July 1896' quoted in C H S Fifoot, *Frederic William Maitland* (Harvard University Press, 1971) 143.

invite the student to think about law in some larger context' alongside Law and Culture and Law and Humanities modules.[52] As John McLaren has put it:

> knowledge of the development of law, legal institutions and legal ideology in the context of political, social and economic forces is essential to an understanding of legal culture (especially one's own), and that historical understanding increasingly provides the context in which lawyers are called upon to apply their intellectual talents and skills to live problems.[53]

Grasp of history allows us to understand where we are going by showing us where we have come from. This should not be about instilling a linear narrative of progress. And it is about method as well as content. Appreciation of history encourages critical and contextual thinking developing 'the ability to understand and evaluate the historical, social, and economic forces that, in one way or another, helped shape a particular result'.[54] In the words of Jim Phillips, Legal History teaches 'law students not only analytical skills and substantive knowledge, but also a deeper understanding of the nature of law'.[55]

Second, Legal History is an exercise in comparative law. Comparative law is the study of the similarities and differences between two or more jurisdictions which enables the jurist 'to broaden his field of research and to increase the knowledge of the foundations of his own legal system'.[56] While comparative law traditionally does this by exploring different legal systems across space, Legal History does it across time.[57] Insisting on Legal History as being comparative is distinct from the argument as to the value of comparative Legal History: that is, the historical comparison of more than one jurisdiction.[58] Insisting on Legal History as being a form of comparative law means recognising that it uses the past to highlight the nature and form of the current law and to critique it by showing that other ways of doing things have been possible. This not only means seeing the past as something that can be learnt from but also seeing the

52 Robin L West, *Teaching Law: Justice, Politics and the Demands of Professionalism* (Cambridge University Press, 2014) 191.

53 John McLaren 'The Legal Historian, Masochist or Missionary? A Canadian's Reflection' (1994) 5 *Legal Education Review* 67.

54 Robert M Jarvis, Phyllis G Coleman and Gail L Richmond, 'Contextual Thinking: Why Law Students (and Lawyers) Need to Know History' (1995–1996) 42 *Wayne Law Review* 1603.

55 Jim Phillips, 'Why Legal History Matters' (2010) 41 *Victoria University of Wellington Law Review* 293, 294.

56 Geoffrey Samuel, *An Introduction to Comparative Law Theory and Method* (Hart, 2014) 8, citing Ronald Drago, 'Droit Compare' in Dennis Alland and Stephanie Rials (eds) *Dictionnaire de la Culture Juridique* (Presses Universitaires de France, 2003) 45.

57 For an application and discussion of this, see John H Baker, *English Law under Two Elizabeths: The Late Tudor Legal World and the Present* (Cambridge University Press, 2021).

58 On which see David Ibbetson, 'The Challenges of Comparative Legal History' (2013) 1(1) *Comparative Legal History* 1 and subsequent articles in that journal.

past as being different.[59] To quote LP Hartley, it is about remembering that 'the past is a foreign country: they do things differently there'.[60] This requires us to consider the past in its own terms and to become immersed in the past to such an extent that this 'forces us to probe our beliefs, compare them to the features we encounter elsewhere, and expose our assumptions to scrutiny and evaluation'.[61] A historical approach, therefore, unlocks 'the recognition of the cultural relativity of the law and its institutions'.[62]

Third, placing law into its context underlines that law is contingent not fixed. As Phillips notes, Legal History shows that law 'is not a set of abstract ahistorical and universal principles'.[63] A historical approach shows how law changes and how the actual changes that occur are not inevitable. It can show that similar experiences have occurred in the past. A historical approach can reveal precedents to current legal problems which are often presented as being new and unique. For example, a historical approach underlines that notions of legal pluralism (the notion that 'it is normal for more than one "legal" system to co-exist in the same social arena'[64]) are not new; indeed, the fact that the medieval period was characterised by a 'radical state of legal pluralism' reveals that it is state centralist notions (the notion that only state law is law) that are novel.[65] The study of Legal History therefore challenges the way in which every generation thinks that the challenges they face are unique. It overcomes the danger of presentism. Jonathan Clarke defined presentism as 'a privileging of the present' and wrote that 'presentism in popular culture involves the reversion to a more restricted mental world' whereby the phrase 'that's old' no longer means 'that originated some time ago' but means 'that is vexatious' and 'that's history no longer means that is important because it has made us what we are' but means 'that is laughably irrelevant to us'.[66] Legal History, by showing how the law is a historical construction, highlights the importance of understanding that construction as we seek to re-construct the law in the light of new challenges.

Fourth, Legal History highlights the necessity of legal change. It teaches us that the current law is not perfect and is not necessarily the finished product. The way in which legal actors have grappled with problems over time in different

59 Jonathan Rose, 'Studying the Past: The Nature and Development of Legal History as an Academic Discipline' (2010) 31(2) *The Journal of Legal History* 101, 101–102.

60 L P Hartley, *The Go-Between* (Penguin, 2004) 5.

61 Jeremy Webber 'The Past and Foreign Countries' (2006) 10 *Legal History* 1.

62 John McLaren 'The Legal Historian, Masochist or Missionary? A Canadian's Reflection' (1994) 5 *Legal Education Review* 67, 74.

63 Jim Phillips, 'Why Legal History Matters' (2010) 41 *Victoria University of Wellington Law Review* 293, 295.

64 Brian Z Tamanaha, *A General Jurisprudence of Law and Society* (Oxford University Press, 2001) 171.

65 Ibid 180, citing Harold J Berman, *Law and Revolution: The Formation of the Western Legal Tradition* (Harvard University Press, 1983) and Walter Ullmann, *The Medieval Idea of Law* (Barnes & Noble, 1969).

66 Jonathan Clark, *Our Shadowed Present* (Atlantic Books, 2003) 2, 7.

social conditions shows the pragmatic and therefore ultimately unpolished nature of Law. As John McLaren put it, Legal History 'provides a valuable antidote to the arrogant belief that we are likely to produce a legal regime of innate comprehensibility, completeness, intellectual perfection and practical attractiveness'.[67] More optimistically it also shows that the legal landscape is not predetermined and that significant amounts of legal change can occur. The study of the current law in isolation tends to suggest that only modest legal change can occur within the confines of the system. Yet, a historical approach shows that the system itself is not universal and modest incremental development of the status quo is not the only option. Legal change is possible on a greater scale than what is often imagined possible. Frederic Maitland expressed this well in a letter:

> The only direct utility of legal history … lies in the lesson that each generation has an enormous power of shaping its own law. I don't think that the study of legal history would make men fatalists; I doubt that it would make them conservatives. I am sure that it would free them from superstitions and teach them that they have free hands.[68]

Fifth, in addition to revealing the potential for legal change, a historical approach enables an understanding of the nature of legal change. As Alan Watson has argued, historical approaches can provide a 'way to measure the speed – or absence thereof – of a response to changed circumstances'.[69] The historian is concerned with the complex relationship between change and continuity; how paradoxically everything changes while everything remains the same. This should include understanding of 'why a legal change did not occur when society changed', something which is often ignored by legal historians who 'tend to concentrate on change and innovation'.[70] Historical viewpoints can therefore aid understandings of social and legal changes and can critique generalisations that occur within the legal literature. Historical perspectives and methods can question linear simplifications that reduce legal and social change to straightforward sequences of cause and effect and that overplay the intentional evolution of legal and social change, ignoring how every cause arose in instances where a range of choices were possible.[71] History presented in all its complexity can question the tales of progress told by 'bad' history where, as Rosemary Auchmuty put it, 'there is always a sense in that law is essentially benevolent and will get there in the end'.[72] A historical approach showing the ebbs and flows of legal change can be used to question simplistic and misleading narratives of progress.

67 John McLaren 'The Legal Historian, Masochist or Missionary? A Canadian's Reflection' (1994) 5 *Legal Education Review* 67, 83.

68 Frederic W Maitland, 'Maitland to AV Dicey, c. July 1896' quoted in C H S Fifoot, *Frederic William Maitland* (Harvard University Press, 1971) 143.

69 Alan Watson, *Legal Origins and Legal Change* (Hambledon Press, 1991) 72.

70 Ibid 70–71.

71 For discussion of this see, e.g., E H Carr, *What Is History?* (Palgrave, 1961) chapter IV; Richard J Evans, *In Defence of History* (Granta, 1997) chapter 5.

72 Rosemary Auchmuty, 'Land Law and Equity and Trusts' in Caroline Hunter (ed) *Integrating Socio-Legal Studies into the Law Curriculum* (Palgrave, 2012) 69, 76.

Sixth, a historical approach questions the relationship between the legal and the social. It raises the question of the extent to which legal change is the product of internal developments within the legal system or of external social and political influences. A historical approach provides a concrete way to study ways in which law is separate from but related to other social institutions and societal norms and values. As John McLaren observed, a historical approach allows legal change to be understood 'in a way which is sensitive not only to doctrinal and institutional development' but also recognises 'the political, social and economic forces which have shaped or affected the law, and what that may suggest about the relationship between legal development and those influences in our own era'.[73] A historical approach can be used to critique the claim that law is entirely autonomous (a game of chess played in a vacuum) while recognising that legal institutions and actors are distinct and that law has its own discourse.[74] Legal History therefore has much to contribute to questions in jurisprudence concerning how law should be defined and distinguished from other forms of social control.[75] It also sheds light on questions in the sociology of law concerning the nature of law and the importance of human agency.[76] As Rosemary Auchmuty has pointed out, a historical approach can highlight 'the power struggles, the opposition to reform and the agency of those campaigners who ultimately succeeded, or not'.[77] It can therefore correct the way that 'students are led to believe that the law has evolved through internal reform rather than as a result of radical movements'.[78]

Seventh, these reasons for the importance of a historical approach to law cumulatively suggest that a historical approach serves as a critique. As Rowan Williams has commented:

> good history makes us think again about the definition of things we thought we understood pretty well, because it engages not just with what is familiar but with what is strange.[79]

73 John McLaren 'The Legal Historian, Masochist or Missionary? A Canadian's Reflection' (1994) 5 *Legal Education Review* 67, 87.

74 The autonomy and completeness of the law can be seen as 'a central – perhaps the central – jurisprudential commitment to legalism': Robin L West, *Teaching Law: Justice, Politics and the Demands of Professionalism* (Cambridge University Press, 2014) 67.

75 Recent years have seen renewed interest in the relationship between Legal History and legal theory. See Chloë Kennedy, 'Immanence and Transcendence: History's Roles in Normative Legal Theory' (2017) 8(3) *Jurisprudence* 557 and the essays in Maksymilian Del Mar and Michael Lobban (eds) *Legal Theory and Legal History* (Ashgate, 2014) and Maksymilian Del Mar and Michael Lobban (eds) *Law in Theory and History: New Essays on a Neglected Dialogue* (Hart, 2016).

76 For discussion on the interplay between Legal History and the Sociology of Law see Chloë Kennedy, 'Sociology of Law and Legal History' in Jiří Přibáň (ed) *Research Handbook on the Sociology of Law* (Edward Elgar, 2020) 31.

77 Rosemary Auchmuty, 'Land Law and Equity and Trusts' in Caroline Hunter (ed) *Integrating Socio-Legal Studies into the Law Curriculum* (Palgrave, 2012) 69, 76.

78 Ibid 77.

79 Rowan Williams, *Why Study the Past?* (Longman and Todd, 2005) 1.

It makes us question what we know by showing that law is contingent, malleable and capable of change; it questions the 'presentist' dividing lines that law students are socialised into including the idea that law is autonomous and objective. A historical approach can therefore be subversive. On the face of it, Legal History does not seem to be subversive. Stereotypes suggest the opposite. The subject can be easily caricatured as a conservative Cambridge-dominated pursuit. The field seems archaic, often being stereotyped as a hobbyhorse for ageing law professors. Yet, a historical approach to law has the potential to be anarchic. As Jim Phillips points out, it shows us that what 'we think of as the law today, and then assume to have always been the case, has in fact not always predominated' and this underlines that 'ways of thinking other than conventional wisdom are possible'.[80] A historical approach to law could and should be inherently subversive. The study of Legal History shows that the law and legal institutions are not fixed, that every line drawn in the law and everything the law holds as sacred are arbitrary and that the environment that law students are socialised into is a historical construct.[81] Seen in this light, Legal History is troubling to the Law School orthodoxy. As Morton Horwitz noted, a historical approach reveals that 'principles of mainstream scholars are historically contingent' and this unsettles the orthodox approach which 'regards history as subversive because it exposes the rationalising enterprise'.[82] This approach, known as Critical Legal History, was developed for some time by a group of scholars based mainly in the United States. The leading British exponent of such an approach, David Sugarman, went as far as to argue that Legal History should 'take on the mantle of an all-purpose subversive, illuminating the connections between legal, socio-economic and political change, thereby enlarging and supplementing the study of law'.[83]

Towards a Subversive Legal History

This book will argue that this is exactly how the historical study of law needs to be reconceptualised: as a subversive critique.

This chapter has outlined the benefits of a historical approach to law, suggesting how history can place law into its context. By providing an exercise in comparative law (but over time rather than space), a historical approach to law highlights the potential for change and provides a way to understanding

80 Jim Phillips, 'Why Legal History Matters' (2010) 41 *Victoria University of Wellington Law Review* 293, 310.

81 In the words of Peter Fitzpatrick, law is presented as mythical: Peter Fitzpatrick, *The Mythology of Modern Law* (Routledge 1992).

82 Morton J Horwitz, 'The Historical Contingency of the Role of History' (1981) 90 *Yale Law Journal* 1057.

83 David Sugarman, 'Writing "Law and Society" Histories' (1992) 55(5) *Modern Law Review* 292.

change while shedding further light upon the interactions between the legal and the social. As William Holdsworth put it, a historical approach to law sheds light upon:

> the manner in which the law is shaped and developed by the changing needs and ideas of different ages, and conversely, the extent to which the law has helped shape these needs and ideas; [and] the permanence and adaptability of legal rules.[84]

Legal History can do more than provide context, however. It can be more than just descriptive. A historical approach can and should serve as critique. Legal History is inherently subversive showing that every legal feature and every dividing line is a human construct that has been, and therefore could, be designed differently. However, the ghettoisation and marginalisation of Legal History as a specialist subject in Law Schools (both in terms of research and teaching) has meant that Legal History has not reached its potential.

One key reason for the comatose state of Legal History is that its subversive capacity has not been appreciated. The stereotypical view of Legal History as being archaic and academic in the worst sense of that word makes it easy to sideline. In Law Schools under pressure to treat students as consumers and with one eye on the requirements of professional regulatory bodies, spending time on context is a luxury. The focus instead is on the learning and application of rules.[85] Legal History does not fit easily into the twenty-first century Law School curriculum. Indeed, the potential of Legal History as a subversive critique is discomforting for twenty-first century Law Schools. The subversive nature of historical analysis flies in the face of the Law School curriculum and student expectations that value legal certainty and regard the legal system as being autonomous and timeless. A historical approach blurs the careful lines constructed around each Law School module. It reveals that the entrenched narratives are invariably one-sided stories that often project a myth of progress by simplifying legal and social processes of change and their effect and by silencing minority, dissenting and alternative viewpoints, experiences and questions. This discomfort is precisely why Legal History is important. It is time for Legal History to embrace its subversive nature. It is this subversive character that underlines the importance of a historical approach in Law Schools critiquing the assumptions, values and

84 William S Holdsworth, 'The Place of English Legal History in the Education of English Lawyers: A Plea for Its Further Recognition' in A L Goodhart and H G Hanbury (eds) *Sir William S Holdsworth: Essays in Law and History* (Clarendon Press, 1946) 20, 35–36.

85 As Alan Harding notes, 'the lawyer's textbook looks more like a chemistry book than a history book: the law is divided up into a number of elements or rules, and when these are traced back to their origins through strings of cases the logical pattern remains dominant and the separate strands of development are not woven into coherent history': Alan Harding, *A Social History of English Law* (Penguin, 1966) 9.

biases told in the story of law and underscoring how law is contingent, constantly interacting with society and that large scale change is possible. Legal History is anarchic not archaic.

This book argues there is a need for Subversive Legal History to become central to Law School activity. Subversive Legal History is not a type of Legal History but is a characteristic. At heart, the argument that this book makes is twofold. First, it argues that being subversive is a necessary characteristic of Legal History if it is to be relevant. And second, it contends that it is this potentially subversive characteristic that makes such a historical approach necessary in Law Schools. In making these arguments, this book draws upon the largely American literature of Critical Legal History but develops that work, noting that the critical turn in law was a product of its time and has had a minimal lasting impact upon the heart of Law School activity in England and Wales in the twenty-first century.[86] These arguments will be developed in the chapters that follow. The next chapter, Chapter 2: 'The Problem with Legal History', asks why Legal History has become marginalised and ghettoised. It critically explores the distinctions often drawn in the field between 'internal' and 'external' approaches, exploring how these have contributed to the marginalisation of Legal History. The following chapter, Chapter 3: 'Subversive Legal History', then begins to provide the solution to overcoming the existing impasse. It unveils the two principles of Subversive Legal History. The first principle is that Subversive Legal History needs to recognise the value and complementary nature of different forms of Legal History and that this can be achieved by recasting the usual internal-external distinction to suggest instead that Legal History has at least both an intellectual history and a social history dimension. The second principle is that we need to go beyond these two dimensions and Legal History needs to be both critical and transformative. This draws upon but develops the work of Critical Legal History and the wider Critical Legal Studies movement, including Robert W Gordon's definition of critical history as:

86 There are, of course, many other works that have argued for a historical approach to law, most notably by advocates of 'historical jurisprudence' on which see Lorren Eldridge, 'Gone and Forgotten: Vinogradoff's Historical Jurisprudence' (2021) *Legal Studies* 194. For a discussion of their work see Laura Cahillane, 'The Use of History in Law: Avoiding the Pitfalls' in Laura Cahillane and Jennifer Schweppe (eds) *Legal Research Methods: Principles and Practicalities* (Clarus Press, 2016) 57, 58–61 and Michael Lobban, 'The Varieties of Legal History' (2012) 5 *Clio@Themis* 1, 4–6. For modern applications of this or similar approaches see the work of Markus D Dubber (Markus D Dubber, 'New Historical Jurisprudence: Legal History as Critical Analysis of Law' (2015) 2(1) *Critical Analysis of Law* 1; Markus D Dubber, 'Legal History as Legal Scholarship: Doctrinalism, Interdisciplinary and Critical Analysis of Law' in Markus D Dubber and Christopher Tomlins (eds) *The Oxford Handbook of Legal History* (Oxford University Press, 2018) 99) and Brian Z Tamanaha, (Brian Z Tamanaha, 'The Third Pillar of Jurisprudence: Social Legal Theory' (2015) 56 *William and Mary Law Review* 2235). This book is not intended to be exhaustive or comprehensive. It does not seek to contain reference to every work that there has been on the interaction of law and history.

> any approach that produces disturbances in the field – that inverts or scrambles familiar narratives of stasis, recovery or progress; anything that advances rival perspectives (such of those as the losers rather than the winners) for surveying developments, or that posits alternative trajectories that might have produced a very different present – in short any approach that unsettles the familiar strategies that we use to tame the past in order to normalize the present.[87]

The chapter will begin to explore why such an approach is better styled as being subversive rather than critical. The fourth chapter, 'The F in Feminist Legal History', develops this by providing a case study of what a subversive approach offers. Drawing upon the developing field of Feminist Legal History, it asks how a focus on gender can subvert conventional historical-legal understandings. It suggests that subverting Legal History on the basis of gender can enable three important 'disturbances' to occur. The first is a disturbance in the narrative. A feminist approach can reveal the missing 'stories' that have been made invisible. Focusing on the question of power complicates linear accounts of progression and rewrites conventional accounts to emphasise the agency of disadvantaged individuals both in terms of campaigning for reform and also in using use law strategically. The second disturbance affects sources. By utilising a much wider range of primary and secondary materials it can be asserted that law cannot be understood in isolation. The third disturbance impacts on disciplinary identities. In exposing the architecture of law as an academic field and the construction of sub-divisions made within law, a feminist approach scrutinises the construction of fields of knowledge, including processes of inclusion and exclusion, on assumptions made, on the authority given to certain voices and the importance afforded to particular topics and arguments.

The remaining chapters further develop Subversive Legal History by returning to these three disturbances. Chapter 5, 'The Perils of Periodisation', looks further at how a subversive approach to Legal History can disturb, debunk and challenge the narrative of historical accounts of law. It explores how periodisation (the splitting up of history into set periods) perpetuates a particular story which simplifies the account of the past to provide a narrative of progress. The chapter proposes an alternative to the assumption of evolutionary progress that underpins the way we understand law: while orthodox accounts of law are based around what Robert W Gordon called evolutionary functionalism,[88] a subversive approach suggests that what I will call 'entropic complexity' is the default state. This is developed further in the next chapter, Chapter 6, 'Counterfactual Legal History', which examines how a subversive approach disturbs the sources and methods conventionally used by legal scholars. It does this by examining the

87 Robert W Gordon, 'The Arrival of Critical Historicism' (1997) 49 *Stanford Law Review* 1023, 1024.

88 Robert W Gordon, 'Critical Legal Histories' (1984) 36 *Stanford Law Review* 57.

potential value of a particular – and controversial – historical method: counterfactual history. The chapter explores the development, use and purpose of counterfactual history. It introduces 'Counterfactual Legal History' to explore whether constructing counterfactual histories should be an approach that a Subversive Legal History could employ to highlight and question the 'stories' given by conventional historical accounts.

Chapters 7 and 8, in different ways, explore the ramifications that a subversive approach has upon disciplinary identities. Chapter 7, 'The Parallel World of Legal Geography', pauses to provide an alternative way of looking at the themes of this book. It compares the development of Legal History to the field of legal geography. It explores how that field has developed, the differences and similarities with Legal History and what insights can be developed to further refine Subversive Legal History. The book then closes with Chapter 8, titled 'We Are all Legal Historians Now'. This develops the arguments of the previous chapters to provide a provocative manifesto that can be used to help reshape legal education. This chapter stresses the need for Subversive Legal History to be seen as an approach to law that needs to be used and applied by all students and teachers. In the non-stop world of the twenty-first century, where Higher Education in general and Law Schools in particular are under increased pressures and pulled in numerous directions, there is a need to rediscover the subversive and transformational nature and power of legal education. Subversive Legal History provides a step in that direction, placing a new revitalised form of historical engagement with and critique of law at the heart of teaching and research. There is a need to place Subversive Legal History at the heart of Law School activity. It is about time.

2 The Problem with Legal History

In three autumnal Oxbridge lectures over the course of a century, three eminent legal historians lamented the fading of their discipline.

On 13 October 1888 at Cambridge, Frederic W Maitland gave his inaugural lecture entitled 'Why the History of English Law has not been Written'.[1] A self-confessed 'long and dismal discourse', the lecture explored why Legal History was 'not flourishing quite as it ought to flourish'.[2] For Maitland, Legal History was not being constrained 'by any lack of evidence'; rather it was 'the limits of our leisure, our strength, our studiousness, our curiosity'.[3] Maitland regretted how the English legal historian was 'overburdened by our materials' and so 'has but flitted over the surface'.[4]

On 22 October 1910 at Oxford, William S Holdsworth gave a lecture, in which he echoed Maitland's disappointment.[5] For Holdsworth, while the nineteenth century was 'notable as the century of the renaissance of historical study', the 'one great exception, which the historian of our age will note with surprise, is the law of England'. He commented that the absence of a 'complete history of English law' (which his work would attempt to fill) and 'the absence of general legal history from the list of subjects in which the law student must satisfy his examiners' would be seen as 'a very curious phenomenon' were we all not so familiar with these oddities.[6]

On 14 October 1998 at Cambridge, John H. Baker's inaugural lecture on 'Why the History of English Law has not been Finished' repeated these concerns.[7]

1 Frederic W Maitland, 'Why the History of English Law Has Not Been Written' in H AL Fisher (ed) *Collected Papers of Frederic William Maitland, Downing Professor of the Laws of England* (Cambridge University Press, 1911) Vol. 1, 480.

2 Ibid 497, 480.

3 Ibid 481.

4 Ibid 483.

5 William S Holdsworth, 'The Place of English Legal History in the Education of English Lawyers: A Plea for Its Further Recognition' in AL Goodhart and HG Hanbury (eds) *Sir William S Holdsworth: Essays in Law and History* (Clarendon Press, 1946) 20.

6 Ibid 21.

7 John H Baker, 'Why the History of English Law Has Not Been Finished' (2000) 59 (1) *Cambridge Law Journal* 62, reproduced in John H Baker, *Collected Papers on English Legal History* (Cambridge University Press, 2013) chapter 83.

A century on from Maitland's inaugural, Baker noted that he had heard it said that 'with so many changes taking place in the law and the legal world, Legal History is becoming a less important branch of legal scholarship and less relevant to a student's needs'.[8] Instead, he observed, career prospects seemed to be advanced more 'by flamboyant essays stating either the obvious or the absurd in fashionable jargon' with citation indexes rewarding work that is 'deservedly attacked' over work that is 'silently approved'. He warned:

> The new information technology may soon provide us with instant access to every piece of legal information throughout the globe; but it will not equip us with the wisdom to understand it. And surely, if civilisation is cut away from its roots, it will wither for want of sustenance.[9]

These autumnal ruminations over the course of a century suggest that there is a question mark over the importance and relevance of Legal History. They also reveal that these three eminent legal historians all agreed that a historical approach to law was important. For Maitland, Holdsworth and Baker, history provided a valuable perspective on law; a concrete means by which to trace, evaluate and critique legal and social change. Maitland regarded technical legal documents as being 'the best, often the only evidence that we have for social and economic history, for the history of morality, for the history of practical religion'.[10] Holdsworth saw legal texts as providing 'the best evidence of its ideas at any given period upon such matters as the forms and modes of its government, its attitude to religion, its economic ideas, its social structures, its views as to property structures'.[11] And Baker noted that 'few other fields apart from archaeology can offer as much opportunity to delve into unbroken ground and recover lost worlds' which would be invaluable in 'keeping alive an understanding of the laws of England in a rapidly changing world'.[12] As Holdsworth put it:

> Legal history, in fact, sheds a brilliant light upon all sides of national life. The light is shed, it is true, from a single, and that a technical standpoint. But it is an important standpoint; for if legal rules reflect the general course and general tendencies of national life, those legal rules, when firmly established give a permanent concrete shape to these tendencies, and thus,

8 Ibid 62–63.

9 Ibid 77.

10 Frederic W Maitland, 'Why the History of English Law Has Not Been Written' in H AL Fisher (ed) *Collected Papers of Frederic William Maitland, Downing Professor of the Laws of England* (Cambridge University Press, 1911) Vol. 1, 480, 486.

11 William S Holdsworth, 'The Place of English Legal History in the Education of English Lawyers: A Plea for Its Further Recognition' in AL Goodhart and HG Hanbury (eds) *Sir William S Holdsworth: Essays in Law and History* (Clarendon Press, 1946) 20, 21.

12 John H Baker, 'Why the History of English Law Has Not Been Finished' (2000) 59(1) *Cambridge Law Journal* 62, 77.

in the long run, have had no small share in the creation of distinct national characteristics.[13]

Yet Maitland, Holdsworth and Baker disagreed as to the place of Legal History and in particular the role of Law Schools. In his inaugural lecture Maitland made it clear that the reason the history of English law was not written was that legal and historical approaches were distinct. Maitland suggested that the lawyer and the historian used 'two different logics, the logic of authority, and the logic of evidence': 'what the lawyer wants is authority and the newer the better; what the historian wants is evidence and the older the better'.[14] For Maitland, studying law with 'purely practical intentions' would not result in an appreciation of history since 'what is really required of the practising lawyer is not, save in the rarest of cases, a knowledge of medieval law as it was in the middle ages, but rather a knowledge of medieval law as interpreted by modern courts to suit modern facts'.[15] This meant that while it would be an exaggeration to say that the study of modern law and the study of Legal History had nothing to do with each other, it is true that it is possible to 'be an excellent lawyer and know little of the remoter parts of history'.[16]

Given these 'irreconcilable contradictions' between legal and historical practice,[17] it might seem surprising that Maitland's inaugural lecture stressed that the history of English law could only be written by legal practitioners. Maitland opined that 'a thorough training in modern law is almost indispensable for any one who wishes to do good work on legal history'.[18] He seemed to suggest that this was not only due to the substance but also to the nature of the work. He questioned whether anyone would 'have the patience to study medieval procedure and conveyancing unless he has had to study modern procedure and modern conveyancing and to study them professionally'.[19] This led Maitland to the conclusion which he dubbed 'the heart of the matter'. For Maitland, the only

13 William S Holdsworth, 'The Place of English Legal History in the Education of English Lawyers: A Plea for Its Further Recognition' in A L Goodhart and H G Hanbury (eds) *Sir William S Holdsworth: Essays in Law and History* (Clarendon Press, 1946) 20, 22.

14 Frederic W Maitland, 'Why the History of English Law Has Not Been Written' in H AL Fisher (ed) *Collected Papers of Frederic William Maitland, Downing Professor of the Laws of England* (Cambridge University Press, 1911) Vol. 1, 480, 491.

15 Ibid 490.

16 Ibid 493. Indeed, as Plucknett noted, this has become even truer since Maitland's day given that medieval precedents and language are less present in the modern law and given the way in which law is often studied on its own and is often the student's 'first and only experience of systematic thought': T F T Plucknett, *Early English Legal Literature* (Cambridge University Press, 1958) 14.

17 Ibid 11.

18 Frederic W Maitland, 'Why the History of English Law Has Not Been Written' in H AL Fisher (ed) *Collected Papers of Frederic William Maitland, Downing Professor of the Laws of England* (Cambridge University Press, 1911) Vol. 1, 480, 493.

19 Ibid 494.

persons able to complete such work were practitioners and ironically the nature of their work meant that they would be physically unable to do it:

> The only persons in this country who possess very fully one of the great requisites for the work are as a rule very unlikely to attempt it. They are lawyers with abundant practice or hopes of abundant practice; if they have the taste they have not the time, the ample leisure, that is necessary for historical research.

For Maitland, developing the historical study of law in the way he envisaged it could not fall to Law Schools. He was of the view that 'the object of a law school must be to teach law, and this is not quite the same thing as teaching the history of law'. He came to the reluctant conclusion that 'in the ordinary teaching of law school there is little room for history, hardly any for remote history'.[20] And he asserted that 'we should not wish to see a professor of law breaking and entering the close of the professor of history'.[21]

Yet, Maitland's conclusion was reached at a time when legal education in the universities was at its infancy. As Baker noted, in Maitland's day 'there were few academic lawyers of any kind,... the only legal history taught at Oxford or Cambridge was Roman, and... the only expertise in ancient legal records was to be found among practising barristers in the inns of court'.[22] Maitland, therefore, had a very narrow understanding of legal education.[23] Moreover, a legal practitioner approach to Legal History which starts from the current law and works backwards would be dangerous in that 'it can harden the teleological attitudes and manners of reflection habitual with lawyers'.[24] As Theodore Plucknett has argued, Maitland's lecture had itself shown that the material, practice and logic of the historian and the lawyer 'were incompatible, and that there was no necessity for a lawyer, *qua* lawyer, bothering with history'.[25] This led Plucknett to the conclusion that 'to make legal history the preserve of professional lawyers is indeed to condemn it to its extinction'.

Contrary to Maitland's inaugural, Holdsworth's lecture concluded that Law Schools were the place, or at least a place, for Legal History. He said that a historical insight to law was to be 'acquired in a lawyer's student days' which could then be 'added to in later years; for historical methods and historical evidence will be familiar things, and the history of the law will not be a sealed book

20 Ibid 495.

21 Ibid 494.

22 John H Baker, 'Why the History of English Law Has Not Been Finished' (2000) 59(1) *Cambridge Law Journal* 62, 63.

23 See further Frederic W Maitland, 'Law at the Universities' in HAL Fisher (ed) *Collected Papers of Frederic William Maitland, Downing Professor of the Laws of England* (Cambridge University Press, 1911) Vol. 3, 419, 427.

24 G R Elton, *F W Maitland* (George Weidenfeld and Nicolson 1985) 22.

25 T F T Plucknett, *Early English Legal Literature* (Cambridge University Press, 1958) 13.

written in an unknown tongue'.[26] He reasoned that if Legal History was generally taught then it could 'be recognized by the profession as the basis of a scientific knowledge of the law'. Holdsworth argued that it was the vocational nature of legal education that was to blame for the marginalisation of Legal History.[27] An 'intensely practical and professional education' perpetuated 'the prevailing ignorance of the history of English law'.

In his lecture, Baker took another approach again. He argued for the academic value of Legal History. Baker said that unless law was 'no more than a body of randomly changing rules, its history must be an essential element in its study'.[28] He asserted that 'the history of English law must also be an essential dimension in the social and intellectual history of this country, as well as being a key to understanding much of the available evidence of the past'. However, despite this, Baker interpreted Maitland as reminding 'us that legal history is history rather than law'. He endorsed:

> Maitland's approach to legal history, which we all now take for granted, [which] was to uncover as far as possible the original records and writings that constitute the body of contemporary evidence, and then to interpret them according to the social and intellectual setting in which they were produced.[29]

Baker, like Maitland, saw the main work of Legal History as 'record work', 'uncovering the raw material' and editing primary sources.

All three lecturers shared a vision of what Legal History entailed: it was the doctrinal legal study of the past. Although Baker saw Legal History as contributing to wider social and intellectual history, he nevertheless saw Legal History as a separate entity. For these three lecturers, Legal History was the study of legal materials from a bygone age; its primary purpose was to edit and interpret primary legal materials. This understanding of Legal History rendered it a specialist pursuit. Baker concluded that 'there is no need for historians of English law to fear redundancy' since there 'is more than enough to keep them in the forefront of legal scholarship for the next hundred years'.[30] Yet, even if such work was to be completed, it is questionable whether it would be at 'the forefront of legal scholarship'. The two competing pressures on Law Schools have meant that Legal History has been doubly relegated. The vocational hold upon Law Schools has meant that the history of law has been curtailed to being simply a part of

26 William S Holdsworth, 'The Place of English Legal History in the Education of English Lawyers: A Plea for Its Further Recognition' in AL Goodhart and HG Hanbury (eds) *Sir William S Holdsworth: Essays in Law and History* (Clarendon Press, 1946) 20, 36.

27 Ibid 25.

28 John H Baker, 'Why the History of English Law Has Not Been Finished' (2000) 59(1) *Cambridge Law Journal* 62.

29 Ibid 64.

30 Ibid 62.

the quest for authority. Maitland's identification of the different logics of law and history as practices still runs true. Moreover, the academic hold upon Law Schools has also led to the neglect of Legal History given that pure doctrinal work is no longer the main focus of legal scholarship.

The answer is to do what Maitland did rather than what he said. As Plucknett put it, his inaugural lecture reflects Maitland's then undeveloped and 'imperfect view of the place of legal history' and 'his later career must be read as the gradual abandonment of the propositions laid down in 1888'.[31] Maitland's subsequent career shows how the historical study of law can prosper as an academic rather than as a practitioner pursuit. Maitland, as a professor of law, did break and enter into the close of the historian, writing and contributing works of general history. He would not have thought of himself as an interdisciplinary scholar but he was; his work freely danced across disciplinary divisions with Maitland authoring works that drew upon and became works in other forms of history and political science.[32] As H E Bell has noted, Maitland's work 'was never channelled in a single groove or pointed to a single end; he has a lively, flexible mind that was always ready to follow a hint from the data that it happened to be processing'.[33] This included the questioning of received wisdoms and the 'spirit which causes one to go around looking for skeletons in closets which might be exposed'.[34] Indeed, in his inaugural lecture Maitland actually recognised that history provided a critique from outside the legal system. As he put it, 'the lawyer must be orthodox otherwise he is no lawyer' but an 'orthodox history seems to me a contradiction in terms'. As Elton has noted, for Maitland, 'historical enquiry demanded the subversion of what had been said before'.[35] This suggests that a historical approach to law needs to operate outside the paradigm of law. It highlights how the history of law can be an academic and interdisciplinary pursuit.

Yet, it is not this version of Maitland that has influenced the development of English Legal History as a field. Rather, it is Maitland's reputation for the doctrinal excavation of old legal texts that has had traction. As Ian Ward has noted, although legal historical work dates back much further, the idea of Legal History as 'a distinct sub-discipline of law is rather more "modern"'.[36] It can be traced back to the second half of the nineteenth century and to the work of Maitland, especially his two major works of doctrinal Legal History, his *History*

31 T F T Plucknett, *Early English Legal Literature* (Cambridge University Press, 1958) 13.

32 For discussion of how Maitland's work in political theory needs to be read in conjunction with his Legal History work see James Kirby, 'History, Law and Freedom: FW Maitland in Context' (2019) 16(1) *Modern Intellectual History* 127.

33 H E Bell, *Maitland: A Critical Examination and Assessment* (Adams & Charles Black, 1965) 108.

34 'Perhaps it is putting it too strongly to imply that Maitland had a polemic spirit, but there is no doubt that when he thought he saw a historical truth, he hewed to the line and let the chips fall where they might': J R Cameron, *Frederick William Maitland and the History of English Law* (University of Oklahoma Press, 1961) 65.

35 G R Elton, *F W Maitland* (George Weidenfeld and Nicolson 1985) 21.

36 Ian Ward, *English Legal Histories* (Hart, 2019) 11.

of English Law and posthumous publication of his lectures on the history of the constitution.[37] For Ward, Legal History 'was born of the same positivist impulse that drove forward modern historiography and historical writing'.[38] And this approach has stuck: 'The tendency to write this history around statutes and cases, the icons of "black letter" law, has ... endured'.[39] As Ward noted:

> In the introduction to his *Letters and Speeches of Oliver Cromwell*, Thomas Carlyle counselled against history which forgets "faces". The risk is nowhere greater than in the writing of legal history.[40]

This is how Legal History continues to be seen in Law Schools. The representation of Legal History in Maitland and Baker's inaugural lectures as a specialist doctrinal exercise in excavation has endured. Legal History is not generally seen as an interdisciplinary field or as a form of critique. This is not to deny, however, that there are scholars whose work uses history as a form of interdisciplinary critique of law. But their work has not entered the canon of Legal History or at least is not seen as epitomising Legal History as a sub-discipline. Indeed, many Law School academics whose research has a historical dimension would not call themselves legal historians – and much more work is of course done outside the Law School. From the end of the twentieth century onwards, there has been an increase of this more socio-legal historical work. However, not only has such work typically not engaged with the more doctrinal scholarship, but it has also often been presented as being in opposition to it. There has been a division within historical work on law which has contributed to the marginalisation of Legal History.[41]

This division between what may broadly be styled doctrinal and socio-legal approaches to the history of law is often characterised as a distinction between the 'old' or 'internal' Legal History on the one hand and the 'new' or 'external'

37 Frederick Pollock and Frederic W Maitland, *The History of English Law* (2nd ed, Cambridge University Press, 1968); Frederic W Maitland, *The Constitutional History of England* (Cambridge University Press, 1941).

38 Ian Ward, *English Legal Histories* (Hart, 2019) 11.

39 Ibid 12. For a detailed account of the development of Legal History see K J M Smith and J P S McLaren 'History's Living Legacy: An Outline of "Modern" Historiography of the Common Law' (2001) 21 *Legal Studies* 251 and Michael Lobban, 'The Varieties of Legal History' (2012) 5 *Clio@Themis* 1.

40 Ian Ward, *English Legal Histories* (Hart, 2019) 12.

41 As Sarah E Hamill has noted, Legal History has become a 'disparate and often jurisdictionally divided field': Sarah E Hamill, 'Review of Legal History' (2019) 28(4) *Social & Legal Studies* 538. This mirrors problems in other areas of history. As Judith M Bennett has noted, 'classicists, medievalists and early modernists are themselves partly to blame for history's waning attention to distant pasts. Classicists long ago began to pursue their work within distinctive interdisciplinary homes; medievalists have built many similar programmes in the last half century; and early modernists are beginning now to follow suit. These interdisciplinary programmes offer many intellectual and pedagogical benefits, but they can also become enclaves that encourage scholars of early eras to remain apart from colleagues working in more modern times': Judith M Bennett, 'Forgetting the Past" (2008) 20(3) *Gender & History* 669, 671.

Legal History on the other hand.[42] In the first camp work explores the doctrinal development of legal ideas, concepts and institutions. Though this is most commonly referred to as the 'internal' or 'old' Legal History,[43] a number of other labels are used such as 'orthodox',[44] 'classical'[45] or 'textual'[46] Legal History.[47] And in the second camp, work explores how law exists as one of many social institutions and how law is shaped by (and shapes) other social institutions and society as a whole. This work is often by those who would not call themselves legal historians (this includes those who work both inside and outside Law Schools). This is the 'external' or 'new'[48] Legal History, also sometimes called 'socio-legal history',[49] 'the social history of law'[50] or 'contextual' Legal History.[51] The difference between the internal and external approaches has been articulated by Robert W Gordon as follows:

> The internal legal historian stays as much as possible within the box of distinctive-appearing legal things; his sources are legal, and so are the basic matters he wants to describe or explain, such as changes in pleading rules, in the jurisdiction of a court, the texts assigned to beginning law students, or the doctrine of contributory negligence. The external historian writes about the interaction between the boxful of legal things and the wider society of which they are a part, in particular to explore the social context of law

42 As with all classifications, however, it is a simplification. As Jonathan Rose has noted: 'To some extent, each type of legal history builds on and reacts to what preceded it in the revisionist tradition. Moreover, the types should not be compartmentalized and are not mutually exclusive, producing hybrid scholarship. But the succeeding types do not replace their predecessors and each type persists, reflecting different scholarly and ideological perspectives and resulting controversies': Jonathan Rose, 'Studying the Past: the Nature and Development of Legal History as an Academic Discipline' (2010) 31(2) *The Journal of Legal History* 101, 117–118.

43 e.g., David Ibbetson, 'What Is Legal History a History of?' in Andrew Lewis and Michael Lobban (eds) *Law and History* (Oxford University Press, 2004) 33.

44 Alan Hunt, 'The New Legal History: Prospects and Perspectives' (1986) 10 *Contemporary Crises* 201, 202.

45 Jonathan Rose, 'Studying the Past: The Nature and Development of Legal History as an Academic Discipline' (2010) 31(2) *The Journal of Legal History* 101, 117.

46 Russell Sandberg and Norman Doe, 'Textual and Contextual Legal History' in Norman Doe and Russell Sandberg (eds) *Law and History: Critical Concepts* (Routledge, 2017) 1.

47 See also the work of Rosemary Hunter which distinguishes *Legal* History which 'focuses on primarily on statutes, cases and judges and legal practice' and Legal *History* which 'explores the legal dimension of historical problems': Rosemary Hunter, 'Australian Legal History in Context' (2003) 21 *Law and History Review* 607, 613.

48 Alan Hunt, 'The New Legal History: Prospects and Perspectives' (1986) 10 *Contemporary Crises* 201.

49 Christopher W Brooks, *Lawyers, Litigation and English Society since 1450* (Hambledon Press, 1998) 179.

50 Michael Lobban, 'The Varieties of Legal History' (2012) 5 *Clio@Themis* 1, 20.

51 Russell Sandberg and Norman Doe, 'Textual and Contextual Legal History' in Norman Doe and Russell Sandberg (eds) *Law and History: Critical Concepts* (Routledge, 2017) 1.

> and its social effects, and he is usually looking for conclusions about those effects.[52]

It is the emphasis and entrenchment of the differences between these two approaches to Legal History which has led to its neglect. This chapter explores how this has occurred. It falls into three sections. The first two sections will outline the characteristics of the two forms of Legal History in turn, which for convenience will be referred to as Internal Legal History and External Legal History. It will explore how these two camps have developed in isolation from and in opposition to one another and will suggest that this has led to the marginalisation of Legal History. The third and final section will contend that this is misguided and will explore the reasons why both approaches complement one another and why both are required.

Internal Legal History

Traditionally the dominant approach to Legal History in Law Schools has been the 'internal' doctrinal 'examination of the evolution of legal doctrine'.[53]

Internal Legal History is 'preoccupied with the genealogy of legal doctrine'.[54] Its approach is 'internal to the extent that it is based on primary sources that are legal', that is, sources such as reported cases, actions in the plea rolls and yearbooks, statutes and early legal literature.[55] It examines 'law on its own terms', exploring 'the law that would have been recognized by lawyers in its times'.[56] Such an approach tends to see 'the law as developing autonomously'.[57] As Jim Phillips put it, such work tends to be preoccupied with the '"origins" of those subjects',[58] stressing how legal changes were mostly the result of domestic innovations internal to the common law. Works of Internal Legal History invariably prioritise the legal. They tend to 'select and organise their material around those

52 Robert W Gordon, 'J. Willard Hurst and the Common Law Tradition in American Legal Historiography' (1975) 10 *Law & Society Review* 9, 11.

53 Christopher W Brooks, *Lawyers, Litigation and English Society since 1450* (Hambledon Press, 1998) 1. 'The tendency to focus on the legal to the exclusion of the social also characterized much twentieth-century legal history writing. Legal developments may have been meticulously chronicled but their non-legal causes and effects less so': Rosemary Auchmuty and Erika Rackley, 'Feminist Legal Biography: A Model for *All* Legal Life Stories' (2020) 41(2) *The Journal of Legal History* 186, 191.

54 David Sugarman, 'Promoting Dialogue between History and Socio-Legal Studies: The Contribution of Christopher W Brooks and the "Legal Turn in Early Modern English History"' (2017) 44(S1) *Journal of Law and Society* S37.

55 Jonathan Rose, 'Studying the Past: The Nature and Development of Legal History as an Academic Discipline' (2010) 31(2) *The Journal of Legal History* 101, 118–119.

56 David Ibbetson, 'What Is Legal History a History of?' in A Lewis and M Lobban (eds) *Law and History* (Oxford University Press, 2004) 33, 34.

57 Michael Lobban, 'The Varieties of Legal History' (2012) 5 *Clio@Themis* 1, 10.

58 Jim Phillips, 'Why Legal History Matters' (2010) 41 *Victoria University of Wellington Law Review* 293, 295–296.

institutions that are distinctively "legal", thereby replicating the core categories and assumptions of modern substantive law'.[59]

Internal Legal History tends to be carried out in Law Schools rather than history departments.[60] As Michael Lobban noted, academic lawyers 'tend to focus their attention on the history of the legal doctrines whose contemporary manifestation they (or their colleagues) also teach'.[61] Internal legal historians therefore replicate the doctrinal method which is prevalent in Law School teaching. This method consists of 'assembling the appropriate cases, reconciling any differences among them, explaining away the irreconcilable, and demonstrating that the evolution of legal doctrine was susceptible to scientific inquiry'.[62] This is the approach taken in traditional Legal History classes on the historical development of the common law as articulated in both the general and area of law specific student textbooks.[63] Such work has tended to focus more upon the role of the common law (as opposed to statute law) in civil law matters (as opposed to criminal law matters) during the medieval and early modern periods.

As noted above, this scholarship grew out of the work of Frederic Maitland, hailed as the father of modern Legal History ('the legal historian's historian').[64] The method of painstakingly examining primary legal sources is often dated back to him, not only because of his works but also given his role in the foundation of the Selden Society which continues to epitomise the internal approach. Maitland's work not only laid the foundation for the classical Legal History works that followed in the first half of the twentieth century (the works of Paul Vinogradoff, William Holdsworth and Theodore Plucknett among others) but also inspired the next generation of historians 'who were interested not in the doctrines of law as such, but who were interested in law as one of the means of

59 David Sugarman, 'Writing "Law and Society"' Histories' (1992) 55(5) *Modern Law Review* 292, 293.

60 Indeed, this is often the focus of critique by historians: Laura Cahillane, 'The Use of History in Law: Avoiding the Pitfalls' in Laura Cahillane and Jennifer Schweppe (eds) *Legal Research Methods: Principles and Practicalities* (Clarus Press, 2016) 57, 61.

61 Michael Lobban, 'The Varieties of Legal History' (2012) 5 *Clio@Themis* 1, 9.

62 Richard A Cosgrove, *Scholars of the Law: English Jurisprudence from Blackstone to Hart* (New York University Press, 1996) 11.

63 John H Baker, *An Introduction to English Legal History* (5th ed, Oxford University Press, 2019), S F C Milsom. *Historical Foundations of the Common Law* (2nd ed, Butterworths, 1981), A W Brian Simpson, *An Introduction to the History of Land Law* (2nd ed, Oxford University Press, 1986), A W Brian Simpson, *History of the Common Law of Contract* (Clarendon Press, 1987), David J Ibbetson, *A Historical Introduction to the Law of Obligations* (Oxford University Press, 1999) and Ann Lyon, *Constitutional History of the United Kingdom* (2nd ed, Routledge, 2016).

64 K J M Smith and J P S McLaren 'History's Living Legacy: An Outline of "Modern" Historiography of the Common Law' (2001) 21 *Legal Studies* 251, 261. Maitland was not, of course, the first writer on Legal History. Maitland's contribution can be contrasted with the 'historical jurisprudence' of Friedrich Carl von Savigny and Henry Sumner Maine.

governance in medieval society'.[65] This included the likes of Frank M Stenton, Doris M Stenton, TF Tout, HG Richardson, Helen Cam and GO Sayles, and was ironic given how Maitland's inaugural lecture saw this work as being best suited to practising lawyers. The same thing happened in the late twentieth century with Maitland's influence extending not only to the legal historians working in Law Schools, most notably SFC Milsom, Brian Simpson, David Ibbetson, and John Baker but also a number of 'non-lawyer legal historians such as James Holt, Paul Hyams, Paul Brand, and John Hudson'.[66]

For Michael Lobban, however, it was Milsom's work which brought about 'the real revolution' within Internal Legal History.[67] He noted that, 'unlike Maitland and his followers in history faculties, Milsom was only interested in the history of the law itself, rather than in how it worked in a broader polity and society'. Moreover, Milsom's work reinvigorated Internal Legal History by regarding it as an intellectual puzzle, the purpose of which was not to shed light on the current law but rather to re-construct a different earlier legal world. As Lobban put it, Milsom 'liberated it from being the handmaiden of current doctrinalists':[68]

> The great lesson taught by Milsom was that legal historians who wanted to understand the "internal" history of the law – its doctrine and practices – had to attempt to think like a lawyer of the age they were studying. They should not look at past law through the lenses of contemporary legal doctrine. For Milsom, legal history was therefore a form of intellectual history. In undertaking it, one had to grasp the fact that terms and concepts which hold one meaning for us held a different meaning in different times. Milsom took up Maitland's lesson that the historian had to study the past on its own terms, and through careful, focused archival work. He took up Maitland's point that only the lawyer could properly understand medieval legal records. But his message seemed in one sense to "out-Maitland" Maitland: for he seemed to say that it was not the legally trained scholar who understood *current* law who could make sense of it: but only the lawyer who had the imagination and historical skill to get inside the medieval lawyer's mind.[69]

A further innovation in Internal Legal History can be found in Brian Simpson's later work. As Ian Ward has noted, 'whilst he was perfectly capable of writing traditional, almost crypto-positivist texts on the history of contract or property, his originality lay elsewhere'.[70] Late in his career Simpson pioneered an approach

65 Michael Lobban, 'The Varieties of Legal History' (2012) 5 *Clio@Themis* 17.

66 Jonathan Rose, 'Studying the Past: The Nature and Development of Legal History as an Academic Discipline' (2010) 31(2) *The Journal of Legal History* 101, 118–119.

67 Michael Lobban, 'The Varieties of Legal History' (2012) 5 *Clio@Themis* 1, 11.

68 Ibid 13.

69 Ibid 11.

70 Ian Ward, *English Legal Histories* (Hart, 2019) 13.

often referred to as 'legal archaeology'. This entailed focusing upon a leading case and then re-constructing 'the exact factual matrices, the personalities and the clashes which led to the famous decisions'.[71] As Simpson put it, although there are differences to archeology (including that legal historians do not tend regularly to destroy their evidence), this approach can be likened to archaeology in that it seeks to 'reconstruct and make sense of the past': 'Cases need to be treated as what they are, fragments of antiquity, and we need, like, archaeologists, gently to free these fragments from the overburden of legal dogmatic, and try, by relating them to other evidence, which has been sought outside the law library, to make sense of them as events in history and incidents in the evolution of the law'.[72] Such an approach has defied categorisation. For Ward, it not only set Simpson apart from Internal Legal History,[73] but also from the professionalisation of history since Maitland.[74] For Smith and McLaren, by contrast, it provided a way of dovetailing internal and external approaches, using 'strongly contextualised examples of micro(case) histories to blunt relatively sharp-edged general legal theory or to reveal passing, but crucially influential, subtexts of prominent legal events'.[75] Although a number of studies of legal archaeology have followed,[76] these have not been incorporated into the Legal History canon. As Ward noted, 'Simpson and his anecdotes were cast to the margins. Which to some might seem diminishing; but to others, conversely a mark of esteem'.[77]

It is Milsom's approach that has defined how Internal Legal History has operated. Following Milsom internal legal historians have narrowed their gaze. As Lobban has noted, 'legal scholars following Milsom have largely concentrated on those areas which have generated the most legal doctrine, and the knottiest problems for lawyers to wrestle with'.[78] Several commentators have been critical of the narrowness and parochialism of internal legal historical work for focusing upon 'a past that ended usually with the 1535 Statute of Uses although which sometimes extended as far forward as the Glorious Revolution of 1688'.[79]

71 Sarah E Hamill, 'Review of Legal History' (2019) 28(4) *Social & Legal Studies* 538, 542.

72 A W Brian Simpson, Leading Cases in the Common Law (Oxford University Press, 1995) 12.

73 'Simpson's histories were everything that positive history was not; contextually rich, intensely human, thoroughly engaging': Ian Ward, *English Legal Histories* (Hart, 2019) 13.

74 'The reception, amongst critics, was occasionally hostile, more generally doubtful [and] neither did it look like proper history; too many "bits and pieces", all a bit "foxy"': ibid.

75 K J M Smith and J P S McLaren 'History's Living Legacy: An Outline of "Modern" Historiography of the Common Law' (2001) 21 *Legal Studies* 251, 315.

76 Sarah E Hamill, 'Review of Legal History' (2019) 28(4) *Social & Legal Studies* 538, 542. See, notably, Cynthia S Gorman, 'Feminist Legal Archaeology, Domestic Violence and the Raced-gendered Juridical Boundaries of U.S. Asylum Law' (2019) 51(5) *EPA: Economy and Space* 1050.

77 Ian Ward, *English Legal Histories* (Hart, 2019) 13.

78 Michael Lobban, 'The Varieties of Legal History' (2012) 5 *Clio@Themis* 1, 12.

79 Jim Phillips, 'Why Legal History Matters' (2010) 41 *Victoria University of Wellington Law Review* 293, 295–296.

Internal accounts have 'tended to focus on the medieval and early modern periods'.[80] As Stuart Anderson has written of practitioners of Internal Legal History:

> Their interest has mainly been in enunciated changes in legal doctrine, and not in whether those changes made a substantial difference to litigants nor, except in a most general sense, in any connection between such changes and underlying social or economic forces. The discipline is "formal," stresses change rather than continuity and emphasises the autonomy of the legal system. ...It is a self-contained discipline.[81]

In Law Schools, this is how Legal History is seen: Legal History is Internal Legal History.[82] The study of the history of law was characterised by academic isolationism. It is 'a history unconcerned with the vast swathe of issues which concerned historians outside the law' meaning that, for example, 'it was possible to write a history of land law without reference to the economic situation of the gentry, or their dynastic concerns, or their place in national politics'.[83] To a large extent, this is how Legal History continues to be seen. Yet, in the late twentieth century, an important change occurred. However, this change affected more the research mission of the Law School as a whole, rather than the research and teaching of Legal History.

External Legal History

For Alan Hunt, 'the emergence of the "new legal history" is one of the most significant trends in recent legal scholarship'.[84]

Since the 1970s, as Ian Ward has noted, 'a broader inter-disciplinary and contextual approach began to gain a foothold in the academy' and 'people started to

80 Philip Handler, 'Legal History' in Dawn Watkins and Mandy Burton (eds) *Research Methods in Law* (2nd ed, Routledge, 2018) 103, 104. It has been claimed that such work has provided 'little sustained attention to the place of legal change in the formative period of industrial capitalism' and has rather 'focused attention on the medieval formation of the common law system and have seen subsequent legal history as the working out of this best of all systems': Alan Hunt, 'The New Legal History: Prospects and Perspectives' (1986) 10 *Contemporary Crises* 201.

81 Stuart Anderson, 'The Lawyer as Historian' (1981) 44 *Modern Law Review* 227. However, compare David Sugarman who wrote of 'old' Legal History 'emphasizing continuity and de-emphasizing change and contingency': David Sugarman, 'Great Beyond His Knowing: Morton Horwitz's Influence on Legal Education and Scholarship in England, Canada, and Australia' in DW Hamilton and A L Brophy (eds) *Law, Ideology and Methods: Essays in Honor of Morton J Horwitz* (Harvard University Press, 2010) 504, 510.

82 The general picture was that English Legal History was narrow and parochial, 'preoccupied with the origins of legal doctrines and institutions': ibid.

83 Jim Phillips, 'Why Legal History Matters' (2010) 41 *Victoria University of Wellington Law Review* 293, 296.

84 Alan Hunt, 'The New Legal History: Prospects and Perspectives' (1986) 10 *Contemporary Crises* 201.

matter'.[85] This transformed the study of the history of law.[86] Two (connected) shifts occurred.[87] The first shift was that in Law Schools, attention began to be paid to the importance of extra-legal factors upon legal change. Socio-legal studies was born. Legal History as traditionally understood became regarded and attacked as an exemplar of the purely doctrinal approach. As David Sugarman pointed out, Legal History 'attracted the suspicion of socio-legal scholars in that it underpinned and legitimated a preoccupation with the narrow technicalities of the law and the treatment of law as largely divorced from the society, politics, and economy in which it operated'.[88] This meant that for many advocating a socio-legal approach 'the moral was clear: the less history the better'. Such scholars generally 'set their sights on the present, and against the past'.[89]

The second shift occurred within, in history departments where a new social history was born. This paid attention to the lived lives of ordinary people in the past and took a much more grounded approach. Law became a facet of this social history. As Smith and McLaren observed, the work of E P Thompson and his protégés at Warwick 'opened up interest in the legal history of the eighteenth and nineteenth centuries' and encouraged scholars to consider how law was experienced within society and especially by the poor and unenfranchised, raising a host of awkward questions about the claimed objectivity and rationality of law in history'.[90] It was this approach to history that proved attractive to the few socio-legal writers who embraced history. Rather than embracing the orthodox doctrinal internal approach of Legal History, such scholars were inspired by the new social history that 'brought the relationships between law and class, race and gender to the fore'.[91] Socio-legal scholars interested in history embraced the methodologies of social historians.[92] As Sugarman noted:

85 Ian Ward, *English Legal Histories* (Hart, 2019) 11.

86 Smith and McLaren note that, before that, 'arguably the only out and out attempt at an "external" narrative account of the full span of English legal history was Alan Harding's *A Social History of English Law* (Penguin, 1966)': K J M Smith and J P S McLaren 'History's Living Legacy: An Outline of "Modern" Historiography of the Common Law' (2001) 21 *Legal Studies* 251, 272.

87 Jim Phillips, 'Why Legal History Matters' (2010) 41 *Victoria University of Wellington Law Review* 293, 297.

88 David Sugarman, 'Promoting Dialogue between History and Socio-Legal Studies: The Contribution of Christopher W Brooks and the "Legal Turn in Early Modern English History"' (2017) 44(S1) *Journal of Law and Society* S37, S38.

89 'in England, history is still not as fully integrated within socio-legal studies as it is in, say, Canada and the United States': ibid S41.

90 K J M Smith and J P S McLaren 'History's Living Legacy: An Outline of "Modern" Historiography of the Common Law' (2001) 21 *Legal Studies* 251, 308.

91 Jim Phillips, 'Why Legal History Matters' (2010) 41 *Victoria University of Wellington Law Review* 293, 298.

92 Laura Cahillane, 'The Use of History in Law: Avoiding the Pitfalls' in Laura Cahillane and Jennifer Schweppe (eds) *Legal Research Methods: Principles and Practicalities* (Clarus Press, 2016) 57, 61.

> They were energized by history's reading of law as a social, political, and cultural formation that could only be understood over time; the contingency of particular legal arrangements; that ordinary people contributed by their conscious efforts to the making of history; and that law and legal practices were systematically structured by economic, cultural, and political power, thereby reinstating facets of the past that were otherwise marginalized.[93]

For Sugarman, this amounted to 'an important but largely unnoticed change in the character of English legal history: namely, its growing recognition that while legal doctrine is important, so too is the real impact of law on society'.[94] However, the reason why this change was 'largely unnoticed' was because Legal History as a sub-discipline in Law Schools was largely unaffected: the specialist legal historians by and large continued to produce works of internal doctrinal Legal History. It was the socio-legal scholars in Law Schools and the social historians outside the Law School who were largely responsible for this new scholarship. Their differing backgrounds and perspectives as well as their often unwillingness to be regarded as legal historians meant that this new external approach neither became a key component of Legal History, the legal sub-discipline, nor became a body of scholarship in its own right.[95]

This external approach to law, then, studies 'the history of law as embedded in its context, typically its social or economic context; the history of the law in action'.[96] Laura Cahillane has noted that 'in as much as the internal approach is described as doctrinal, we can refer to the external approach as looking at "the

93 David Sugarman, 'Promoting Dialogue between History and Socio-Legal Studies: The Contribution of Christopher W Brooks and the "Legal Turn in Early Modern English History"' (2017) 44(S1) *Journal of Law and Society* S37, S38. This interest, however, has often not been reciprocated. 'While historians increasing resort to legal records and engage in law-related research, socio-legal scholarship is usually off their radars' (ibid S41). As Sugarman notes, 'the linkages between history and socio-legal studies are complex and paradoxical' (ibid S37).

94 Ibid S59.

95 As Sugarman has noted, Law and History 'were competitors for academic legitimacy, cultural authority, student numbers, and material support, making boundary maintenance part of their raison d'être' (ibid S38). And history and socio-legal studies have different methods and assumptions: 'Socio-legal scholars may treat history as largely a repository of examples and data that they can draw upon for their own purposes. But historians may regard this as ransacking secondary sources in order to "theorize the facts", an exercise whose potential pitfalls include over-simplification': ibid S39–S40.

96 David Ibbetson, 'What Is Legal History a History of?' in A Lewis and M Lobban (eds) *Law and History* (Oxford University Press, 2004) 33.

law in action" – almost a historical version of the socio-legal approach'.[97] External Legal History is:

> not confined just to explications of doctrinal and institutional evolution [but] extends to investigation of the cultural factors, social forces and values, ideological and intellectual impulses and political and economic realities on the development of law, legal institutions and attitudes towards law.[98]

Anthony Musson wrote that the 'new legal history' moved 'beyond the somewhat restrictive or myopic view of the law and legal institutions afforded in many conventional interpretations'.[99] Such work has explored 'the interface between the legal and the social' and has brought about a 'veritable renaissance to the writing of legal history'. Although this might be seen as an overstatement in that most socio-legal work still gravitates to the social sciences rather than to history, External Legal History has become much more fashionable than the internal doctrinal approach. As Sarah E Hamill has put it: '"Good" legal history is no longer an endless "and then" of judicial decisions but a "why this at this time" approach. Legal historians are expected to read around the law and capture the contexts which shaped it'.[100] The tenor of this comment is telling: External Legal History is regarded by its adherents as a necessary corrective to the internal approach which is dismissed, if not as 'bad' history then at least as inferior. As Alan Harding provocatively put it, the external approach 'does at least try to be real history; to relate the development of law as a whole, and forwards, to the development of English society not to race backwards as a bundle of legal doctrines'.[101] External Legal History has engaged with periods and areas of law that were previously neglected in the Legal History literature. Although David Sugarman has noted that the 'the boundaries of the subject have spread in almost every conceivable direction',[102] certain areas and topics have achieved particular attention. While Internal Legal History focused on the medieval and early modern periods and the development of the laws of property and obligations under the common law, External Legal History has focused on

97 Laura Cahillane, 'The Use of History in Law: Avoiding the Pitfalls' in Laura Cahillane and Jennifer Schweppe (eds) *Legal Research Methods: Principles and Practicalities* (Clarus Press, 2016) 57, 61.

98 John McLaren 'The Legal Historian, Masochist or Missionary? A Canadian's Reflection' (1994) 5 *Legal Education Review* 67, 70–71.

99 Anthony Musson, *Medieval Law in Context* (Manchester University Press, 2001) 3.

100 Sarah E Hamill, 'Review of Legal History' (2019) 28(4) *Social & Legal Studies* 538, 540.

101 Alan Harding, *A Social History of English Law* (Penguin, 1966) 9. Christopher Brooks stated that 'thanks to the general interest over the past half century in so many aspects of social history, including questions about the political awareness and "agency" of the people outside the landed elite, any study of law that concentrates only on high politics is bound to seem unsatisfactory and myopic': Christopher W Brooks, *Law, Politics and Society in Early Modern England* (Cambridge University Press, 2008) 9.

102 David Sugarman, 'Writing "Law and Society" Histories' (1992) 55(5) *Modern Law Review* 292, 299.

modern history,[103] with a particular focus upon criminal justice,[104] exploring the political, social, economic and cultural causes and effects of changes, including a number of works that focus on inequalities such as race and gender,[105] as well as the importance of other non-legal developments.[106] The different focus of internal and external legal historians is striking. While Milsom exemplified the approach of Internal Legal History by asserting that 'the miserable history of crime in England can be shortly told. Nothing worth-while was created',[107] it has been claimed by an external legal historian that 'much of the existing contribution to legal history within socio-legal studies can be found concentrated in the field of criminal justice'.[108] This underlines how the two camps within Legal History rarely talk to each other.

There is also a notable difference in method and approach between the internal and external camps. In part this results from their differing focuses. As Steve Hedley has observed, 'there is no call for weighty tomes on "the law of contract in the 1890s"; anyone who wishes to know about it can consult the weighty tomes written at the time'.[109] This has meant that accounts of modern Legal History have 'retreated from the black-letter tradition'. Historians of modern Legal History 'have for the most part either turned away from the Law Reports altogether, or attempted something more challenging within them: the search

103 See, e.g., A H Manchester, *Modern Legal History* (Butterworths, 1980); William R Cornish and Geoffrey de N Clark, *Law and Society in England 1750–1950* (Sweet and Maxwell, 1989) [A new edition of this was published as William R Cornish *et al.*, *Law and Society in England 1750–1950* (2nd ed, Hart, 2019)] and the work cited by David Sugarman and G R Rubin, 'Towards a New History of Law and Material Society in England 1750–1914' in G R Rubin and David Sugarman (eds) *Law, Economy & Society* (Professional Books, 1984) 1.

104 There has also been a notable 'turn to history' in constitutional and international law as well as in the development of Law and Literature and legal biographies: David Sugarman, 'Promoting Dialogue between History and Socio-Legal Studies: The Contribution of Christopher W Brooks and the "Legal Turn in Early Modern English History"' (2017) 44(S1) *Journal of Law and Society* S37, S41.

105 See, for instance, Laura Gowing, *Domestic Dangers: Women, Words and Sex in Early Modern London* (Oxford University Press, 1996) and Garthine Walker, *Crime, Gender and Social Order in Early Modern British History* (Cambridge University Press, 2009).

106 Leading works include E P Thompson, *Whigs and Hunters* (Allen Lane, 1975); Douglas Hay *et al.*, *Albion's Fatal Tree* (Allen Lane, 1975). There has also been a focus on the history of the legal professions, though Brooks was critical of the lack of the literatures on the history of crime and the history of the legal profession 'either to communicate much with each other or to make a significant impact on the social and political history of the England between 1500 and 1800': Christopher W Brooks, *Lawyers, Litigation and English Society since 1450* (Hambledon Press, 1998) 179.

107 S F C Milsom. *Historical Foundations of the Common Law* (2nd ed, Butterworths, 1981) 403.

108 Lorie Charlesworth, 'On Historical Contextualisation: Some Critical Socio-Legal Reflections' (2007) 1 *Crimes and Misdemeanours* 1, 18.

109 Steve Hedley, '"Superior Knowledge or Revelation": An Approach to Modern Legal History' (1987) 18 *Anglo-American Law Review* 177.

for values in legal reasoning'. As Carolyn Steedman has put it, practitioners of social history are interested in 'legal proceedings as stories or narrative sources':

> Social historians love legal records – a court report, a notebook like the ones a lord chief justice kept – because they allow them to reconstruct a personhood, an identity. Social historians are far more interested in the possibilities this legal record offers for their own narrative – the one they will write, in some history or other – than in the narratological analysis of a few words that were probably not spoken in that way. Social historians love legal records because they are useful; their love is born of utility.[110]

This different focus has not only led to an emphasis on non-legal developments and sources but has also led to a wider understanding of what law includes. For instance, work on and concerning legal pluralism[111] has seen the 'traditional ambit of historical interest in the institution of the laws, namely the courts and judges' expanded not only to cover 'the political and cultural significance of courts and judges' but also the recognition 'that knowledge of the law and legal institutions and visions of legality is not confined to the agents of the law'.[112] This means that it can be 'difficult to discern the clear boundaries' of External Legal History;[113] indeed it is often difficult to distinguish such work as Legal History as opposed to social or political history.[114] Similarly in some socio-legal works there is a historical dimension to the analysis but it is questionable whether that renders the work itself a historical or legal historical work.[115] The diversity of External Legal History is ever-increasing: for instance, there is a growing theoretical literature including the exploration of the relationship between Legal History and legal theory.[116]

It is important, however, that the internal and external division is not overstated. Michael Lobban has noted that 'a number of English lawyers have turned their attention more towards broader, contextual questions, applying the

110 Carolyn Steedman, *History and the Law: A Love Story* (Cambridge University Press, 2020) 221.

111 See, especially, H W Arthurs, *'Without the Law': Administrative Justice and Legal Pluralism in Nineteenth Century England* (University of Toronto Press, 1985).

112 John McLaren 'The Legal Historian, Masochist or Missionary? A Canadian's Reflection' (1994) 5 *Legal Education Review* 67, 78, 81.

113 Philip Handler, 'Legal History' in Dawn Watkins and Mandy Burton (eds) *Research Methods in Law* (2nd ed, Routledge, 2018) 103, 105.

114 Indeed, the external approach is based on the premise that 'the law's past cannot be separated from the host of other pasts that historians concerns [sic] themselves with – social history, political history, economic history, cultural history, gender history' and so on. Jim Phillips, 'Why Legal History Matters' (2010) 41 *Victoria University of Wellington Law Review* 293, 296.

115 Sarah E Hamill, 'Review of Legal History' (2019) 28(4) *Social & Legal Studies* 538, 540.

116 Again, Simpson's work was the catalyst for this: A W Brian Simpson, 'The Common Law and Legal Theory', in A W Brian Simpson (ed) *Oxford Essays in Jurisprudence* (Oxford University Press, 1973) 77–99. See, further, the essays in Maksymilian Del Mar and Michael Lobban (eds) *Law in Theory and History: New Essays on a Neglected Dialogue* (Hart, 2016).

technical skills of the legal historian to broader historical questions'.[117] Such works fuse both doctrinal and socio-legal approaches but tend to be found in discrete areas of law and are seen as part of the literature in that area rather than as Legal History.[118] There are also examples of such work outside the Law School. Jonathan Rose names 'the work of non-lawyer historians such as Wilfrid Prest and Christopher Brooks' as falling under the label of 'the social history of law'.[119] David Sugarman has highlighted the work of Brooks in particular as the example of an historian 'who transcended the boundaries of social, political, and legal history, and placed law centre-stage'.[120] Although it is true that 'the new social history had been seriously engaged with legal records for some time',[121] most of this work has used legal materials as a source of evidence about society and has not been interested in the law itself. Brooks' work, by contrast, was concerned with the detail of the law and saw law as more than just a vehicle for oppression. Contrary to the prevalent focus on criminal law, Brooks focused on the civil litigation levels and the lower branches of the legal profession in particular,[122] showing how law was used by people.[123] His work was concerned with the 'constitutive and penetrative character of law throughout society by mapping

117 Michael Lobban, 'The Varieties of Legal History' (2012) 5 *Clio@Themis* 1, 20.

118 Lobban notes that: 'examples range from crime through to family law and the poor law' and cites as examples: Stephen Cretney, *Family Law in the Twentieth Century: A History* (Oxford University Press, 2003); and Rebecca Probert, *Marriage Law and Practice in the Long Eighteenth Century: A Reassessment* (Cambridge University Press, 2009); Lorie Charlesworth, *Welfare's Forgotten Past: A Socio-Legal History of the Poor Law* (Routledge, 2010).

119 Jonathan Rose, 'Studying the Past: The Nature and Development of Legal History as an Academic Discipline' (2010) 31(2) *The Journal of Legal History* 101, 119–120.

120 'He demonstrated that law exercised a fundamental role in mediating and constituting social, political, and economic relationships at all levels of society throughout the sixteenth and seventeenth centuries. He investigated both elite and popular legal consciousness on an almost unparalleled scale, adopting top-down and bottom-up approaches that revealed the trickle-up, as well as trickle-down, diffusion of legal ideas': David Sugarman, 'Promoting Dialogue between History and Socio-Legal Studies: The Contribution of Christopher W Brooks and the "Legal Turn in Early Modern English History"' (2017) 44(S1) *Journal of Law and Society* S37, S41.

121 Michael J Braddick, 'Christopher Brooks's Contribution to Early Modern History' in Michael Lobban, Joanne Begiato and Adrian Green (eds) *Law, Lawyers and Litigants in Early Modern England: Essays in Memory of Christopher W Brooks* (Cambridge University Press, 2019) 11, 13.

122 His main works were Christopher W Brooks, *Pettyfoggers and Vipers of the Commonwealth: The 'Lower Branch' of the Legal Profession in Early Modern England* (Cambridge University Press, 1986); Christopher W Brooks, *Lawyers, Litigation and English Society since 1450* (Hambledon Press, 1998); Christopher W Brooks, *Law, Politics and Society in Early Modern England* (Cambridge University Press, 2008).

123 He noted that 'some of the most compelling accounts of early modern social history have been written without exploring the legal dimension in detail, largely because it has been taken for granted that that the law, especially the civil as opposed to the criminal law, was of little consequence for, or offered little in the way of the agency to, the vast majority of the population': Christopher W Brooks, *Lawyers, Litigation and English Society since 1450* (Hambledon Press, 1998) 5.

the creation, transmission, and reception of legal thought'.[124] He sought 'to re-integrate the history of law, legal institutions and the legal professions with the general and social history of the period'.[125] Although he was critical of doctrinal Legal History,[126] Brooks took part in Legal History conferences and worked with internal legal historians.[127] Moreover, his work on litigation levels 'deployed legal history, social history, and law and society scholarship to pursue his distinctive agenda and to challenge conventional wisdom'.[128] His work 'demonstrated that law had social, political, and legal dimensions of considerable significance, and that legal, social, and political historians had largely neglected those dimensions and, crucially, their interaction'.[129] The approach of Brooks and others on the social history of law shows the benefits of transcending the internal-external division in Legal History scholarship. Sugarman asserted that 'the work of both socio-legal scholars and historians would benefit from greater cross-fertilization, and from taking the social history of law itself more seriously'.[130] The same could be said to apply to doctrinal legal historians: they could both benefit from and contribute to this literature. As Lobban has argued, Brooks' work also underscored the valuable contribution that internal legal historians can make:

> Although there has often been a temptation among some historians to disparage the narrowness of doctrinal history, historians have become increasingly aware of the relevance of legal doctrine for much social and economic history. Private law is an important instrument of governance: law provides a framework within which power is exercised by individuals and groups on society. While some parts of law are developed through legislatures after much public debate and as a result of conscious choice and political struggle,

124 David Sugarman, 'Promoting Dialogue between History and Socio-Legal Studies: The Contribution of Christopher W Brooks and the "Legal Turn in Early Modern English History"' (2017) 44(S1) *Journal of Law and Society* S37, S49.

125 Christopher W Brooks, *Law, Politics and Society in Early Modern England* (Cambridge University Press, 2008) 1. Elsewhere he described it as 'an attempt to reconstruct the social history of lawyers': Christopher W Brooks, *Lawyers, Litigation and English Society since 1450* (Hambledon Press, 1998) 1.

126 He wrote that the 'lack of interest which accounts for the relative paucity of work on the subject since the late nineteenth century, is frequently, and with some justification, blamed on the insularity and sterility of what is usually described as doctrinal legal history': Christopher W Brooks, *Law, Politics and Society in Early Modern England* (Cambridge University Press, 2008) 2–3.

127 David Sugarman, 'Promoting Dialogue between History and Socio-Legal Studies: The Contribution of Christopher W Brooks and the "Legal Turn in Early Modern English History"' (2017) 44(S1) *Journal of Law and Society* S37, S49.

128 David Sugarman, 'Law, Law-Consciousness and Lawyers as Constitutive of Early Modern England: Christopher W Brooks's Singular Journey' in Michael Lobban, Joanne Begiato and Adrian Green (eds) *Law, Lawyers and Litigants in Early Modern England: Essays in Memory of Christopher W Brooks* (Cambridge University Press, 2019) 32, 41.

129 David Sugarman, 'Promoting Dialogue between History and Socio-Legal Studies: The Contribution of Christopher W Brooks and the "Legal Turn in Early Modern English History"' (2017) 44(S1) *Journal of Law and Society* S37, S54–55.

130 Ibid S41.

> very much is developed either through the practices of lawyers drafting documents and instruments, or through legal contestations in court. One of the tasks of the legal historian speaking to a wider historical audience is to remind them that the language which lawyers and legal officials use, and the operation of their institutions play a crucial part in the governance of society and in structuring private relations. Legal historians can explain how these fundamentals of governance work in any given historical society; and to show how they change.[131]

However, the fact that such an approach remains exceptional underscores how entrenched the division is. It is also notable that Brooks came from outside the Law School. The prevalent perception of Legal History as taught and researched in Law Schools remains predominantly internal and doctrinal. The external approach, though fashionable, has neither replaced nor co-exists with the internal approach as representing, let alone epitomising, how Legal History is seen as an academic field. The internal-external division has had a significant detrimental effect that has furthered the stagnation of the historical study of law in English Law Schools and so it cannot be simply ignored.

The Need for Both

To outsiders, Legal History is still seen as being synonymous with the internal approach.

The main trappings of Legal History as a legal sub-discipline (its specialist journals, book series and conferences) all mostly reflect the internal tradition. However, the criticism by the external approach, coupled with similar movements within academia as a whole seems to have resulted in a retreat of internal legal historical scholarship, which has meant that Legal History has become less visible. While there has been an increase in External Legal History, this is not often presented as Legal History. Indeed, while External Legal History has been quick to focus on areas and topics ignored by the internal legal historians, it has been less keen to revisit areas that have been examined in detail by internal accounts. Legal History is still seen as being synonymous with the internal doctrinal tradition and this is seen as neither the basis for cutting edge legal scholarship nor as proper history. In both respects, this results from the inattention to methodology that is often ascribed to internal legal historians.

These criticisms and the caricaturing of the Internal Legal History mainstream have led to a hesitation on their part to engage in with the external approach. David Sugarman has accepted that 'it is difficult not to share the unease of many a historian' given the 'more *avantgarde* proponents of "newness"'.[132]

131 Michael Lobban, 'The Varieties of Legal History' (2012) 5 *Clio@Themis* 1, 21.

132 David Sugarman, 'Writing "Law and Society" Histories" (1992) 55(5) *Modern Law Review* 292, 300.

The result has been that the internal legal historical approach – and Legal History as a sub-discipline – has become ghettoised. There has been a decrease in the appetite to produce doctrinal Internal Legal History in a way that is accessible enough for non-specialists in Legal History. A vicious circle has been created: the denigration of internal doctrinal Legal History has meant that such work is being produced in a way that is unattractive to advocates of socio-legal studies. As Lorie Charlesworth has noted, Internal Legal History is dominated by of 'a close-knit group of mostly (male) academics who took their law degrees from the Universities of Cambridge, Oxford and London where they occupy prestigious law chairs, some of which have always been designated for legal historians'. This has led to the area being unattractive to outsiders.[133]

This has affected the general reputation of Legal History and limited interdisciplinary interactions. David Sugarman has noted that belittling law in general and Legal History in particular has become 'fair sport among historians' who have often 'stigmatized law and legal historians (with some notable exceptions) as intrinsically unhistorical, given their preoccupation with reading the past in the light of modern legal doctrine'.[134] As Sarah E Hamill has noted, this 'has resulted in historians being dismissive of some legal history as bad history or at least not useful history with utility being work that historians will use themselves'.[135] As Sugarman has noted, external legal historians have often contributed to keeping law and Legal History at arm's length from historians by perpetuating the notion that 'the fog of the law, with its highly technical and arcane persona, is regarded with some justification as obscure and daunting'.[136] This, too, has contributed to the decline of Legal History since the overall picture has been the 'limited contribution of legal history to general history'.[137]

These developments are unfortunate. The internal-external distinction tends to caricature the nature and scope of internal work and depicts a binary watertight distinction between two forms of history and two types of historian that is reductionist, trite and incorrect. Jonathan Rose has argued that much work within the Internal Legal History tradition has ceased to be entirely internal and positivist: 'Much of it involves political, social, and economic contexts, as internal legal sources cannot be fully understood in a vacuum that ignores

133 Lorie Charlesworth, 'On Historical Contextualisation: Some Critical Socio-Legal Reflections' (2007) 1 *Crimes and Misdemeanours* 1, 27.

134 He also noted a key reason for this: 'Divorcing history from law and legal history spoke to the self-identity of modern professional historians': David Sugarman, 'Promoting Dialogue between History and Socio-Legal Studies: The Contribution of Christopher W Brooks and the "Legal Turn in Early Modern English History"' (2017) 44(S1) *Journal of Law and Society* S37, S39.

135 Sarah E Hamill, 'Review of Legal History' (2019) 28(4) *Social & Legal Studies* 538, 541–542.

136 David Sugarman, 'Promoting Dialogue between History and Socio-Legal Studies: The Contribution of Christopher W Brooks and the "Legal Turn in Early Modern English History"' (2017) 44(S1) *Journal of Law and Society* S37, S39.

137 Christopher W Brooks, *Lawyers, Litigation and English Society since 1450* (Hambledon Press, 1998) 5.

the external context'.[138] This reflects the move in law generally whereby extra-legal factors and methods from other disciplines are used alongside doctrinal research methods. Indeed, Smith and McLaren observed that it was possible to identify both internal and external approaches in Legal History long before the 1970s.[139] They gave the example of the work of CHS Fifoot which not only was concerned with doctrinal development but was also 'deeply immersed in the broader swathe of contemporary ideas. Jurists and judges are set alongside social scientists, historians and political philosophers. Intellectual influences, or linkages, are speculated upon, often to be dismissed'. The same is obviously true of works on legal biography; these cannot be described simply as being either internal or external.[140] Institutional Legal History, 'the history of courts, of literature, of the legal profession',[141] is also difficult to classify in this way. Furthermore, even the most internal analysis does not occur in a vacuum and is shaped by (either explicitly or implicitly) the world in which the development occurred and the world in which the author lives. As Michael Lobban has noted, even the most doctrinal of legal historians 'have shown that one cannot understand the nature and developments of legal concepts in the past without having some idea of their social contexts'.[142]

This point can be illustrated by reference to the work of the legal historians who are seen to epitomise the Internal Legal History tradition. As we have seen, the internal approach to law is often dated back to the work of Frederic Maitland, arguably the leading nineteenth century legal historian, who did more than anyone else to articulate the development of legal ideas in the medieval period. Yet, as Rose points out, even though his most doctrinal work *The History of English Law*[143] 'focuses on institutional and doctrinal development, it is not purely legal, as he understands the relationship of law to a broader social and

138 Jonathan Rose, 'Studying the Past: The Nature and Development of Legal History as an Academic Discipline' (2010) 31(2) *The Journal of Legal History* 101, 118–119.

139 K J M Smith and J P S McLaren 'History's Living Legacy: An Outline of "Modern" Historiography of the Common Law' (2001) 21 *Legal Studies* 251, 272.

140 This is a growing field as documented by David Sugarman, 'From Legal Biography to Legal Life Writing: Broadening Conceptions of Legal History and Socio-legal Scholarship' (2015) 42 *Journal of Law and Society* 7; William Cornish, *Life Stories and Legal Histories* (Selden Society, 2015). There have been numerous biographies of judges, legal practitioners and famed legal writers. These include some twentieth century figures (see Nicola Lacey, *A Life of H L A Hart: The Nightmare and the Noble Dream* (Oxford University Press, 2006) and Fiona Cownie, 'The United Kingdom's First Woman Law Professor: An Archerian Analysis' (2015) 42(1) *Journal of Law and Society* 127).

141 David Ibbetson, 'What Is Legal History a History of?' in Andrew Lewis and Michael Lobban (eds) *Law and History* (Oxford University Press, 2004) 33.

142 Michael Lobban, 'Sociology, History and the "Internal" Study of Law' in R Nobles and D Schiff (eds) *Law, Society and Community: Socio-Legal Essays in Honour of Roger Cotterrell* (Ashgate, 2014) 39, 54. Cf. Anthony Bradney, 'Law as a Parasitic Discipline' (1998) 25(1) *Journal of Law and Society* 71, 72.

143 Frederick Pollock and Frederic W Maitland, *The History of English Law* (2nd ed, Cambridge University Press, 1968 [1898]).

political context'.[144] And this is even more true of his work as a whole which 'is extensive, varied, and eclectic, abounding in ideas, insights, and concepts'.[145] As Michael Lobban has pointed out, it is ironic that proponents of both Internal and External Legal History 'would probably trace their professional genealogy to one man, FW Maitland'.[146] Yet, it is not only Maitland who straddled the division. Even the work of SFC Milsom, arguably the greatest internal legal historian of the twentieth century,[147] shows a degree of overlap between the internal and external approaches. While Milsom's work provides possibly the best example of a history of legal ideas, this did not mean that Milsom viewed law as an autonomous system operating in a vacuum. Rather, his work focused on how the legal system – as a system made up of people – functioned over time; how in each age practitioners sought to get their client out of the legal difficulties of the day. Milsom's internal analysis of the primary legal materials led him to call for a greater appreciation of the social context in which the law operated.[148] Classifying Milsom as an internal legal historian shows the limits of the internal-external distinction and its underestimation of the value and importance of the internal approach.

A tempting response to the problematic internal-external distinction is to disregard it, especially given that a purely internal approach as envisaged by much of the external critique rarely if ever exists. However, this would ignore the fact that the internal-external division in Legal History broadly reflects the distinction within law as a whole between doctrinal and socio-legal methods. Ignoring the distinction would likely undermine the importance of the two approaches which look at law from different angles and take divergent approaches, which are both needed. Indeed, the strengths of one approach often help to rectify the weaknesses of the other approach. The particular, technical and grounded evidence unearthed by Internal Legal History complements and is complemented by the contextual, wider and interdisciplinary insights gleaned through External Legal History. Internal and external responses should not be placed in opposition to one another; they are necessarily complementary. There is value to both internal

144 Jonathan Rose, 'Studying the Past: The Nature and Development of Legal History as an Academic Discipline' (2010) 31(2) *The Journal of Legal History* 101, 114.

145 See further R A Houston, '"The Hard Rind of Legal History": F W Maitland and the Writing of Late Medieval and Early Modern British Social History' in Michael Lobban, Joanne Begiato and Adrian Green (eds) *Law, Lawyers and Litigants in Early Modern England: Essays in Memory of Christopher W Brooks* (Cambridge University Press, 2019) 58.

146 Michael Lobban, 'The Varieties of Legal History' (2012) 5 *Clio@Themis* 1, 4.

147 David Ibbetson, 'Milsom's Legal History' (2017) 76(2) *Cambridge Law Journal* 360.

148 Milsom's self-confessed heretical critique of Maitland's account emphasised the continuing importance of the feudal courts and the localisation of justice and suggested that the early writs did little to replace this. Milsom's main contributions can be found in S F C Milsom, *The Legal Framework of English Feudalism* (Cambridge University Press, 1976), his introduction to Frederick Pollock and Frederic W Maitland, *The History of English Law* (2nd ed, Cambridge University Press, 1968) and integrated within S F C Milsom, *Historical Foundations of the Common Law* (2nd ed, Butterworths, 1981).

and external approaches. Internal approaches explore the legal ideas and practices that constitute social ideas and practices while external approaches examine, for instance, what legal change 'tells us about power relationships in society, or tracing whether the rule was enforced or not, or if it was resisted, avoided, or challenged by the communities at which it was aimed'.[149] Legal and social understandings influence one another and develop over time.

This means that there is a need for the doctrinal internal analysis of legal materials alongside external approaches. There is fault on both sides for the lack of dialogue between the different camps. Writers on Internal Legal History need to recognise this and question the assumptions and biases underpinning their work. It also needs to be borne in mind that even the most doctrinal work requires interpretation and that this ought to be subject to further scrutiny and reassessment.[150] As Carolyn Steedman reminds us, 'all manner of scholars, including legal scholars write autoethnography'; that is, 'a scholar uses self-reflection and personal experience to explore wider cultural, social and political meanings and understandings'.[151] Writers of Internal Legal History also need to be conscious that doctrinal legal study on its own will only provide 'an understanding of the interactive nature of legal assumptions and ideas of the various legal agents and agencies most immediately engaged in the process'.[152] It needs to be recognised that such work needs to be built upon in order to answer broader macro questions about the role of law in social, political and cultural change and particular micro questions about the non-legal motivations for legal developments.[153] Internal legal historians need to be aware that any speculation about social, political and cultural causes and effects will be just that: mere speculation. An academic output is no place for 'man in pub' philosophising; the making of sociological, philosophical or political statements without reference to or the recognition of any of the research found in those respective disciplines.[154] But external legal historians also need to remember that new and critical approaches need to build upon, rather than replace, doctrinal legal scholarship. Any work that does not do so is likely to run the risk of being like a house built on sand; of producing a 'law-lite' account that is likely to include simplifications and can even be

149 Michael Lobban, 'Sociology, History and the "Internal" Study of Law' in Richard Nobles and David Schiff (eds) *Law, Society and Community: Socio-Legal Essays in Honour of Roger Cotterrell* (Ashgate, 2014) 39, 54.52.

150 As Simon Schama has observed, 'even in the most austere scholarly report from the archives, the inventive faculty – selecting, pruning, editing, commenting, interpreting, delivering judgements – is in full play': Simon Schama, *Dead Certainties* (Granta, 1991) 322. See further, e.g., John Tosh, *The Pursuit of History* (5th ed, Pearson 2010) chapter 6.

151 Carolyn Steedman, *History and the Law: A Love Story* (Cambridge University Press, 2020) 24.

152 K J M Smith and J P S McLaren 'History's Living Legacy: An Outline of "Modern" Historiography of the Common Law' (2001) 21 *Legal Studies* 251, 312.

153 Smith and McLaren give the example of the work of Simpson using 'strongly contextualised examples of micro(case) histories to blunt relatively sharp-edged general legal theory or to reveal passing, but crucially influential, subtexts of prominent legal events': ibid 315.

154 Russell Sandberg, *Religion, Law and Society* (Cambridge University Press, 2014) 259.

premised upon errors, given that the initial impressions of the legal problems can be questioned by the meticulous analysis of case law and statute.[155]

A problem seems to be the way in which each camp misunderstands the other and the distance between their approaches. This has resulted in the antagonistic tone and the resultant anxieties. Although newer work will often question and debunk the arguments and findings of older works, that is not to say that they should denigrate the method, approach and ambition of that work. And care needs to be taken as to identifying precisely what has been debunked. As John Baker has observed, 'the discovery of new pieces of material may greatly change the picture and lead us to abandon explanation designed to fit the imperfect previous knowledge' but 'it is very rare for new material to disprove completely what went before'.[156] As he rightly states, 'historical work builds on what has gone before'.

This idea of constructively building upon previous work is crucial. Even acts of demolition need to be both preceded by and followed by dialogue. External approaches need to build upon internal accounts and writers of doctrinal Legal History need to be aware that their work can be built upon either by themselves or by other scholars. This interaction goes both ways. It is not a question of either approach being preferable. Both have their advantages and their flaws. It is rather about recognising that they are not as far apart as it might first appear and that they can complement each other. This approach has the potential to lead to a renaissance in Legal History. Smith and McLaren suggest that this has already occurred.[157] They write that Legal History 'has been revivified and transformed into a broad-based art, lending itself to a multiplicity of objectives through a diversity of methodologies, each offering particular revelations and additions to our knowledge of the past, and, consequently, our self knowledge'. This seems too optimistic, however. The quantity and quality of research monographs, journal articles and conference presentations may point towards such transformation. But this is only part of the picture. The declining place of history in the Law School curriculum and therefore in the education of those who will practice law is of concern. There is little point having 'revived and transformed' Legal History if it exists as a specialism of the few at the margins. Smith and McLaren's optimistic conclusion leads them to dismiss the need to explore further the nature of Legal History:

> Rather than through sterile, not to say futile, exercises in stipulating the necessary hallmarks of all forms of legal historiography, weighing the worth of any contribution should, in large measure, entail asking just how far any such enterprise achieves its own express or implicit claims and objectives.

155 Ibid 257–258.

156 John H Baker, 'Reflections on "Doing" Legal History' in Anthony Musson and Chantal Stebbings (eds) *Making Legal History* (Cambridge University Press, 2012) 7, 18, 17.

157 K J M Smith and J P S McLaren 'History's Living Legacy: An Outline of "Modern" Historiography of the Common Law' (2001) 21 *Legal Studies* 251, 324.

Smith and McLaren are entirely correct to say that each work should be judged on its own merits against its own research questions and that there is value in all various forms of Legal History. There should be no attempt to produce a definition of Legal History or a list of characteristics or functions if the purpose is to produce homogenisation. To do otherwise would be an abuse of academic freedom, devaluing or even censuring particular approaches and constraining innovation. Yet, there is a need to reflect further on the nature of Legal History. This is not to produce a straitjacket of characteristics for the discipline but rather to correct current misunderstandings. Such reflection is needed to bridge the damaging divisions that currently exist and to stress the importance and ambition of the historical study of law. This chapter has shown that the divided state of historical scholarship in Law Schools has contributed to the decline of Legal History.[158] The sub-discipline is still institutionally defined by the Internal Legal History of yesteryear, which is now seen as passé. Although external forms of Legal History have grown, they have done so outside the sub-discipline and often have either not made reference to or have been hostile to the internal tradition. A gap has grown between the two approaches and this gap has led to the decline of Legal History as a field of study. This gap needs to be overcome because both approaches are needed and are complementary to one another. This suggests that a new categorisation is needed that moves beyond the internal-external dichotomy. This will be the focus of the next chapter which will explore how a Subversive Legal History can develop that draws upon but transcends the achievements of the internal and external approaches and which would go some way to overcome the concerns of Maitland, Holdsworth and Baker about the decline of Legal History. Subversive Legal History seeks to reclaim the historical study of law as an integral feature of legal scholarship and education.

158 This is not to say that it is the only cause. Developments in legal education and the marketisation of higher education more generally have played a part. Richard A Cosgrove has also cited how the 'pervasive bromide that the events of the Glorious Revolution in 1688 and its aftermath somehow "settled "the constitution"' and how the 'inward turn of jurisprudence from social analysis to legal theory since the 1880s' has contributed to the 'the decline of legal history's claims': Richard A Cosgrove, *Scholars of the Law: English Jurisprudence from Blackstone to Hart* (New York University Press, 1996) 208–209. Carolyn Steedman has noted that the rhetoric of timelessness that underpins the common law has also widened the gap between law and history. The way in which history 'proposed the radical disjuncture of then from now' has meant that law 'did not care for historians. It didn't then, and it doesn't now. Law will never take notice of you, no matter how much you hang around the bike shed after school, hoping for just one look, just one glance sent your way': Carolyn Steedman, *History and the Law: A Love Story* (Cambridge University Press, 2020) 9.

3 Subversive Legal History

The two main principles of Subversive Legal History are derived from the two main reasons for the comatose state of Legal History in Law Schools in England and Wales.

As discussed in the last two chapters, although there are some notable exceptions, Legal History has largely been absent in Law Schools for two main reasons. First, as Chapter 2 explained, the divisions within Legal History and the development of historical work on law outside the sub-discipline have contributed to Legal History's marginalisation by creating division. Second, as discussed in Chapter 1, the subversive nature of Legal History means that it is unsettling to law students and teachers in that it flies in the face of the Law School curriculum and student expectations which value legal certainty and regard the legal system as being autonomous. This chapter will contend that these two causes of the death of Legal History actually point the way to its resurgence.

The two main principles are as follows. First, Subversive Legal History needs to recognise the value and complementary nature of different forms of Legal History. The divisions should not be overlooked but need to be built upon. As will be argued below, Subversive Legal History has to recognise and needs to develop at least an intellectual history dimension and a social history dimension. Second, Subversive Legal History needs to be critical and transformative; and in this respect this chapter will argue that it needs to draw upon and develop the Critical Legal History approach. As we will see, Critical Legal History is often regarded as a type of External Legal History and is portrayed as being in opposition to the internal doctrinal tradition. However, this chapter will argue that this is misguided and that all Legal History should be critical. Crucially, this includes not only External Legal History but also Internal Legal History – or to use the language that will be proposed here, the social history and intellectual history dimensions should both be critical. Indeed, the association of Critical Legal History with the external approach is one of the reasons why that term is problematic. This chapter will contend that the term 'Critical' is both vague and loaded and it will be suggested that the term 'Subversive' is to be preferred instead.

This chapter falls into three parts. The first two parts examine, in turn, the two principles of Subversive Legal History. The final part develops this by examining and insisting that the subversive nature applies as much to the intellectual history dimension of Legal History as it does to the social history dimension. It discusses Roger Cotterrell's seminal essay 'Why Must Legal Ideas be Interpreted Sociologically?'[1] from a Legal History perspective, asking: why must legal ideas be interpreted historically?

The First Principle: The Intellectual History and Social History Dimensions of Legal History

The first principle of Subversive Legal History is that the division between internal and external approaches needs to be reconceptualised to see the historical study of law as having necessarily both an intellectual history dimension and a social history dimension.

At the end of the last chapter, it was argued that divisions in the field between the internal mainstream Legal History canon and the fragmented external work on historical approaches to law should not be ignored and cannot be healed simply by cheering the plurality and diversity of approaches.[2] There is a need to recognise the different approaches and their contributions and also to reconceptualise the relationship between them. The aim is to capture more accurately the nature of the two approaches and to regard them both as essential parts of the historical analysis of law.

This is not just about a change of names, though current labels are insufficient and counterproductive in terms of the aim of transforming the historical study of law and placing it at the centre of Law School activities. The juxtaposing of the 'old' and 'new' labels, though roughly correct in identifying the development of a fresh approach over time, perpetuates the notion that newer approaches would supplant the allegedly inferior and limited older approaches. The terms 'internal' and 'external', though useful in reflecting wider debates about the nature of studying law, suggest an unhelpful and inaccurate binary distinction. The terms 'textual' and 'contextual' too imply the inferiority of the first approach and fail to capture the richness and diversity of the endeavours approached by both camps: the textual label suggests that those scholars are simply studying the interpretation of primary sources in social isolation; the contextual label says very little about what that approach embodies and the nature of it.

As a result, in what follows a different approach will be taken. Inspiration will be derived from the development of history as a discipline to suggest that the two forms of Legal History that internal-external dichotomy represents (which are by no means the only forms and are not completely distinct from each other)

1 Roger Cotterrell, 'Why Must Legal Ideas be Interpreted Sociologically?' (1998) 25 *Journal of Law and Society* 171, reprinted as Roger Cotterrell, *Law, Culture and Society* (Ashgate, 2006) chapter 3.

2 Cf. K J M Smith and J P S McLaren 'History's Living Legacy: An Outline of "Modern" Historiography of the Common Law' (2001) 21 *Legal Studies* 251, 324.

can be seen as legal-historical approaches that derive and develop from the intellectual history and social history traditions respectively. This is inspired by a throw-away remark by John Baker that 'Law flits uncomfortably between intellectual and social history'.[3] The discussion in the previous chapter is very much the account of that uncomfortable flit. However, from the articulation and defence of the two approaches provided there and the argument that they are complementary and linked, it is now possible to extrapolate what it means to say that Legal History includes at least dimensions that derive from the intellectual history of the law and the social history of the law. It must be stressed at the outset, however, that the words 'at least' here are important. Other approaches are, of course, not to be excluded.[4] Moreover, this articulation should not be taken as requiring both of the approaches to be present at all times. Individual works and indeed individual authors may rely on one approach at the expense of the other. That is entirely unobjectionable. The approach taken should reflect the research questions of the particular piece of work. It should also be stressed that there is no clear dividing line between the two dimensions of intellectual and social history: some work will straddle the two. The two dimensions are raised in order to underscore that they are both valid and complementary to each other. The contention is that, as a whole, Legal History needs to include and value both approaches.

Intellectual history is often seen as being synonymous with the 'history of ideas'; though Robert Darnton has also defined it as including 'the study of informal thought, climates of opinion and literary movements'[5] As Richard Whatmore has put it, while 'historians cannot avoid ideas', intellectual history can be distinguished as being the 'systematic study of the content of those ideas and of their transmission, translation, diffusion and reception'.[6] Internal legal historians have long appreciated that their interest is in the development of legal ideas.[7] Indeed, Maitland wrote that: 'The History of law must be a history of ideas. It must represent, not merely what men have done and said, but what men have thought in bygone ages'.[8] Assaf Likhovski has noted that to study the intellectual

3 John H Baker, 'Criminal Courts and Procedure, 1550–1800' in J S Cockbourn (ed) *Crime in England 1500–1800* (Methuen, 1977) 15.

4 The Oxford Handbook of Legal History takes a slightly different approach to what is proposed here. It has a section dedicated to approaches to Legal History which includes chapters on Legal History as legal scholarship, social history, political history, intellectual history, doctrinal history, cultural history, economic history as well as a number of related chapters: Markus D Dubber and Christopher Tomlins (eds) *The Oxford Handbook of Legal History* (Oxford University Press, 2018).

5 Robert Darnton, 'Intellectual and Cultural History' in M Kammen (ed) *The Past Before Us: Contemporary Historical Writing in the United States* (Cornell University Press, 1980) 337. He also includes the social history of ideas and cultural history under the umbrella of intellectual history.

6 Richard Whatmore, *What Is Intellectual History?* (Polity Press, 2016)13–14.

7 See, e.g., the essays in (2016) 64 *Buffalo Law Review*.

8 Frederic W Maitland, *Domesday Book and Beyond* (Fontana 1960) 415.

history of law is to examine 'the history of legal ideas and concepts'.[9] The reference to 'intellectual' does not mean intellectuals. As Robert Gordon put it:

> we shouldn't limit intellectual history to the high falutin' theorizers, the high mandarins of the system, the philosophers or several steps down from the philosophers, the producers of legal thought, or the producers of legal doctrine or writers or treatises. We are interested in intellectuals in the vernacular, people who are arguing, justifying, categorizing and often simply describing history.[10]

The intellectual history dimension of Legal History includes the everyday development of legal ideas both in doctrine and in practice.[11] John Baker introduced his book in *The Oxford History of the Laws of England* series by stating that the focus of the book and of the series was 'the intellectual and institutional framework within which the lawyers' opinions were formed and their arguments devised, the processes of litigation managed and recorded, and the legislative changes achieved'.[12] Baker's distinction between the 'intellectual and institutional' should not be taken to mean that intellectual history of law is simply the history of doctrine. It clearly includes this:[13] the study of how legal ideas are developed in legal education and through texts.[14] However, the intellectual history of law actually includes everything Baker describes: it includes the institutional, exploring legal ideas as developed through the legal system. This includes what Michael Lobban described as the study of law as 'a specialist intellectual technique':[15] the study of law as interpretation and reinterpretation, of legal argumentation and of the development of legal discourse. This was the main contribution of Milsom, who explored how legal ideas changed over time

9 Assaf Likhovski, 'The Intellectual History of Law' in Markus D Dubber and Christopher Tomlins (eds) *The Oxford Handbook of Legal History* (Oxford University Press, 2018) 151.

10 Robert W Gordon, 'Some Final Observations on Legal Intellectual History' (2016) 64 *Buffalo Law Review* 215.

11 The same is true of intellectual history generally. It is the study of 'what people in the past meant by the things they said and what these things "meant" to them': John Burrow, cited in Richard Whatmore, *What Is Intellectual History?* (Polity Press, 2016)13.

12 John H Baker, *The Oxford History of the Laws of England, Vol VI, 1483–1558* (Oxford University Press, 2003) vi.

13 On which see Joshua Getzler, 'Legal History as Doctrinal History' in Markus D Dubber and Christopher Tomlins (eds) *The Oxford Handbook of Legal History* (Oxford University Press, 2018) 171.

14 As Assaf Likhovski noted: 'Intellectual historians of law are also interested in the history of legal education and the production of academic and other legal texts, in changes in the abstract structures that underlie the thought and discourse of lawyers in a given era': Assaf Likhovski, The Intellectual History of Law' in Markus D Dubber and Christopher Tomlins (eds) *The Oxford Handbook of Legal History* (Oxford University Press, 2018) 151.

15 Michael Lobban, 'Sociology, History and the "Internal" Study of Law' in Richard Nobles and David Schiff (eds) *Law, Society and Community: Socio-Legal Essays in Honour of Roger Cotterrell* (Ashgate, 2014) 39, 51.

through the way in which cases were argued and decided. Milsom recognised that Legal History can be understood as part of intellectual history. For Milsom, the history of law is 'not just part of social and economic history. To use uncomfortably large words, it is the intellectual history of society'.[16] It is not only that Legal History can be seen as part of intellectual history but also that there is an intellectual history tradition within Legal History. Referring to Internal Legal History as the intellectual history tradition provides a useful step forward in that while the label Internal Legal History suggests that it is concerned with the way that historical research is conducted (the doctrinal examination of legal materials), referring to this as an intellectual history approach instead highlights the focus of the analysis (the development of legal ideas).[17] This means that, unlike Internal Legal History as conventionally understood, an intellectual history of law is interested in legal ideas both inside and outside 'the box of distinctive-appearing legal things'.[18] It is not limited to legal materials. It includes the study of how law has been impacted by non-law influences (political, social and cultural changes) and what is revealed about the nature and operation of law.[19] The intellectual history of law includes popular understandings of law: what Assaf Likhovski refers to as 'the history of legal consciousness – that is, the study of the ideas that laypersons have about law and its institutions'.[20] It requires the study of particular communities at particular times and how they understand, distinguish and perpetuate legal ideas.[21] As Robert Gordon has noted:

> an intellectual history of a body of law will try to reconstruct the conceptual world of its creators, to describe their system of thought and the courses they assembled to create it, and perhaps also to reveal its intellectual context, its relation to other contemporary systems of thought.[22]

Crucially, the intellectual history dimension of Legal History is, then, the study of an authored practice. It underlines that law – legal institutions, legal doctrine,

16 S F C Milsom, 'Maitland' (2001) 60(2) *Cambridge Law Journal* 265, 270.

17 An intellectual history approach seeks 'to produce causal explanations for the appearance (and disappearance) of those ideas, to trace the influence of a given idea over time, and to defamiliarise current ideas and concepts about law as a first step in the process of reforming them': Assaf Likhovski, 'The Intellectual History of Law' in Markus D Dubber and Christopher Tomlins (eds) *The Oxford Handbook of Legal History* (Oxford University Press, 2018) 151.

18 Robert W Gordon, 'J. Willard Hurst and the Common Law Tradition in American Legal Historiography' (1975) 10 *Law & Society Review* 9, 11.

19 Michael Lobban, 'Sociology, History and the "Internal" Study of Law' in Richard Nobles and David Schiff (eds) *Law, Society and Community: Socio-Legal Essays in Honour of Roger Cotterrell* (Ashgate, 2014) 39, 43.

20 Assaf Likhovski, 'The Intellectual History of Law' in Markus D Dubber and Christopher Tomlins (eds) *The Oxford Handbook of Legal History* (Oxford University Press, 2018) 151.

21 Richard Nobles and David Schiff, 'Introduction' in Richard Nobles and David Schiff (eds) *Law, Society and Community: Socio-Legal Essays in Honour of Roger Cotterrell* (Ashgate, 2014) 1, 4.

22 Robert J Gordon, 'Book Review: *Tort in America: An Intellectual History*' (1980–1991) 94 *Harvard Law Review* 903, 908.

legal theories and so on – are constructs and are capable of change. An intellectual history approach includes the study of how law has been understood and presented over time and so is the study of works on law as well as of the law itself, scrutinising the question of authorship and possible unreliable narration in relation to both. This can include the study of particular figures and their impact. As noted in the previous chapter, there has been an increase in interest in biographical writing in Legal History and in socio-legal studies more generally.[23] Therefore, although an intellectual history approach to law includes the 'the intellectual history of legal history as such',[24] it is not restricted to the study of how legal ideas have been developed by legal actors. It is much wider than that and concerns all ways and all contexts within which legal ideas are developed. As John Burrow has noted, 'intellectual history attends… to the reflective communal life of human beings, in the past; to their assumptions, arguments, enquires, ruminations about the world and themselves… And the various vocabularies and rhetorics in which they conducted these'.[25] An intellectual history of law focuses on legal communications but does not limit these to settings and contexts that are already deemed to be legal.

The other dimension of Legal History derives from social history. In the words of Trevelyan, social history entails the study of 'the daily life of the inhabitants of the land in past ages'.[26] As Louise A Tilly has noted, social history 'covers a lot of ground' but can be defined as being 'the study of economic, political, and social structures, the analysis of collectivities – groups defined by class, occupation, sex, family position, geographic location, ethnicity, religion, etc. – in the past'.[27] She wrote that 'one of the key impulses of social history's development is (was) a populist vision that aims (aimed) to seek out how ordinary people lived and acted in the past'. Social history 'adds new stories or new voices and characters to old stories' and 'deepens and broadens the contexts of our stories'. As Kali Murray puts it, 'social history widens the scope by focusing on a broader range of actors'.[28]

23 However, since the 1960s intellectual historians have increasingly focused on the 'study of communities of knowledge' rather than on the lives of 'great minds' (Assaf Likhovski, 'The Intellectual History of Law' in Markus D Dubber and Christopher Tomlins (eds) *The Oxford Handbook of Legal History* (Oxford University Press, 2018)151, 161), an approach that has to date had less influence on legal scholarship. However, see the essays in Michael Lobban and Ian Williams (eds) *Networks and Connections in Legal History* (Cambridge University Press, 2020). A further exception to this can be found in histories of learned societies, most notably Fiona Cownie and Raymond Cocks, *'A Great and Noble Occupation!' The History of the Society of Legal Scholars* (Hart, 2009). There has also been work on pressure and campaign groups such as Sharon Thompson's work on the Married Women's Association: Sharon Thompson, ***Family Law Reformers: The Story of the Married Women's Association*** (Hart, forthcoming).

24 John W Cairns, 'Intellectual History and Legal History' in Richard Whatmore and Brian Young (eds) *A Companion to Intellectual History* (John Wiley, 2016) 213.

25 John W Burrow, 'Intellectual History in English Academic Life: Reflections on a Revolution' in Richard Whatmore and Brian Young (eds) *Intellectual History* (Palgrave, 2006) 11.

26 G M Trevelyan, *English Social History* (Longmans, 1944) vii.

27 Louise A Tilly, 'Social History and Its Critics' (1980) 9(5) *Theory and Society* 668.

28 Kali Murray, 'Serendipity and Care: Cultural and Social History in Property Law' in Susan Bright and Sarah Blandy (eds) *Researching Property Law* (Palgrave, 2016) 77, 78.

As the last chapter explained, the rise of social history was itself a cause of the rise of External Legal History. It is not a far step to say that a social history approach is the defining characteristic of this kind of Legal History scholarship. It is the history of law as one social institution among other social institutions (such as the economy, family, education, media, religion and so on) and within the setting of society as a whole. It is the study of how law interacts with its social environment and how its social environment interacts with law. It is the historical study of the non-legal origins, causes, motivations, assumptions and consequences that are of relevance to the history of law. It is the study of non-legal sources and their relationship with legal sources, using a blend of methodologies. As Laura F Edwards notes, 'moving beyond the written records, legal officials, and designated institutions usually associated with the law's presence and influence, legal historians extend law into the realm of social history'.[29]

Social history can be empirical in that it is concerned with 'real life' and the histories of non-elites. It can also be theoretical. The opening editorial of the *Social History* journal noted that: 'Social historians increasingly offer explanations at the level of theory.... Many of the methods currently deployed by social historians are broadly derived from the social sciences'.[30] Although there are some criticisms of the use of social science research methods,[31] Charles Tilly has argued that:

> Far from being sopped up by the sponge of social science, however, social history – retrospective and prospective – has an opportunity to clean up the social sciences. The greatest need of the social sciences today is for historically grounded theories and analyses. By "historically grounded" I mean taking place and, especially, time explicitly and seriously into consideration.[32]

Social history can play a similar grounding role in relation to law. Social history places law into its temporal and sociological context. However, this process is two-way. As Laura F Edwards pointed out, reference to law is integral and transformational for social history: 'legal history then changes our view of social history, by exposing the law's presence in places and relationships that most historians imagine to be far distant from anything remotely legal'.[33] For Edwards, 'because people's use of the law also reshaped it..., social history and legal history are inseparable'. This insight is key to many pieces of work on External Legal History which already blend social history and legal analyses, most

29 Laura F Edwards, 'Law as Social History' in Markus D Dubber and Christopher Tomlins (eds) *The Oxford Handbook of Legal History* (Oxford University Press, 2018) 119, 120.

30 'Editorial' (1976) 1 *Social History* 1.

31 See Louise A Tilly, 'Social History and Its Critics' (1980) 9(5) *Theory and Society* 668.

32 Charles Tilly, 'Two Callings of Social History' (1980) 9(5) *Theory and Society* 679, 680.

33 Laura F Edwards, 'Law as Social History' in Markus D Dubber and Christopher Tomlins (eds) *The Oxford Handbook of Legal History* (Oxford University Press, 2018) 119, 120.

notably the work on the 'social history of law',[34] epitomised by the scholarship of Christopher Brooks as discussed in the previous chapter. Yet, reconceptualising such work as being the social history dimension of Legal History will underscore the need for lawyers doing such work to draw upon social history. Indeed, it will underline this as a methodological choice and recognise that other forms of history also impact upon and are impacted by law.[35]

This re-conceptualisation regarding Legal History as including at least an intellectual history dimension and a social history dimension underlines the need to move away from a binary distinction. Individual works and individual historians are likely to cross the line between the two. By emphasising that some Legal History work occurs in the intellectual history tradition while other takes place in the social history tradition, the intention is not to entrench differences between the two. Rather, it is to suggest the overlap and interrelated nature of historical work on law while simultaneously recognising the diversity of approaches and the value of both doctrinal and socio-legal analyses. Unlike the internal-external divide described in the last chapter or the focus on doctrinal and socio-legal methods, highlighting two dimensions of history does not provide a binary division. It is commonly accepted that the fields of intellectual and social history complement one another rather than battle one another. Richard Whatmore underlined that 'intellectual historians accept that… ideas are social forces'.[36] Robert Gordon has noted that 'the history of legal ideas is an important branch of the history of political and economic thought, of the way in which people try to explain, justify and rationalize the social arrangements under which they live'.[37] John Burrow has noted that the term 'intellectual history' is to be preferred over the term 'history of ideas' because this stresses how it complements other historical dimensions, 'registering, by analogy with "political" or "economic" history, an attention to forms of human activity'.[38] And Louse A Tilly has written that different forms of history can be dealt with separately and 'it is not everyone's task to integrate the two'.[39]

It is, therefore, not a question of one approach to Legal History superseding the other. The rigorous scholarship resulting in a volume of medieval case transcripts published by the Selden Society is as important as the scrupulous research that underpins a monograph applying social scientific research methods to reveal

34 Jonathan Rose, 'Studying the Past: The Nature and Development of Legal History as an Academic Discipline' (2010) 31(2) *The Journal of Legal History* 101, 119–120.

35 As Christopher Brooks noted, 'The intriguing thing about "the law" is that it appears to offer a tantalising opportunity to transcend the divide between political and social history': Christopher W Brooks, *Law, Politics and Society in Early Modern England* (Cambridge University Press, 2008) 10.

36 Richard Whatmore, *What Is Intellectual History?* (Polity Press, 2016) 9.

37 Robert J Gordon, 'Book Review: *Tort in America: An Intellectual History*' (1980–1991) 94 *Harvard Law Review* 903, 906.

38 John W Burrow, 'Intellectual History in English Academic Life: Reflections on a Revolution' in Richard Whatmore and Brian Young (eds) *Intellectual History* (Palgrave, 2006) 11.

39 Louise A Tilly, 'Social History and its Critics' (1980) 9(5) *Theory and Society* 668, 669.

the biographical experiences of litigants. Both add to our knowledge of how law was lived and both are subject to future revision. As John Baker has argued, 'historical work builds on what has gone before'.[40] Moreover, it needs to be accepted that they are different forms of Legal History and the fact that a study in intellectual history is not a social history (and vice versa) should not be used as a criticism against such work. It also needs to be noted that this approach would not mean that Legal History will cease to exist with such work becoming part of either intellectual history or social history. This is unlikely to happen because such work will still have a distinct legal focus. Work that is part of the intellectual history dimension of Legal History will be distinct from general intellectual history in that it will focus upon legal ideas. Similarly, work in the social history dimension of Legal History will be distinct from social history generally in that it focuses on interactions with law. The use of this language should, however, increase interaction and collaboration with historians with expertise in intellectual and social history. But it should not mean that these fields of history would replace Legal History. Legal History would continue to be understood as the study of the history of law, including its intellectual history and its social history. What is important is that both forms of work are carried out in the field as a whole and that the two forms are seen as part of the legal historian's toolkit. This understanding is designed to overcome existing divisions and to stress the value of and need for both approaches. It is not a question of one being newer than the other, or more sophisticated than the other, or, as will now be discussed, of one being more critical than the other.

The Second Principle: The Critical Character of Legal History

The second principle is that Subversive Legal History needs to be critical and transformative, drawing upon and developing the Critical Legal History tradition.

The rise of Critical Legal History can be understood as part of two wider (and related) developments. The first was the postmodern turn[41] within the

40 John Baker, 'Reflections on "Doing" Legal History' in Anthony Musson and Chantal Stebbings (eds) *Making Legal History* (Cambridge University Press, 2012) 7, 17.

41 There are various different understandings of the term postmodernity originating from a range of disciplines. For an entertaining introduction to several postmodernist theorists see Arthur A Berger, *Postmortem for a Postmodernist* (Sage, 1997). As Lyotard wrote, 'simplifying to the extreme', the term postmodern can be defined as 'incredulity towards metanarratives' and the term postmodern age can be used to describe a 'transition [that] has been under way since at least the end of the 1950s'. The concept of postmodernity may be understood as the rejection of the meta-narratives of modernity. Postmodernism is characterised by the 'breaking up of grand narratives', a rejection of positivism and the rise of pluralism and cultural relativism: Jean-Francois Lyotard, *The Postmodern Condition* (Manchester University Press, 1984) xxiv, 3, 15. As Bauman has put it, postmodernity is a rejection of 'the typically modern view of the world' as 'one of an essentially ordered totality': Zigmunt Bauman, *Legislators and Interpreters*

humanities and social sciences in general and in history in particular.[42] The second was the rise of Critical Legal Studies[43] within law which has been described as 'essentially "an historical enterprise" devised to destabilise or subvert accepted legal constructions'.[44] Critical Legal History, then, was both 'a product of the Critical Legal Studies movement' as well as the result of 'the ascendancy of radical thought in the broader academy'.[45] It describes a school of thought epitomised in the US in the work of Morton Horwitz and Robert Gordon and in the UK by David Sugarman.[46] Yet, like Critical Legal Studies and postmodernism, there are 'considerable variations in the style, focus and method of work produced' under the label of Critical Legal History.[47] Indeed, the very notion that there is one 'correct' theory or method is anathematic to critical scholars.[48]

For Jonathan Rose, Critical Legal History can be described as being 'conceptual and jurisprudential', 'strongly revisionist' in its attack of traditional juristic concepts and scholarly ideas and of viewing law 'as inherently historical and

(Polity, 1987) 3. See, further Zigmunt Bauman, *Intimations of Postmodernity* (Routledge, 1992) chapter 9.

42 Sugarman has referred to how 'the basic assumptions, principles and methodologies of history writing and the status of historical knowledge have been questioned by, amongst others, Geertz, Habermas, Gadamer, Foucault and Derrida in ways which, despite their abstraction and jargon, are increasingly difficult to ignore': David Sugarman, 'Writing "Law and Society" Histories' (1992) 55(5) *Modern Law Review* 292, 300. See further Ian Ward, *English Legal Histories* (Hart, 2019) 6–10.

43 For discussion of Critical Legal Studies and its impact upon law generally see, e.g., Roberto Mangaberia Unger, *The Critical Legal Studies Movement: Another Time, A Greater Task* (Verso, 2015); Ian Ward, *Introduction to Critical Legal Theory* (2nd ed, Cavendish, 2004); Alan Hunt, 'The Theory of Critical Legal Studies' (1986) 6 *Oxford Journal of Legal Studies* 1; Jiři Přibaň, 'Sharing the Paradigms? Critical Legal Studies and the Sociology of Law' in Reza Banakar and Max Travers (eds) *An Introduction to Law and Social Theory* (Hart, 2002) 119; and the essays collected in J Boyle (ed) *Critical Legal Studies* (Dartmouth, 1994) and (1987) 14(1) *Journal of Law and Society*.

44 K J M Smith and J P S McLaren 'History's Living Legacy: An Outline of "Modern" Historiography of the Common Law' (2001) 21 *Legal Studies* 251, 277.

45 Jonathan Rose, 'Studying the Past: The Nature and Development of Legal History as an Academic Discipline' (2010) 31(2) *The Journal of Legal History* 101, 120–121.

46 See Morton J Horwitz, *The Transformation of American Law 1780–1860* (Harvard University Press, 1977), Morton J Horwitz, *The Transformation of American Law 1870–1960: The Crisis of Legal Orthodoxy* (Oxford University Press 1992), R W Gordon, 'Critical Legal Histories' (1984) 36 *Stanford Law Review* 57, David Sugarman and G R Rubin. 'Towards a New History of Law and Material Society in England, (1750–1914)' in G R Rubin and David Sugarman (eds) *Law, Economy & Society* (Professional Books, 1984) 1.

47 Cf. Peter Fitzpatrick and Alan Hunt, 'Critical Legal Studies: Introduction' (1987) 14(1) *Journal of Law and Society* 1.

48 Fitzpatrick and Hunt asserted that 'Critical legal studies seeks to provide an environment in which radical and committed scholarship can thrive in diversity with no aspiration to lay down a "correct" theory or method': ibid.

with an ideological role'.[49] Like Critical Legal Studies generally, Critical Legal History can be understood as a critic of the orthodox legal position. Alan Hunt has written that Critical Legal Studies is a critique of liberalism and in particular:

> The liberalism against which critical theory directs its critical energies is the liberal theory which has generated the philosophy of legalism and the associated jurisprudence of legal positivism that has so decisively implanted itself in the academic, the political and the popular discourse of contemporary capitalist democracies. The central features of this powerful doctrine of legalism are: (a) the separation of law from other varieties of social control, (b) the existence of law in the form of rules which both define the proper sphere of their own application and (c) which are presented as the objective and legitimate normative mechanism whilst other normative types are partial or subjective, and (d) yield determinant and predictable results in their application in the juridical process.[50]

In short, a critical approach questions law's autonomy, objectivity and certainty. For instance, a major preoccupation of Critical Legal History is a particular focus upon the relationship between Law and economics[51] exploring 'whether law is a passive reflection of economic change or whether it has any degree of autonomous causal impact upon economic change'.[52] Critical Legal History is political not in the sense that it takes a particular political stance but in that it is directly concerned with questions of power. As Jim Phillips observed, 'there is a politics… in the sense that it requires rejection of the position that law stands entirely separate from society. But beyond that it is possible to write Legal History from a variety of political stances'.[53] Writing in this tradition often articulates, emphasises and directs critical fire at power imbalances. It realises that conventional historical narratives are constructs. This is reflected in Ben Golder's call for a 'critical genealogy': 'a mode of history writing that self-consciously operates on the level of narrative construction and not positive truth, beckoning us to think critically about its own narrative and the political stakes and conditions that give rise to it'.[54] Such an approach highlights that these orthodox constructs have not given voice to alternative and often minority approaches.

49 Jonathan Rose, 'Studying the Past: The Nature and Development of Legal History as an Academic Discipline' (2010) 31(2) *The Journal of Legal History* 101, 121.

50 Alan Hunt, 'The Theory of Critical Legal Studies' (1986) 6 *Oxford Journal of Legal Studies* 1, 4.

51 On which see, e.g., Ron Harris, 'The History and Historical Stance of Law and Economics' in Markus D Dubber and Christopher Tomlins (eds) *The Oxford Handbook of Legal History* (Oxford University Press, 2018) 23 and Anne Fleming, 'Legal History as Economic History' in ibid 207.

52 Alan Hunt, 'The New Legal History: Prospects and Perspectives' (1986) 10 *Contemporary Crises* 201, 203.

53 Jim Phillips, 'Why Legal History Matters' (2010) 41 *Victoria University of Wellington Law Review* 293, 301.

54 Ben Golder, 'Contemporary Legal Genealogies' in Justin Desautels-Stein and Christopher Tomlins (eds) *Searching for Contemporary Legal Thought* (Cambridge University Press, 2017) 80, 96.

As David Sugarman put it, 'selectivity, omissions and interpretations of many long-standing unifying frameworks are no longer accepted'.[55]

Alan Hunt has argued that Critical Legal History's 'primary target is a Whig interpretation of legal history which perceives the past as the forebear of the contemporary legal system through a unilinear trajectory'.[56] The label 'Whig History', originated by Herbert Butterfield,[57] describes a mode of 'big history' writing which long outlasted the Whig Party.[58] This approach presented a meta-narrative of 'the past as a journey to democracy or the past as a story of class struggle'.[59] As Ian Ward noted:

> Whig historians and jurists continued to write a narrative that placed the "great" Reform Act at the culmination of a long and "glorious" history stretching back through the "great and Glorious Revolution of 1688 to the "Great Charter" of 1215. A series of "great" things accounted for the past of English constitutional history, and the same past assured the future.[60]

This approach, which Critical Legal History set itself in opposition to, emphasised a narrative of evolutionary progress.[61] This was explored further in Robert W Gordon's now classic essay, 'Critical Legal Histories'.[62] This sought to describe the 'distinctive mode of legal history being written by scholars' affiliated with Critical Legal Studies and also had the broader aim of 'trying to tease out and make explicit a set of background assumptions (here called "evolutionary

55 David Sugarman, 'Writing "Law and Society" Histories' (1992) 55(5) *Modern Law Review* 292, 299.

56 Alan Hunt, 'The New Legal History: Prospects and Perspectives' (1986) 10 *Contemporary Crises* 201, 202–203.

57 Herbert Butterfield, *The Whig Interpretation of History* (G Bell & Sons, 1931).

58 Ian Ward, *English Legal Histories* (Hart, 2019) 4. Indeed, writing in 2012 Robert W Gordon noted that 'Whiggish modernization theories have recently rebounded in force'. He accredited the fall of the Soviet Union and the Iron Curtain as bringing back Whig progress narratives in particularly 'reductive and triumphalist forms': 'Now liberal capitalism on the **US** model was seen as the only viable outcome of modernization' (Robert W Gordon, '"Critical Legal Histories Revisited": A Response' (2012) 37 *Law & Social Inquiry* 200, 211).

59 David Sugarman, 'Writing "Law and Society"' Histories (1992) 55(5) *Modern Law Review* 292, 299.

60 Ian Ward, *Writing the Victorian Constitution* (Palgrave, 2018) 19.

61 Robert W Gordon has distinguished between narratives of recovery, progress and teleology: 'A narrative of recovery, often accompanied by a jeremiad lamenting recent lapses and corruptions, is one in which the legal system is seen as ready to be guided to recover the purity of its original principles. By contrast, a narrative of progress is one in which the legal system is seen as obeying a long-term process of historical transformation – e.g. from feudalism to liberal capitalism, status to contract, subordination to equality. Finally, a teleological narrative is one which shows legal forms working themselves pure over time to reveal their core of immanent principle': Robert Gordon, 'The Arrival of Critical Historicism' (1997) 49 *Stanford Law Review* 1023, 1024.

62 Robert W Gordon, 'Critical Legal Histories' (1984) 36 *Stanford Law Review* 57, reprinted as chapter 11 of Robert W Gordon, *Taming the Past: Essays on Law in History and History in Law* (Cambridge University Press, 2017). All subsequent references are to the reprint.

functionalism")[63] about the course of western History, that American legal scholars tended to take for granted, and to challenge those assumptions'.[64] In an introduction to the reprint of the essay, Gordon identified that, although Critical Legal Studies 'was never a unified thing', there was nonetheless 'a common agreement around the idea that the way law was taught in American Law Schools, rationalized in legal scholarship, and deployed in legal arguments and decision-making', that contributed to two ideas.[65] These were 'false legitimation', that is, 'the complacent idea that the legal system in force is about as efficient, just and rational a system that it could be' and 'false necessity' and the idea that the legal system 'could not be reformed except in minor ways without risking economic and political catastrophe'.

Gordon identified five common threads which underpinned the dominant vision of what he referred to as 'evolutionary functionalism'.[66] The first thread stresses the autonomy of law and emphasises the word 'and' in the phrase 'law and society'.[67] This is often denoted by reference to law's 'closure': the presentation of law as an autonomous phenomenon.[68] As Gordon put it, this representation portrays '"law" and "society" as separate special categories, each describable independently from the other but related to each other through various mechanisms of casual linkage'.[69] The second thread emphasises the pressures and limits upon society, that 'societies have needs'. This 'is the functionalist heart of the dominant vision': the Durkhemian[70] understanding of societies as having

63 The concept was referred to as 'adaptation theory' in Gordon's earlier work: Robert W Gordon, 'Historicism in Legal Scholarship' (1981) 90 *Yale Law Review* 1017, reprinted as chapter 10 of Robert W Gordon, *Taming the Past: Essays on Law in History and History in Law* (Cambridge University Press, 2017).

64 Ibid 221. The word 'background' here is key: 'in strictly legal writing the theory is usually inexplicit: it lurks as a set of background assumptions rather than being explicitly set forth and argued for': Robert W Gordon, '"Critical Legal Histories Revisited": A Response' (2012) 37 *Law & Social Inquiry* 200, 202.

65 Robert W Gordon, *Taming the Past: Essays on Law in History and History in Law* (Cambridge University Press, 2017) 220.

66 The scope and ambition of this analysis is breathtaking. As Christopher Tomlins has noted, 'in forty-odd pages, Gordon assimilates the totality of prior sociolegal theorizing – indeed, the totality of prior social science since the Enlightenment – to a single template or orthodoxy, which he then eviscerates in order to clear the ground'. He shows that 'Evolutionary functionalism is the dominant and enduring account of the relationship between legal and social change embraced in one form or another in enlightened opinion since the late eighteenth century': Christopher Tomlins, 'What Is Left of the Law and Society Paradigm after Critique? Revisiting Gordon's "Critical Legal Histories"' (2012) 37 *Law & Social Inquiry* 155, 159.

67 Robert W Gordon, *Taming the Past: Essays on Law in History and History in Law* (Cambridge University Press, 2017) 224.

68 For discussion, see, for instance, the essays in Alan Norrie (ed) *Closure or Critique: New Directions in Legal Theory* (Edinburgh University Press, 1993).

69 Robert W Gordon, *Taming the Past: Essays on Law in History and History in Law* (Cambridge University Press, 2017) 224.

70 Interestingly, his name call of the 'functionalist sociological legal history omits Durkheim: see ibid 227.

universal and specific needs which 'operate both as pressures and constraints' being 'motors driving the society to find means for their fulfilment' and setting 'the limits on the possibilities of social experimentation'.[71] The third thread develops this and states that all societies follow 'an objective, determined progressive social evolutionary path' in a way that is 'natural (in the sense that some version of it will happen in every society unless "artificial" constraints force a deviation)'. Although 'different generations have described these evolutionary processes somewhat differently',[72] the narrative employed is that of evolutionary progress.[73] Gordon noted that:

> What all these histories have in common is their determinist teleologies, whose elemental parts – the "extension of the market," the "breakdown of traditional communities and status hierarchies," the "shift from ascribed to achieved social status," the "triumph of the middle class," the "revolution of production in the factory system," the "rise of the administrative state," and the "development of the multi-divisional form of corporate organization" – are all linked together in a master process of social evolution.[74]

Gordon noted that while lawyers 'once played a moderately important role in actually writing these histories', now legal writing 'is more likely just to assume that some objective, generally understood process of development has been working away in the background, and to leave the actual details of the process to vague implication'.[75] In other words, this narrative of progress is not only implicitly accepted, it is also not questioned. Gordon's fourth thread is that that legal systems are 'described and explained in terms of their functional responsiveness to social needs'; the analysis is whether 'legal forms and institutions have satisfied, or failed to satisfy, the functional requirements of each stage' in social development. The fifth thread is that 'the legal system adapts to changing social needs' in that, although legal changes 'can be dysfunctional for short periods', adaption is the normal course'.[76] This is reflected in the idea that the 'common law over time tends to work itself pure', that legal doctrine has become 'ever more certain and predictable as well as more adaptable to social needs'; and that

71 Ibid 225.

72 Later Gordon noted that: 'Nobody ever thought this modal form was universal: some societies have deviated into fascism, others into communism; still others reverted to theocracy or virulent ethnic nationalism, and many have simply stagnated in traditional or primitive phases': Robert W Gordon, '"Critical Legal Histories Revisited": A Response' (2012) 37 *Law & Social Inquiry* 200, 200–201.

73 On which see further, Peter Stein, *Legal Evolution: The Story of an Idea* (Cambridge University Press, 1980) and Allan C Hutchinson, *Evolution of the Common Law* (Cambridge University Press, 2005).

74 Robert W Gordon, *Taming the Past: Essays on Law in History and History in Law* (Cambridge University Press, 2017) 220, 226–227.

75 Ibid 227.

76 Ibid 228.

the law has 'become more and more efficient'.[77] As he later put it, this functionalist part of the argument is 'that law and legal systems are best understood as facilitative technologies that are adaptive responses to social needs and demands resulting from these modernizing processes: law basically follows evolving custom'.[78] Gordon's argument is that the pervasive functionalism has turned both 'law' and 'society' into 'ahistorical, universal types'.

Evolutionary functionalism therefore lives up to its label. It describes a number of ideas and assumptions that are dominant and entrenched which assemble around two ideas: evolution – a basic Darwinian understanding that regards history as a constant, linear process of progress and improvement – and functionalism – the underlying values of the functionalist school of sociological thought, dated to Emile Durkheim[79] and Talcott Parsons,[80] that understands society as being comprised of agencies of socialisation that perform different functions in order for society as a whole to operate through consensus. As Gordon notes, this vision 'has been kept going much longer in legal thought than in social thought generally'.[81] He notes that: 'The notion that law always is, or at least ought to be, functionally adapting to evolving social needs is so deeply embedded in standard legal speech that one isn't likely to make a legal argument of any length without at least mentioning it'. Evolutionary functionalism is so entrenched that it is almost unnoticeable. The effect it has upon how Law Schools understand and portray law is significant. This is especially true of how Law Schools understand legal change and Legal History: evolutionary functionalism's 'essential working assumptions misleadingly objectify history, making highly contingent developments appear to have been necessary'.[82] It promotes the idea that the development of the law is orderly, inevitable and, to be blunt, dull. The prevalence of evolutionary functionalism represses the potential of Legal History to underline the contingency of law and the vast scope of legal change.

As Gordon noted, the critical approach counters evolutionary functionalism by arguing:

77 Ibid 229.

78 Robert W Gordon, '"Critical Legal Histories Revisited": A Response' (2012) 37 *Law & Social Inquiry* 200, 200–201.

79 Durkheim's conception of law is aptly summed up by a chapter title used in Roger Cotterrell's *The Sociology of Law*: 'Law as an Integrative Mechanism': Roger Cotterrell, *The Sociology of Law* (2nd ed, Butterworths, 1992). See also Roger Cotterrell, *Emile Durkheim: Law in a Moral Domain* (Stanford University Press 1999).

80 On which see A Javier Trevino, *Talcott Parsons on Law and the Legal System* (Cambridge Scholars Publishing 2008). Parsons' work has also been afforded little attention in the sociology of law: Reza Banakar and Max Travers, 'Systems Theory' in Reza Banakar and Max Travers (eds) *Law and Social Theory* (2nd ed, Hart. 2013) 53. This work has been developed more recently into the social systems theory identified with the works of Niklas Luhmann, which is further discussed in Chapter 5.

81 Robert W Gordon, *Taming the Past: Essays on Law in History and History in Law* (Cambridge University Press, 2017) 231.

82 Ibid 233.

> that by taking the world as we know it as largely determined by impersonal social forces, evolutionary-functionalists obscure the ways in which these seemingly inevitable processes are actually manufactured by people who claim (and believe themselves) to be only passively adapting to such processes.

This has some similarities with Marxist critiques of false consciousness but differs in that it does not come from a particular political perspective (though critical approaches derive from the Left generally)[83] and places more emphasis upon agency. In 'Critical Legal Histories' Gordon presented various different 'partial critiques' that provided variations upon evolutionary functionalism,[84] before providing a seven-part summary from these of a 'set of partial critiques' which 'most people who accept themselves as doing critical legal historiography would probably accept'.[85] These were as follows. First, social life and the course of historical development are 'not determined by any uniform evolutionary path'.[86] Second, there is no determined link between social and legal change: 'Comparable social conditions (both within the same and across societies) have generated contrary legal responses, and comparable legal forks have produced contrary social effects'. Third, law is neither 'an objective response to objective historical processes' nor 'a neutral technology adapted to the needs of that particular society'. Rather, 'legal forms and practices are political products that arise from the struggles of conflict'. Fourth, legal forms and practices do not 'shift with every realignment of the balance of political forces' but are embedded in 'relatively autonomous' structures. Fifth, these 'relatively autonomous' structures have their own internal ideologies and rituals that have an effect upon 'the realm of consciousness' meaning that legal forms and practices cannot 'be explained completely by reference to external political/social/economic factors'. Sixth, this impacts upon our accustomed way of thinking about the history of law whereby we simply project our 'parochial categories onto the past'.[87] Seventh, this can be overcome by realising that the conventional views of the historical development of law 'are mediated by familiar narrative story-lines that are so deeply entrenched in our consciousness that we are often unaware of their rule over our conception of reality'.

83 For Christopher Tomlins, Gordon's essay 'is deeply haunted by Marxism' in that 'there runs throughout the essay, expressed almost wholly offhand, in asides and footnotes, a constant distancing from, and disavowal of, Marxist history and theory': Christopher Tomlins, 'What is Left of the Law and Society Paradigm after Critique? Revisiting Gordon's "Critical Legal Histories"' (2012) 37 *Law & Social Inquiry* 155, 159.

84 See Robert W Gordon, *Taming the Past: Essays on Law in History and History in Law* (Cambridge University Press, 2017) 234–260.

85 Gordon pointed out that these critiques did not originate with Critical Legal Studies but that Critical Legal Studies scholars have combined these critiques, attempt to go beyond them and have applied the results to the historiography of legal doctrines and institutions: ibid 261.

86 Ibid 260.

87 Ibid 261.

Gordon concluded by arguing that the Critical Legal History critique could be generalised and deepened in three ways.[88] First, the distinction between law and society can be blurred further by emphasising 'the fundamentally constitutive character of legal relations in social life'.[89] Law and society are 'inextricably mixed';[90] after all, 'it is just about impossible to describe any set of "basic" social practices without describing the legal relations among the people involved'.[91] Second, it can be argued that law is constitutive of consciousness: this is the 'claim not only that law figures as a factor of the power relationships of individuals and social classes but also that it is omnipresent in the very marrow of society'.[92] Indeed, 'legal categories affect social perceptions' to such an extent that law persuades that 'the world described in its images and categories is the only attainable world in which a sane person would want to live'. For Gordon, a critical approach highlights this and supersedes it by showing that the social effect of law is contingent and exploring 'counterfactual trajectories':

> Another way of looking at what seems to be the key difference of approach between functionalists and their Critical opponents is that the functionalist examines what has actually happened and explains how it all "works," how each development fits into the pattern created by all the others, while the Critic takes each event as situated not on a single developmental path but on multiple trajectories of possibility, the path actually chosen being chosen not because it had to be but because the people pushing for alternatives were weaker and lost out in their struggle or because both winners and losers shared a common consciousness that set the agenda for all of them, highlighting some possibilities and suppressing others completely. How can one identify the counterfactual trajectories, the roads not taken? From the experience of other societies, from the hopes of those who lost the struggle, from routine practices that the same society has tried in other spheres of life without ever dreaming they might be applied to the situation at hand, and from imagination disciplined, as one hopes, by the knowledge of past failures.[93]

Gordon suggested here that a Critical approach rejects the single-trajectory view of socio-legal change by showing how that change was not pre-determined but was the result of agency and chance. This element of chance is developed in the

88 Susanna L Blumenthal has argued that 'these aspects of the Critique are best understood as overstatements of the sort made in the throes of a generational revolt': Susanna L Blumenthal, 'Of Mandarins, Legal Consciousness, and the Cultural Turn in US Legal History' (2012) 37 *Law & Social Inquiry* 167, 174.

89 Robert W Gordon, *Taming the Past: Essays on Law in History and History in Law* (Cambridge University Press, 2017) 263.

90 Ibid 266.

91 Ibid 262.

92 Ibid 267.

93 Ibid 271.

third way in which he suggested a Critical approach can be furthered.[94] Gordon suggested that: 'The same body of law, in the same context, can always lead to contrary results because law is indeterminate at its core, in its inception, not just in its applications'.[95] For Gordon, this 'indeterminacy exists because legal rules derive from structures of thought, the collective constructs of many minds, that are fundamentally contradictory'.[96] Law is 'founded upon contradictions' and its chief job is 'to keep those oppositions from becoming too starkly obvious'.[97] Legal History written in the evolutionary functionalist mode seeks to hide and/ or normalise this. By contrast, Legal History written in the critical mode seeks to highlight and question this. As Gordon put it, critical legal historiography becomes 'the intellectual history of the rise and fall of paradigm structures of thought designed to mediate contradictions'.[98] Critical Legal Historians need to strive towards providing 'thickly described accounts of how law has been imbricated in and has helped to structure the most routine practices of social life'.[99]

Over a decade later, in an introduction to a symposium on critical histories, Gordon provided further guidance on how this was to be achieved. In his short essay 'The Arrival of Critical Historicism', he provided a broader account of what a critical approach entailed.[100] Gordon there described 'critical history' as 'any approach to the past that produces disturbances in the field – that inverts or scrambles familiar narratives of stasis, recovery or progress; anything that advances rival perspectives'. [101]

Christopher Tomlins has called this approach 'utterly subversive'.[102] Read in conjunction with 'Critical Legal Histories', it can be said that Critical Legal History is a disturbance that seeks to unsettle and critique the notion that law is autonomous, objective and predictable and complicates accounts of legal and

94 Christopher Tomlins has argued that this is the decisive departure, 'the point of no return': Christopher Tomlins, 'What Is Left of the Law and Society Paradigm after Critique? Revisiting Gordon's "Critical Legal Histories"' (2012) 37 *Law & Social Inquiry* 155, 158.

95 Ibid. As Laura F Edwards has noted, Gordon's world is one where 'change is circuitous, illogical, and even accidental; in which even the most informed actions did not always produce intended consequences; in which similar political currents produced different outcomes in different places. People then could not control their world, and we are even less equipped to comprehend past societies now. Our efforts to represent the past will always be partial because the logic of that world, to the extent that logic guided it at all, is now lost': Laura F Edwards, 'The History in "Critical Legal Studies"' (2012) 37 *Law & Social Inquiry* 187, 190.

96 Robert W Gordon, *Taming the Past: Essays on Law in History and History in Law* (Cambridge University Press, 2017) 271–272.

97 Ibid 273.

98 Ibid 274.

99 Ibid 281.

100 Christopher Tomlins, 'What Is Left of the Law and Society Paradigm after Critique? Revisiting Gordon's "Critical Legal Histories' (2012) 37 *Law & Social Inquiry* 155, 163.

101 Robert Gordon, 'The Arrival of Critical Historicism' (1997) 49 *Stanford Law Review* 1023, 1024.

102 Christopher Tomlins, 'After Critical Legal History: Scope, Scale, Structure' (2012) 8 *Annual Review of Law and Social Science* 31, 37.

social change that are based upon these liberal expectations. It challenges progress myths of legal evolution and the associated conservative belief that legal change can occur within the system. Some of the principles put forward by Gordon would now be accepted by a significant number of legal scholars. For instance, this is true of the focus on power relationships and the contention that 'law, society, culture and economy are not external to each other; they are part of a larger common complex'.[103] However, Gordon's critical approach goes further than the now common calls to place law in context.

As Roger Cotterrell put it, 'a critique of law must put all taken-for-granted assumptions about the nature of law in issue'.[104] Critical Legal History 'shows the way in which our most basic legal categories and distinctions (e.g. that between "public" and "private" realms) are both the product of, and themselves give rise to, political and ideological struggles among different people'.[105] It is inherently revisionist, necessarily challenging and invariably contentious, controversial and divisive.

This controversial and divisive nature also applies to the 'critical' label itself. The word is both vague and loaded. The term is vague in that the word 'critical' is used to refer to any sort of judgment. As Panu Minkkinen has noted, '"critical judgment" is a generic intellectual skill that all researchers are supposed to be able to apply'.[106] A critical approach is also by definition always a response to something else: 'to be critical is always to be critical *of* something'.[107] And this means that it is shaped by the assumptions, values and content of whatever is being criticised. A critique runs the risk of being merely an act of de-construction.[108] It does not necessarily enable the necessary next step of re-construction. Writing over twenty years after the publication of 'Critical Legal Histories', Gordon conceded that 'the potential contributions of historical learning to rebuilding society – as contrasted simply to combating the fatalistic sense that no change is possible – are still not so clear'.[109] This is at least in part attributable to the label 'critical' and the form and ambition of analysis that it denotes.

103 David Sugarman, 'Writing "Law and Society" Histories' (1992) 55(5) *Modern Law Review* 292, 298.

104 Roger Cotterrell, 'Power, Property and the Law of Trusts: A Partial Agenda for Critical Legal Scholarship' (1987) 14(1) *Journal of Law and Society* 77, 79.

105 Charles Barzun, 'Causation, Legal History, and Legal Doctrine' (2016) 64 *Buffalo Law Review* 81, 86.

106 Panu Minkkinen, 'Critical Legal "Method" as Attitude' in Dawn Watkins and Mandy Burton (eds) *Research Methods in Law* (2nd ed, Routledge, 2018) 146.

107 Ibid 150.

108 Gordon noted that works of Critical Legal Studies tended to take the same format: 'orthodoxy synthesized-partial critiques-total critique and transcendence-critique of the critique': Robert W Gordon, *Taming the Past: Essays on Law in History and History in Law* (Cambridge University Press, 2017) 222.

109 Robert W Gordon, 'The Past as Authority and as Social Critic: Stabilizing and Destabilizing Functions of History in Legal Argument' in Terrence J McDonald (ed) *The Historic Turn in the Human Sciences* (University of Michigan Press, 1996) 339, 364–365.

The 'critical' label is also loaded due to its association with Critical Legal Studies. The experience of Critical Legal Studies in England and Wales has differed significantly from in the United States.[110] On this side of the pond, Critical Legal Studies was even more at the margins of legal education. It has been described as 'the *enfant terrible* of contemporary legal studies. It delights in shocking what it takes to be the legal establishment'.[111] It has also been much more associated with Marxism. As Peter Fitzpatrick and Alan Hunt noted, 'in Britain critical legal studies has been less eclectic: the key traditions informing debate have been Marxism, feminism and critical social theory of the Frankfurt variety'.[112] The decline in interest in Marxism has meant that the Critical Legal Studies banner has largely been replaced by particular focuses on critical race, feminist and sexualities studies.[113] The same has happened in the US, where Critical Legal Studies once had a much larger stronghold, and, as Gordon noted, these intellectual movements have prospered because they had the advantage 'of being allied with active movements for social and legal change outside the academy'.[114] Most accounts agree that the Critical Legal Studies movement (if it ever was a movement) was burned out in the 1990s, though 'the echoes of its intervention are still audible in legal scholarship'.[115] The same is true of Critical Legal History, which again was far more established in America than it ever was in Britain. Even in America, where the 'greatest long-term influence and success' of Critical Legal Studies was in Legal History,[116] this too has declined. As Christopher Tomlins has noted, 'the conjunction of history of law has proceeded more prosaically. Contextualizing debates have been rampant' and there

110 Roger Cotterrell, 'Power, Property and the Law of Trusts: A Partial Agenda for Critical Legal Scholarship' (1987) 14(1) *Journal of Law and Society* 77.

111 Alan Hunt, 'The Critique of Law: What is "Critical" about Critical Legal Theory?' (1987) 14(1) *Journal of Law and Society* 5.

112 Peter Fitzpatrick and Alan Hunt, 'Critical Legal Studies: Introduction' (1987) 14(1) *Journal of Law and Society* 1, 2.

113 Christopher Tomlins concluded that 'Marxism has never had more than a fringe presence in legal history' and that 'legal historians need to discover what makes Marxist legal history useful and attractive is less that it is a particular way of doing legal history that produces specific outcomes than that it is an explicitly *historical* method': Christopher Tomlins 'Marxist Legal History' in Markus D Dubber and Christopher Tomlins (eds) *The Oxford Handbook of Legal History* (Oxford University Press, 2018) 515, 537, 538.

114 Robert W Gordon, '"Critical Legal Histories Revisited": A Response' (2012) 37 *Law & Social Inquiry* 200, 204.

115 Christopher Tomlins, 'What Is Left of the Law and Society Paradigm after Critique? Revisiting Gordon's "Critical Legal Histories"' (2012) 37 *Law & Social Inquiry* 155, 156. As Brenna Bhandar has noted, 'while critical legal studies in American legal academe is now a school of thought that is seen in historical terms, it continues to have a generative and productive life in the Anglophone world (in particular, the UK, Ireland, and Australia)': Brenna Bhandar, 'Critical Legal Studies and the Politics of Property' in Susan Bright and Sarah Blandy (eds) *Researching Property Law* (Palgrave, 2016) 60, 62.

116 Christopher Tomlins, 'What Is Left of the Law and Society Paradigm after Critique? Revisiting Gordon's "Critical Legal Histories"' (2012) 37 *Law & Social Inquiry* 155, 163.

has been the 'dominion of social history in legal history research'.[117] For Tomlins, this has resulted in 'complacency' and a field 'awaiting redemption':[118] 'The "subversive" conjunction between history and critical legal studies… has ended' and this is 'a marker of intellectual exhaustion'.[119]

This book argues, however, that there is much life left in a subversive approach. Critical Legal Studies has left a legacy upon twenty-first century Law Schools. There are critical research networks, critical modules and critical alternative textbooks but their ideas continue to seldom trouble the mainstream. They remain a niche alternative. Although many of the ideas and principles of the Critical Legal Studies movement have become widely accepted, this is typically in areas that are peripheral to Law Schools. Moreover, this mostly relates to particular critiques within the legal system as opposed to a critique of the system as a whole. This book argues, therefore that there is a need to revisit the bolder original works. This is not about turning the clocks back to the debates of the late twentieth century but about learning from them by going back to the original works by Gordon. The 'critical' label is unhelpful here because it invokes Critical Legal Studies with all its baggage. Rather than turning to the Critical Legal Studies tradition as a whole, there is a need to revisit Gordon's foundational work and to develop further what he referred to as 'the subversive tendencies of critical history'.[120] Gordon's work actually shows that such an approach is not a further example of the new and external approaches to Legal History (as many accounts have assumed Critical Legal History to be).[121] The last few pages of 'Critical Legal Histories' argue that it actually applies more to Internal Legal History, understanding this as a form of intellectual history which is critically informed. The two principles of Subversive Legal History outlined in this chapter therefore overlap. Legal History should be understood as having at least an intellectual history and a social history dimension – and both of these dimensions need to be critical. The subversive approach is not limited to work in the social history dimension; it also applies to the conventional mainstream doctrinal legal histories that this chapter has re-characterised as being the intellectual history dimension of Legal History. The final section will explore this further: with reference to Gordon as well as to Roger Cotterrell's seminal essay 'Why Must Legal Ideas be

117 Christopher Tomlins, 'Law and History' in Keith E Whittington, R Daniel Kelemen and Gregory A Calderia (eds) *The Oxford Handbook of Law and Politics* (Oxford University Press, 2008) 723, 728.

118 Ibid 731.

119 Ibid 730.

120 Robert W Gordon, 'The Arrival of Critical Historicism' (1997) 49 *Stanford Law Review* 1023, 1026.

121 See, e.g., Jonathan Rose, 'Studying the Past: the Nature and Development of Legal History as an Academic Discipline' (2010) 31(2) *The Journal of Legal History* 120 and Russell Sandberg and Norman Doe, 'Textual and Contextual Legal History' in N Doe and R Sandberg (eds) *Law and History: Critical Concepts* (Routledge, 2017) 1, 8 *et seq.*

Interpreted Sociologically?',[122] it will explore how a critical approach applies to Internal Legal History.

Why Must Legal Ideas be Interpreted Historically?

Ironically, work on why a sociological approach to law should be favoured over all others provides an argument for why law needs history and why this requires both internal and external approaches.

In twenty-first century Law Schools it is uncontroversial (at least in terms of research) to suggest that law should be understood in its context and, although law has a number of potential disciplinary bedfellows and the choice of partner is shaped by subject, question and personal preference/experience, invariably the suitor is some form of social science discipline. This is so taken for granted that it has aroused little comment. However, the work of Roger Cotterrell about the need for the Sociology of Law has cast some attention on this. Although Cotterrell explored why a sociological approach to law is required, his work has been interpreted and developed by Michael Lobban to argue for the historical study of law. Moreover, this argument shows that Cotterrell's argument applied especially to internal doctrinal study provided that this is reconceptualised as a form of intellectual history.

A shift in Cotterrell's thinking can be identified that broadened his understanding of what a sociological approach to law entailed. Cotterrell's early work clearly visualised law and sociology as two disciplines that could complement one another. He wrote how they shared 'a fundamentally similar subject matter': 'norms, rules, institutions, social relations, authority, social control, civil rights, power, conflict and conflict resolution and the relationship between the public and private spheres'.[123] For Cotterrell, the fact that sociology is concerned with the very values, patterns and ideologies that are embodied in law as substantive rules meant that the two disciplines were 'similarly comprehensive' and it was:

> this common concern of law and sociology with the whole range of social relations which makes a sociological perspective on law potentially more generally fruitful than, for example, a perspective drawn from economics, or some other discipline concerned with a particular category of human relationships.[124]

By contrast, Cotterrell's later work, particularly in his essay 'Why Must Legal Ideas be Interpreted Sociologically?', went beyond arguments for cooperation between law and sociology. His argument became that legal and sociological

122 Roger Cotterrell, 'Why Must Legal Ideas be Interpreted Sociologically?' (1998) 25 *Journal of Law and Society* 171, reprinted as Roger Cotterrell, *Law, Culture and Society* (Ashgate, 2006) chapter 3. All subsequent references will be to the reprint.

123 Roger Cotterrell, *The Sociology of Law* (2nd ed, Butterworths, 1992) 5–6.

124 Ibid 5.

understandings of law are 'inseparable'.[125] His later work emphasised how 'legal and other social ideas interpenetrate each other'.[126] For Cotterrell, legal ideas are not only the cause and the product of social reality (and vice versa) but the two are constantly interacting: 'Sociological insight is simultaneously inside and outside legal ideas, constituting them and interpreting them, sometimes speaking through them and sometimes speaking about them, sometimes aiding, sometimes undermining them'. He argued that to understand legal ideas sociologically is to understand legal ideas as 'a means of structuring the social world', recognising both 'power and their limits'.[127]

The use of the word 'Ideas' in the title 'Why Must Legal Ideas be Interpreted Sociologically?' is, therefore, telling. Cotterrell is doing more than rejecting the classic distinction between law as behaviour studied by sociologists and law as doctrine studied by lawyers. Cotterrell is arguing that law as doctrine should also be studied sociologically since it is the study of ideas. His argument is not just that law can have social affects and be shaped by the social. Rather, it is that legal ideas themselves are social phenomena and need to be studied as such. The use of Cotterrell's argument here might appear to be perverse since he was arguing that legal ideas needed to be understood sociologically not historically.

Cotterrell's later argument developed (but did not cite) the first of the three ways in which Gordon argued that the Critical Legal History critique could be generalised and deepened.[128] As Gordon later noted, this had come to form 'an alternative conception to functionalism' which was 'called – rather mystifyingly and not always helpfully – a "constitutive" theory of law-society relations' whereby 'law (partially) constitutes society and society constitutes law'.[129] Indeed, this notion of law and society as mutually constitutive is one of the Critical Legal Studies tenets that have become commonplace.[130]

This is important in that it completely disregards and explodes the internal-external binary distinction. Susanna L Blumenthal has argued that Gordon's 'Critical Legal Histories' discards the law-box model that Gordon had previously

125 Roger Cotterrell, *Law, Culture and Society* (Ashgate, 2006) 45.

126 Ibid 54.

127 Ibid 63.

128 Robert W Gordon, *Taming the Past: Essays on Law in History and History in Law* (Cambridge University Press, 2017) 263.

129 Robert W Gordon, '"Critical Legal Histories Revisited": A Response' (2012) 37 *Law & Social Inquiry* 200, 203. See also Alan Hunt, *Explorations in Law and Society: Towards a Constitutive Theory of Law* (Routledge, 1993).

130 Laura F Edwards, 'The History in "Critical Legal Studies"' (2012) 37 *Law & Social Inquiry* 187, 188. As Cynthia Nicoletti has put it: 'new works of history are less interested in cordoning off the realm of the explicitly "legal". Law and society are not necessarily distinct anymore in a meaningful way, or at least legal historians perceive the two realms as mutually constitutive of one another, such that it no longer makes sense to draw a sharp demarcation between the two. The boundary between the legal and the non-legal is porous and difficult to pinpoint with a great deal of precision': Cynthia Nicoletti, 'Writing the Social History of Legal Doctrine' (2016) 64 *Buffalo Law Review* 121.

described,[131] since 'law and society were now understood to be inextricably connected'.[132] Likewise discarded is the sociological and jurisprudential distinction between law as behaviour (studied by sociologists) and law as doctrine (as studied by lawyers).[133] Moreover, this also discards the distinction between Internal and External Legal History: as Gordon pointed out, contrasting the 'history of legal ideas' with 'the history of the law's effects on actual behaviour in the real world' is just 'another version of the false law/society dichotomy'.[134] The mutually constitutive argument goes further than saying that both perspectives are needed and are complementary.[135] It is no longer a question of needing both dimensions. It is that both dimensions are interlinked. There is no separate box of law; rather the legal and the social constantly interpenetrate one another. Crucially, this means that the two approaches cannot ignore each other. This means that it is impossible to study law in isolation from society. Moreover, the reverse is also true. As Michael Lobban has argued, this approach contends that 'those who study society without paying serious attention to what is distinctively "legal" within it impoverish their very understanding of that society'.[136] The mutually constitutive argument therefore shows why it is important to analyse law internally. Understanding law and society as being mutually constitutive requires understanding the legal and the social. Michael Lobban has built upon this to argue that historical approaches to law provide a preferable way of exploring law internally. Reviewing sociological and philosophical ways of examining law internally by comparing the 'internal perspectives' put forward by the likes of Herbert Hart, Brian Tamanaha and Niklas Luhmann, Lobban suggested that although these theories explore 'how to identify the distinct realm of law, by considering "internal" perspectives which invite us to think about what people *mean* by law' they do not go 'quite far enough in identifying what is law and how it works'.[137] For Lobban, these theories do not 'look at the ways in which

131 Robert W Gordon, 'J. Willard Hurst and the Common Law Tradition in American Legal Historiography' (1975) 10 *Law & Society Review* 9, 11.

132 Susanna L Blumenthal, 'Of Mandarins, Legal Consciousness, and the Cultural Turn in US Legal History' (2012) 37 *Law & Social Inquiry* 167, 174.

133 As Niklas Luhmann put it, 'sociologists observe the law from the outside and lawyers observe the law from the inside': Niklas Luhmann, *Law as a Social System* (Oxford University Press, 2004) 59. For further discussion of the distinction see, e.g., Brian Z Tamanaha, *Realistic Socio-Legal Theory* (Oxford University Press, 1997) chapter 6 and Reza Banakar, *Merging Law and Sociology: Beyond the Dichotomies in Socio-Legal Research* (Galda and Wilch Verlag, 2003) chapter 2.

134 Robert W Gordon, 'Critical Legal Histories' in Robert W Gordon (ed) *Taming the Past: Essays on Law in History and History in Law* (Cambridge University Press, 2017) 274.

135 For example, Luhmann came to this conclusion on the basis that each perspective 'sees more, but sometimes less' than the other: Niklas Luhmann, *A Sociological Theory of Law* (2nd ed, Routledge, 1983/2014) 286.

136 Michael Lobban, 'Sociology, History and the "Internal" Study of Law' in Richard Nobles and David Schiff (eds) *Law, Society and Community: Socio-Legal Essays in Honour of Roger Cotterrell* (Ashgate, 2014) 39, 39–40.

137 Ibid 51.

law is used and developed; and it is here that the historical approach can be of particular use'. There is a need to consider both 'law as rule' (law as 'a mechanism of power') and also 'law as interpretation' ('law as a specialist intellectual technique'). And law as interpretation 'can be usefully studied with the tools of intellectual history', which explores the development of legal ideas and legal technique. Lobban maintains that a historical approach is particularly useful in understanding law internally since it provides a detailed empirical study which is able to trace and explain change and its internal and external causes, including the way in which 'incremental economic and social changes may also have an impact on "internal" doctrine'.[138] Law provides concrete evidence of political, social, economic and cultural change. It provides records which, although seemingly technical, are also loaded with the values and assumptions of the time in which they were written.

This argument can be taken further to show that internal historical approaches to law can themselves be critical. This really subverts the prevalent image of the internal-external distinction in Legal History as captured in the previous chapter. Internal approaches are stereotyped and dismissed as being part of the 'old' Legal History which newer and critical approaches will supersede. Alan Hunt has somewhat dramatically described the 'evolutionary doctrinalism' of orthodox Legal History as 'the major tradition which the new legal history seeks to supersede' and as its 'enemy'.[139] Alan Hunt, like other critical legal theorists, tends to position their approach in opposition to doctrinal legal studies. Writing with Peter Fitzpatrick, he wrote that an 'element of cohesion' among critical theorists can be found in the 'shared rejection of the dominant tradition of Anglo-American legal scholarship, the expository orthodoxy or, more crudely, the "black-letter law" tradition'.[140] Critical Legal History, then, is usually seen as an example of the new external approach. However, Michael Lobban has shown that histories of internal doctrine can actually be critical. Internal historical analysis can reveal that the position 'is less stable and coherent than is sometimes assumed'.[141] As he put it, to study legal doctrine is to study of how 'judges and 'jurists constantly strive for doctrinal coherence'. It is to study law as a human-construct. Indeed, as Lobban points out, re-constructing the internal 'entails getting inside the mind of actors within the "system"'.[142] This approach is reflected in the development of internal Legal History as a dimension of intellectual history, as discussed above. It is also reflected in Gordon's 'Critical Legal Histories', the idea that Legal History in the critical tradition actually points to rather than conceals the contradictions and general grubbiness of legal interactions.

138 Ibid 54, 55.

139 Alan Hunt, 'The New Legal History: Prospects and Perspectives' (1986) 10 *Contemporary Crises* 201, 203.

140 Peter Fitzpatrick and Alan Hunt, 'Critical Legal Studies: Introduction' (1987) 14(1) *Journal of Law and Society* 1.

141 Michael Lobban, 'Sociology, History and the "Internal" Study of Law' in Richard Nobles and David Schmidt (eds) *Law, Society and Community: Socio-Legal Essays in Honour of Roger Cotterrell'* (Ashgate, 2014) 39.

142 Ibid 56.

It is often underappreciated that Gordon's 'Critical Legal Histories' is an article which sought to develop internal doctrinal legal-historical scholarship. Yet, the article began by stating that critical legal writers had 'probably devoted more pages to historical description – particularly the intellectual history of legal doctrine – than to anything else, even law and economics', noted that this was 'at first glance surprising' and asked: 'What could conceivably be radical – or, as some unkindly ask, even interesting – about rewriting the history of doctrine?'[143] It is true that the article was critical of the conventional internal approach but this was only in so far as the approach implicitly accepted evolutionary functionalism.[144] Gordon was not dismissive of such work *per se* but wrote that such historians 'are partly to blame for the ways in which their work has been misunderstood' because they sometimes wrote 'without paying nearly enough attention to the applications to which these doctrines were put in everyday practical reasoning or to the specific controversies or political events that suddenly opened up the doctrines to question'.[145] Critical Legal History was intended to redress this and did this by re-casting rather than abandoning doctrinal Legal History. It is notable that Gordon's third way in which the Critical Legal History critique could be generalised and deepened portrayed Critical Legal History as being 'the intellectual history of the rise and fall of paradigm structures of thought designed to mediate contradictions' and Gordon stated that 'this special kind of doctrinal history is surely the most distinctive Critical contribution'.[146] As Gordon later explained, he wanted to show that:

> This new doctrinal history of legal fields structured by "contradictions" was not a reactionary reversion to traditional "internal" modes of legal historiography, but an interesting and illuminating way of approaching the social study of legal consciousness.[147]

Gordon was arguing for a very different approach than 'the usual sort of internalist doctrinal history that showed how a legal concept – such as "consideration" in contract doctrine – had developed from some medieval or Roman embryo into its splendidly mature form'; rather he was arguing for:

> [a] history that showed how jurists came to assemble a whole coherent system of doctrine in the late-nineteenth century, and how that system cracked

143 Robert W Gordon, *Taming the Past: Essays on Law in History and History in Law* (Cambridge University Press, 2017) 221–222.

144 Gordon noted that the functional tradition in historiography had 'done most to nurture and inspire [his] own work' and that 'one could do worse than to keep trying to imitate the practices of the great functionalist figures even after one has stopped accepting their theories': ibid 223.

145 Ibid 276.

146 Ibid 274.

147 Robert W Gordon, '"Critical Legal Histories Revisited": A Response' (2012) 37 *Law & Social Inquiry* 200, 203. He noted that 'doctrinal history was an especially efficient tool for helping dissolve notions of legal functionalism, for if the law were rooted in such structural contradictions, it could inherently be made functional to radically divergent forms of social ordering'.

open under the pressure of its own contradictions, as well as savage political and intellectual attacks from outside.[148]

In short, he was looking for a critical version of what was described above as the intellectual history dimension of Legal History.

Crucially, 'Critical Legal Histories' did not argue that the study of doctrinal legal sources be abandoned but argued 'for studying law embedded in everyday practice as well'.[149] Indeed, the essay made what Gordon later called a 'half-hearted' argument for the study of internal legal sources – which he referred to as 'mandarin materials'.[150] It was argued that the study of such materials made 'a certain amount of sense' for three reasons: first, such materials were 'relatively accessible'; second, such materials exhibited 'an exceptionally refined and concentrated version of legal consciousness' which was 'the prototype speech behind many different dialect discourses in the society';[151] and third, this focus gave 'students alternative ways of thinking about the very materials that law teachers have traditionally cared about: the core doctrinal subjects'.[152] Gordon argued that in so doing the critics 'have engaged traditional doctrinalists on their own turf and have in the process stirred up a fabulous ruckus'. In short, a critical approach can use doctrinal methods to explore law's ideology while at the same time critiquing the role played by the common law system in perpetuating that ideology. Doctrinal legal study is limited only where it is uncritical, where it does not realise and seek to question its evolutionary functionalist setting. Doctrinal study which is alert to this is a necessary part of the analysis.

Yet, as Susanna L Blumenthal has noted, it is striking how few of Gordon's followers have pursued this line of inquiry.[153] Instead, work following Gordon has tended to situate itself in the external camp and in opposition to doctrinal Legal History. Gordon's critics have disparaged his focus on doctrine,[154] while Gordon himself has backtracked a little, claiming that he was writing for

148 Ibid 205.

149 Ibid 208.

150 That is, 'case law and treatise literature produced by the high mandarins of the legal system'. Robert W Gordon, '*Taming the Past: Essays on Law in History and History in Law* (Cambridge University Press, 2017) 277.

151 Ibid. As Laura F Edwards put it, 'The study of law, conceived of in this way, required attention to mandarin texts because those were what defined its structure. Such an approach would then illuminate the complex, seemingly perverse developments that characterized both law and society – and, according to Gordon, that had so bedeviled the scholarship in sociolegal studies': Laura F Edwards, 'The History in "Critical Legal Studies"' (2012) 37 *Law & Social Inquiry* 187, 188.

152 Robert W Gordon, *Taming the Past: Essays on Law in History and History in Law* (Cambridge University Press, 2017) 278.

153 Susanna L Blumenthal, 'Of Mandarins, Legal Consciousness, and the Cultural Turn in US Legal History' (2012) 37 *Law & Social Inquiry* 167, 177–178.

154 'Critical Legal History' has been criticised as providing an 'unqualified endorsement of legal history as the history of doctrine', which left 'little basis for a legal history that was not the history of doctrine': Christopher Tomlins, 'What is Left of the Law and Society Paradigm after

a specific audience and 'was not trying to privilege the history of legal doctrine over other kinds of legal history' and 'not identifying "critical" history with the history of doctrine'.[155] It is true that his work, together with the argument of Lobban and the re-casting of Internal Legal History as a dimension of intellectual history, does not privilege this form of Legal History but it does insist that it is of the same importance as other forms. Indeed, synthesising the arguments of Gordon and Cotterrell underscores that no distinction can be drawn between internal and external approaches since they interpenetrate one another. As Alan Hunt has argued, a critical approach necessarily involves an internal approach to law because it involves the study of ideology: by 'problematising the attitudes, beliefs and values of legal actors' a critical approach:

> makes it possible to ask questions about the formation of the consciousness of legal actors, about the internal relations between the constituents of their beliefs and also to make the consequences that flow from these beliefs a central focus of legal theory.[156]

A critical approach cannot be understood as being purely external 'if "external" is treated as involving the adoption of a detached behaviouralism which self-consciously chooses to ignore the meanings associated with the consciousness of legal actors'. For Hunt, Critical Legal Studies was external only 'in the sense... of maintaining a critical distance from the self-conceptions of legal professionals'.[157]

This chapter has shown that since a division between the legal and the social cannot and should not be made, then it follows that the internal-external dichotomy needs to be abandoned. Ironically Cotterrell's argument on why legal ideas should be understood sociologically provides a ringing endorsement of the need to study law internally and shows that history is well equipped to do this. However, exploring what Cotterrell meant by sociological is enlightening here. In Cotterrell's later argument, law and sociology were no longer conceptualised as two disciplines. Indeed, Cotterrell was adamant that in using the term 'sociological' he was not invoking 'adherence to the distinct methods, theories or outlook of the academic discipline called sociology'.[158] For Cotterrell, 'sociological understanding of legal ideas is transdisciplinary understanding and the

Critique? Revisiting Gordon's "Critical Legal Histories' (2012) 37 *Law & Social Inquiry* 155, 160.

155 Robert W Gordon, '"Critical Legal Histories Revisited": A Response' (2012) 37 *Law & Social Inquiry* 200, 205.

156 Alan Hunt, 'The Critique of Law: What is "Critical" about Critical Legal Theory?' (1987) 14(1) *Journal of Law and Society* 5, 12.

157 Ibid 13.

158 Roger Cotterrell, *Law, Culture and Society* (Ashgate, 2006) 54. He used the term 'to keep firmly in mind certain definite foci in interpreting law, but these foci and their authoritative definition are not the property of any particular academic discipline': ibid 50.

essence of a sociological interpretation of legal ideas lies in three postulates'.[159] The first is that 'law is an entirely social phenomenon': this means that law 'as a field of experience is to be understood as an aspect of social relationships in general, as wholly concerned with the coexistence of individuals in social groups'. Legal ideas 'can be understood as the outcome of historical, cultural, political or professional conditions which sociological studies are able to describe and explain'.[160] The second is that 'the social phenomena of law must be understood *empirically* through detailed examination of variation and continuity in actual historical patterns of social coexistence, rather than in relation to idealized or abstractly imagined social conditions'.[161] The third postulate is that legal ideas 'must be understood systematically, rather than anecdotally or impressionistically'.[162] There is a tension between the second and third postulates but for Cotterrell, 'the never-ending activity of balancing the empirical and the systemic' was the 'task of interpreting law' and this task required the 'drawing on continually changing conceptions of law's nature as a social phenomenon, an aspect of social life to be related to other aspects'.[163]

Michael Lobban has argued that these three postulates suggest that Cotterrell's transdisciplinary approach to law was in some respects as close to a historical analysis as it was to a sociological one.[164] Cotterrell's understanding of law as a social phenomenon insisted on legal ideas as being historically informed. It regarded law not as a 'universal abstract entity' but as existing 'only in the practices of people in specific times and places'. Cotterrell's emphasis upon empirical experience was, for Lobban, 'music to the ears of the historian'.[165] And historical work is systemic with the difference being that generalisations tend to be the consequence of the 'bottom up' empirical investigation rather than the 'top-down' scientific hypotheses provided by grand theory.[166] For Lobban, a

159 Ibid 54–55.

160 Ibid 47.

161 He noted that this needs to be 'based on the observation of the diversity and detail of historical experience. Speculation about the nature of or the meaning of legal ideas that does not relate its inquires to historical experience in this way is impractical and may lack point since it ignores the specificity of the contexts in which the meanings of legal doctrine are shaped': ibid 57.

162 'The aim is to broaden understanding from the specific to the general. It is able to assess the significance of particularities in a wider perspective, to situate the richness of the unique in a broader theoretical context and so to guide its interpretation': ibid 55.

163 Ibid 58.

164 Michael Lobban, 'Sociology, History and the "Internal" Study of Law' in Richard Nobles and David Schiff (eds) *Law, Society and Community: Socio-Legal Essays in Honour of Roger Cotterrell* (Ashgate, 2014) 39.

165 Ibid 43.

166 By contrast, Cotterrell himself thought that the third postulate would not apply to history because 'history is usually determinedly empirical and richly related to the understanding of social life, but may limit its effort to be explicitly systemic or generalized in its portrayal of the social, in order to achieve a multifaceted insight into particular people, actions, developments or events similar to that offered by the rich evocations and descriptions of great fiction': Roger Cotterrell, *Law, Culture and Society* (Ashgate, 2006) 56.

historical perspective can provide a better understanding of 'the distinct nature of legal thought and its different operation in different eras and contexts':[167]

> Rather than asking how "law" impacts on "society" in general, we may learn more by looking at particular aspects of law impacting on particular aspects of society. For such an enterprise, the historian's method – with its keen focus on the particular context and its scepticism for grand theory – seems in many ways the most useful one.[168]

This is not a defence of the status quo in Legal History, however. Robert W Gordon distinguished between two different ways in which this empirical grounded historical work can exist in Legal History.[169] First, there is the 'conservative' approach, also held by 'some liberal historians', which seeks 'to identify with the lawyers and judges and jurists they write about, or at least with their situation'. For such legal historians:

> history is in part professional training in statecraft: we look to past masters to see what to emulate, what mistakes they made, and what to avoid and to learn maxims of prudential wisdom. Law making has often been misguided, but well-made law, sound doctrine, and sensible policy is basically benign.

Such an approach accepted and perpetuated evolutionary functionalism and with it a reduced capacity for legal change and a limited role for Legal History. Second and conversely, there is the 'radical-populist' approach which 'sees law from the bottom up, from the perspectives of oppressed or disempowered groups'. Legal History 'in this mode is a dialectical story of progressively self-conscious but repeatedly thwarted subordinated group insurgency'. In such accounts, law is characterised 'as both a medium of ruling-class oppression and as a practically effective expression of the ideal of limits of such oppression'.[170] Law appears as the 'broken promises' of 'universally good norms of equal rights' which 'have been twisted and manipulated by dominant groups to their own advantage'. For Gordon, this approach allowed for a much greater role for legal historians, freeing them 'from one of the besetting diseases of legal history, its filiopietism towards tradition and the heroic lawyers and judges of the past'.[171] This approach also transforms how the relationship between law and society is seen. It markedly

167 Michael Lobban, 'Sociology, History and the "Internal" Study of Law' in Richard Nobles and David Schiff (eds) *Law, Society and Community: Socio-Legal Essays in Honour of Roger Cotterrell* (Ashgate, 2014) 39, 48.

168 Ibid 56–57.

169 Robert W Gordon, 'The Past as Authority and as Social Critic: Stabilizing and Destabilizing Functions of History in Legal Argument' in Terrence J McDonald (ed) *The Historic Turn in the Human Sciences* (University of Michigan Press, 1996) 339, 350.

170 Ibid 351.

171 Ibid 352.

changes the portrayal of the background social forces by emphasising 'the suffering and violence underlying what had been told as the story of gradual and impersonal social changes – "evolution", "modernization" and "development"'.

Moreover, Gordon noted that a 'set of critics' among American legal scholars had moved this analysis on further:[172] using the methods of social, cultural and intellectual history 'to undermine the very idea of authoritative traditions'.[173] Their project 'is to show legal ideas, rules, institutions and procedures as contingent products of time and circumstances', with the purpose of trying to show that 'the jumble of forms of legal-social life and thought that we have become used to are not the ones that we are stuck with':

> The premise is that if we can show how past forms were made and unmade, and how present forms in their turn came to be put together, we can make the present seem more plastic, more amenable to present reimagination and change.

This approach sits well with Gordon's later description of critical history as 'any approach that produces disturbances in the field'.[174] In his earlier work Gordon wrote that the aim of his preferred approach was 'to displace altogether ruling modes of legal thought, past and present, from their privileged position on center stage' and 'to replace their master narratives with alternative stories whose heroes and heroines ensure and resist dominant ideas of legality and struggle to forge their own normative orders'.[175] The 'critical' label does not really cover this. The label of Subversive Legal History is a preferable way of describing this 'bottom up' approach of shaking the legal world as if it were a snow globe, disorientating and re-orientating everything.

This chapter has argued that history can play a vital role in questioning, de-constructing and re-constructing law provided that the field of Legal History is re-conceptualised to move beyond the internal-external division. Subversive Legal History describes not a particular type of legal-historical study but an approach. It is an approach that is inclusive and regards the diversity of approaches within the historical study of law as being necessary and complementary. This chapter has re-conceptualised internal and external approaches to Legal History to underscore their roots in the intellectual history and social history traditions

172 Gordon noted that this 'picture of law as a historical instrument of class, race, and gender subordinated and even more of its history as a story of thwarted progress and broken promises' remained 'very important to the projects of lawyers, judges and politicians' but that the 'scholarly enterprise' of 'left-of-centre' Legal History had 'moved somewhat beyond this set of concerns': ibid 353.

173 Ibid 359.

174 Robert Gordon, 'The Arrival of Critical Historicism' (1997) 49 *Stanford Law Review* 1023, 1024.

175 Robert W Gordon, 'The Past as Authority and as Social Critic: Stabilizing and Destabilizing Functions of History in Legal Argument' in Terrence J McDonald (ed) *The Historic Turn in the Human Sciences* (University of Michigan Press, 1996) 339, 359.

respectively and insisted that both are needed and are intertwined. This has been underlined by insisting that all forms of Legal History adopt a critical approach. The Critical Legal Studies movement of which Critical Legal History was a key part was 'a disruptive engagement in a particular circumstance'.[176] Now is not the time to re-enact old battles. However, Gordon's foundational works can inspire a new and fresh way forward. They point to a need for disturbances which critique evolutionary functionalist narratives. However, this needs to go further than a critical approach characterised by de-construction. Subversion should also lead to re-construction. This can be achieved by subverting the current position by altering the lens from the dominant narrative of progress. This can be achieved by what Natalie Zemon Davis has described as decentering history:

> Decentering involves the stance and the subject matter of the historian. The decentering historian does not tell the story of the past only from the vantage point of a single part of the world or of powerful elites, but rather widens his or her scope, socially and geographically, and introduces plural voices into the account.[177]

There are many ways to decentre law. One could say, to subvert law. This can be shown by the various literatures that focus on race, class, religion, sexualities and gender inequalities. This work is in many ways the heir to the Critical Legal Studies movement. The next chapter will focus on the last of these literatures as a case study. It explores what is known as Women's Legal History or as Feminist Legal History and will examine what sort of disturbance can be achieved by subverting law on the basis of gender. This will develop further the articulation of Subversive Legal History by contending that a feminist approach to law illustrates what a Subversive Legal History can achieve.

176 Roberto Mangaberia Unger, *The Critical Legal Studies Movement: Another Time, A Greater Task* (Verso, 2015) 4.

177 Natalie Zemon Davis, 'Decentering History: Local Stories and Cultural Crossings in a Global World' (2011) 50 *History and Theory* 188, 190.

4 The F in Feminist Legal History

Although the word 'history' does not actually come from the fusion of the words 'his' and 'story', it often seems that it does.

History – and Legal History in particular – is invariably presented as if it is one unified story. It is often forgotten that it is one among many stories. It is overlooked that it is an authored interpretation. It is not seen as a partial account that comes from a particular observer, a selective viewpoint coming complete with loaded assumptions. As Carole Pateman noted in her seminal work *The Sexual Contract*, typically only half of the 'story or conjectural history is given'.[1] The half story that is commonly told invariably comes from the white, male, moneyed perspective. This means, as Pateman's work showed, that the conjectural history told and assumed excludes the subordination suffered by women. As Pateman put it, 'We hear an enormous amount about the *social* contract; a deep silence is maintained about the *sexual* contract'. Her work showed that the focus on a 'story of freedom' ignores the 'story of subjection' found in the sexual contract, which shows 'how men's patriarchal right over women is established through contract' because, rather than being universal, 'civil freedom is a masculine attribute and depends upon patriarchal right'.[2]

The conventional story told about gender by law presents gender as being in the words of Joanne Conaghan a historic trace, as 'remnants of a patriarchal legal past which law is gradually casting off', as 'a mistake to be corrected within the conception of law as an essentially benign and progressive institution'.[3] Yet, Pateman, by telling a different story, reveals that law perpetuates disadvantage: 'contract is far from being opposed to patriarchy; contract is the means by which modern patriarchy is constituted'.[4] Her insistence that the invisible story of the sexual contract be told and the orthodox account be questioned and debunked provides an example of what a subversive approach to law can reveal by telling the untold story; by making visible what was previously invisible. A focus on gender provides what Robert W Gordon labelled as a Critical History approach since it

1 Carole Pateman, *The Sexual Contract* (Polity Press, 1988) 1.

2 Ibid 2.

3 Joanne Conaghan, *Law and Gender* (Clarendon, 2013) 77.

4 Carole Pateman, *The Sexual Contract* (Polity Press, 1988) 2.

'produces disturbances in the field – that inverts or scrambles familiar narratives of stasis, recovery or progress'.[5] It provides one way of highlighting, questioning and departing from the linear progress narratives of evolutionary functionalism that are prevalent in legal discourse. Placing gender to the fore is subversive in that it alters the lens in which the law is seen; it disturbs and then supersedes the orthodox narrative. There are, of course, other different lenses that could be applied (most notably focusing on race, religion, class or sexualities). Applying such lenses, like focusing on gender is transformative. Gender is barely visible in conventional narratives and conceptualisations of law; rather, law is conventionally seen as being independent of gender.[6]

Such an approach is not common in Law Schools. Although there is a significant body of work in North America and elsewhere,[7] it remains true that Legal History 'scholarship in the UK and Ireland largely ignores women' in that 'at best it plays down women's perspectives and agency and at worst reduces mentions of women to the occasional paragraph'.[8] Yet, in recent years, particularly in the United States but also on this side of the Pond,[9] a growing literature has developed that emphasises gender and that focuses on these missing stories.[10] This has sometimes been referred to as 'engendering' Legal History: that

5 Robert Gordon, 'The Arrival of Critical Historicism' (1997) 49 *Stanford Law Review* 1023, 1024.

6 Joanne Conaghan, *Law and Gender* (Clarendon, 2013) 71.

7 For a comparison between the USA and the UK see Maria Drakopoulou, 'Feminist Historiography of Law: An Exposition and Proposition' in Markus D Dubber and Christopher Tomlins (eds) *The Oxford Handbook of Legal History* (Oxford University Press, 2018) 603.

8 Erika Rackley and Rosemary Auchmuty, 'Women's Legal Landmarks: An Introduction' in Erika Rackley and Rosemary Auchmuty (eds) *Women's Legal Landmarks: Celebrating the History of Women and Law in the UK and Ireland* (Hart, 2018) 1, 4. 'English legal history has – almost in its entirety – been written as history of "great men"': Rosemary Auchmuty and Erika Rackley, 'Feminist Legal Biography: A Model for *All* Legal Life Stories' (2020) 41(2) *Journal of Legal History* 186, 194. See also Erika Rackley and Rosemary Auchmuty, 'The Case for Feminist Legal History' (2020) 40(4) *Oxford Journal of Legal Studies* 878, 880–886 and the introduction to Gwen Seabourne, *Women in the Medieval Common Law, c.1200-1500* (Routledge, 2021).

9 In the UK this is now epitomised by the project and book on Women's Legal Landmarks (Erika Rackley and Rosemary Auchmuty (eds) *Women's Legal Landmarks: Celebrating the History of Women and Law in the UK and Ireland* (Hart, 2018) and Rosemary Auchmuty (ed) *Great Debates in Law and Gender* (Palgrave, 2018) which is structured around legal sub-disciplines with each chapter 'identifying gender issues in traditional legal subject areas' such as property law, contract law and tort law, including a chapter on Legal History by Auchmuty herself. These works are the tips of an emerging literature within UK Law Schools that includes work by Rosemary Auchmuty, Erika Rackley, Joanne Conaghan, and Sharon Thompson.

10 In a recent agenda-setting article Erika Rackley and Rosemary Auchmuty posit that it 'may be that we are witnessing a highpoint of interest in the lives of early women lawyers, and women's legal history generally, both within and outside the academy, fuelled by the twin centenaries of the (partial) extension of the vote to women in 1918 and the formal admission of women to the legal profession the following year'. However, they warn that 'without a strong scholarly method, politics and purpose, there is a danger that these celebrations will also encourage the proliferation of well-meaning but uncritical heroine narratives replete with myths and anecdote': Erika Rackley and Rosemary Auchmuty, 'The Case for Feminist Legal History' (2020) 40(4) *Oxford Journal of Legal Studies* 878, 879.

is, integrating 'the stories of women into the dominant history of the law [to] reconstruct the assumed contours of history'.[11] This entails asking what Rosemary Auchmuty called the 'woman question': asking 'where are the women in this account?'[12] And then 'including women's stories, experiences, and voices (often hidden, ignored and silenced in dominant narratives) and locating men's position – their opposition or support – within these'.[13] Such an approach develops the existing 'one dimensional' historical accounts by 'adding new events, providing new details, and suggesting alternative explanations for the traditional historical narrative'.[14] This has mostly been achieved in relation to the histories of women's rights and such accounts have questioned the evolutionary functionalist dominant narrative by documenting the actual lived 'ebb and flow of women's empowerment' which contrasts with the conventional understanding of incremental, but linear, progress toward the eradication of barriers to women's empowerment'.[15] Engendering the narrative has shown 'how women used their own experience to transform gendered legal norms'.[16] This involves 'establishing women as agents rather than simply subjects of law'.

However, engendering Legal History requires more than just writing women into the history of law, it recognises a new timeline. As Felice Batlan has argued, 'it produces a new history, creating possibilities of re-narrations and the

11 Tracy A Thomas and Tracey J Boisseau, 'Introduction: Law, History, and Feminism' in Tracy A Thomas and Tracey J Boisseau (eds) *Feminist Legal History: Essays on Women and Law* (New York University Press, 2011) 1.

12 Erika Rackley and Rosemary Auchmuty, 'Women's Legal Landmarks: An Introduction' in Erika Rackley and Rosemary Auchmuty (eds) *Women's Legal Landmarks: Celebrating the History of Women and Law in the UK and Ireland* (Hart, 2018) 1, 5; Erika Rackley and Rosemary Auchmuty, 'The Case for Feminist Legal History' (2020) 40(4) *Oxford Journal of Legal Studies* 878, 889–891. This also 'involves exploring whether a statement, law or situation applies to both sexes or only to one and that where it applies to both sexes, the question involves asking how their experiences of the same phenomena differs': Rosemary Auchmuty, 'Recovering Lost Lives: Researching Women in Legal History' (2015) 42 *Journal of Law and Society* 34, 42–43.

13 Erika Rackley and Rosemary Auchmuty, 'Women's Legal Landmarks: An Introduction' in Erika Rackley and Rosemary Auchmuty (eds) *Women's Legal Landmarks: Celebrating the History of Women and Law in the UK and Ireland* (Hart, 2018) 1, 5.

14 Tracy A Thomas and Tracey J Boisseau, 'Introduction: Law, History, and Feminism' in Tracy A Thomas and Tracey J Boisseau (eds) *Feminist Legal History: Essays on Women and Law* (New York University Press, 2011) 1, 2, 12.

15 Ibid 13. As Erika Rackley and Rosemary Auchmuty put it, such work consists of 'challenging assumptions of unabated progress and liberal incrementalism by showing that legal reform is often messy, disjointed and episodic, that there is very often a backlash and regrouping by opponents, and that hard-won gains are easily lost as momentum and focus shift elsewhere': Erika Rackley and Rosemary Auchmuty, 'Women's Legal Landmarks: An Introduction' in Erika Rackley and Rosemary Auchmuty (eds) *Women's Legal Landmarks: Celebrating the History of Women and Law in the UK and Ireland* (Hart, 2018) 1, 5.

16 Tracy A Thomas and Tracey J Boisseau, 'Introduction: Law, History, and Feminism' in Tracy A Thomas and Tracey J Boisseau (eds) *Feminist Legal History: Essays on Women and Law* (New York University Press, 2011) 1, 2; Felice Batlan, 'Engendering Legal History' (2005) 30(4) *Law & Society Inquiry* 823, 830.

potential for fresh interpretations'.[17] It is an act of creation rather than mere revision. And this will often require revisiting existing structures and starting again from scratch. Moreover, engendering Legal History requires more than just re-writing legal stories where women already exist albeit invariably at the margins. As Batlan contended, engendering Legal History is not only valuable in relation to areas such as domestic relations and family law where 'issues of women and gender readily appear'. It is also useful – possibly even more useful – when applied to 'those areas of law that on the surface appear to be ungendered'.[18] This is likely to produce an even more radical transformation since 'gendered readings of seemingly ungendered categories change our narratives of legal history, complicating our assumptions'.[19] All areas of Legal History are therefore ripe for engendering; as Batlan comments, 'after all, court cases are about men and women who live gendered lives'.[20]

Engendering Legal History can be said to have three main effects. First, it questions assumptions. As Batlan has written, focusing on gender 'makes us question some of our basic assumptions about legal history'.[21] It serves as 'a mode of analysis [that] can expose and controvert some of our basic assumptions about citizenship, law and the construction of the liberal state'.[22] She gave the example of 'what happens to liberalism's vaunted protection of property and deference to contract when coverture is read into the law?'[23] Reinstating the missing story of gender re-orientates the analysis questioning assumptions about the public-private divide by revealing how 'family structure reflects public life and public life informs the family'.[24] It questions the usual evolutionary functionalist narratives by changing the focus and the angle. The usual macro 'top-down' focus is replaced by a micro perspective that places what was previously at the margins at the centre of the analysis.[25] As Sandra Harding puts it, 'to make sense of any actual woman's life or the gender relations in any culture, analyses must

17 Ibid 823.

18 Ibid 837.

19 Ibid 842.

20 Ibid 837. For a discussion of this in the medieval context see Gwen Seabourne, *Women in the Medieval Common Law c.1200-1500* (Routledge, 2021).

21 Felice Batlan, 'Engendering Legal History' (2005) 30(4) *Law & Society Inquiry* 823, 832.

22 Ibid 824.

23 That is, the common law doctrine whereby 'a woman's property and income became her husband's on marriage': Sharon Thompson, *Prenuptial Agreements and the Presumption of Free Choice* (Hart, 2015) 40. On this see further, Mary L Shanley, *Feminism, Marriage and the Law in Victorian England* (Princeton University Press, 1989) and the essays in Tim Stretton and Krista Kesselring (eds) *Married Women and the Law: Coverture in England and the Common Law World* (McGill-Queen's University Press, 2013).

24 Felice Batlan, 'Engendering Legal History' (2005) 30(4) *Law & Society Inquiry* 823, 833.

25 The process of engendering questions the common portrayal of law as 'a series of top-down reforms responding to, at best, individual challenges': Rosemary Auchmuty, 'Recovering Lost Lives: Researching Women in Legal History' (2015) 42 *Journal of Law and Society* 34, 52.

begin in real, historical women's lives'.[26] This recasts the traditional approach of law and of Legal History.[27]

Second, engendering Legal History questions the explanations that have previously been given for legal and social change. It may replace or supplement existing justifications. Gender may provide an explanation for legal and social changes that have previously been attributed to internal legal changes or economic factors. As Batlan put it, 'How does gender account for changes in law that historians have traditionally interpreted as the result of economic change? How does our understanding of the individual's' relationship to the state change when domestic relations law stands not at the periphery of law, but at its core?'[28] In so doing, a different level of explanation is often provided, again focusing on the micro rather than the macro level. As Harding notes, this creates 'the need for explanation to bear on assumptions and practices that appear natural or unremarkable from the perspective of the lives of men in the dominant groups. Thinking from the perspectives of women's lives makes strange what had appeared familiar'.[29] Moreover, as Gwen Seabourne has argued that 'in undertaking studies of women and the common law, legal historians should be prepared to embrace complexity and nuance rather than seeing attention given to women (or other groups other than the standard free, non-"foreign" male) as a distraction likely to produce regrettable derogation from neat narratives, such as those of the "rises" of centralisation and professionalization of the common law'. [30]

Third, and crucially, engendering Legal History brings to the fore the issue of power dynamics. The questioning of assumptions and explanations enables legal historians to 'uncover the many mechanisms by which men have retained power for themselves in law'.[31] As Harding puts it, it takes 'the perspective from the lives of people on the "other side" of gender battles, offering a view different from the "winner's stories" about nature and social life which men's interpretations of men's lives tend to produce'.[32] Focusing on gender also shows how 'power becomes effectuated – that is, made real and material'; like race, religion,

26 Sandra Harding, *Whose Science? Whose Knowledge?* (Cornell University Press, 2013) 151.

27 'Since time immemorial, the history of the common law has been the history of "great men" and their ideas – their "truths". Judgments today still tend to invoke one of a number of "stock" legal stories to reframe the litigants' experiences into recognised legal narratives and excludes ambivalent or complicating detail and other grievances. The effect is to shape the story (and, often, the character of the people concerned) to fit the formal categories of law, many of them not designed to work for women, and allow counsel to formulate an argument that is selective, or even silent, as to facts, omitting those deemed to be irrelevant': Erika Rackley and Rosemary Auchmuty, 'The Case for Feminist Legal History' (2020) 40(4) *Oxford Journal of Legal Studies* 878, 892.

28 Felice Batlan, 'Engendering Legal History' (2005) 30(4) *Law & Society Inquiry* 823, 824.

29 Sandra Harding, *Whose Science? Whose Knowledge?* (Cornell University Press, 2013) 150.

30 Gwen Seabourne, *Women in the Medieval Common Law c.1200-1500* (Routledge, 2021) 158–159.

31 Rosemary Auchmuty, 'Recovering Lost Lives: Researching Women in Legal History' (2015) 42 *Journal of Law and Society* 34.

32 Sandra Harding, *Whose Science? Whose Knowledge?* (Cornell University Press, 2013) 150.

class and sexuality, gender 'is at least one way through which power becomes systematized, articulated and legitimized'.[33] It also questions the myths of law, dispelling notions that law is based on equity and fairness. This makes engendering Legal History an exercise in feminism in that it is more than just the revealing of missing stories; engendering Legal History is feminist in that it uses those stories to highlight and critique the defects in existing accounts and to challenge and change the assumptions and explanations of the conventional linear evolutionary functionalist narratives. It requires the asking of why the stories have become invisible and the adoption of a permanent shift in perspective that means that the once invisible and marginal becomes visible and central. The act of engendering becomes truly critical – utterly subversive – when the focus on power means that fire is directed at the entire edifice.

This chapter argues that such an approach needs to be designated as Feminist Legal History rather than as Women's Legal History.[34] As June Purvis has noted, women's history is 'a history that takes women as its subject matter but is not necessarily informed by the ideas and theories that would constitute a feminist analysis'.[35] Feminist Legal History, by contrast, draws upon the 'well established and vigorously theorized sub-discipline of feminist history' and goes beyond the collecting and assembling of the facts in that it 'seeks to produce a new, accurate, inclusive account'.[36] As Erika Rackley and Rosemary Auchmuty have succinctly put it: 'Women's legal history simply adds women to the story;

33 Felice Batlan, 'Engendering Legal History' (2005) 30(4) *Law & Society Inquiry* 823, 825.

34 'The cultural processes that have produced "women" have also produced "men". Gender is the concept in our current practice that encompasses this relational dynamic. It seems useful to shift the name of the field, from women's history to gender history, to reflect this': Jeanne Boydston, 'Gender as a Question of Historical Analysis' (2008) 20(3) *Gender & History* 558.

35 June Purvis, 'Doing Feminist Women's History: Researching the Lives of Women in the Suffragette Movement in Edwardian England' in Mary Maynard and June Purvis (eds) *Researching Women's Lives from a Feminist Perspective* (Taylor & Francis, 1994) 166, 167. However, it is worth noting that there is no watertight distinction between the two concepts which has led some commentators to question: 'Is feminist legal history simply women's legal history rebranded?' (Erika Rackley and Rosemary Auchmuty, 'The Case for Feminist Legal History' (2020) 40(4) *Oxford Journal of Legal Studies* 878, 888). Indeed: 'However defined, historians continue to explore and publish research categorised as women's and as gender history and, in many instances, the distinction between them is false'. Indeed, issues of gender 'were already present in women's history and feminist scholarship in the 1960s and 1970s' (Alexandra Shepard and Garthine Walker, 'Gender, Change and Periodisation' (2008) 20(3) *Gender & History* 453, 455).

36 Erika Rackley and Rosemary Auchmuty, 'Women's Legal Landmarks: An Introduction' in Erika Rackley and Rosemary Auchmuty (eds) *Women's Legal Landmarks: Celebrating the History of Women and Law in the UK and Ireland* (Hart, 2018) 1, 4–5. It also draws upon women's Legal History: 'in practice, the stories and narratives of women 'in', 'and' and 'of' law – what we might call "women's legal history" – are the building blocks of feminist legal history. It is through these histories that feminist legal history is able to expose and contest': Erika Rackley and Rosemary Auchmuty, 'The Case for Feminist Legal History' (2020) 40(4) *Oxford Journal of Legal Studies* 878, 889.

feminist legal history seeks to change it'. Their work has argued that the purpose of Feminist Legal History 'is transformative, not descriptive':

> It requires its authors to commit not only to uncovering the silences and the silenced and to locating the specific in the general, but also to take a further step and use these histories to challenge and change the dominant narrative not only of the past, but also of the future.[37]

This chapter falls into three sections which collectively and cumulatively demonstrate how Feminist Legal History can serve as an example and template for Subversive Legal History.[38] The first section will explore how feminism and Feminist Legal Studies has been understood; the second section will then identify and elucidate five features of Feminist Legal Studies; the third and final section will then focus on Feminist Legal History as an exemplar of Subversive Legal History, arguing that a feminist re-construction of Legal History on the basis of gender can enable three important disturbances to occur.

37 Erika Rackley and Rosemary Auchmuty, 'Women's Legal Landmarks: An Introduction' in Erika Rackley and Rosemary Auchmuty (eds) *Women's Legal Landmarks: Celebrating the History of Women and Law in the UK and Ireland* (Hart, 2018) 1, 4–5. As they put it elsewhere: 'Anchored in a commitment to disciplinary, social and political change, feminist legal history seeks not only to inform about women in law in the past, to uncover new histories, but also to challenge, and ultimately transform, our understandings of the past and present, and indeed the future' (Erika Rackley and Rosemary Auchmuty, 'The Case for Feminist Legal History' (2020) 40(4) *Oxford Journal of Legal Studies* 878, 879).

38 The following will draw upon works of feminist legal scholarship as well as Feminist Legal History scholarship because most of the discussion of the feminist contribution to law comes from the former. Rackley and Auchmuty note that 'the *doing* of feminist legal history as an academic discipline and method remains largely undeveloped in the UK': Erika Rackley and Rosemary Auchmuty, 'The Case for Feminist Legal History' (2020) 40(4) *Oxford Journal of Legal Studies* 878, 879. Maria Drakopoulou has suggested that this 'virtual absence of feminist legal historians in the UK can be largely accounted for by the manner in which the feminist project in law was conceived' with Feminist Legal Studies emphasising the present and positing 'legal arrangements affecting living women as those most worth of consideration': Maria Drakopoulou, 'Feminist Historiography of Law: An Exposition and Proposition' in Markus D Dubber and Christopher Tomlins (eds) *The Oxford Handbook of Legal History* (Oxford University Press, 2018) 603, 606. (See also Maria Drakopoulou, 'Clio's Forgotten Consciousness: History and the Question of Feminist Critique in Law' (2013) 38(1) *Australian Feminist Law Journal* 3.) However, this chapter will show that much work on feminist legal scholarship emphasises the importance of history to the extent that a neat line cannot be drawn between feminist legal scholarship and Feminist Legal History. For instance, Erika Rackley and Rosemary Auchmuty have suggested that the transformative nature of Feminist Legal History means that it is focused on the future: 'while its substance may require the author to look back, the motivation of feminist legal history is forward-looking': Erika Rackley and Rosemary Auchmuty, 'Women's Legal Landmarks: An Introduction' in Erika Rackley and Rosemary Auchmuty (eds) *Women's Legal Landmarks: Celebrating the History of Women and Law in the UK and Ireland* (Hart, 2018) 1, 5.

The F Word

Although the word 'feminism' conjures up a variety of different meanings and reactions from different people and in divergent contexts, it remains possible to identify some recurring characteristics of Feminist Legal Studies.

The field of Feminist Legal Studies arose in the 1980s 'virtually simultaneously in Canada, the US, Britain, Australia and Scandinavia' and can be understood as being both 'an off-shoot of critical legal studies' and 'a development from the women's movement more generally'.[39] Its influence upon British Law Schools was slowly felt but formed part of what Emily Jackson and Nicola Lacey have referred to as the 'gradual intellectualisation of law schools' and the 'increased openness to interdisciplinary study'.[40] This meant that by the dawn of the new millennium, Feminist Legal Studies constituted 'a significant body of scholarship, competing with other jurisprudential theories for distinguished journals and texts'.[41] Indeed, it became one of the heirs and possibly even the successor to the Critical Legal Studies movement. Feminism is now seen as one of, if not the main, critical approaches used in Law Schools. As Joanne Conaghan has noted, 'few areas of law, no matter how musty or arcane, have remained immune from the feminist legal challenge'. Yet, the influence of feminist approaches upon legal scholarship has been uneven and varied.

There are a wide range of perspectives and traditions within feminist thought. A taxonomy of schools of feminist thought such as the liberal, radical, cultural and postmodern is often identified.[42] However, as Vanessa Munro has convincingly argued, talk of such classifications runs the risk that we 'lose sight of the basic and fundamental convictions that continue to animate and unite theorists across these divides'.[43] Although feminists are wary of attempts to identify

39 Joanne Conaghan, 'Labour Law and Feminist Method' (2017) 33(1) *International Journal of Comparative Labour Law* 93; M D A Freeman, *Lloyds Introduction to Jurisprudence* (9th ed, Sweet & Maxwell, 2014) 1079. Though it has been noted that by the 1980s, it was 'the substance – though not yet the discipline – of law' that was 'well within feminist historians' purview', with most work coming from outside English and Welsh Law Schools: Erika Rackley and Rosemary Auchmuty, 'The Case for Feminist Legal History' (2020) 40(4) *Oxford Journal of Legal Studies* 878, 887.

40 Emily Jackson and Nicola Lacey, 'Introducing Feminist Legal Theory' in James Penner, David Schiff and Richard Nobles (eds) *Introduction to Jurisprudence and Legal Theory* (Butterworths, 2002) 779, 780.

41 Joanne Conaghan, 'Reassessing the Feminist Theoretical Project in Law' (2000) 27(3) *Journal of Law and Society* 351, 352.

42 Patrica A Cain, 'Feminism and the Limits of Equality' (1990) 24 *Georgia Law Review* 803. See also, e.g., Emily Jackson and Nicola Lacey, 'Introducing Feminist Legal Theory' in James Penner, David Schiff and Richard Nobles (eds) *Introduction to Jurisprudence and Legal Theory* (Butterworths, 2002) 779, 794–834 and Hilaire Barnett, *Introduction to Feminist Jurisprudence* (Cavendish, 1998) chapters 6–9.

43 Vanessa Munro, *Law and Politics at the Perimeter: Re-evaluating Key Debates in Feminist Theory* (Hart, 2007) 11. Carole Pateman has suggested that such 'classification of feminists … suggests that feminism is always secondary, a supplement to other doctrines': Carole Pateman, *The Sexual Contract* (Polity Press, 1988) x.

essential or fundamental principles,[44] this does not mean that identifying trends and general features of feminism is impossible.[45] As Joanne Conaghan has argued, 'despite the breadth and variety of feminist scholarship',[46] including the range of methodologies employed,[47] it remains possible and 'useful to identify some common, recurring features of feminist academic engagement with law and to do so without either essentializing feminism or denying the complexity and contestability of the features thus described'.[48] Yet, feminism is not to be understood as a discrete approach characterised by a fixed set of principles.[49] Rather, it is a dynamic '*process* of engagement or interaction – a dynamic *movement* of ideas',[50] which 'places distinctive substantive issues on the agenda of legal scholarship and legal theory'.[51]

The main distinctive issue is that a feminist approach focuses on gender as a structural and ideological means of subordination and exclusion.[52] For Vanessa

44 As Joanne Conaghan has noted, 'Feminists, in keeping with other dissonant traditions, have not been generally receptive to efforts to impose upon them conceptual, classificatory and/or other normative orderings. The inclination rather has been to resist such efforts and to voice concerns about their disciplinary and normalising effects: Joanne Conaghan, 'The Making of a Field of the Building of a Wall? Feminist Legal Studies and Law, Gender and Sexuality' (2009) 17 *Feminist Legal Studies* 303, 304.

45 Vanessa Munro's 'hefty disclaimer' does, however, apply to this chapter: 'there is no such thing as a united feminist jurisprudence, nor a universally shared feminist legal method. Aligned under the banner of modern feminism are a diversity of perspectives regarding the causes and consequences of unequal gender power relations, the ways in which the law and state have played a role in their creation and maintenance, and the most effective strategies for their eradication': Vanessa Munro, 'The Master's Tools? A Feminist Approach to Legal and Lay Decision-Making' in Dawn Watkins and Mandy Burton (eds) *Research Methods in Law* (2nd ed, Routledge, 2018) 194–195.

46 Joanne Conaghan, 'Reassessing the Feminist Theoretical Project in Law' (2000) 27(3) *Journal of Law and Society* 351, 358–359.

47 Conaghan's work on labour law shows how feminists use 'a multitude of methods to interrogate labour law – empirical, doctrinal, textual, and so on' and share methodology with other critical theoretical approaches: Joanne Conaghan, 'Labour Law and Feminist Method' (2017) 33(1) *International Journal of Comparative Labour Law* 93, 95.

48 Joanne Conaghan, 'Reassessing the Feminist Theoretical Project in Law' (2000) 27(3) *Journal of Law and Society* 351, 358–359. See also Heather Wishtik's framework for inquiry for feminist jurisprudence: Heather Wishnik, 'To Question Everything: The Inquiries of Feminist Jurisprudence (1986) 1 *Berkeley Women's Law Journal* 64, 72–75.

49 Emily Jackson and Nicola Lacey, 'Introducing Feminist Legal Theory' in James Penner, David Schiff and Richard Nobles (eds) *Introduction to Jurisprudence and Legal Theory* (Butterworths, 2002) 779, 789; Joanne Conaghan, 'Reassessing the Feminist Theoretical Project in Law' (2000) 27(3) *Journal of Law and Society* 351, 356.

50 Ibid 356 fn 17. See also Rosemary Hunter and Ruth Fletcher, 'Law, Gender and Sexuality: The Making of a Field – Introduction' (2009) 17 *Feminist Legal Studies* 289 and the other articles in that special edition.

51 Emily Jackson and Nicola Lacey, 'Introducing Feminist Legal Theory' in James Penner, David Schiff and Richard Nobles (eds) *Introduction to Jurisprudence and Legal Theory* (Butterworths, 2002) 779, 789.

52 For discussion of how 'the use of gender as a category of (historical) analysis is not unproblematic' see the discussion by Erika Rackley and Rosemary Auchmuty, 'The Case for Feminist Legal History' (2020) 40(4) *Oxford Journal of Legal Studies* 878, 888.

Munro, feminism 'is committed at its most fundamental level to highlighting the historical and contemporary sites of women's exclusion and/or subordination, to exploring the material and ideological conditions that create and perpetuate this condition and to making demands for their eradication'.[53] It achieves this by emphasising gender. As Joanne Conaghan puts it, a feminist approach 'presupposes that gender has a much greater structural and/or discursive significance than is commonly assumed, a significance which is ideologically but not practically diminished by its relative invisibility'.[54]

In feminist work, gender has been increasingly used as a frame of analysis rather than focusing on 'women's rights'.[55] It is possible to identify a shift in feminist legal literature moving on from identifying a particular 'women's perspective' to instead regarding 'the framework of gender divisions as a general category for critical legal analysis' that has 'opened up the possibility that law's contribution to the gendering of its subjects might interact with other social forces'.[56] However, this does not mean that feminist research is synonymous with research about gender. Research about gender does not have to use feminist legal theory at all.[57] And feminist scholarship does not presume that gender is always relevant. Rather, as Conaghan points out, the proposition that it is a category of significance is the very hypothesis that such scholarship is seeking to explore. As she puts it, feminist method entails 'the application of gender as a category of analysis to a field of knowledge in order to generate new questions capable of informing and transforming research agendas'.[58] Feminist Legal Studies focuses and highlights 'the ways in which law is implicated, in the twenty-first century, in all of these complicated, sometimes sophisticated, but always resolute structures of gender'.[59]

53 Vanessa Munro, *Law and Politics at the Perimeter: Re-evaluating Key Debates in Feminist Theory* (Hart, 2007) 11.

54 Joanne Conaghan, 'Reassessing the Feminist Theoretical Project in Law' (2000) 27(3) *Journal of Law and Society* 351, 359–360.

55 Pivotal to this was Joan W Scott, 'Gender: A Useful Category of Analysis' (1986) 91 *American Historical Review* 103. Focusing on gender includes both women and men and, of course, does not frame the analysis in binary terms. Erika Rackley and Rosemary Auchmuty pointed out that 'feminist legal history also requires us to go back and look at the legal men, and at men's place in women's legal history, as supporters of women's rights, opponents or passive beneficiaries of the gendered legal regime': Erika Rackley and Rosemary Auchmuty, 'The Case for Feminist Legal History' (2020) 40(4) *Oxford Journal of Legal Studies* 878, 893.

56 Katherine O'Donovan's 1985 book *Sexual Divisions in Law* (Weidenfeld & Nicolson, 1985) is said to have 'represented a watershed in British feminist legal scholarship': Emily Jackson and Nicola Lacey, 'Introducing Feminist Legal Theory' in James Penner, David Schiff and Richard Nobles (eds) *Introduction to Jurisprudence and Legal Theory* (Butterworths, 2002) 779, 781.

57 Sharon Thompson, 'Are Methods in Law a Feminist Issue?' (Paper presented at the Gender Rules conference on 20th June 2016, available on the Law and Gender YouTube channel at: <https://youtube.com/channel/UCLpBO6KARuD5mAskawbl4NQ >).

58 Joanne Conaghan, 'Labour Law and Feminist Method' (2017) 33(1) *International Journal of Comparative Labour Law* 93, 100.

59 Alison Diduck and Katherine O'Donovan, 'Feminism and Families' in Alison Diduck and Katherine O'Donovan (eds) *Feminist Perspectives on Family Law* (Routledge, 2006) 1, 6.

As Conaghan argues, this requires more than simply taking account of gender.[60] Gender is not seen as being 'external to law, carrying empirical and distributional, not conceptual or theoretical, significance'. Rather, gender is 'analytically central' and 'deeply constitutive' of law. This accepts and furthers Cotterrell's argument that the legal and the social cannot be separated because legal and social ideas constantly penetrate one another. Ideas about gender are both affected by and effect legal ideas. By choosing to explicitly recognise this, issues of power are placed at the core of the discussions rather than on the margins.[61] A feminist approach alters the lens in which we see law and the social world by shedding light on structural and entrenched gendered disadvantages that are perpetuated.[62] This shows up implicit assumptions found within legal ideas and legal culture. A focus on gender reveals that 'the value, integrity and justice of our historical and present day society, and its practices and institutions, is undermined by a pervasive tendency to privilege the interest and experiences of men over women'.[63] For Conaghan, 'the application of a gender lens works to: (1) expose the operation of gender bias and neglect; (2) destabilise the normative and conceptual infrastructure; and (3) historicise and contextualise the field'.[64]

The feminist approach, therefore, is one of critique.[65] This can take several forms.[66] However, regardless of the exact form or method, feminist methods 'aim to disrupt; to question; to render problematic the "objective", 'the neutral" and the "normal"'.[67] The target includes the intellectual development of law, what Maria Drakopoulou referred to as 'the language, reason and practice of law' as well as what she has called 'law's morphological power': 'the pivotal acts

60 Joanne Conaghan, 'Labour Law and Feminist Method' (2017) 33(1) *International Journal of Comparative Labour Law* 93, 98.

61 Sharon Thompson and Russell Sandberg, 'Multicultural Jurisdictions: The Need for a Feminist Approach to Law and Religion' in Russell Sandberg (ed) *Leading Works in Law and Religion* (Routledge, 2019) 179, 184–185.

62 By focusing on gender, feminist legal scholars seek to highlight and explore the gendered content of law and to probe characterizations positing themselves as neutral and, more specifically, ungendered': Joanne Conaghan, 'Reassessing the Feminist Theoretical Project in Law' (2000) 27(3) *Journal of Law and Society* 351, 359.

63 Vanessa Munro, *Law and Politics at the Perimeter: Re-evaluating Key Debates in Feminist Theory* (Hart, 2007) 11.

64 Joanne Conaghan, 'Labour Law and Feminist Method' (2017) 33(1) *International Journal of Comparative Labour Law* 93, 100.

65 A feminist approach to law 'aspires to produce a critical interpretation of legal practices: Emily Jackson and Nicola Lacey, 'Introducing Feminist Legal Theory' in James Penner, DavidSchiff and Richard Nobles (eds) *Introduction to Jurisprudence and Legal Theory* (Butterworths, 2002) 779, 785.

66 Hilaire Barnett identified four methods 'which intersect and are by no means mutually exclusive [and which] may be labelled: (a) consciousness raising/unsilencing women; (b) asking "the woman question"/critique/textual de-construction; (c) theorising law's gendered nature; (d) feminist practical reasoning': Hilaire Barnett, *Introduction to Feminist Jurisprudence* (Cavendish, 1998) 19, 23.

67 Alison Diduck and Katherine O'Donovan, 'Feminism and Families' in Alison Diduck and Katherine O'Donovan (eds) *Feminist Perspectives on Family Law* (Routledge, 2006) 1.

of separation, isolation and delineation it authoritatively performs and which designate who and what inhabits its empire, where its limits lie, and what exists beyond them'.[68] A feminist approach is, in the words of Emily Jackson and Nicola Lacey, 'an interpretative approach which seeks to get beyond the surface level of legal doctrine and legal discourse, and which sees traditional jurisprudence as ideological – and hence as an apologia for the status quo'.[69] The key characteristic of feminist legal scholarship, as a form (and as a successor) of Critical Legal Studies, is that it highlights, challenges and disrupts evolutionary functionalist understandings about law by its focus on gender as a site of subordination and exclusion.

Five Features of Feminist Legal Studies

In focusing upon how gender as a means of subordination and exclusion can challenge conventional stories of law, five features of Feminist Legal Studies may be identified.[70]

First, feminism is a grounded approach. A feminist lens dispenses with the usual 'top-down' analysis to instead focus on actual lived experiences, operating from the bottom up.[71] As Joanne Conaghan put it, feminist theory is built 'from the ground up, from the shared experience of women talking from personal testimonies, story-telling, consciousness-raising, and other revelatory techniques aimed at highlighting perspectives ignored by traditional narratives'.[72] This involves examining the everyday experiences of how women interact with the law. June Purvis reminded us that 'where possible, finding women's own words on the past is a critical aspect of "feminist" research'.[73] A focus on the concrete 'is one of

68 'This power is a creative one, rather than one enforced within its territory and upon its subjects'; 'Located in acts of separation and engendering, the morphological power of law manifests law's role in the creation and sustenance of difference and, as such, makes certain questions particularly pertinent to the feminist critique of law': Maria Drakopoulou, 'Clio's Forgotten Consciousness: History and the Question of Feminist Critique in Law' (2013) 38(1) *Australian Feminist Law Journal* 3, 20.

69 Emily Jackson and Nicola Lacey, 'Introducing Feminist Legal Theory' in James Penner, David Schiff and Richard Nobles (eds) *Introduction to Jurisprudence and Legal Theory* (Butterworths, 2002) 779, 789–790.

70 See also the 'six substantive and methodological characteristics of feminist legal history' identified by Erika Rackley and Rosemary Auchmuty, 'The Case for Feminist Legal History' (2020) 40(4) *Oxford Journal of Legal Studies* 878, 889–902.

71 There is 'a rejection of abstraction and commitment to the importance of context: Vanessa Munro, 'The Master's Tools? A Feminist Approach to Legal and Lay Decision-Making' in Dawn Watkins and Mandy Burton (eds) *Research Methods in Law* (2nd ed, Routledge, 2018) 194, 196.

72 Joanne Conaghan, 'Reassessing the Feminist Theoretical Project in Law' (2000) 27(3) *Journal of Law and Society* 351, 364.

73 June Purvis, 'Doing Feminist Women's History: Researching the Lives of Women in the Suffragette Movement in Edwardian England' in Mary Maynard and June Purvis (eds) *Researching Women's Lives from a Feminist Perspective* (Taylor & Francis, 1994) 166, 167.

the things that clearly demarcates feminist jurisprudence from mainstream legal theory'.[74] This is summed up by the conviction that the personal is the political.

Second, feminist scholarship exposes binary understandings about gender roles and social life. It shows how identity and social roles are defined by understandings of femininity that are pervasive in a masculine-dominated public discourse. Persuasive stereotypes about gender roles perpetuate two neat binary understandings: contrasting male and female and the public and private spheres. As Vanessa Munro noted, 'women are identified with domestic and family life, with reproduction and with passive but accessible (hetro) sexuality'.[75] A feminist legal approach shows how these gendered understandings are articulated in law – 'the myriad ways in which law constructs gender by invoking images of 'woman''[76] – and how this leads to and perpetuates structural disadvantage.[77] A feminist perspective insists upon the connectedness and integrated nature of human existence and that 'lives that are not splintered between private or public, personal or professional'.[78] This re-casts not only the terrain but also the options that are available.

Third, feminist approaches highlight how ideas are gendered. It is not just legal structures and institutions (and subjective understandings of such structures and institutions) that are gendered. A feminist approach can uncover the gendered nature of legal concepts and ideas themselves (and their application). As Joanne Conaghan noted, a feminist approach can show how 'legal concepts are gendered not just in their application, but also in their meaning and scope'.[79] This can involve unpacking the gendered assumptions present in legal concepts. This can include taking 'a sceptical approach towards claims of law's rationality and neutrality'.[80] This may show that the gendering of law is more subtle than

74 M D A Freeman, *Lloyds Introduction to Jurisprudence* (9th ed Sweet & Maxwell, 2014) 1081.

75 Vanessa Munro, *Law and Politics at the Perimeter: Re-evaluating Key Debates in Feminist Theory* (Hart, 2007) 12. The theory of performativity pioneered by Judith Butler, has highlighted how gendered understandings are perpetuated by women's subjective understandings of themselves and the construction and re-construction of their social and legal identities: Judith Butler, *Gender Trouble: Feminism and the Subversion of Identity* (Routledge, 1990); Judith Butler, *Bodies that Matter: On the Discursive Limits of 'Sex'* (Routledge, 1993).

76 Joanne Conaghan, 'Reassessing the Feminist Theoretical Project in Law' (2000) 27(3) *Journal of Law and Society* 351, 361.

77 For instance, 'Family law perpetuates an inadequate system of private economic support for women and children whilst constituting an obstacle to the development of a more adequate public system of support and benefit': Carol Smart, *The Ties That Bind: Law, Marriage and the Reproduction of Patriarchal Relations* (Routledge 1984) 230.

78 Marie A Failinger, Elizabeth R Schlitz and Susan J Stabile, 'Foreword' in Marie A Failinger, Elizabeth R Schlitz and Susan J Stabile (eds) *Feminism, Law, and Religion* (Ashgate, 2013) xiii, xv.

79 Joanne Conaghan, 'Reassessing the Feminist Theoretical Project in Law' (2000) 27(3) *Journal of Law and Society* 351, 360–361.

80 Vanessa Munro, 'The Master's Tools? A Feminist Approach to Legal and Lay Decision-Making' in Dawn Watkins and Mandy Burton (eds) *Research Methods in Law* (2nd ed, Routledge, 2018) 194, 196. A feminist critique can 'challenge key assumptions about the operation of legal reason, for example, that the application of legal rules is a logic-driven process producing

it first appears especially when the analysis moves away from obviously gendered categories such as the reasonable man or the role played by battered women's syndrome in the criminal law on loss of control. For instance, the idea of the 'individual rights-bearer' can be critiqued as resting upon and perpetuating a liberal legal idea of the autonomous rational person. This approach 'invites the application of a gender lens to a seemingly genderless space or operation and 'helps to flush out any hidden norms lurking unacknowledged behind a gender-neutral façade'.[81] It shows how gender is actually 'analytically central' to and 'deeply constitutive' of law.

Fourth, feminist approaches can emphasise the agency of those experiencing disadvantage, subordination and exclusion.[82] As Vanessa Munro observed, 'the claim that society, and its institutions, are patriarchal is central to feminist analysis'.[83] However, talk of patriarchy can often ironically lead to paternalistic conclusions that present women as victims without agency.[84] There is a need to go further than saying that law is a male construct and that women are subjects of male oppression. A feminist approach needs to explore the power dynamics at play in particular situations. As Sharon Thompson has put it, 'a feminist perspective is useful because it does not aim to present men as *necessarily having* an oppressive role…, but it recognises that there *is a power dimension* between men and women'.[85] This needs to take into account not only multiple forms of

---

objectively determinable answers and/or that the conceptual structures and categorical schemes which support law are value-neutral, the purely intellectual product of disembodied minds': Joanne Conaghan, 'Labour Law and Feminist Method' (2017) 33(1) *International Journal of Comparative Labour Law* 93, 103.

81 Ibid 101.

82 However, as Rosemary Auchmuty and Erika Rackley insist, while this is 'about uncovering the lives of women missing from legal history', this is 'not about creating heroines'. They note that 'heroine narratives' all 'follow a formulaic structure designed, in this case, to overcome the challenge of honouring women who did something they were not supposed to do: that is, step outside the conventional realm of women, the private sphere, into the public sphere which belonged to men, and succeed in spite of all opposition'. Such narratives 'offer (over-simplified) versions of women's lives that can be harnessed for a political purpose': 'Women who succeed do so on men's terms. They are absorbed into patriarchal society rather than transforming it': Rosemary Auchmuty and Erika Rackley, 'Feminist Legal Biography: A Model for *All* Legal Life Stories' (2020) 41(2) *Journal of Legal History* 186, 204, 205. See, further, Erika Rackley and Rosemary Auchmuty, 'The Case for Feminist Legal History' (2020) 40(4) *Oxford Journal of Legal Studies* 878, 897–900.

83 Vanessa Munro, *Law and Politics at the Perimeter: Re-evaluating Key Debates in Feminist Theory* (Hart, 2007) 12. See also, for instance, the literature discussed in Hilaire Barnett, *Introduction to Feminist Jurisprudence* (Cavendish, 1998) chapter 3.

84 As Munro notes, an argument based on patriarchy stresses 'that the processes by which women's interests have been (re)presented, historically and currently, have been mediated (or "refracted") by male interpretations and understandings': Vanessa Munro, *Law and Politics at the Perimeter: Re-evaluating Key Debates in Feminist Theory* (Hart, 2007) 12.

85 Sharon Thompson, *Prenuptial Agreements and the Presumption of Free Choice: Issues of Power in Theory and Practice* (Hart, 2015) 9.

oppression but also crucially emphasises the agency of women.[86] As Thompson has argued, 'it is important not to presume a lack of agency when there is evidence of oppression or systematic subordination'.[87] Rather relationships need to be looked at as a whole and there is a need to pay attention 'to the tacit understandings affecting intimate relationships'.[88] One way of achieving this is to take a relational approach, as shown by Thompson's Feminist Relational Contract Theory, which focuses on the relationships between people and their power relations.

Fifth, a feminist approach is normative. A feminist approach seeks to bring about social change. As Joanne Conaghan put it, feminism is concerned 'not just with describing or interpreting social arrangements but also with changing them, that is, with prescribing and effecting transformation, informed by a range of normative ideals including sexual equality, social justice, and individual self-development'.[89] Feminism's 'history, focus, concepts, methodologies, political and intellectual objectives are all imbued with an overriding sense of wrongfulness, of violation, exploitation and repression, of silenced voices and excluded Others'. This means that feminist scholarship can, and often does have, a political dimension.[90] As Erika Rackley and Rosemary Auchmuty noted: 'Feminist legal history is a call to arms to anyone who cares about the position of women in law, and society generally'.[91] However, academic feminism has a different 'validatory framework' than feminism as a political movement: as Conaghan pointed out, while 'as a scholarly engagement, feminism (seeks to) acquire(s) respectability and legitimacy through its explanatory and interpretative power; as a political movement, however, it gains its legitimacy through its ability visibly to bring

86 This is overlooked in traditional legal histories where women are 'portrayed as the passive recipients of legal and social change, as subjects rather than initiators of legal reform'. Conventional accounts instead present 'hard-fought-for legal change, for example, as a simple response to shifts in "social attitudes"': Erika Rackley and Rosemary Auchmuty, 'The Case for Feminist Legal History' (2020) 40(4) *Oxford Journal of Legal Studies* 878, 884, 881.

87 Sharon Thompson, 'Feminist Relational Contract Theory: A New Model for Family Property Agreements' (2018) 45(4) *Journal of Law and Society* 617, 627.

88 Ibid 629.

89 Joanne Conaghan, 'Reassessing the Feminist Theoretical Project in Law' (2000) 27(3) *Journal of Law and Society* 351, 375.

90 For Erika Rackley and Rosemary Auchmuty, 'Feminist legal history is, then, at root a political project': Erika Rackley and Rosemary Auchmuty, 'Women's Legal Landmarks: An Introduction' in Erika Rackley and Rosemary Auchmuty (eds) *Women's Legal Landmarks: Celebrating the History of Women and Law in the UK and Ireland* (Hart, 2018) 1, 5. However, as Conaghan pointed out: 'The feminist unpacking of the largely hidden gendered content of law has operated in tandem with its strategic deployment to advance women's interests': Joanne Conaghan, 'Reassessing the Feminist Theoretical Project in Law' (2000) 27(3) *Journal of Law and Society* 351, 362.

91 Erika Rackley and Rosemary Auchmuty, 'The Case for Feminist Legal History' (2020) 40(4) *Oxford Journal of Legal Studies* 878, 902.

about political change'.[92] This means that 'feminism in the academy, then, is both expressive and interrogative of feminist politics'.[93]

The diverse and dynamic nature of feminism means that care must be taken not to express these five features in too dogmatic terms. Moreover, two important points need to be stressed. The first point is that, although feminism is a critique, this does not mean that it necessarily has to exist in opposition to other approaches. Feminist analysis is often placed as being critical of liberalism and its emphasis upon individual autonomy and rational choice. As Vanessa Munro noted, 'much feminist commentary has been critical of the key tenets of the liberal tradition – lamenting in particular its tendency to abstraction and its assumption of individualism'.[94] However, it is also true, as Munro pointed out, that emphasising this conflict between feminism and liberalism can actually hamper the development of feminist legal scholarship. She warned of the danger of 'the tendency in too much feminist work to "lump together" disparate liberal approaches or to "straw-man" its liberal target' and is concerned about the 'lack of engagement with the liberal tradition on its own terms' which threatens 'to substantially weaken the feminist critique'.[95] This is especially unfortunate given that, as Munro pointed out, liberal thought can be understood to actually emphasise connectedness or relationality. She cited the work of Martha C Nussbaum for emphasising that 'the essence of liberalism is in fact fundamentally relational, since it is about respect for *others* as individuals'.[96] It is important, therefore, not to deny the extent to which liberal understandings of law have already ensured that 'in some areas at least, legal reasoning is already relational albeit perhaps in the more negative sense that "it privileges certain kinds of relationships"'.

The point here is that a feminist perspective should not necessarily be placed in opposition to conventional accounts. Instead, it can improve those accounts. Feminism serves as an exercise in de-construction and re-construction. Feminist scholarship does not simply diagnose; its grounded nature means that it is especially well-placed also to be the needed medicine that rebuilds, re-strengthens and improves. As Conaghan put it, 'the role of feminism here has been at once destructive and constructive'.[97] This invariably means that while 'feminist interventions have contributed to the instability and uncertainty' that afflicts the law they have also provided 'the promise and potential of feminist scholarship to aid the refashioning of a field widely acknowledged to be in disarray'.[98]

92 Joanne Conaghan, 'Reassessing the Feminist Theoretical Project in Law' (2000) 27(3) *Journal of Law and Society* 351, 355.

93 Ibid 356.

94 Vanessa Munro, *Law and Politics at the Perimeter: Re-evaluating Key Debates in Feminist Theory* (Hart, 2007) 4.

95 Ibid 53.

96 Ibid 54, citing Martha C Nussbaum, *Sex and Social Justice* (Oxford University Press, 1999) 57.

97 Joanne Conaghan, 'Labour Law and Feminist Method' (2017) 33(1) *International Journal of Comparative Labour Law* 93, 105.

98 Ibid 108.

The second point is that, although this chapter focuses on gender as a subversive means to critique the stories told by law, this is not to deny that other focuses such as upon race, religion, class or sexuality could perform similar and equally necessary correctives. Indeed, this has been partially recognised within Feminist Legal Studies in the growing the literature on intersectionality whereby the focus has 'shifted away from the concept of gender as an isolated category of analysis towards a concern with the way in which gender intersects with other categories of identity for purposes of understanding and combating inequality'.[99] This literature emerged as a result of the '"essentialism" critique on feminist jurisprudence during the 1990s'.[100] This was the assumption that 'women *qua* women share a common essence, experience, predicament or perspective'.[101] This focus represents 'a growing recognition of the need to broaden the representational base of feminism to take better account, substantively and strategically, of differences between women' buoyed by a 'a keen suspicion of categories in general and of the category "woman" in particular'.[102] However, Joanne Conaghan has been critical of the literature on intersectionality for being premised upon identity 'as a core unit of analysis, with gender, race and other inequality "grounds" being repositioned as "dimensions" of identity which law fails adequately to capture and reflect'.[103] She is concerned that this has 'had the unfortunate effect of directing feminist efforts away from concrete, empirically-based legal research with a socio-economic or distributive focus towards more abstract theoretical encounters with gendered cultural and legal representations'.[104]

Although focusing on other grounds of subordination and exclusion is undoubtedly important, these require analysis in their own right. Feminist approaches cannot be blind to them but their focus is upon gender inequalities. Feminist Legal History is not synonymous with Subversive Legal History. Rather, it is one type of Subversive Legal History. It is desirable that other forms of Subversive Legal History – focusing on race, religion, class, sexuality and other stories that are marginalised in the conventional conjectural histories of law – also take place. These will have different characteristics, will move the analysis in different ways and will provoke diverse disturbances. However, the types of disturbances that occur are likely to be

99 Joanne Conaghan, 'Intersectionality and the Feminist Project in Law' in Emily Grabham, Davina Cooper, Jane Krishnadas and Didi Herman (eds) *Intersectionality and Beyond: Law, Power and the Politics of Location* (Routledge, 2009) 21.

100 Emily Jackson and Nicola Lacey, 'Introducing Feminist Legal Theory' in James Penner, David Schiff and Richard Nobles (eds) *Introduction to Jurisprudence and Legal Theory* (Butterworths, 2002) 779, 847. On which see also Hilaire Barnett, *Introduction to Feminist Jurisprudence* (Cavendish, 1998) 20 *et seq.*

101 Vanessa Munro, *Law and Politics at the Perimeter: Re-evaluating Key Debates in Feminist Theory* (Hart, 2007) 7.

102 Ibid 23.

103 Ibid 30.

104 Joanne Conaghan, 'Reassessing the Feminist Theoretical Project in Law' (2000) 27(3) *Journal of Law and Society* 351, 370.

the same. The next section will, with reference to Feminist Legal History as an exemplar, outline the three major types of disturbances that a subversive approach will bring about.

The Three Disturbances

A feminist approach is subversive in that it causes three important disturbances to occur.

The first disturbance is that Feminist Legal History is about disturbing the narrative of Legal History by focusing on the question of power, complicating linear accounts of progression and re-writing conventional accounts to emphasise the agency of individuals and movements both in terms of campaigning for reform and also in using law strategically. It provides an alternative story which not only identifies, challenges and disrupts the dominant narrative but also supersedes it. A feminist approach results in the engendering of Legal History:[105] questioning the assumptions and explanations of the conventional account and refocusing on the question of power relations by moving the subordinated and excluded from the periphery to the core. Feminist Legal Studies has long made use of historical analysis. As Joanne Conaghan notes, although feminists 'have no monopoly on history' nevertheless 'feminist scholars have found it helpful to apply historical perspectives to legal terrain':

> What history does is render the present contingent so that arrangements which present themselves as natural and universally determined are revealed to be the contrivances of past processes and events, not timeless but time-bound.[106]

A feminist account can allow the subversive potential of Legal History to come to the fore, showing that law is contingent, that the seemingly prescribed parameters of legal change are malleable constructions and that alternative ways of doing law are possible. Refocusing the lens to place gender at the fore allows us to see beyond the conventional stories of law and therefore allows us to glimpse a wider range of possibilities. As Anne Bottomley points out, a historical approach can be valuable because 'recovering histories, genealogies, of law allows us to examine foundational claims, but also the processes which made possible those assertions'.[107] Feminist Legal History subverts the picture to create a new history. In the words of Tracey J Boisseau, 'this mission to think counter-intuitively about the past' constitutes 'a direct and purposeful assault on conventional thinking about the relationship between law, gender relations and

105 Ute Gerhard and Karen Offen, 'Preface' in Sara L Kimble and Marian Rowekamp (eds) *New Perspectives on European Women's Legal History* (Routledge, 2017) I.

106 Joanne Conaghan, 'Labour Law and Feminist Method' (2017) 33(1) *International Journal of Comparative Labour Law* 93, 109.

107 Anne Bottomley, 'Introduction' in Anne Bottomley (ed) *Feminist Perspectives on the Foundation Subjects of Law* (Cavendish, 1996) 1, 3.

women's lives that is often directly undercutting what our legal system, stuck in a blind present, generally imagines to be natural or to have always been true'.[108] This attack is an action not only of de-construction but also of re-construction. A corrected history can be used not only to improve our understandings of the law but also crucially inform calls for reform. As Tracy A Thomas and Tracey J Boisseau put it, 'Feminist Legal History attempts to provide [a] useable past with the hope it will impact future changes in the law that are responsive to the lived realities of women'.[109]

The second disturbance is that a feminist approach disturbs the sources of Legal History. The mantra that the personal is political, the focus on bottom-up lived experiences and the agency of those without power and its insistence that binary distinctions such as those between private and public and between the legal and the social are patriarchal constructs means that a feminist approach requires a much wider range of primary and secondary materials than those normally used in legal studies. As Felice Batlan pointed out, works that seek to engender Legal History use:

> A blend of source material, which reaches far beyond court cases. Like much of the new legal history, they rely on legislative proceedings, administrative hearings, bar minutes, newspapers, letters, speeches, church proceedings, the writings of participants in social movement, fiction, and the flotsam of popular culture.[110]

This is in itself subversive. As Rosemary Auchmuty and Erika Rackley have noted, 'to undertake in-depth research into secondary sources written by historians as well as non-legal records, runs counter to the training of many legal scholars, who are not only not familiar with this material, but have been trained to disregard it – to rely only on strictly legal sources'.[111] They have argued that:

> It is incumbent upon feminist legal historians to recover and present women's own stories of their encounters with law: to search out women's voices in autobiographical accounts, oral histories, the press, fiction even; to look beyond self-referential legal historical accounts and to immerse ourselves in secondary sources, often written by social historians and biographers, which reconstruct and account for the law in its political and social context,

108 Tracey J Boisseau, 'Preface' in Tracy A Thomas and Tracey J Boisseau (eds) *Feminist Legal History: Essays on Women and Law* (New York University Press, 2011) ix, x.

109 Tracy A Thomas and Tracey J Boisseau, 'Introduction: Law, History, and Feminism' in Tracy A Thomas and Tracey J Boisseau (eds) *Feminist Legal History: Essays on Women and Law* (New York University Press, 2011) 1, 26.

110 Felice Batlan, 'Engendering Legal History' (2005) 30(4) *Law & Society Inquiry* 823, 847. See, further, Rosemary Auchmuty, 'Recovering Lost Lives: Researching Women in Legal History' (2015) 42 *Journal of Law and Society* 34, 41.

111 Rosemary Auchmuty and Erika Rackley, 'Feminist Legal Biography: A Model for *All* Legal Life Stories' (2020) 41(2) *Journal of Legal History* 186, 192.

> and provide insights into not only what was going on but also, crucially for our purposes, *what it was like* for women then. This is important not simply because it adds women's perspectives, hitherto absent, to the historical account, but because it helps to avoid imposing the understandings of the present on to the past.[112]

A feminist approach goes further than requiring the study of non-legal sources alongside legal sources. It requires an understanding that there is no such thing as a purely legal source. Rather, in the words of Batlan, a feminist approach understands that 'law reflects societal understandings of gender while simultaneously constructing such understandings'.[113] It questions 'where law can be located and what constitutes law, denying that law is in any way a closed or autonomous system'. It is not a question of studying law 'and' society but law 'in' society and society 'in' law. Indeed, a feminist approach subverts the analysis to such an extent that the old discourse of 'law and society' is outmoded. This means that new methodological approaches are required that can transcend conventional understandings of what is meant by legal and indeed socio-legal research.

The third and final disturbance is that Feminist Legal History disturbs the assumptions and explanations concerning disciplines of knowledge. The feminist questioning of the story of the law does not only critique what goes on in legislatures and courtrooms. The conventional narrative is also perpetuated in Law Schools. As Nicola Lacey put it, a feminist critique questions 'a number of assumptions common to positivistic and liberal legal scholarship': notions that legal reasoning is neutral, that law is a system of enacted norms or rules that have a unity and coherence and are rational neutral, objective, autonomous and central to social relations.[114] Work of a critical persuasion has the problem of often finding itself part of the very thing that it is seeking to criticise. As Sharon Thompson pointed out, the question of how feminism can operate within law to produce solutions given that law is part of the problem is perhaps the greatest challenge for a feminist methodological approach in law.[115] Joanne Conaghan has written of:

> A recurrent anxiety – evident within feminist legal studies in particular – about whether and where to locate feminist scholarship within broader fields of the discipline. For example, is feminist legal studies best positioned at the

112 Erika Rackley and Rosemary Auchmuty, 'The Case for Feminist Legal History' (2020) 40(4) *Oxford Journal of Legal Studies* 878, 892.

113 Felice Batlan, 'Engendering Legal History' (2005) 30(4) *Law & Society Inquiry* 823, 847.

114 Nicola Lacey, *Unspeakable Subjects: Feminist Essays in Legal and Social Theory* (Hart, 1998) 4.

115 Sharon Thompson, 'Are Methods in Law a Feminist Issue?' (Paper presented at the Gender Rules conference on 20th June 2016, available on the Law and Gender YouTube channel at: <https://youtube.com/channel/UCLpBO6KARuD5mAskawbl4NQ>). See also Carol Smart, *Feminism and the Power of Law* (Routledge 1989).

> margins of law (where, arguably, it can more easily retain its critical edge) or should feminist scholars strive towards the absorption and incorporation of feminist perspectives within the legal academic mainstream?[116]

There is a conflict between getting in bed with the enemy or being so far removed from the mainstream that you are unable to influence it. A feminist critique of law cannot operate entirely separate to and outside conventional legal discourse. To transform law, a feminist approach needs to recognise that law and social ideas are inseparable (*pace* Cotterrell) and that the feminist project is shaped by and shapes both. This means, as Hilaire Barnett has put it, that feminist legal methods are able to 'complement traditional legal method by incorporation of alternative views, experiences, perceptions and values which traditional method, in its insistence on logic and deductive thought, may exclude'.[117] A feminist approach subverts the conventional approach and is crucially an act of re-construction as well as de-construction.

This subversive spirit also de-constructs and re-constructs boundaries between areas of knowledge. It disturbs conventional understandings about the formation of intellectual fields and the distinctions made between them to justify their existence. This includes traditional dividing lines between Legal History and Feminist Legal Studies.[118] Erika Rackley and Rosemary Auchmuty observed that this occurs in a context in UK and Ireland, 'where legal history – let alone feminist legal history – remains a relatively niche subject'.[119] Their *Women's Legal Landmarks* project 'sought to carve out a space for feminist legal history, so that it might push at the boundaries of knowledge and critical engagement in legal history and feminist legal studies generally'. Feminist Legal History, then, can provide a disturbance that creates a space and need for a new subversive form of Legal History. A focus on gender in Legal History, then, should not be seen merely as bridging the gap between conventional Legal History and gender

116 Joanne Conaghan, 'The Making of a Field or the Building of a Wall? Feminist Legal Studies and Law, Gender and Sexuality' (2009) 17 *Feminist Legal Studies* 303, 304.

117 Hilaire Barnett, *Introduction to Feminist Jurisprudence* (Cavendish, 1998) 25.

118 Maria Drakopoulou referred to the 'paradox marking feminist legal history' which results from the 'peculiar combination' of asserting its own institutional autonomy as a field yet also being defined by its 'intellectual dependency upon its "sister fields"' of Feminist Legal Studies and feminist history. She argued that Feminist Legal History needs to find its own discursive space rather than bridging the gap to overcome the weaknesses of both law and history. She calls for an '"otherwise feminist" history' which 'although continuing to remain faithful to interdisciplinarity is able to clearly distinguish its own direction of historical research from that of its "sister" fields': Maria Drakopoulou, 'Feminist Historiography of Law: An Exposition and Proposition' in Markus D Dubber and Christopher Tomlins (eds) *The Oxford Handbook of Legal History* (Oxford University Press, 2018) 603, 617, 619. This analysis, however, seems to apply more to the US than the UK where Feminist Legal History remains in an embryonic stage, though it does serve as an important warning.

119 Erika Rackley and Rosemary Auchmuty, 'Women's Legal Landmarks: An Introduction' in Erika Rackley and Rosemary Auchmuty (eds) *Women's Legal Landmarks: Celebrating the History of Women and Law in the UK and Ireland* (Hart, 2018) 1, 5.

history; it actually transforms Legal History.[120] A feminist subversive approach exposes the current narrow conception of legal studies and indeed of socio-legal studies and pushes historical approaches to the fore. As Judith M Bennett noted:

> Feminism needs history, deep history as well as recent history. It is our special brief, as feminist historians, to ensure that history is not only ever-present (even to those feminists who prefer to ignore it) but also rich, plausible and well-informed.[121]

This is just one example of how a feminist approach also exposes the architecture of law as an academic field and of the sub-divisions made within law. As Conaghan noted, the 'blurring of legal disciplinary boundaries is not peculiarly feminist',[122] like any critical approach, a feminist approach 'troubles categories, blurs boundaries, subverts meanings and contests normative priorities'.[123] However, a feminist approach to field-making is also an act of re-construction. A subversive approach not only disturbs the conventional account but also supersedes it. As Conaghan put it, 'law emerges simultaneously *gendered* and *gendering*' both 'a repository of values replicating and reinforcing wider social and cultural arrangements – including gender-based attitudes, practices, and beliefs – and also actively implicated in the construction and maintenance of such arrangements'.[124]

A feminist approach scrutinises the construction of fields of knowledge, including processes of inclusion and exclusion, the assumptions made, the authority given to certain voices and the importance afforded to particular topics and arguments. A feminist approach is not only critical of law as an institutional system but also of law as a discourse, as a body of knowledge. For Conaghan, the practice and effect of field-making is political.[125] Field-making 'lends strength to an intellectual tradition' and 'raises the visibility and enhances the authority of scholarship which might otherwise be excluded or marginalised by the established conceptual or disciplinary infra-structure'. A feminist derived subversive approach not only questions but would also play with and use the process of field-making in order to subvert the field, to question orthodoxies and to reclaim the field as part of the critical tradition. Paying attention to field-making can be far from being a dry semantic question of definition provided that the role of agency is central to field-making.

120 Ute Gerhard and Karen Offen, 'Preface' in Sara L Kimble and Marian Rowekamp (eds) *New Perspectives on European Women's Legal History* (Routledge, 2017) I.

121 Judith M. Bennett, 'Forgetting the Past' (2008) 20(3) *Gender & History* 669, 675.

122 Joanne Conaghan, 'Labour Law and Feminist Method' (2017) 33(1) *International Journal of Comparative Labour Law* 93, 111.

123 Ibid 114.

124 Ibid 112.

125 Joanne Conaghan, 'The Making of a Field or the Building of a Wall? Feminist Legal Studies and Law, Gender and Sexuality' (2009) 17 *Feminist Legal Studies* 303, 304.

A feminist subversive approach re-casts the way in which we look at fields of knowledge by focusing on the personal rather than the institutional. For Ruth Fletcher, 'a field connotes an area of research and teaching, rather than a disciplinary mode of knowledge production, or a collection of academic scholarship'.[126] She wrote of 'intellectual fields as distinguishing themselves from each other as they take on particular logics through the application of key concepts and methods to research terrain'. As Conaghan noted, Fletcher is thinking of the word 'field' as 'as a verb rather than as a noun (as in: to field a player in a sport or a fighter on a battlefield)' in that the focus 'is more on process (or practice in Ruth's conception) than on product, on doing rather than being'.[127] As Alison Diduck put it, it is vital 'not to abstract out of existence the real people who do the work of actively constituting a field'.[128] Drawing upon Fletcher, Diduck sees a field as being more than just 'a place or space'; it is 'as much our actions as it is the products of those actions'.[129] An embodied approach to field-making is similarly interested in the 'stories' of those who work in fields, their experiences, their practices, their assumptions. It is, for Diduck, an exploration of her intellectual 'home' and 'a set of embodied practices in and around a particular home that is undergoing constant renovation'. A subversive feminist approach, then, sees field-making as a creative act, a deliberate act, a human act and so, Conaghan reminds us, it is always and should always be a contestable act:

> To mark out a field, then, is never simply to describe what is already there; it is to create, to produce, to bring forth. Envisioning a field requires a vision, projection or plan, the execution of which involves selection, discrimination, and judgement making. Both the vision and the selection are contestable. Indeed, it is the nature of field-making to engender, often deliberately to provoke, contestation.[130]

A feminist perspective subversively reveals how acts of construction and re-construction have perpetuated disadvantages on grounds of gender. It shows how field-making occurs both explicitly and implicitly. As with the disturbance of the narratives and sources, the disturbance of fields allows hidden stories and perspectives to come to the fore. To the extent that the dominant conventional account questions the existence and nature of fields of knowledge at all, it sees disciplines as being universal, fixed and defined in a top-down way. Legal sub-disciplines in particular are often said to be defined outside of the academy. Areas of law are often said to be defined by statute or by the courts rather than

126 Ruth Fletcher, 'Embodied Practices' (2009) 17 *Feminist Legal Studies* 315, 316.

127 Joanne Conaghan, 'The Making of a Field or the Building of a Wall? Feminist Legal Studies and Law, Gender and Sexuality' (2009) 17 *Feminist Legal Studies* 303, 307.

128 Alison Diduck, 'Doing Home' (2009) 17 *Feminist Legal Studies* 293.

129 Ibid 295.

130 Joanne Conaghan, 'The Making of a Field or the Building of a Wall? Feminist Legal Studies and Law, Gender and Sexuality' (2009) 17 *Feminist Legal Studies* 303, 305.

by those who are active in the field.[131] A feminist approach rebuts this.[132] For Fletcher, fields are collective endeavours which develop as a result of and as part of 'embodied practices'.[133] Field construction is affected both by the political and the social and also by the relationships formed by those within the field relative to each other and relative to those outside the field. In contrast to top-down and sterile narratives of the developments of fields that focus on objective measurements invariably limited to outputs (defining a field by what has been published), seeing field construction and re-construction as an embodied practice allows us to see fields not only as being contested but also as being shaped by such contestation. As Fletcher noted, thinking about 'field-making as embodied practices helps us to acknowledge the ways in which feelings of alienation or excitement at new legal developments become a source of knowledge and a motivation for further investigation' and how 'hunger in turn provoked a rethinking of key concepts and methods'.[134] The construction and re-construction of the field is a dynamic process that is on-going and so, the current construction of a field is neither fixed nor the end.

This provides a further critique of and move away from the evolutionary functionalist narrative. As Fletcher puts it, thinking in terms of embodied practices focuses on how a field 'grows organically in fits and starts, in cycles and flows, rather than in a top-down, even and linear fashion'.[135] A subversive approach then provides a means to highlight and critique the stories that disciplines and sub-disciplines tell about themselves and which they use to constrain their development. Indeed, the very talk of disciplines and sub-disciplines is part of this story. A subversive approach reveals that the construction and often unseen perpetuation of fields of knowledge is an act of subordination and exclusion. Crucially it underlines that the act and its effect are both contingent and contestable. This applies to the story told about law as a discipline and also the story told about Legal History as a sub-discipline.[136] These are authored, partial stories – written by Oxbridge educated straight white men – which are falsely presented

131 Criminal law is defined as the body of law that defies criminal offences; family law is defined as the area of law dealt with by the Family Court etc.

132 As Anne Bottomley notes feminism 'gives rise to the recognition of the contingency of attempting to form, of asserting or claiming, subject status'. This brings about 'a crucial awareness of the process of construction': Anne Bottomley, 'Introduction' in Anne Bottomley (ed) *Feminist Perspectives on the Foundation Subjects of Law* (Cavendish, 1996) 1, 2.

133 Ruth Fletcher, 'Embodied Practices' (2009) 17 *Feminist Legal Studies* 315, 316.

134 Ibid 317.

135 Ibid 316.

136 As Erika Rackley and Rosemary Auchmuty note: 'Legal historians, and the discipline of legal history itself, have been heavily invested in preserving the illusion of legal objectivity, neutrality and inevitability; in maintaining a narrative characterised by progress and liberal incrementalism. The consequence of this pursuit of coherence is that the jumbled reality of law reform – the setbacks, compromises and failures – is lost' (Erika Rackley and Rosemary Auchmuty, 'The Case for Feminist Legal History' (2020) 40(4) *Oxford Journal of Legal Studies* 878, 882).

as universal and fixed. They are ripe for subversive actions of de-construction and re-construction.

Feminist Legal History, then, goes beyond the definition of Critical History of creating 'disturbances in the field'.[137] Rather, it is about three particular forms of disturbance informed by a focus on gender and the five features of feminist legal scholarship described above. A feminist approach disturbs the narrative and the sources used by traditional academic accounts, before critiquing the formation of academic knowledge itself. These disturbances are all directly concerned with questions of power and focusing upon the agency of those that conventional accounts invariably overlook. Maria Drakopoulou has argued that a historical approach to law can help develop Feminist Legal Studies, calling for a new alliance between history and law 'which is capable of generating new questions to ask of law and about law, and thus a new way of thinking critically about law':

> This alliance of law and history is capable of bearing further gifts to feminist legal scholarship; for the necessity and the validity of the search for new ways of thinking about law can only pass through a historical account of what has gone before. And it is to the alliance between critique and history that the feminist legal scholar should again take recourse. The study of women and law has come a long way and the time is now ripe to take a pause and, before setting off towards new directions, contemplate its own historicity.[138]

For Drakopoulou, this can only be achieved 'through the historicization of the feminist project in law':

> It is only through critical reflection upon its own history and the conditions which made it possible that feminist legal scholarship can develop a deeper understanding of its current predicament; why it has asked these questions of law and not others, and why it has developed these modes of critique and not others.

This insight can be applied to legal scholarship generally. This, in short, is what Subversive Legal History seeks to achieve. As Tracy A Thomas and Tracey J Boisseau put it, a feminist approach provides 'a kind of applied legal scholarship [which] seeks to make history directly relevant to modern legal discourse'.[139] It also rejects the assumptions of evolutionary functionalism that are at the heart of

137 Cf. Robert Gordon, 'The Arrival of Critical Historicism' (1997) 49 *Stanford Law Review* 1023, 1024.

138 Maria Drakopoulou, 'Clio's Forgotten Consciousness: History and the Question of Feminist Critique in Law' (2013) 38(1) *Australian Feminist Law Journal* 3, 21.

139 Tracy A Thomas and Tracey J Boisseau, 'Introduction: Law, History, and Feminism' in Tracy A Thomas and Tracey J Boisseau (eds) *Feminist Legal History* (New York University Press, 2011) 1, 26.

modern legal discourse. As Erika Rackley and Rosemary Auchmuty have argued, 'feminist legal history seeks to resist and debunk the idea that legal history – and women's legal history in particular – is inherently and inexorably progressive'.[140] They argue that because 'another version of what has happened has become embedded in the public consciousness', Feminist Legal History is not about the production of 'alternative interpretations to sit alongside the conventional texts'.[141] Rather than being 'a niche companion to, or "perspective on", the objective canon', Feminist Legal History 'aims to write women (back) into legal history and thus force the discipline to confront the issue of women's long exclusion and marginalisation'. They warn that:

> As long as feminist legal history is ghettoised, and its content not incorporated into mainstream historical accounts; as long as the legal curriculum and textbooks ignore history generally, or harness it only in the service of the status quo; as long as everything a woman does is regarded as less important than the actions of men (or entirely unimportant), then the knowledge and understandings that have been uncovered, publicised and become visible in one generation can and will disappear before the next comes along.[142]

A feminist approach to Legal History therefore reshapes historical approaches away from being a specialism and towards being at the beating heart of what Law Schools do. A historical approach is needed to identify, challenge, de-construct and re-construct the stories that are told about law. A subversive approach is therefore inherently and necessarily historical. A historical approach is no longer seen as the preserve of a distinct and select sub-discipline within legal studies called Legal History. It is not even regarded as an exercise in interdisciplinary borrowing from the academic discipline of history. All these terms – law, history, Legal History and so on – are mere labels. Subversive Legal History is therefore

140 Erika Rackley and Rosemary Auchmuty, 'The Case for Feminist Legal History' (2020) 40(4) *Oxford Journal of Legal Studies* 878, 900. Feminist Legal History instead reveals 'a complex patchwork of gains and losses, failed attempts, pyrrhic victories, compromises and uneasy alliances. Progress is never linear, but ebbs and flows' (ibid 901): 'Feminist legal history offers a more realistic account of the unfolding pageant of the past. It reveals a tale of two steps forward, one step back, as forces of reaction consistently regroup to return the situation to the status quo, and of advances lost, often more easily than they were gained. It calls out the notion of cumulative legal progress for the myth that it is: one that encourages us to believe that things are getting better all the time; that, if things were unjust in the past, they are not only much better now, but also will continue to get better if we just wait long enough. ... Feminist history tell us that advances in the position and status of women do not just happen; rather, they are the result of years – often decades – of argument, activism and renewed activism, largely (though not solely) by women, resisted largely (but not solely) by men' (ibid 901–902).

141 Ibid 903, 902.

142 This means that 'Feminist legal history is thus part historical record, part guidebook. From its pages we learn not only the stories of women's legal history, and of the women and men who made and sometime failed to make history, but also potential strategies of feminist law reform': ibid 903.

not a new label for a sub-discipline within law but is rather the name given for convenience to a movement. It denotes a new means of doing law that should become prevalent.

Subversive Legal History challenges and supersedes the conventional dominant history which is imbued with evolutionary functionalist assumptions and explanations. It changes the lens not only to de-construct but also to re-construct. SFC Milsom notably likened Legal History to 'that children's game in which you draw lines between numbered dots, and suddenly from the jumble a picture emerges'.[143] Subversive Legal History questions whether we ought to be playing the game of drawing lines at all, it asks who is advantaged and disadvantaged from that game and it questions what it means to win. Subversive Legal History shows that law is not fixed, certain or universal; it reveals that law is constructed, authored and contingent. This chapter has provided an illustration of what Subversive Legal History can achieve by reference to Feminist Legal History as an exemplar of this approach. The three disturbances described here will be reflected upon and developed further in the chapters that follow. The following chapters will explore further possibilities that exist if a subversive approach is taken. The next two chapters will further examine respectively how the narrative and methods of law can be disturbed before the final two chapters focus upon the effect upon disciplines of knowledge.

143 S F C Milsom, *Historical Foundations of the Common Law* (2nd ed, Butterworths, 1981) 8.

5 The Perils of Periodisation

The Law School is like a monastery.

Monasteries are self-contained communities that perpetuate themselves through order, through the stories they repeat, through their rules and most importantly by their isolation from what may be called the real world. The Law School operates in a similar way. Year after year, the same chants can be heard. In lecture halls up and down the country, lecturers repeat the similar intonations that make up each foundational module, which are scribbled down and learnt by students. The law student becomes accustomed to and disciplined to the language, the abstraction and the scale of their task: to learn the law, to analyse it within its own parameters and then to apply it to neat but highly fictionalised hypothetical scenarios. The study of doctrine becomes indoctrination.[1] Students forget that they are hearing stories. They do not realise that these stories have authors. Textbooks (which, of course, are authored but become dehumanised in the classroom) repeat structures, concepts, ideas and chronologies presenting them as planned, as structured, as being universal. Shelves after shelves of books with virtually identical tables of contents by different authors perpetuate the same canon. There are, of course, exceptions: lecturers, modules and textbooks that do not stick to the script. But these remain the exceptions that prove the rule.

Law is presented in a particular way, within a narrative of progress.[2] As E P Thompson put it: 'The greatest of all legal fictions is that the law itself evolves, from case to case, by its own impartial logic, true to its own integrity'.[3] This

1 As Peter Goodrich put it: 'In studying law it is necessary first to believe in it and then to praise it': Peter Goodrich, 'Poor Illiterate Reason: History, Nationalism and Common Law' (1992) 1 *Social and Legal Studies* 7, 19.

2 'Law continues to present itself as a progression towards justice and equality and celebrates the winners in the doctrinal war – the statute that passed, the principle that succeeded – excluding 'irrelevant' detail that does not fit the chosen legal narrative': Rosemary Auchmuty and Erika Rackley, 'Feminist Legal Biography: A Model for *All* Legal Life Stories' (2020) 41(2) *The Journal of Legal History* 186, 191.

3 E P Thompson, *Whigs & Hunters: The Origins of the Black Act* (Penguin, 1990) 250. As Brian Simpson noted, 'There is, of course, a sense in which nobody really believes this anymore, but it remains the case that much legal behaviour proceeds on the assumption that law is like that': A W Brian Simpson, *Leading Cases in the Common Law* (Oxford University Press, 1995) 10.

presentation of the autonomy of law suggests that law only tends to get stuck because of an unforeseen circumstance or a change outside its control (it is rarely law's fault but where it is then a particular defect is to blame). The solution almost always comes from a part of the political or legal system. The end result is never perfect, but it is always better. It is the story of continual improvement with occasional corrective measures. The flow, the direction, the existence, the purpose are rarely questioned. Law is assumed to be logical, certain and fair. Law is assumed to be capable to deal with its imperfections. Law cleanses itself. The law student learns to accept this. They question what they are allowed to question, not the structure or purpose but the detail; the imperfections which they are allowed to critically analyse. They discuss reform but on the law's own terms and on the assumption that any such reform would be performed by law's own heroes. Legal reform is the role of legislatures, the product of official law reform bodies. In limited circumstances only, it is the role of judges. Lived experiences can only ever potentially trigger legal change through official means: through the courts or through engagement with the official channels. Activism exists outside the law. Non-legal solutions and possibilities exist outside the law. Questioning the need for law exists outside the law.

There is a paradox here in that the Law School both distinguishes itself from and says that it prepares students for the world of legal practice. The Law School, therefore, perpetuates its own autonomy, its own self-contained community. On the one hand, the Law School emphasises the need for a liberal education and the malleable phrase socio-legal research where it needs to separate itself from the legal profession. While on the other hand, it emphasises the nature of legal reasoning and its real life application where it needs to distinguish itself from the rest of the academy. In being torn between two masters (the profession and the university), the Law School ultimately chooses to satisfy neither. Law students are inducted into a specific, very self-contained community. Writing doctrinal essays is unlikely to prepare them well either for a career in legal practice or for further academic study.

Law students deserve more than a monastic education. Subversive Legal History – using history to disturb law – provides a way of doing this. A hallmark of Subversive Legal History is the critical disturbance (de- and re-construction) of the conventional stories that Law Schools perpetuate. This reveals that the stories Law Schools tell are authored stories and are therefore constructed, biased and partial. Moreover, Subversive Legal History reveals that the stories that are told are all imbued with similar values: they are founded upon what Robert Gordon called evolutionary functionalism.[4] This is not surprising since evolutionary functionalism – the idea of linear progress – is itself a historical construct. As Dorothy Ross has argued, this understanding of historical progress 'emerged in the eighteenth century, with its confidence in human powers and

4 Robert W Gordon, 'Critical Legal Histories' (1984) 36 *Stanford Law Review* 57.

unidirectional sense of time'.[5] She referred to it as a 'major step', 'closely bound with the process of secularization' whereby:

> The changing earthly world had to be loosened from the eternal world of God and his immutable truth. Value and meaning had to be found in the secular world, and secular modes of understanding historical change had to gain authority. Moreover, change itself had to be understood as a real change – as a succession of qualitatively different phenomena – and not merely as random variations, the surface appearance of essentially unchanging things, or the recurring cycle of an endless wheel. The past had to be both decisively different and causally linked to the present. … The result was a view of history in which time moved ever forward, early causes were sufficient to explain its motion, and those causes were seen to operate in a succession of qualitatively different historical contexts.[6]

This perception of history has, of course, been questioned. Ross noted that it was 'no sooner stated… than it came under attack'.[7] However, while that critique has been heard in professional history; it has gone unchallenged in the ubiquitous type of history that has become prevalent; the progress myth of evolutionary functionalism is so deep rooted as to render it virtually invisible. This is the understanding of history which is endemic in the monastic Law School. Indeed, it is not seen as history at all. It is simply the way in which legal change is presented: the linear story of one thing building upon another on a forward-moving path to progress. For a time, Critical Legal Studies highlighted the issue and provided a critique.[8] However, this was short-lived. As Unger has noted, 'Critical legal studies was never intended to generate a permanent genre of legal writing, or to take its place among a standing cast of schools of legal theory. It was a disruptive engagement in a particular circumstance'.[9] Critical Legal Studies did not provide a permanent disruption, a complete process of re-construction as well as de-construction. A subversive historical approach is needed to critique the historical construct of bad history. A subversive approach can highlight and move

5 Dorothy Ross, 'Historical Consciousness in Nineteenth Century America' (1984) 89(4) *American Historical Review* 909, 911.

6 Ibid 910.

7 Ibid 924.

8 See, e.g., Robert W Gordon, 'The Past as Authority and as Social Critic: Stabilizing and Destabilizing Functions of History in Legal Argument' in Terrence J McDonald (ed) *The Historic Turn in the Human Sciences* (University of Michigan Press, 1996) 339, 344: 'lawyers' uses of history have generally been apologetic, designed to endow currently dominant claims to entitlements and distributions of legal advantage and modes of legitimating property and power with the authority of the past'.

9 Roberto Mangaberia Unger, *The Critical Legal Studies Movement: Another Time, A Greater Task* (Verso, 2015) 4.

us on from the evolutionary functionalism which has always had Law Schools in its grasp.[10]

This chapter illustrates how Subversive Legal History can be used to disturb and supplant the omnipresent evolutionary functionalist legal narrative.[11] It will do so by critically examining the practice of periodisation (the splitting up of history into set periods) as a manifestation of evolutionary functionalist thinking before exploring whether an alternative exists to the forward-moving focus on periodisation and the underpinning narrative of evolutionary functionalism. This chapter will fall into three sections. The first will explore the concept of periodisation and the criticisms of it. Following on from the last chapter, this will pay particular attention to feminist criticisms. The second section explores Kathryn McNeilly's work on 'untimely evolution' as a means of developing and superseding evolutionary functionalism.[12] However, it will be argued that, although McNeilly's work provides a significant advance, its evolutionary focus means that it continues to normalise development and advancement. The third and final section therefore draws upon social entropy, chaos and complexity theories to suggest that it is 'entropic complexity' rather than evolutionary functionalism that is the norm. Overall, this chapter will suggest that superseding the narrative of evolutionary functionalism, as entrenched by periodisation, requires not only the highlighting and de-construction of evolutionary functionalism but also its replacement and that this is a vital contribution of the Subversive Legal History approach.

The P Word

Periodisation is endemic but hidden in legal discourse.

As Padma Anagol has pointed out, the focus on chronological divisions is what distinguishes history from other disciplines.[13] Yet, periodisation is a popular

10 Indeed, Legal History itself has not been immune from this affliction. Milsom's famous critique of Maitland attacked how 'Maitland saw England as a legal Galapagos insulating native evolution from Roman contamination' and how 'he pressed the Darwinian analogy too far, seeing the whole development of English law in terms of monstrous species, "the forms of action"'. As Milsom pointed out, 'the lawyer's power to impose a simple and convincing pattern upon complex matters' becomes compelling; it becomes 'a creed because it *had* to be right': S F C Milsom, 'Maitland' (2001) 60(2) *Cambridge Law Journal* 265, 268, 269. Though also note how Maitland 'shook up the hardening complacency of evolutionary views of history … to invert the conventional patterns of "progressive" social development' by concluding that 'English law had evolved away from the "individualism" of medieval village societies toward more cooperative and communal forms in modern associational life': Robert W Gordon, 'The Past as Authority and as Social Critic: Stabilizing and Destabilizing Functions of History in Legal Argument' in Terrence J McDonald (ed) *The Historic Turn in the Human Sciences* (University of Michigan Press, 1996) 339, 345.

11 The notion of law as narrative has been explored by the rich literature on law as literature. See, for instance, the essays in Peter Brooks and Paul Gewirtz (eds) *Law's Stories: Narrative and the Rhetoric of Law* (Yale University Press, 1996).

12 Kathryn McNeilly, 'Are Rights Out of Time? International Human Rights Law, Temporality, and Radical Social Change' (2019) 28(6) *Social and Legal Studies* 817.

13 Padma Anagol, 'Agency, Periodisation and Change in the Gender and Women's History of Colonial India' (2008) 20(3) *Gender & History* 603, 609.

form of categorisation in legal discourse too. Some periodisations are borrowed from other disciplines, such as reference to the medieval period or postmodernity, or exist outside law in some way, usually linked to centuries or decades or the time in office of particular figures, be they monarchs, prime ministers or chairs of notable committees. Other periodisations are more law specific, being often defined by particular legal events, before and after a particular statute or case or after some other legal or political change such as the reorganisation of legal-political bodies. The prevalence of periodisation in legal discourse is unsurprising; after all, periodisations are used as part of everyday speech but are invariably overlooked and not questioned.

Leonard Orr's understanding of periodisation 'as the acceptable shared delusionary vision of the past, a consensus kept for its use-value' is more than apt.[14] Like all forms of categorisation, periodisation is by its very nature 'a simplifying, consolidating and universalising process'.[15] This is, after all, what renders it useful. It prevents the whole of history happening at once. As Jeanne Boydston noted, its purpose 'is to bring order and meaning to an otherwise unruly tangle of data and permit us to hold steady the otherwise constant flurry of difference and change'.[16] Yet, in so doing, the act of periodisation divorces the material 'from "real" time and space' and instead locates it 'in a type of critical utopia'. As Boydston put it, periodisation tends 'to reduce the mess and variability of lived experience to a few elements that are allowed to stand, falsely, as a substitute for that experience, and to collapse complicated and distinct historical processes into stable, materialised representations. When we use a category of analysis, we authorise that process of reduction, with all of its numerous and inevitable concealments and misrepresentations'.[17] Periodisations also become entrenched. It means that a particular understanding of 'the past is constantly reified and

14 Leonard Orr, 'Modernism and the Issue of Periodization' (2005) 7(1) *CLCWeb: Comparative Literature and Culture* 2. Criticism of periodisation is by no means new or novel. In his 1830 essay 'on History', Thomas Carlyle wrote that: 'Our clock strikes when there is a change from hour to hour; but no hammer in the Horologe of Time peals through the universe when there is a change from Era to Era': Alan Shelston (ed) *Thomas Carlyle: Selected Writings* (Penguin, 1971) 54. And Lord Acton in his Cambridge inaugural lecture of 1895, told his listeners to 'study problems in preference to periods': Lord Acton, 'Inaugural Lecture on the Study of History' (1895) <oll.libertyfund.org/title/2533>.

15 Jeanne Boydston, 'Gender as a Question of Historical Analysis' (2008) 20(3) *Gender & History* 558, 560.

16 Ibid. Even those writers who raise objections to periodisation nevertheless use them as a framing device, particularly for pedagogical purposes. Orr commented that this is true of even the most cutting edge work; he noted that ironically the schemas found in postmodernist post-structuralist writers such as Jean Baudrillard and Michel Foucault are in keeping and are reliant upon traditional periodisations. Baudrillard 'manages to be traditional and un-historical simultaneously', while Foucault has been called 'our most-notorious periodiser'. Leonard Orr, 'Modernism and the Issue of Periodization' (2005) 7(1) *CLCWeb: Comparative Literature and Culture* 2; Marshall Brown, 'Periods and Resistances.' (2001) 62(4) *Modern Language Quarterly* 309, 314.

17 Jeanne Boydston, 'Gender as a Question of Historical Analysis' (2008) 20(3) *Gender & History* 558, 560.

reconstituted in the present'.[18] In the words of Padma Anagol, 'conventional chronologies hamper fresh thinking; naturalise particular views of history; and are often value-laden, preventing critical scrutiny of their assumptions and agendas'.[19] As Robert Rehder put it, 'period terms do our thinking for us'.[20]

However, periodisation is an especially problematic categorisation because periodisation brings with it a particular meaning: it demarcates and provides a neat end and a new beginning. Moreover, it establishes that this new beginning is marked more by change compared to the previous period than continuity. Merry E Wiesner-Hanks has argued that periodisations are sound where there is a large body of scholarship that has considered both change and continuity in structures and processes and has concluded that change outweighs continuity.[21] However, periodisations are often used without this rigorous process being carried out.[22] What makes matters even more questionable is that invariably each chronological period is presented not only as new but also as an advance. Periodisation, therefore, provides a means by which the past is simplified to provide a narrative of progress. Periodisation emphasises the difference between junctures in time and presents, in the words of Emmanuel Melissaris, it presents legal change as being 'linear and forward-facing': 'The movement is from the past to the future in the way of the movement of an arrow'.[23]

While presented as a natural explanatory device, periodisation is a construct and a choice. Every decision as to which unit of periodisation to use, how to label it, how to apply it are all important parts of the creation (and perpetuation) of a particular narrative. Kathleen Davis defined periodisation as 'not simply the drawing of arbitrary boundaries through time but a complex process of conceptualizing categories, which are posited as homogenous and proactively validated by the designation of a period divide'.[24] She argued that the units of periodisation 'exercise exclusionary force' in that they 'impose homogeneities' that not only mask (say) 'the existence of "modern" characteristics in the Middle Ages and "medieval" characteristics in modernity, but also distort the histories of

18 Lynn Abrams, 'The Unseamed Picture: Conflicting Narratives of Women in the Modern European Past' (2008) 20(3) *Gender & History* 628, 640.

19 Padma Anagol, 'Agency, Periodisation and Change in the Gender and Women's History of Colonial India' (2008) 20(3) *Gender & History* 603.

20 Robert Rehder, 'Periodization and the Theory of Literary History' (1995) 22 *Colloquium Helveticum: Cahiers Suisses de Littérature Comparée* 117, 120–121.

21 Merry E Wiesner-Hanks, 'Do Women Need the Renaissance?' (2008) 20(3) *Gender & History* 539, 545.

22 As Robert Rehder noted, we invariably 'continue to employ and defend a classification that is without any intellectual justification and whose assumptions have never been examined': Robert Rehder, 'Periodization and the Theory of Literary History' (1995) 22 *Colloquium Helveticum: Cahiers Suisses de Littérature Comparée* 117, 120–121.

23 Emmanuel Melissaris, 'The Chronology of the Legal' (2005) 50 *McGill Law Journal* 839, 843–844.

24 Kathleen Davis, *Periodization & Sovereignty: How Ideas of Feudalism & Secularization Govern the Politics of Time* (University of Pennsylvania Press, 2008) 3.

fields'.[25] In the same way that constructing and perpetuating a field of knowledge is an often overlooked exercise in power, so too is every act of periodisation. As Kathleen Davis put it, periodisation 'does not refer to a mere back-description that divides history into segments, but to a fundamental political technique – a way to moderate, divide and regulate – always rendering its services *now*'.[26]

Periodisation serves as a mechanism of inclusion and exclusion and of prioritisation, deciding what story is being told. This means that, in the words of Ludmilla Jordanova, periodisation hinges on the privileging of particular vantage points and the selection of 'symbolic markers' and thus constitutes 'a form of classification of the past'.[27] This has been the focus of the feminist critique of periodisation. A landmark and influential publication on periodisation from a feminist perspective was Joan Kelly's famous essay questioning whether women had a renaissance, which began by stating that: 'One of the tasks of women's history is to call into question accepted schemas of periodization'.[28] For Kelly, existing periodisations focus on 'the historical development of men' and often 'have quite different, even opposite, effects upon women'. She proposed an 'ideological index' which would compare the quality of women's historical experience vis-à-vis men: the 'regulation of female sexuality', 'women's economic and political roles',[29] women's cultural roles and ideologies about women 'in particular the sex-role system displayed or advocated in the symbolic products of the society, its art, literature, and philosophy'. Although later work has provided some refinements of this index,[30] Kelly's essay remains a 'blue print' for the scholarly response to the gendered nature of periodisation. As Natalie Zemon Davis put it, the essay demonstrates 'how to *do* women's history, about the big questions to ask, and the tools and variables and resources to turn to in trying to answer them'.[31] As Emily Grabham and Sian M Beynon-Jones have noted: 'Feminist and postcolonial thought has long been significant for challenging linear time and developmental historicism by dismantling apparently "natural", homogenous or teleological concepts of time'.[32]

25 Ibid 3–4.

26 Ibid 5.

27 Ludmilla Jordanova, *History in Practice* (Arnold, 2000) 127, 132.

28 Joan Kelly, 'Did Women have a Renaissance?' in Renate Bridenthal and Claudia Koonz (eds) *Becoming Visible: Women in European History* (Houghton Mifflin Co, 1977) 20.

29 'i.e., the kind of work they performed as compared with men, and their access to property, political power, and the education or training necessary for work, property, and power': ibid.

30 As Theresa Coletti has noted, subsequent work has 'exposed the complexities of Kelly's question' requiring 'more nuanced assessments' taking into account, for instance, the 'extraordinary range and variety of early modern women's cultural agency and creativity': Theresa Coletti, '"Did Women Have a Renaissance?" A Medievalist Reads Joan Kelly and Aemilia Lanyer' (2013) 8 *Early Modern Women* 249.

31 Natalie Zemon Davis, 'Forum: Revisiting Joan Kelly's "Did Women Have a Renaissance?"' (2013) 8 *Early Modern Women* 241, 247.

32 Emily Grabham and Sian M Beynon-Jones, 'Introduction' in Sian M Beynon-Jones and Emily Grabham (eds) *Law and Time* (Routledge, 2019) 1, 3–4.

However, as Alexandra Shepard and Garthine Walker have noted, the focus of the feminist critique of periodisation has changed over time.[33] First, 'the question of where women fitted into conventional accounts of change over time was rapidly reframed to ask, first, *did* women fit into such historical narratives at all, and second, were such changes positive or negative for women?'[34] This led feminist historians to lament the 'inadequacies, limitations and inapplicability of existing explanatory and theoretical frameworks within academic history'.[35] Second, feminists began to question what would happen if the lens was shifted to place the position of women to the fore. As Lynn Abrams has noted, this entails prioritising women's own understanding of their past' and this 'forces one to think hard about the organising concepts with which we have become familiar and acculturated'.[36] The grounded feminist method creates 'a patchwork of contiguous and sometimes competing histories which may be resistant to overarching narratives of continuity and change. The turning points, periodisations and conceptual frameworks that may work for broad-ranging syntheses have limited applicability when one takes a microscope to a place exhibiting different tendencies'.[37] Focusing on gender is likely to challenge and de-centre the conventional narratives. It has the potential 'both to complicate and, more fundamentally, to revise received narratives of change'.[38]

As Lynn Abrams noted, 'the deliberate prioritising of women's voices and interpretations in the local context provides a version of women's pasts that may jar with more familiar narratives of continuity and change'.[39] She wrote that this dissonance 'should be taken seriously' rather than placing the women's story 'on the margins and... as peripheral to the core story'. Placing gender to the fore will create new narratives. As Abrams wrote, weaving individual local histories:

> into the smooth fabric of the narrative of European women's history creates more than colour and texture. It offers new and perhaps surprising points of contrast; it encourages us to look closer at the familiar stories; it disrupts

33 Alexandra Shepard and Garthine Walker, 'Gender, Change and Periodisation' (2008) 20(3) *Gender & History* 453.

34 Ibid 454.

35 Ibid 455.

36 Lynn Abrams, 'The Unseamed Picture: Conflicting Narratives of Women in the Modern European Past' (2008) 20(3) *Gender & History* 628, 638.

37 Ibid, 640.

38 Alexandra Shepard and Garthine Walker, 'Gender, Change and Periodisation' (2008) 20(3) *Gender & History* 453. This is not straightforward. As Merry E Wiesner-Hanks points out, there remain 'doubts about whether chronological categories derived from the experience of *some* women can be applied to women's history as a whole, or whether change that is generally seen as only tangential to gender relations should qualify as a major turning point: Merry E Wiesner-Hanks, 'Do Women Need the Renaissance?' (2008) 20(3) *Gender & History* 539.

39 Lynn Abrams, 'The Unseamed Picture: Conflicting Narratives of Women in the Modern European Past' (2008) 20(3) *Gender & History* 628, 641.

> narratives of continuity and change and chronologies and offers unfamiliar parallels.

For Abrams, 'gender history must have the confidence to create its own narratives which may sit alongside, challenge or be incorporated in the overarching interpretations'.[40]

The word 'narratives' in the plural is crucial. It is not a question of producing a new meta-narrative focusing on women. As Abrams points out, 'history should not be subsumed within a universal European women's history narrative, because it would disappear or at the very least exist as an interesting exoticism; and that is not good enough'.[41] It is imperative that one progress narrative imbued with evolutionary functionalism is not replaced by another by, for instance, constructing a narrative of 'women's emancipation as the standard by which 'progress' for women is evaluated'.[42] Rather, a plurality of narratives needs to be embraced, remembering that they are precisely that: narratives. As Kathleen Canning has put it, gender history should 'confidently admit the possibility of disparate temporalities. Rather than attempting to fit gender back into established chronologies and categories, its more productive outcome may be to allow dissonance within grand narratives'.[43] This dissonance requires what Mary Nash has called the 'need to recognise the heterogeneity of expressions of women's historical trajectories...in a way that does not subordinate this task to the categories of mainstream history – whether this means national histories or even women's history itself'.[44]

The importance of a feminist or otherwise subversive critique of periodisation is not only to criticise the labels used but also the way in which the periodisations are arrived at. Such a critique insists that change does not always occur in a top-down fashion, is not invariably linear and ordered and does not originate from official actors within the system but from outside, through lived experiences and through activism. It highlights the complex interplay between change and continuity and, crucially, insists that nothing is fixed or universal. Conventional units of periodisation are one way in which the potential for legal change is narrowed. As Emily Grabham and Sian M Beynon-Jones convincingly argued, a critical approach is 'necessary for unmooring essentialist knowledge practices that maintain colonial orders or particular configurations of gender, sexuality and race as

40 Ibid 628–629.

41 Ibid 641.

42 Alexandra Shepard and Garthine Walker, 'Gender, Change and Periodisation' (2008) 20(3) *Gender & History* 453, 454.

43 Kathleen Canning, *Gender History in Practice: Historical Perspectives on Bodies, Class and Citizenship* (Cornell University Press, 2006) 61.

44 Mary Nash, 'Rethinking Narratives in European Women's History: Motherhood, Identities and Female Agency in Twentieth-Century Spain' in Terry Brotherstone, Deborah Simonton and Oonagh Walsh (eds) *Gendering Scottish History: An International Approach* (Cruithne Press, 1999) 113.

"timeless", "modern" or "advanced"'.[45] A subversive critique of periodisation problematises and revaluates the concept of time itself.

Recent years have witnessed a burgeoning interdisciplinary literature on time, including the budding specialist literature on law and time.[46] This literature has argued that the prevalent tendency in legal scholarship has been to naturalise time, 'time is often assumed to exist as though it were a natural phenomenon, unfolding effortlessly and inconspicuously as the backdrop to social and political life'.[47] As John Harrington noted, 'time is central to the classical liberal model of law as unified, fixed, and self-sufficient'.[48] Writers on law and time have argued that this has overlooked 'law's production of time, instead exteriorising time as something distinct from law itself'.[49] The law and time literature has sought to correct this by highlighting the various ways in which time is produced by social practices and constructed by law. Identifying that time is constructed has enabled the development of a contrary understanding of time 'as social, plural, and rhetorical'.[50] Emily Grabham and Sian M Beynon-Jones advocated conceiving of time as being 'made or co-produced, not pre-existing and separate'.[51] As they put it, 'time results from power and agency and is shared, collective and contested'.[52] They argue that 'studying legal temporalities should involve understanding how times as well as laws and legal knowledges are constituted; how they come to matter'.[53] This inserts a much needed focus on agency: showing that time itself is constructed and authored.

45 Emily Grabham and Sian M Beynon-Jones, 'Introduction' in Sian M Beynon-Jones and Emily Grabham (eds) *Law and Time* (Routledge, 2019) 1, 6.

46 As Emily Grabham and Sian M Beynon-Jones note, there has been 'a flourishing, over recent years, in critical, socio-legal scholarship on law's temporalities. Such scholarship has begun to take seriously time's effects on law and social ordering: ibid 1. Elen Stokes has noted, however, that law has yet contributed little to the scope of 'future studies;' which has been developed by several disciplines across the arts, humanities, and social sciences: Elen Stokes, 'Beyond Evidence: Anticipatory Regimes in Law' (2021) 43(1) *Law and Policy* 73.

47 Renisa Mawani, 'Law as Temporality: Colonial Politics and Indian Settlers' (2014) 4 *Irvine Law Review* 65, 70.

48 For example, 'the doctrine of precedent, which binds the present to the past, is an important example of the law producing its own time. The law of contract, which binds the present to the future, is another': John Harrington, 'Time as a Dimension of Medical Law' (2012) 20 *Medical Law Review* 491, 498, 496.

49 Emily Grabham and Sian M Beynon-Jones, 'Introduction' in Sian M Beynon-Jones and Emily Grabham (eds) *Law and Time* (Routledge, 2019) 1.

50 John Harrington, 'Time as a Dimension of Medical Law' (2012) 20 *Medical Law Review* 491.

51 Emily Grabham and Sian M Beynon-Jones, 'Introduction' in Sian M Beynon-Jones and Emily Grabham (eds) *Law and Time* (Routledge, 2019) 3.

52 Ibid 19.

53 Ibid 22. This is encapsulated in Emmanuel Melissaris' concept of 'chronos' which referred to the 'shared normative experience' whereby participants in legal communities assume the 'possibility to grasp and control time, to synchronize the imaginary temporality of the normative world with the time of the real world'. For Melissaris, chronos was 'the way that participants in a legal discourse make sense of time and their ability to ascribe it normative meaning and control it in common'.

The critique of periodisation reveals that, like all categorisations, periodisation is a necessary evil. As David Perkins put it, 'we cannot write history without periodising it'.[54] Yet, this does not mean that a critical approach should not be taken. Indeed, Perkins has argued that this is why periodisation is necessary: 'we require the concept of a unified period in order to deny it, and thus make apparent the particularity, local difference, heterogeneity, fluctuation, discontinuity, and strife that are now preferred categories for understanding any moment of the past'. A critical appreciation of periodisation is therefore a prerequisite to the act of subversion. There is a need to question and debunk but this can only be done if there is an artifice to subvert and crucially if it is accepted that the artifice is constructed and therefore subject not only to de-construction but to a radically different re-construction. In the same way that a critical approach needs something to be critical of, a subversive approach needs something to subvert. The difference, however, is that once the object is subverted, it is necessarily transformed. Subversive Legal History, therefore, goes further than simply highlighting the problematic nature of periodisation in general and of particular periodisations in general. Subversive Legal History changes the lens, creates new periodisations and shows that periodisations are constructed. Far from being natural, universal labels of convenience, periodisations are transformed into contested vehicles for power relations. A subversive approach underscores how loaded specific periodisations and periodisation in general are. Perhaps most notably, this reveals how periodisations play a key role in the perpetuation of the progress narrative of evolutionary functionalism. Subversive Legal History is crucial in highlighting and de-constructing this, especially given how prevalent and routine evolutionary functionalism is in Law Schools. However, a subversive approach needs to go beyond such a critique; it needs to be re-construction too. This raises the question of whether there are alternatives to the progress narrative of evolutionary functionalism which could be used to contest and improve periodisations that have been adopted.

Alternatives to Evolutionary Functionalism: (i) Untimely Evolution

The critique of periodisation raises the question of whether it is possible to move away from narratives imbued with evolutionary functionalism.

The literature on the history of international law provides an identification and clarification of one alternative to linear forward-moving progress narratives. This can be found in the work of Kathryn McNeilly, in particular,[55] her article 'Are Rights Out of Time? International Human Rights Law, Temporality, and

54 David Perkins, *Is Literary History Possible?* (Johns Hopkins University Press, 1992) 65.

55 See also Kathryn McNeilly, *Human Rights and Radical Social Transformation: Futurity, Alterity, Power* (Routledge, 2017).

Radical Social Change',[56] which developed, applied and furthered feminist work on temporalities, most notably the work of Elizabeth Grosz.[57]

McNeilly noted that the argument is often made that human rights have become *passé*: 'human rights are out of time, that their time as an emancipator vision for the future is up and that they are no longer the discourse of the moment that we are living in'.[58] Her article responds to this argument by arguing that 'international human rights law is not out of time, but it should be'. McNeilly's argument is not that the time of human rights has ended or that they are no longer useful, rather it is that we need to think of human rights as being 'untimely'. By this, she means that human rights are 'out of step or out of time, which goes beyond a linear and progressive relation between past, present and future'. Following Grosz,[59] McNeilly wrote that:

> Untimeliness thought in this way requires abandoning commitment to linearity, progression and predictability in understanding international human rights. In contrast, this area of law must be apprehended as operating via a conception of the future that does not necessarily follow progressively from the past or present, that is unknown and out of control of the present, and that better foregrounds the continual elaboration of the new.[60]

An 'untimely' approach, then, presents the future of rights as being 'not knowable – outlined in relevant declarations, treaties and other instruments – nor progressively following from the present'. As McNeilly pointed out, 'this means giving up the presumption that the future follows straightforwardly from the past and resisting setting agendas for a knowable future in favour of embracing newness and the possibilities this may bring'.[61] She wrote that international human rights:

> can only be of use if they are conceived not as concepts drawn upon in the present for a predictable and linear future, but as untimely politico-legal

56 Kathryn McNeilly, 'Are Rights Out of Time? International Human Rights Law, Temporality, and Radical Social Change' (2019) 28(6) *Social and Legal Studies* 817.

57 Most notably, Elizabeth Grosz, *The Nick of Time: Politics, Evolution and the Untimely* (Duke University Press, 2004) and Elizabeth Grosz, *Time Travels: Feminism, Nature, Power* (Duke University Press, 2005). See also Elizabeth Grosz (ed) *Becomings: Exploration in Time, Memory, and Futures* (Cornell University Press, 1999).

58 Kathryn McNeilly, 'Are Rights Out of Time? International Human Rights Law, Temporality, and Radical Social Change' (2019) 28(6) *Social and Legal Studies* 817, 818.

59 Elizabeth Grosz, 'The Untimeliness of Feminist Theory' (2010) 18(1) *NORA: Nordic Journal of Feminist and Gender Research* 48, 49.

60 Kathryn McNeilly, 'Are Rights Out of Time? International Human Rights Law, Temporality, and Radical Social Change' (2019) 28(6) *Social and Legal Studies* 817, 818.

61 Ibid 823.

> concepts orientated towards a future which, like human life itself, is endlessly becoming.[62]

This is unsettling 'opening up to the unknown and its uncertainties'. This is very much in keeping with what has been called here as a subversive approach. The value of McNeilly's article is that, in dialogue with Grosz, she explored the possibilities for such an 'untimely' approach. She asserted that in the international human rights law context, an 'untimely' approach would shift the focus away from the refinement of texts towards responding to the unexpected and being able to respond to that in novel ways. As she put it:

> this means that international human rights law becomes less about laying down legal obligations and pursuing ever increasing state adherence to such, and more about exploring how, legally and politically, rights can uncover the unexpected and help usefully break with the past or present.

She is correct to assert that while 'this assertion stems from theory, it has profoundly practical implications'. It highlights the extent to which legal discourse is orientated to and focused upon the past. The system of precedent, which is foundational to the common law tradition, is based upon a timely understanding of linear forward-progress which severely limits the options available. Legal change in the common law tradition operates like water through a series of pipes; these pipes often narrow and rarely change direction. Moreover, lawyers operate as plumbers: always looking for solutions within the system; the solutions we look for are always within a narrow range of options; they are all internal to the system. McNeilly's critique highlights that we do not question whether there is a need for a wider range of options, a different system to the plumbing.

For McNeilly, an 'untimely' approach is one which 'requires a return to the basics'.[63] As she noted, this can take different forms but she argued that 'a productive place to begin is by re-approaching the developmental narrative of this discourse: how human rights in international law are understood as concepts which have developed, and which continue to do so'. In other words, there is a need to explore how ideas and concepts have developed over time and how they have been developed in the discourse. This sounds similar to the need for an intellectual history of law discussed in the previous chapters. In order to realise the possibilities, there is a need to explore how legal ideas have developed over time. Usefully McNeilly developed this insight by discussing and applying Grosz's work which reinterpreted Charles Darwin's concept of evolution by natural selection in an untimely way.[64] Darwinian evolution, for Grosz, 'is a fundamentally

62 Ibid 825.

63 Ibid 826.

64 See Elizabeth Grosz, *The Nick of Time: Politics, Evolution and the Untimely* (Duke University Press, 2004) chapters 1–3 and Elizabeth Grosz, *Time Travels: Feminism, Nature, Power* (Duke University Press, 2005) chapters 1–3.

open-ended system which pushes toward a future with no real direction, no promise of any particular result, no guarantee of progress or improvement, but with every indication of inherent proliferation and transformation'.[65] As McNeilly noted, it therefore provides an exemplar of an 'untimely' approach in that it 'provides an account of endless variation and difference towards a future which is not constrained by the past, although informed by it, that is inherently unpredictable and eschews the notion of progress'.[66] In Darwinian evolution, 'time is not linear, but deep and vast, an almost limitless reservoir where innumerable variations can play out'.[67] This means that, according to McNeilly, 'the overarching principles of Darwinian evolution read as stressing temporal dispersion, variation and an unknown future – are useful in thinking about the developmental narrative of international human rights law'.[68] However, she cautioned that this does not amount to a call for a wholesale or straightforward application of Darwinian theory, rather what she is calling for is that 'some of Darwin's underpinning principles, thought in a Groszian manner as demonstrating untimely evolution, can be reformulated and deployed to bring a new perspective to this area'.

McNeilly therefore developed the notion of 'untimely evolution'. This approach has two important ramifications. The first is that it necessitates the rejection of simplistic and certain origin stories. Applying Darwinian underpinning principles in the way McNeilly advocated stresses the concept of variation and therefore calls into question attempts to identify a fixed trajectory and origin. McNeilly made it clear that this would have significant effects upon the understanding of international human rights law. As she put it:

> The importance of perceiving current species as produced through variation, as opposed to having a fixed origin, can also be brought to reflection on international human rights law to reframe its developmental trajectory. Rather than aiming to locate an "origin" – be this the 1940s post-War period or some other point in history – this politico-legal discourse can be embraced as having, at a basic level, no origin. Let me be clear: this does not

65 Grosz saw 'Darwin as providing an ingenious temporal machine for the production of the new, which constrains the new only through the history that made it possible and the present which it actively transforms, but which leaves its directions, parameters, and destinations unknown and unknowable': Elizabeth Grosz, *The Nick of Time: Politics, Evolution and the Untimely* (Duke University Press, 2004) 25, 26.

66 Kathryn McNeilly, 'Are Rights Out of Time? International Human Rights Law, Temporality, and Radical Social Change' (2019) 28(6) *Social and Legal Studies* 817, 827.

67 Ibid. This corresponds with what Michel Serres described as the way in which 'time percolates or flows in turbulent ways': Emily Grabham and Sian M Beynon-Jones, 'Introduction' in Sian M Beynon-Jones and Emily Grabham (eds) *Law and Time* (Routledge, 2019) 1, 16. See Michel Serres and Bruno Latour, *Conversations on Science, Culture, and Time* (University of Michigan Press, 1995) 49.

68 Kathryn McNeilly, 'Are Rights Out of Time? International Human Rights Law, Temporality, and Radical Social Change' (2019) 28(6) *Social and Legal Studies* 817, 827.

> mean that international human rights law emerged from nowhere. Quite the opposite, it means that such has come into being through a long process of repetition and variation in contingent contexts. These contexts shape the future for rights, albeit the future remains unknown and is not constrained by the past or present.

Instead of looking for origins, 'the development of international human rights can be understood as one of descent with modification whereby rights ideas are reproduced and adaptively change in prevailing socio-legal and political landscapes in an ongoing and unpredictable way'.[69] This has clear application outside the human rights context.

Origin stories and quests for such origins are prevalent in doctrinal Legal History. Historians of the common law have often embarked upon the quest for the origin of common law developments and a debate has often resulted about whether such concepts are solely the internal product of the legal system or were shaped by external events, perhaps being transplanted from another jurisdiction.[70] A subversive approach – embracing Cotterrell's insistence that the legal and the social constantly constitute one another – would present and critique any articulation of a neat origin story as being mythical.[71] As McNeilly put it, this would situate the mutation of legal ideas as part of 'productive processes of transformation and change' and would transform not only the historical analysis but future application since this too would then not be 'an exclusive search for legal solutions'.[72]

69 Ibid 828.

70 See, for instance, the debate as to the origin of consideration. John Baker has written that 'no other doctrine in English law can compete with 'consideration' for the greatest diversity and complexity of historical explanations' and that 'anyone who attempts to augment, even by a few pages, all that has already been written on this vexed subject must at the outset acknowledge his own foolhardiness': John Baker, 'Origin of the Doctrine of "Consideration" in M S Arnold *et al.* (eds) *On the Laws and Customs of England: Essays in Honor of S E Thorne* (University of North Carolina Press, 1981) 336, 336–337. It seems, however, that legal historians are increasingly heeding this warning. As Fifoot noted, scholarship has now shown that the doctrine is 'neither an exotic imported from a more luxurious jurisprudence, nor though a domestic invention of the common law. ... The "mystery of consideration" which the Victorian lawyers found so fascinating becomes no more than a practical answer to an urgent problem': C H S Fifoot, *History and Sources of the Common Law* (Stevens & Sons, 1949) 399. Milsom concluded that 'with this subject as with many others we have tried to be too precise, to trace the later meaning of a legal word back to some single source; and we have complicated the task by supposing that even in the later law the word had a meaning in the sense of representing an idea': S F C Milsom, *Historical Foundations of the Common Law* (2nd ed, Butterworths, 1981) 357.

71 This would underline the work of Milsom. His scholarship notably debunked talk of '"the origin of trespass" in the simple sense once thought' presenting the proposed causes instead as 'clearly part of a story which cannot be understood without it': ibid 357–358.

72 Kathryn McNeilly, 'Are Rights Out of Time? International Human Rights Law, Temporality, and Radical Social Change' (2019) 28(6) *Social and Legal Studies* 817, 829.

The second ramification of 'untimely evolution' is that 'just as there is no origin, there is also no end point'.[73] McNeilly was insistent that 'human rights can never be viewed in terms of linear progress towards a final achievement'.[74] Untimely evolution therefore provides an alternative approach to the common 'progressive narrative' whereby developments 'continue, or begin, a forward-pushing evolutionary trajectory inevitably facilitating a more equal shaping of social life'.[75] It shows that there is a greater potential for change and that change does not always equate to progress. It presents an 'ongoing, messy development' which includes 'what might be perceived as regressive as well as progressive movements'. It provides a disturbance and creates the need for a process of de-construction and re-construction. McNeilly gave the example of how untimely evolution applies to women's rights. She observed that:

> This requires rethinking the familiar chronology of women's rights. Rather than a story of progressive realization from the 1940s onward, the development of international human rights pertaining to sex/gender should be understood as a process of never-ending repetition and variation responding to contingent contexts and not necessarily moving progressively between past, present and future. Following untimely Darwinian principles, the ongoing descent with modification of this discourse is a blind process and may move "forward" as well as "backwards". Embracing such means understanding that future development in this area may in fact involve going backwards in order to go forward.[76]

For McNeilly, this does not necessarily guarantee 'a more radical evolution' but it does mean that 'new conceptual possibilities emerge and offer new ways of thinking in a moment when discussion on sex, gender and sexuality is changing in international human rights law to include issues and identities' that go beyond existing ideas, frameworks and formulations.[77]

However, although the form of evolution adopted is no longer linear and progressing, it remains progressive. McNeilly conceded that untimely evolution still views 'development as always ongoing'. Her work revisited Darwin and removed the most problematic elements of evolutionary theory but her untimely evolution does not go quite far enough. It still normalises progress and advancement albeit in a looser, messier, multi-dimensional way. For McNeilly, untimely

73 Ibid 828.

74 For McNeilly, 'the untimeliness inherent in Darwin's evolution assists us to view development as always ongoing – a long-term activity – but not in the sense of progressing, guided to a significant extent by contexts, contingency and chance rather than controlled by states, the UN, international lobbyists, non-governmental organizations or others towards a final end or goal'. The concept of untimeliness, therefore, means that more characters – including non-legal actors, are part of the narrative.

75 Ibid 830.

76 Ibid 831.

77 Ibid 833.

evolution provided a step forward because it 'fundamentally rejects progress as a driving force. Evolution, rather, is a blind process, at times moving forward, at others appearing to move backwards'. This, however, still presents a particular progressive direction of change as being the norm by contrasting it with a regressive direction.

McNeilly's concept of untimely evolution serves as a valuable critique of periodisation: it rejects the notion of fixed origins and end points. It also rejects elements of evolutionary functionalism in that it replaces linearity with the notion of blind processes. However, this does not go quite far enough. The concept of evolution, though refined, remains in her work. Although there is no end point and although movement goes both backwards and forwards, there remains a norm that there is movement and an expected travel direction, albeit one that is not always followed. The concept of evolution, albeit untimely, emphasises that change is expected, albeit that the change may not be an advance. Although untimely evolution recognises variation, it stops short of regarding it as a norm. Indeed, it recognises it as an exception to the norm. This is because the scientific basis that McNeilly uses, Darwinian evolution, continues to normalise development and advancement. Therefore, in seeking to move away from narratives imbued with evolutionary functionalism, a further step needs to be taken.

Alternatives to Evolutionary Functionalism: (ii) Entropic Complexity

In moving beyond evolutionary functionalism, a different scientific basis needs to be adopted: the concept of entropy.

The concept of entropy denotes the gradual decline into disorder. The development of the concept of entropy dates back to the second law of thermodynamics and the development of modern thermodynamics in the nineteenth century'.[78] The second rule states that the entropy of an isolated system increases; in other words 'disorder will tend to increase if things are left to themselves'.[79] As Niall Ferguson has noted, 'this is of profound historical importance, not least because it implies an ultimate and disorderly end to the history of human life and indeed the universe'. It also underscores how a lack of order and predictability is the norm.

Traditionally, social scientists and humanities scholars have been slow to use the concept of entropy, instead using the concept of equilibrium. As Kenneth

78 Kenneth D Bailey, *Social Entropy Theory* (University of New York Press, 1990) 52. 'The second law of thermodynamics states that all physical processes are irreversible (meaning one-directional) because some energy is always spent or dissipated as heat. The amount of dissipated energy in a system is referred to as entropy': David Collins, 'The Chaos Machine: The WTO in a Social Entropy Model of the World Trading System' (2014) 34(2) *Oxford Journal of Legal Studies* 353.

79 Niall Ferguson 'Introduction – Virtual History: Towards a "Chaotic" Theory of the Past' in Niall Ferguson (ed) *Virtual History: Alternatives and Counterfactuals* (Papermac, 1998) 1, 72.

D Bailey noted, while equilibrium (the idea of a return to normalcy) exists 'as a comforting thought', entropy 'in contrast, has no such comforting intuitive understandability and no notion of balance'.[80] This may be why social theorists have paid it little attention. Until recently, 'the concept of entropy lay slumbering in the shadows of sociology for decades while its sibling concept of equilibrium was widely applied in functionalism'.[81] However, the critical and postmodernist attack on functionalism has meant that, although the concept of equilibrium is still widely used, 'entropy has arisen from its slumber'. A number of different but complementary literatures have emerged such as social entropy theory,[82] chaos theory[83] and complexity theory.[84] By drawing on these theories, and in particular works that have applied these theories in the context of law,[85] it is possible to go further than Kathryn McNeilly's work on 'untimely evolution' to

80 Kenneth D Bailey, *Social Entropy Theory* (University of New York Press, 1990) 72.

81 Ibid 73.

82 Most notably ibid and Kenneth D Bailey, *Sociology and the New Systems Theory: Toward a Theoretical Synthesis* (University of New York Press, 1994) which developed the Living Systems Theory, as propounded by J G Miller, *Living Systems* (McGraw Hill, 1978). On their relationship see Kenneth D Bailey, 'Living Systems Theory and Social Entropy Theory' (2006) 23 *Systems Research and Behavioral Science* 291.

83 Chaos theory began as 'a branch of mathematics that deals with nonlinear dynamical systems.' Systems are nonlinear where 'due to feedback or multiplicative effects between the components, the whole becomes something greater than the mere sum of its individual parts'. They are dynamical because 'the system changes over time based on its current state'. Moreover, 'over time, these systems can produce wildly unpredictable, divergent and fractal (i.e., infinitely detailed and self-similar without ever actually repeating) behaviour. … Chaos fundamentally indicates that there are limits to knowledge and prediction because some futures may be unknowable with any precision: Geoff Boeing, 'Visual Analysis of Nonlinear Dynamical Systems: Chaos, Fractals, Self-Similarity and the Limits of Prediction' (2016) 4(37) *Systems* 1. Chaos theory has had a 'huge impact in science and philosophy': Lena C Zuchowski, *A Philosophical Analysis of Chaos Theory* (Palgrave, 2017) 1. It has even attracted popular attention: James Gleick, *Chaos* (Sphere Books, 1988) and Leonard Smith, *Chaos: A Very Short Introduction* (Oxford University Press, 2007).

84 As Jamie Murray, Thomas E Webb and Steven Wheatley note, 'the origins of complexity theory can be traced back to early work on cybernetics and information technology … but the notion of a distinctive theory of complexity is normally credited to the Belgian physical chemist Ilya Prigogine, who won the Nobel Prize for Chemistry in 1977 for his work on far from equilibrium systems': Jamie Murray, Thomas E Webb and Steven Wheatley, 'Encountering Law's Complexity' in Jamie Murray, Thomas E Webb and Steven Wheatley (eds) *Complexity Theory and Law: Mapping an Emergent Jurisprudence* (Routledge, 2019) 3, 8. Although there is 'no general science or philosophy of complexity and no agreed on final definition of the subject' (ibid 4), today complexity theory is 'a scientific field with many branches': John H Holland, *Complexity: A Very Short Introduction* (Oxford University Press, 2014) 1. For discussion of the theory as applied within the social sciences see David Byrne, *Complexity Theory and the Social Sciences: An Introduction* (Routledge, 1998).

85 Respectively David Collins, 'The Chaos Machine: The WTO in a Social Entropy Model of the World Trading System' (2014) 34(2) *Oxford Journal of Legal Studies* 353; Robert E Scott, 'Chaos Theory and the Justice Paradox' (1993) 35 *William& Mary Law Review* 329; and Jamie Murray, Thomas E Webb and Steven Wheatley (eds) *Complexity Theory and Law: Mapping an Emergent Jurisprudence* (Routledge, 2019).

suggest that it is 'entropic complexity' rather than evolutionary functionalism that is the norm.

Although these theories overlap and can be drawn together, the three theories (social entropy theory, chaos theory and complexity theory) do provide distinct focuses that 'entropic complexity' will consolidate. Social entropy theory regards controlling the level of entropy to be the main the role of social systems such as law. As David Collins put it, 'complex modern societies are themselves systems that have a number of distinct features which operate to ensure that entropy levels remain below the maximum or equilibrium, meaning that they remain organized and do not devolve into chaos or anarchy'.[86] Seen this way 'social entropy theory is therefore a descriptive model for understanding the phenomenon in which social systems and the institutions within them tend towards a state of disorganization'. In his article which applies the theory to law, Collins argued that the world trading system can therefore be understood as a model of social entropy, with his work 'examining how the law of the World Trade Organization (WTO) is failing to counter the entropic tendencies that have emerged in the system of international trade'.

However, while Collins may see entropy as something to be overcome, for present purposes entropy can instead be seen as the prevalent, default setting. Entropy, a natural state of disorganisation and chaos, can be used as alternative to the progress narrative. In his article, Collins identified certain developments of the world trading system that are indicative of entropy such as randomness, the prevalence of disputes regarding legal entitlements and the domination of local groups rather than of any central leadership with more general and long-term goals.[87] While the narrative of evolutionary functionalism would see such developments as needing to be corrected in the path to progress and while McNeilly's 'untimely' approach would see them as backward movements, an approach based upon entropy would see such chaos – such uncertainty, nuance and flexibility – as normal. This reverses the usual approach to the common law which 'assumes that although the law may appear to be irrational, chaotic and particularistic, if one digs deep enough and knows that one is looking for, then it will soon become evident that the law is an internally coherent and unified system of rules'.[88] Chaos theory shows that the first impressions of the chaos of law were not mistaken. This does not make history, including Legal History, redundant. Quite the opposite: the task of tracing developments becomes more complex and multi-causal, reflecting the lack of a clear distinction between the social and the legal. In a state of entropy, no regard is to be had for such distinctions.

86 David Collins, 'The Chaos Machine: The WTO in a Social Entropy Model of the World Trading System' (2014) 34(2) *Oxford Journal of Legal Studies* 353, 354.

87 Ibid 358, 361, 365.

88 David Sugarman, 'Legal Theory, the Common Law Mind and the Making of the Textbook Tradition' in William Twining (ed) *Legal Theory and the Common Law* (Blackwell, 1986) 26.

Chaos theory supplements this approach, stressing the chaotic state is normal. The suggestion that what historians study is chaotic is by no means novel. In his 1830 essay 'on History', Thomas Carlyle wrote:

> Actual events are nowise so simply related to one another as parent and offspring are; each single event is the offspring of not one, but of all other events, prior or contemporaneous and will in its turn combine with others to give birth to new: it is an ever-living, ever-working Chaos of being, wherein shape after shape bodies itself forth from innumerable elements. And this Chaos... is what the historian will depict and scientifically gauge.[89]

Chaos theory entails the acceptance of entropy. As Robert E Scott has put it, chaos theory 'can best be described as a form of zen, stressing as it does the acceptance of tensions in life and physical processes'.[90] Applied to law, chaos theory 'tells us to accept the contradictions, the disorder, in our legal system. All systems, including the legal system, are unpredictable and erratic'. For Scott, this reinforces 'the best lessons taught' by Critical Legal Studies: 'Chaos in law describes human life. Thus, we in law must continuously be self-conscious, self-criticizing, self-analyzing, but above all, patient and accepting of the limits of our discipline'.[91] By this he meant that chaos theory makes us aware of the limits of law. It shows that 'law is not a linear process; we cannot solve the equation. It backtracks on, recycles and redefines old concepts in order to deal with new dilemmas'.[92] Moreover, this realisation is healthy: it presents the system as being dynamic in that it 'is the very tension whose resolution we seek that keeps our legal system in a dynamic state of continuous renewal and repair'.

Chaos theory is also useful in determining what it means to study chaos historically. As Niall Ferguson has argued, chaos 'does *not* mean anarchy. It does *not* mean that there are no laws in the natural world. It simply means that those laws are so complex that it is virtually impossible for us to make accurate predictions'.[93] An approach based on chaos theory emphasises the importance of random behaviour.[94] Ferguson pointed out that for economists 'chaos theory helps to explain why predictions and forecasts based on linear equations which are the basis for most economic models are so often wrong'.[95] Applied to history, chaos theory questions linear explanations. For Ferguson, 'it reconciles the notions of causation and contingency' by rejecting the extreme positions that there

89 Thomas Carlyle, *Historical Essays* (University of California Press, 2003) 7.

90 Robert E Scott, 'Chaos Theory and the Justice Paradox' (1993) 35 *William & Mary Law. Review* 329, 348.

91 Ibid 349.

92 Ibid 350.

93 Niall Ferguson 'Introduction – Virtual History: Towards a "Chaotic" Theory of the Past' in Niall Ferguson (ed) *Virtual History: Alternatives and Counterfactuals* (Papermac, 1998) 1, 77.

94 Ibid 78.

95 Ibid 77.

is no such thing as cause or effect and that history is predetermined.[96] Rather it shows that there can be 'unpredictable outcomes even when successive events are causally linked'. Chaos theory shows that 'interventions into a system may have unpredictable outcomes even if the intervention is very minor, as tiny effects can compound (or be damped) nonlinearly over time'.[97] This is underlined in the famous 'butterfly effect'[98] which shows how small events can 'compound and irreversibly alter the future of the universe'.[99] This underlines the importance of agency, showing that legal change can be caused in multiple different ways.

Complexity theory brings this together by showing that entropy and chaos is also the direction of travel. It shows that the effect of entropy and chaos is the development of complex systems. A complex system exists where there is emergence. This concept of emergence represents the notion that the whole is more than the sum of its parts and that something new has been created which has an autonomous life of its own.[100] So, it could be said that a complex system exists where it has a life of its own; its own form; its own artificial intelligence. This would mean that legal studies generally (and Legal History in particular) is the study of the artificially intelligent system of law. However, as Jamie Murray, Thomas E Webb and Steven Wheatley have commented, 'complexity theory remains largely absent from legal thinking' and 'there is no standard approach, no jurisprudence of complexity'.[101] They suggested, however, that applying complexity theory to law is necessary because:

> law systems are complex systems and to make better sense of the law we must look to the insights from complexity to develop models that explain what law is and how we should think about the very nature and purpose of law.[102]

96 Ibid 79. Compare the criticism of Richard J Evans (*Altered Pasts: Counterfactuals in History* (Abacus, 2016) 66) that 'those who argue that history is essentially chaotic – that is, predominantly the produce of chance – have always had to concede that larger systems of causation still exist, determining the overall pattern of events though not their precise nature or timing'. This is a flawed criticism since chaos theory does not imply anarchy and does not require the abandonment of causation. Evans' further critique that 'there is no measurable evidence that human affairs are becoming more chaotic, whatever may be happening in the universe out there' also seems to suggest that he sees chaos as being synonymous with anarchy rather than complexity.

97 Geoff Boeing, 'Visual Analysis of Nonlinear Dynamical Systems: Chaos, Fractals, Self-Similarity and the Limits of Prediction' (2016) 4(37) *Systems* 1.

98 Often first attributed to the short story 'A Story of Thunder' by Ray Bradbury, published in Ray Bradbury, *The Golden Apples of the Sun* (Corgi, 1975) 88.

99 Geoff Boeing, 'Visual Analysis of Nonlinear Dynamical Systems: Chaos, Fractals, Self-Similarity and the Limits of Prediction' (2016) 4(37) *Systems* 1, 14.

100 John H Holland, *Complexity: A Very Short Introduction* (Oxford University Press, 2014) 2; Jamie Murray, Thomas E Webb and Steven Wheatley, 'Encountering Law's Complexity' in Jamie Murray, Thomas E Webb and Steven Wheatley (eds) *Complexity Theory and Law: Mapping an Emergent Jurisprudence* (Routledge, 2019) 3, 11.

101 Ibid 6, 11.

102 Ibid 4.

They proposed that:

> Complexity theory understands law as an emergent, self-organising system in which an interactive network of many parts – actors, institutions and "systems" operate with no overall guiding hand, giving rise to complex collective behaviours that can be observed in patterns of law communications.[103]

This would underline the conclusion in previous chapters that Legal History necessitates the study of the system in its own right and how it has developed (an exercise in intellectual history) and also how the system interacts with its environment and other systems (an exercise in social history). Moreover, this approach underscores that the system of law is a construction: even if it appears to have a life of its own it was and is created, authored and shaped by human interaction and is full of the assumptions, biases and values of particular creators, authors and shapers. Legal historians need to be aware of this and need to subvert it: they need to understand and critique law as a constructed complex system.

This can be achieved by understanding how a complex system is likely to operate. It has been suggested that complex systems tend to be characterised by certain characteristics: self-organisation, chaotic behaviour and 'fat-tailed' behaviour (where rare events occur much more often than would be predicted).[104] All of the elements of a complex system are adaptive and are 'non-linear in their operations, which indicates that small changes in conditions can lead to significant alterations in behaviour'.[105] In short, there exists 'an exciting picture of ceaseless creativity'.[106] This does not mean that complex systems are unstable; rather 'their stability is a consequence of dynamic relationships between their many parts'.[107] A complex system is characterised by adaptive interaction (where interactive agents 'modify their strategies in diverse ways as experience accumulates').[108] In short, a complex system hides its own chaos behind an image of stability. The role of the legal scholar is to uncover the chaotic and unpredictable behaviour that is hidden. Complexity theory therefore provides 'a number of insights' including highlighting:

> The unpredictability of legal systems; the idea of the law system as emergent, the result of the interactions between law actors; the ability of law to adapt to changes in its external environment and the functioning of other law

103 Ibid 3.

104 John H Holland, *Complexity: A Very Short Introduction* (Oxford University Press, 2014) 1.

105 Richard Nobles and David Schiff, 'Taking the Complexity of Complex Systems Seriously' (2020) 83(3) *Modern Law Review* 661, 665.

106 Jamie Murray, Thomas E Webb and Steven Wheatley, 'Encountering Law's Complexity' in Jamie Murray, Thomas E Webb and Steven Wheatley (eds) *Complexity Theory and Law: Mapping an Emergent Jurisprudence* (Routledge, 2019) 3, 5.

107 Richard Nobles and David Schiff, 'Taking the Complexity of Complex Systems Seriously' (2020) 83(3) *Modern Law Review* 661, 665.

108 John H Holland, *Complexity: A Very Short Introduction* (Oxford University Press, 2014) 1.

> systems; the importance of context to understanding law; the unclear, contested and open nature of law system boundaries and the way they interface with society; and the fact that practitioners and scholars cannot avoid ethical responsibility in their work.[109]

Such an approach is in line with the dynamic, interpenetrating view of law and society as propounded by Cotterrell. Murray, Webb and Wheatley wrote of complexity theory reflecting the 'the deeply interconnected, perpetually interacting, reiterative nature of social existence.[110] It is also fundamentally a subversive approach in that it questions law's self-presentation as being objective and predictable instead revealing it to be 'a form of information or communication which takes its meaning from its application, in context, through iteration'.[111] Complexity theory 'understands the structures that stabilise system elements as themselves a result of those elements, which means that order is produced from the bottom up, through relationships of attraction, rather than imposed from above, through force or hierarchy'.[112] It can be placed in opposition to the progress narrative provided by evolutionary functionalism since complexity theory 'is opposed to final destinations and only provides descriptions and analysis suitable for the moment'.[113]

However, in some respects, some versions of complexity theory are not subversive enough. Murray, Webb and Wheatley were at pains to stress that complexity theory 'is not a postmodern theory'.[114] Whether or not the term postmodern is used is beside the point; what is of importance is the effect that this had upon their understanding of complexity theory. Murray, Webb and Wheatley seemed to view postmodernism as equating to relativism. They rejected this because 'one of the central lessons of complexity is that, whilst the functioning of complex systems cannot be predicted with absolute certainty, neither are complex systems completely unpredictable'.[115] This is unobjectionable: a subversive approach based on entropy and chaos rejects linearity and problematises without

109 Jamie Murray, Thomas E Webb and Steven Wheatley, 'Encountering Law's Complexity' in Jamie Murray, Thomas E Webb and Steven Wheatley (eds) *Complexity Theory and Law: Mapping an Emergent Jurisprudence* (Routledge, 2019) 3, 11.

110 Ibid 5.

111 It points to the need to pay 'attention to more levels (micro-, meso- and macro-) and their relationships both with each other and the outside environment, as well as a willingness to treat any model (or regulatory regime) as tentative and revisable in light of further information': Richard Nobles and David Schiff, 'Taking the Complexity of Complex Systems Seriously' (2020) 83(3) *Modern Law Review* 661, 665–666.

112 Ibid 665.

113 Jamie Murray, Thomas E Webb and Steven Wheatley, 'Encountering Law's Complexity' in Jamie Murray, Thomas E Webb and Steven Wheatley (eds) *Complexity Theory and Law: Mapping an Emergent Jurisprudence* (Routledge, 2019) 3, 5.

114 Ibid 9.

115 Complexity theory involves a rejection of both the ambition of modernity to understand and explain everything and the claim of post modernity (or at least its characterisation) that everything is contingent and nothing can be explained': ibid 10.

completely destroying predictability. However, what is more problematic is their assertion that complexity theory is not postmodern 'because it is not concerned with doing away with, or otherwise transcending boundaries. It is concerned with the means by which these boundaries – of actor's understanding, of institutions, of systems, of concepts – are constructed, with their justifications and with their responses to stimulation by other boundaries'.[116] The questioning and transcending of boundaries is, however, a characteristic of a subversive approach; the alternative is to reduce the subversive critique as being only within the system and on the system's own terms. Complex theory has the potential to contribute to this but its advocates have limited its reach.

A further problem with complexity theory is that, although it is presented as a critique of functionalism,[117] it continues to be underpinned by functionalist understandings. Like social entropy theory, complexity theory not only critiques but also builds upon functionalism.[118] There is therefore a risk that these theories could suffer from a similar defect to McNeilly's argument in that they continue to be shaped by one half of evolutionary functionalism, the very thing that a subversive approach is positioned in opposition to. While McNeilly's dialogue with Darwin embraces evolution, these theories can be understood as being a development of functionalism. For complexity theory, in particular, the controversy surrounds its relationship with Niklas Luhmann's social systems theory, also known as autopoietic theory, which developed sociological functionalist thought. Social systems theory was developed by Niklas Luhmann and rests upon the notion of functional differentiation; the way in which in modern society a plethora of social systems discharge specific functions as opposed to the pre-modern tendency for one specific institution to discharge a plethora of functions.[119] For Luhmann, modern society is functionally differentiated into autonomous social systems such as law, religion, politics, science and the media. Luhmann saw these social systems as reproducing themselves by communication, rather than following Durkheim and Weber in seeing them as being the product of labour divisions or social action. For Luhmann, social systems are self-referential: he came to refer to them as 'autopoietic' systems on the grounds that they produce and reproduce their own unity. Commentators are divided as to the relationship between complexity theory and social systems

116 Ibid 9.

117 'Complexity theory came into existence following the recognition that the Newtonian model of a clockwork universe that could be taken apart and subjected to reductionist analysis was unable to explain the workings of certain (complex) systems': Ibid 5.

118 Kenneth D Bailey regarded his theory as being 'first and foremost a macrosociological approach' which attempted to 'build upon the best-known macro systems theory in sociology: structural functionalism': Kenneth D Bailey, *Social Entropy Theory* (University of New York Press, 1990) 2, 8.

119 See, most notably Niklas Luhmann, *Social Systems* (Stanford University Press, 1995); Niklas Luhmann, *Theory of Society* (Stanford University Press, 2012); Niklas Luhmann *A Sociological Theory of Law* (Routledge, 1985) and Niklas Luhmann, *Law as a Social System* (Oxford University Press, 2004).

theory: while Murray, Webb and Wheatley have argued that complexity theory 'is qualitatively different from' social systems theory and 'significantly enhances' the study of law;[120] Richard Nobles and David Schiff have responded by asserting that the two theories have much in common and are complementary.[121] Murray, Webb and Wheatley gave four reasons why they considered complexity theory to be different from and superior to social systems theory.[122] First, they asserted that 'complexity theory is better science' in that while social systems theory simply drew upon the work of Maturana and Valera,[123] complexity theory is 'well established in physics, chemistry and biology, and the literature has drawn on a wide range of sources in these disciplines'.[124] Yet, as Nobles and Schiff responded, not only is it the case that complexity theory actually challenges 'many of the approaches that we associate with science',[125] but also the issue is not which theory is 'drawn from more categories of science than the other, but which of them best informs the object to be observed, which in this case is society, and law within society'.[126] Indeed, simply applying a scientific theory without translating it through sociology – as social systems theory does, is likely to be problematic.[127] The problem with social systems theory is not that it is less established in science but rather the science upon which it is based. It is, as Nobles and Schiff note, 'a theory of societal evolution'.[128] It therefore runs the risk of suffering from the same limitations as Kathryn McNeilly's work on untimely evolution.

The second reason given focuses squarely upon the functionalist point. Murray, Webb and Wheatley asserted that, unlike social systems theory, complexity theory 'does not require that communications be framed according to a predetermined list of social functions. And, more importantly, it anticipates that

120 Jamie Murray, Thomas E Webb and Steven Wheatley, 'Encountering Law's Complexity' in Jamie Murray, Thomas E Webb and Steven Wheatley (eds) *Complexity Theory and Law: Mapping an Emergent Jurisprudence* (Routledge, 2019) 3, 6.

121 Richard Nobles and David Schiff, 'Taking the Complexity of Complex Systems Seriously' (2020) 83(3) *Modern Law Review* 661.

122 Jamie Murray, Thomas E Webb and Steven Wheatley, 'Encountering Law's Complexity' in Jamie Murray, Thomas E Webb and Steven Wheatley (eds) *Complexity Theory and Law: Mapping an Emergent Jurisprudence* (Routledge, 2019) 3, 6.

123 Humberto R Maturana and Francisco J Varela, *The Tree of Knowledge: The Biological Roots of Human Understanding* (Shambhala Press, 1987).

124 Jamie Murray, Thomas E Webb and Steven Wheatley, 'Encountering Law's Complexity' in Jamie Murray, Thomas E Webb and Steven Wheatley (eds) *Complexity Theory and Law: Mapping an Emergent Jurisprudence* (Routledge, 2019) 3, 6.

125 'Science normally operates with a reductionist methodology – an assumption that it is possible to identify and break complex wholes into their respective parts, and to model the relationships between those parts': Richard Nobles and David Schiff, 'Taking the Complexity of Complex Systems Seriously' (2020) 83(3) *Modern Law Review* 661, 664.

126 Ibid 668.

127 They noted that 'research uncoordinated by a compatible theoretical framework also raises the spectre that any subsequent findings cannot build into a body of knowledge, but must remain as isolated observations': ibid 663.

128 Ibid 667.

the confluence of communications amongst different actors, institutions and systems – the interface of their respective descriptions strategies, their boundaries of understanding – is the most important aspect of social behaviour to observe for law'.[129] Although Nobles and Schiff responded by saying that this criticism was based on the functionalism found in earlier sociological theories rather than in social systems theory,[130] this does not answer the critique that social systems theory is based upon functionalism. Indeed, Nobles and Schiff commented that the same was true of complexity theory: the shared onus on 'the necessity for problem solving if a particular system within modern complex society is to reproduce' meant that complexity theory and social systems theory 'adopt a similar attitude to functionalism'.[131]

The third reason given raised an often made critique of social systems theory: Murray, Webb and Wheatley commented that 'the dehumanised nature of autopoiesis is highly problematic'.[132] This 'setting aside of the importance of human agency... closes off great swathes of activity which are neither anticipated nor understood at a systematic level'. This criticism is overstated: social systems theory is not dehumanised but rather is a theory of society that focuses on the level of systems.[133] It is questionable whether this does exclude activity which would be analysed by complexity theory. Indeed, Nobles and Schiff argued that complexity theory should embrace this insight from social systems theory since combining the two would enable 'seeing the primary unit of society not as human actors, but as communications, and seeing how humans become

129 Jamie Murray, Thomas E Webb and Steven Wheatley, 'Encountering Law's Complexity' in Jamie Murray, Thomas E Webb and Steven Wheatley (eds) *Complexity Theory and Law: Mapping an Emergent Jurisprudence* (Routledge, 2019) 3, 7.

130 For Nobles and Schiff, this ignored 'the difference between Luhmannian and Parsonian versions of functionalism' because social systems theory did not claim that 'different systems are organised in order to carry out particular functions': 'it is not that communications have to be framed within law in order to ensure that law executes its normative function. Rather, it is that law, with its binary code, presents itself as a system of norms, and in so doing, contributes hugely to the solving of one of the problems which, were it not solved, would prevent society operating at its current and increasing levels of complexity': Richard Nobles and David Schiff, 'Taking the Complexity of Complex Systems Seriously' (2020) 83(3) *Modern Law Review* 661, 673.

131 Ibid 674.

132 Jamie Murray, Thomas E Webb and Steven Wheatley, 'Encountering Law's Complexity' in Jamie Murray, Thomas E Webb and Steven Wheatley (eds) *Complexity Theory and Law: Mapping an Emergent Jurisprudence* (Routledge, 2019) 3, 7.

133 A system and how it develops can be analysed while simultaneously recognising that the system is a human construct and that it is being constantly shaped by the actions of individuals. It is perfectly possible to talk and analyse the legal system or systems within the legal system while recognising that the system is the product of humans thinking and litigating. As Nobles and Schiff noted, a systems theory analysis simply takes a different focus: 'its hermeneutics are rooted not in the intentions of human actors, but in the meanings generated by those actors through their participation as communicators': Richard Nobles and David Schiff, 'Using Systems Theory to Understand Legal Pluralism: What Could Be Gained?' (2012) 46(2) *Law and Society Review* 265, 266–267.

constituted as actors, alongside organisations, and perhaps other entities within systems of communication'.[134]

The fourth reason is the criticism that while social systems theory rests 'on the assumption that, were perfect communication somehow possible, regulatory failure would not occur, by contrast 'complexity theory shows that there is no perfect form of regulation available'.[135] Nobles and Schiff rebutted this as a fallacy on the basis that the fact that social systems theory identifies reasons for regulatory failure does not 'lead to the conclusion that, in their absence, regulation would be perfected'.[136] Rather, they concluded that social systems and complexity theory have much in common and that this included the acceptance of entropy.[137]

The debate on these four reasons therefore actually shows the closeness of the two approaches and the fact that complexity theory (like social entropy theory) has developed as a critique of – and is therefore still informed by – functionalism therefore remains a serious risk. The focus on entropy as opposed to the traditional functionalist focus on equilibrium may provide some help in this respect.[138] And it is to emphasise this, as well as because all three theories (social entropic theory, chaos theory and complexity theory) overlap and are not in isolation sufficient, that the term entropic complexity should be used to describe this second alternative to evolutionary functionalism.

Drawing upon the three theories introduced above, entropic complexity can be said to have the following seven characteristics: First, entropic complexity rejects the evolutionary aspect of evolutionary functionalism. Drawing upon McNeilly's work, law is untimely: it neither operates in linear nor progressive ways. This means that rather than focusing on origins or end points, there is a need to explore the intellectual history of the ebb and flow of legal ideas. Second, entropic complexity rejects the functionalist aspect of evolutionary functionalism. The default is not equilibrium. Law is a complex system and the natural result of

134 Richard Nobles and David Schiff, 'Taking the Complexity of Complex Systems Seriously' (2020) 83(3) *Modern Law Review* 661, 677.

135 Jamie Murray, Thomas E Webb and Steven Wheatley, 'Encountering Law's Complexity' in Jamie Murray, Thomas E Webb and Steven Wheatley (eds) *Complexity Theory and Law: Mapping an Emergent Jurisprudence* (Routledge, 2019) 3, 7.

136 Richard Nobles and David Schiff, 'Taking the Complexity of Complex Systems Seriously' (2020) 83(3) *Modern Law Review* 661, 678–679.

137 'Neither theory presumes that the systems to be analysed are causally closed. Neither theory denies thermodynamics – all systems expend energy, and require ever increasing amounts of energy in order to achieve increased complexity. Both theories acknowledge that a system is affected by its environment (remembering that a system's environment includes other systems). Both theories are directed to systems that do not have a simple input/output relationship with their environment, whereby the same input always leads to the same output, which would allow a given input from the environment to determine the output of the affected system': ibid 674–675.

138 Kenneth D Bailey asserts that 'the limitation of functionalist systems theory stem largely because it is based upon the isolated-system equilibrium theory … rather than on … entropy analysis': Kenneth D Bailey, *Social Entropy Theory* (University of New York Press, 1990) 71.

a complex system is entropy. This means that lack of order and unpredictability are the norm; uncertainty, nuance and flexibility are the default. Third, consequentially, entropic complexity liberates the way in which we understand and analyse law. This all opens up significantly the prospects of legal change on a much wider level. It also underscores the limits of law and that law is not about providing a solution in the same way as solving a mathematical equation. Fourth, this complicates but makes more important the role of the legal historian. Their role is to explore the multiple causes and multiple consequences of legal phenomena, noting that this will be interpenetrated by non-legal phenomena. Prediction is difficult but not impossible since entropic complexity does not result in complete anarchy. Fifth, entropic complexity stresses the need to examine individuals and systems. On the one hand, this approach underlines the importance of agency. Random behaviour can have a significant effect. However, in addition to exploring the experiences of individuals and their social groups, attention needs to be paid to how complex systems develop their own artificial intelligence: how they emerge and develop a life of their own which equates to more than the sum of their parts. Law is an example of this. It is not an objective entity but consists of communication. This communication needs to be an object of study. Sixth, entropic complexity emphasises the dynamic interconnectedness of systems and therefore shows that individual systems cannot be studied in isolation. Complex systems – such as law – are self-organising but not fully autonomous. They have an open and contested interaction with other systems. The legal and the non-legal cannot be adequately distinguished from one another but are interpenetrative. Complex systems are characterised by dynamic relationships and adaptive interaction. Seventh, entropic complexity requires a subversive approach to the analysis of law recognising that the artificial intelligence of law is constructed and shaped by particular people with their own biases, assumptions and values. A subversive approach disturbs the way in which we see the system by focusing on agency, especially the agency of those who have been previously marginalised. It also requires the questioning, de-construction and re-construction of concepts, ideas and boundaries, including those around areas of study.

There are risks to such an approach. Christopher Tomlins has argued that: 'Complexity, now fetishized as such across many scholarly disciplines, has, to be sure, enriched the substance of scholarship; simultaneously it has paralyzed generalizing inquiry'.[139] He wrote that the depressing outcome might 'be that what is left after critique is merely a blur of similitude, as the field of law and society joins all post-critical scholarship in the energetic but sadly pointless pursuit of an essentially bourgeois aesthetic of complexity, of endless, causeless relativity'.[140] This is not inevitable, however. But it does require that a subversive approach pay attention to the question of causation. Susanna L Blumenthal has noted that

139 Christopher Tomlins, 'What is Left of the Law and Society Paradigm after Critique? Revisiting Gordon's "Critical Legal Histories' (2012) 37 *Law & Social Inquiry* 155, 158.

140 Ibid 164.

'legal historians writing post-Critique are noticeably (and perhaps understandably) cagey about matters of causation'.[141] It is important that subversive legal historians do not fall into this trap. An approach based on entropic complexity rather than evolutionary functionalism does not abandon the issue of causation and explanation but it does render it more difficult, complicated and nuanced. As Blumenthal pointed out, such work 'recovers forgotten perspectives and posits alternative trajectories with a strange admixture of moral clarity, ironic distance, and wistfulness as they leave their readers to contemplate unfulfilled promises, accidental republics, and unfinished struggles'. This requires new approaches and new methodologies. The next chapter will provide a taste of this. It will draw upon Blumenthal's reference to 'alternative trajectories' and will also return to Robert W Gordon's suggestion, mentioned in Chapter 2, that the role of a critical approach is not to explain how each event 'works' and fits within the evolutionary functionalism pattern but is to consider the 'multiple trajectories of possibility' showing how the path actually chosen was 'chosen not because it had to be' but was the result of power struggles and amounted to agenda setting.[142] Gordon's question – 'How can one identify the counterfactual trajectories, the roads not taken?' – is the focus of the next chapter. It will explore a specific method – counterfactual history – as an example of how a subversive approach can develop in order to try to ensure that Law Schools can become less like monasteries.

141 Susanna L Blumenthal, 'Of Mandarins, Legal Consciousness, and the Cultural Turn in US Legal History' (2012) 37 *Law & Social Inquiry* 167, 177.

142 Robert W Gordon, *Taming the Past: Essays on Law in History and History in Law* (Cambridge University Press, 2017) 271.

6 Counterfactual Legal History

The historian E P Thompson famously dismissed 'counterfactual fictions' as '*Geschichtenscheissenschlopff*, unhistorical shit'.[1]

This chapter will explore whether and how Subversive Legal History can use counterfactual history, a method common within populist historical works and to some extent in historical academic texts.[2] However, as Thompson's colourful language suggests, counterfactual history is a controversial approach within academic history. This chapter will begin by exploring why this is. It falls into three parts. The first introduces the phenomenon of counterfactual history exploring its development, use and purpose. This will visit the heated debate among academic historians as to the merits of counterfactual analysis. This will conclude that if counterfactual history is to be used as a method of academic analysis then certain precautions and safeguards need to be taken. The second part of the chapter will explore what these precautions and safeguards are by using the instructions given and reflected upon by editors of volumes on counterfactual history to distil the eight main rules of counterfactual historical analysis. The final part of the chapter will explore the usefulness of this approach in relation to law. It will explore how lawyers use counterfactual analysis and the advantages and disadvantages of using counterfactual history in a legal context, whether or not it is 'unhistorical shit'.

The chapter, then, introduces and explores, for the first time, Counterfactual Legal History, asking 'what if' legal developments had occurred differently and

1 E P Thompson, *The Poverty of Theory and Other Essays* (Merlin Press, 1978) 100.

2 Various different labels, such as 'alternative history', '"what if?" history', 'allohistory' and 'alternate history' are used to describe what this chapter will refer to as 'counterfactual history': Simon T Kaye, 'Challenging Certainty: The Utility and History of Counter factualism' (2010) 49 *History and Theory* 38. This chapter will use the term 'counterfactual history' unless an alternative label has been developed by the writer being discussed such as Niall Ferguson's concept of 'virtual history': Niall Ferguson (ed) *Virtual History: Alternatives and Counterfactuals* (Papermac, 1998). The term 'counterfactual history' can be distinguished from 'secret histories' that 'purport to explain the hidden private stories behind the official explanations of historical events' and 'counterhistories' which stress 'the forgotten struggles or viewpoints of those outside the mainstream': Catherine Gallagher, *Telling it Like it Wasn't: The Counterfactual Imagination in History and Fiction* (University of Chicago Press, 2018) 2.

comparing that with what actually happened. It questions how asking and following through on the 'what if' question can shed light upon how law actually developed and how it could develop. Counterfactual Legal History seemingly has the potential to unlock the subversive nature of Legal History. It highlights the connection between change and continuity and assesses the importance of change by exploring changes in a negative sense, asking what would have happened had they not occurred (or had occurred differently). Counterfactual Legal History, by asking what could have been, highlights not only other possible futures (underlining the contingency of law) and also emphasises the importance of agency (showing that other futures are possible and can be achieved). A counterfactual approach provides an assault on a deterministic interpretation of law as being fixed. It provides an opportunity to question and indeed depart from the progress narrative of evolutionary functionalist accounts. This chapter picks up the challenge posed in the previous chapter to explore one possible way in which history can be used imaginatively and creatively to subvert, de-construct and re-construct understandings of law.

Counterfactual History

The person most closely identified with counterfactualism is probably Gwyneth Paltrow.

The 1998 romantic comedy film *Sliding Doors* alternated between two storylines depending upon whether the lead character, played by Paltrow, caught a train or not. As Andrew Roberts has pointed out, the movie 'perfectly enunciates the superiority of accident versus design in history'.[3] *Sliding Doors* has become popular culture shorthand to explain the notion of counterfactuals. Counterfactuals can be defined as 'alternative versions of the past in which one alteration in the timeline leads to a different outcome from the one we know actually occurred'.[4] Counterfactual history can be defined as the exploration of such an alteration in the timeline and the discussion of the effect that this could have had. As Catherine Gallagher put it, the 'definitive characteristic' is existence and pursuance of 'a counterfactual-historical hypothesis', that is, an 'explicit or implicit past-tense hypothetical, conditional conjecture pursued when the antecedent condition is known to be contrary to fact'.[5] Counterfactual history involves asking and following through on the 'what if' question: what if William of Normandy had been defeated at the Battle of Hastings; what if Hitler had been assassinated in the 1930s; what if Paltrow's character had not caught that train.

3 Andrew Roberts, 'Introduction' in Andrew Roberts (ed) *What Might Have Been* (Phoenix, 2004) 1, 2.

4 Richard J Evans, *Altered Pasts: Counterfactuals in History* (Abacus, 2016) xi.

5 Catherine Gallagher, *Telling It Like It Wasn't: The Counterfactual Imagination in History and Fiction* (University of Chicago Press. 2018) 2.

Reviewers of *Sliding Doors*, though generally positive, were quick to note the 'gimmicky feel' of the alternate futures split narrative.[6] Many critics of counterfactual history have been considerably harsher in their denigration. As Niall Ferguson pointed out, 'hostility to counterfactual arguments has been and remains surprisingly widespread among professional historians'.[7] E H Carr saw counterfactualism as a 'purely emotional and unhistorical reaction' and dismissed it as a mere 'parlour game with the might-have-been of history',[8] while Eric Hobsbawm wrote that if we are not concerned with 'what actually happened' then' we are not historians'.[9] For Hobsbawm, conjectural history had a place in the discipline of history but its role 'is to help us assess the possibilities of present and future, rather than past'.[10] Michael Oakeshott saw counterfactualism as 'a pure myth, an extravagance of the imagination'.[11] He regarded it as being 'outside the current of historical thought' and that it did 'not belong to historical thought at all; it is a monstrous incursion of science into the world of history'. Allan Megill noted that authors of such works are better seen as writers of imaginative literature, though he conceded that 'this is not necessarily bad, but it is not history'.[12] And Marc Bloch also saw it as little more than a game. He wrote that: 'We are not forbidden to amuse ourselves with these questions, providing we understand them for what they really are: simple rhetorical devices intended to illuminate the role of contingency and of the unforeseeable in the progress of mankind'.[13]

On the other hand, counterfactualism has its advocates among professional historians. Niall Ferguson, hailed as one of counterfactualism's most read and respected proponents,[14] regards counterfactual history – or 'virtual history' as he dubs it – 'a necessary antidote to determinism'.[15] Similarly, Jonathan Clark wrote that it was counterfactualism that 'promises an historical rehabilitation… which has freed our vision of the world from the overdetermination which underlies all stadial theories, whether modernist or postmodernist'.[16] Lewis B

6 See <https://www.rottentomatoes.com/m/slidingdoors>. The ending of the film also seems to suggest an element of determinism. The means might differ but the end will be achieved no matter what.

7 Niall Ferguson 'Introduction – Virtual History: Towards a "Chaotic" Theory of the Past' in Niall Ferguson (ed) *Virtual History: Alternatives and Counterfactuals* (Papermac, 1998) 1, 5.

8 E H Carr, *What Is History?* (Palgrave, 2001) 92, 91.

9 Eric Hobsbawm, *On History* (Orion, 1997) 105.

10 Ibid 105–106.

11 Michael Oakeshott, *Experience and its Modes* (Cambridge University Press, 1933) 128.

12 Allan Megill, *Historical Knowledge, Historical Error: A Contemporary Guide to Practice* (University of Chicago Press, 2007) 152.

13 Marc Bloch, *The Historian's Craft* (Manchester University Press, 1992) 104.

14 Simon T Kaye, 'Challenging Certainty: The Utility and History of Counter factualism' (2010) 49 *History and Theory* 38, 40.

15 Niall Ferguson 'Introduction – Virtual History: Towards a "Chaotic" Theory of the Past' in Niall Ferguson (ed) *Virtual History: Alternatives and Counterfactuals* (Papermac, 1998) 1, 89.

16 Jonathan Clark, *Our Shadowed Present: Modernism, Postmodernism and History* (Atlantic Books, 2003) 28–29.

Namier went as far to say that 'the enduring achievement of historical study is a historical sense – an intuitive understanding– of how things do not happen'.[17]

It would be fair to say, then, as Philip E Tetlock and Geoffrey Parker noted, that 'counterfactual history polarizes scholars'.[18] For some it is a mere parlour game yet for others it is history's necessary saviour. However, counterfactualism is not confined to history departments. Counterfactual thinking and arguments are part and parcel of everyday life.[19] Counterfactualism is not 'a position or school of thought' but is rather 'a tool, capable of use in many contexts'.[20] As Andrew Roberts pointed out, 'we only have to look at our own lives to appreciate how the alteration of one small thing on one particular day can sometimes have a huge effect on everything else, perhaps for years, perhaps for life'.[21] The point of such thoughts is to better understand our past not to change it. As Ferguson noted, 'we know perfectly well that we cannot travel back in time and do things differently'.[22] 'What if' thoughts about our own lives shed light upon what led us to the present. In the words of Ferguson:

> Because decisions about the future are – usually – based on weighing up the potential consequences of alternative courses of actions, it makes sense to compare the actual outcomes of what we did in the past with the conceivable outcomes of what might have been.

It follows from this that imagining counterfactuals is key to the learning process.[23] The question of what could have been done differently is a counterfactual one. As Simon T Kaye noted, the way in which constructing 'what if' scenarios 'comes naturally to human beings' makes its contested place as a method within academic history odd and questionable.[24]

Although counterfactual history has never been common, there are 'numerous works, especially from the early twentieth century, that have come to form

17 Lewis B Namier, *Avenues of History* (Hamish Hamilton, 1952) 4.

18 Philip E Tetlock and Geoffrey Parker, 'Counterfactual Thought Experiments: Why We Can't Live without Them & How We Must Learn to Live with Them' in Philip E Tetlock, Richard N Lebow and Geoffrey Parker (eds) *Unmaking the West: 'What-If' Scenarios That Rewrite World History* (University of Michigan Press, 2006) 14.

19 Niall Ferguson 'Introduction – Virtual History: Towards a "Chaotic" Theory of the Past' in Niall Ferguson (ed) *Virtual History: Alternatives and Counterfactuals* (Papermac, 1998) 1, 2.

20 Jeremy Black, *What If? Counterfactualism and the Problem of History* (Social Affairs Unit, 1998) 2.

21 Andrew Roberts, 'Introduction' in Andrew Roberts (ed) *What Might Have Been* (Phoenix, 2004) 1.

22 Niall Ferguson 'Introduction – Virtual History: Towards a "Chaotic" Theory of the Past' in Niall Ferguson (ed) *Virtual History: Alternatives and Counterfactuals* (Papermac, 1998) 1, 2.

23 Ibid; See also Jeremy Black, *What If? Counterfactualism and the Problem of History* (Social Affairs Unit, 1998) 18.

24 Simon T Kaye, 'Challenging Certainty: The Utility and History of Counter factualism' (2010) 49 *History and Theory* 38, 40.

something like a canon for counterfactual history'.[25] Such works have increased in number and in sophistication in recent years.[26] Originally, the few works of this type provided ample evidence to support E H Carr's denigration of counterfactualism as a mere 'parlour game'.[27] This was especially true of an early collection of essays edited by JC Squire, *If It Had Happened Otherwise*,[28] which featured a chapter by Winston Churchill among 'a motley crew which, mainly comprised of novelists and journalists' that took a self-deprecating tone.[29] The introduction to the volume concluded that counterfactual history was not of much help 'as nobody is to know' and, as Richard Evans has noted, its light hearted, humorous and nostalgic tone meant that it was more of an 'if only' than a 'what if'.[30] For Niall Ferguson, Squire's volume established counterfactual essay as 'a vehicle for wishful thinking or reductive explanation – and, above all, high table humour' and was responsible for rendering counterfactual history insignificant for a generation.[31] Squire's edited collection and a further collection by Daniel Snowman[32] lacked any methodological discussion or precision in their use of counterfactuals.

A major turning point in the development of counterfactual history as an academic method developed in a specific context and in a particular way: it developed in the field of economic history and in relation to quantitative analysis, chiefly in the work of the US economic historian Winthrop R Fogel.[33] As Ferguson quipped, there was 'no wishful thinking here and certainly no humour'.[34] Fogel's work explored the impact of the development of railroads upon American economic growth but he was not really asking a 'what if' question at all.[35] As Ferguson pointed out, his:

> purpose of calculating the "social savings" afforded by railroads is not to conjure up a plausible alternative history but to test a hypothesis about the

25 Catherine Gallagher, *Telling It Like It Wasn't: The Counterfactual Imagination in History and Fiction* (University of Chicago Press. 2018) 9.

26 For a discussion of earlier precursors see Simon T Kaye, 'Challenging Certainty: The Utility and History of Counter factualism' (2010) 49 *History and Theory* 38, 45 *et seq.* and Richard J Evans, *Altered Pasts: Counterfactuals in History* (Abacus, 2016) chapter 1.

27 Cf. E H Carr, *What Is History?* (Palgrave, 2001) 91.

28 J C Squire, *If It Had Happened Otherwise* (Longmans, 1931).

29 Niall Ferguson 'Introduction – Virtual History: Towards a "Chaotic" Theory of the Past' in Niall Ferguson (ed) *Virtual History: Alternatives and Counterfactuals* (Papermac, 1998) 1, 9.

30 Richard J Evans, *Altered Pasts: Counterfactuals in History* (Abacus, 2016) 88, 16, 18.

31 Niall Ferguson 'Introduction – Virtual History: Towards a "Chaotic" Theory of the Past' in Niall Ferguson (ed) *Virtual History: Alternatives and Counterfactuals* (Papermac, 1998) 1, 14.

32 Daniel Snowman (ed) *If I Had Been … Ten Historical Fantasies* (Harper Collins, 1979).

33 Winthrop R Fogel, *Railroads and American Economic Growth: Essays in Econometric History* (Johns Hopkin Press 1964).

34 Niall Ferguson 'Introduction – Virtual History: Towards a "Chaotic" Theory of the Past' in Niall Ferguson (ed) *Virtual History: Alternatives and Counterfactuals* (Papermac, 1998) 1, 17.

35 Richard J Evans, *Altered Pasts: Counterfactuals in History* (Abacus, 2016) 39.

> role of railroads in economic growth. No one is in fact trying to "imagine" nineteenth century America without railways.[36]

The work of the New Economic Historians such as Fogel highlighted the need to identify and explore multiple causes and possibilities but stopped short of establishing counterfactualism as a method in history. For Ferguson, this meant that up until the 1990s, there were:

> two distinct kinds of counterfactual which have been used by historians: those which are essentially the product of imagination but (generally) lack an empirical basis; and those designed to test hypotheses by (supposedly) empirical means, which eschew imagination in favour of computation.

Richard J Evans agreed that until the 1990s '"what if?" speculations on history remained essentially at the level of entertainment, appeared intermittently and did not demand to be taken particularly seriously'.[37]

However, since the 1990s there has been a steady flow of publications, usually in the form of edited collections on counterfactual history. This was kick-started by a monograph by Geoffrey Hawthorn,[38] which carefully 'worked out three alternate histories and was probably the first serious attempt to move such speculation out of the philosophy departments and into the social sciences since the 1970s',[39] and Ferguson's edited collection,[40] which 'both expressed and boosted a renewed interest in the genre', especially in terms of military history.[41] Counterfactual thinking increased in popularity not just in academic and popular history but within culture generally.[42] And with the increasing quantity of counterfactual history there has been some increase in of the breadth of areas and the matters dealt with. However, a significant amount of this work focused on macro political, military and diplomatic history.[43] Jeremy Black has suggested that this is because such histories focus on short-term changes.[44] By contrast, he noted that counterfactual history is rarely used in social history because 'many subjects in social history tend to be tackled thematically rather than chronolog-

36 Niall Ferguson 'Introduction – Virtual History: Towards a "Chaotic" Theory of the Past' in Niall Ferguson (ed) *Virtual History: Alternatives and Counterfactuals* (Papermac, 1998) 1, 18.

37 Richard J Evans, *Altered Pasts: Counterfactuals in History* (Abacus, 2016) 39.

38 Geoffrey Hawthorn, *Plausible Worlds: Possibility and Understanding in History and the Social Sciences* (Cambridge University Press, 1991).

39 Simon T Kaye, 'Challenging Certainty: The Utility and History of Counter factualism' (2010) 49 *History and Theory* 38, 55.

40 Niall Ferguson (ed) *Virtual History: Alternatives and Counterfactuals* (Papermac, 1998).

41 Richard J Evans, *Altered Pasts: Counterfactuals in History* (Abacus, 2016) 39.

42 Simon T Kaye, 'Challenging Certainty: The Utility and History of Counter Factualism' (2010) 49 *History and Theory* 38, 39.

43 Ibid 153–154.

44 Jeremy Black, *What If? Counterfactualism and the Problem of History* (Social Affairs Unit, 1998) 60.

ically and with an emphasis on trends rather than events'.[45] He added that 'the modest role of counterfactualism in social history arises because agency there tends to be attributed to groups rather than individuals or small cohorts'.

However, this discussion of the development of counterfactual history is only a partial picture. It relates only to explicit works on counterfactual history: edited collections and occasional monographs devoted to the subject. It does not include works which are not 'on' counterfactual history but where counterfactual history happens to be used as a method. Taking a broader picture leads to the conclusion that counterfactuals are endemic in history. Most historical work includes counterfactual considerations. As Max Weber noted, 'in every line of every historical work, indeed in any section of archival and source materials for publication, there are, or more correctly, must be "judgments of possibility"'.[46] Even Eric Hobsbawm noted that 'all history is full of implicit or explicit counterfactuals'.[47] This implicit – or 'veiled' use – of counterfactualism is often said to be present in 'revisionist' works of history given that 'most revisionists tend to be challenging some form of deterministic interpretation'.[48] However, it is more common than that because counterfactual thinking occurs implicitly as 'a by-product of any historical statement that implies causality'.[49] As John Lewis Gaddis points out, counterfactuals are a 'procedure for establishing causation'.[50] They are 'the historian's virtual equivalent of laboratory experimentation'.[51] In other words, 'whenever we draw a cause-effect lesson from the past, we commit ourselves to the claim that, if key links in the causal chain were broken, history would have unfolded otherwise'.[52] This approach means that historical analysis can rarely if ever be free of counterfactual reasoning. For Philip E Tetlock and Geoffrey Parker, history would be 'counterfactual free only if those who study

45 Ibid 45.

46 Edward A Shils and Henry A Finch (ed) *Max Weber on the Methodology of the Social Sciences* (Free Press of Glencoe, 1949) 173.

47 Eric Hobsbawm, *On History* (Orion, 1997) 150. It has been suggested that even advocates of counterfactual history do not fully appreciate 'how ubiquitous what-if reasoning is in historical narrative': Philip E Tetlock and Geoffrey Parker, 'Counterfactual Thought Experiments: Why We Can't Live without Them & How We Must Learn to Live with Them' in Philip E Tetlock, Richard N Lebow and Geoffrey Parker (eds) *Unmaking the West: 'What-If' Scenarios that Rewrite World History* (University of Michigan Press, 2006) 14, 18.

48 Niall Ferguson 'Introduction – Virtual History: Towards a "Chaotic" Theory of the Past' in Niall Ferguson (ed) *Virtual History: Alternatives and Counterfactuals* (Papermac, 1998) 1, 19.

49 Simon T Kaye, 'Challenging Certainty: The Utility and History of Counter factualism' (2010) 49 *History and Theory* 38.

50 John Lewis Gaddis, *The Landscape of History* (Oxford University Press, 2002) 100. For Catherine Gallagher, 'historians implicitly use counterfactuals whenever they make causal statements': Catherine Gallagher, *Telling It Like It Wasn't: The Counterfactual Imagination in History and Fiction* (University of Chicago Press. 2018) 9.

51 John Lewis Gaddis, *The Landscape of History* (Oxford University Press, 2002) 101.

52 Philip E Tetlock and Geoffrey Parker, 'Counterfactual Thought Experiments: Why We Can't Live without Them & How We Must Learn to Live with Them' in Philip E Tetlock, Richard N Lebow and Geoffrey Parker (eds) *Unmaking the West: 'What-If' Scenarios That Rewrite World History* (University of Michigan Press, 2006) 14, 17.

it are prepared to eschew all causal inference and limit themselves to strictly descriptive narratives of what happened. This precludes smuggling in causal claims under the guise of verbs such as influenced, shaped, responded, transformed, triggered, moulded and precipitated'.[53] Counterfactual thinking exists wherever a historian considers the possibility of alternative outcomes even if they do then not go onto explore such alternatives in depth.

There exists, therefore, a contradiction whereby historians on the whole are critical and resistant to counterfactual history but yet use counterfactual reasoning all the time. As Philip E Tetlock and Geoffrey Parker point out, historians cannot 'have it both ways – ridiculing counterfactual history in one place and covertly using it in others'. Yet, there is a difference between the implicit and the explicit use of counterfactualism. There is a difference between recognising that there may have been alternative possible outcomes and actively exploring such outcomes with the same level of analysis as the actual timeline. The tension between the implicit and explicit use of counterfactualism also underscores the uncertainty as to what counterfactual history is. It shows that counterfactual history can cover a broad spectrum, potentially ranging from what Allan Megill considers 'the legitimate, indeed essential, role of counterfactuality in any attempt on the part of the historian to make claims about what caused what in history, and another use of counterfactuality that is closer to imaginative literature than to history'.[54]

This is problematic because it means that historians can often be at cross purposes when they talk about counterfactualism. As with the difference between different camps in Legal History, this can lead to an antagonistic relationship where both sides fail to learn from the work of the others. Jeremy Black, for instance, has presented 'counterfactualism as the nemesis of often stuffy and unreflecting scholars'.[55] While on the other hand, counterfactual history's 'opponents often disparage it as a recent development, little more than a postmodern fad, a right-wing plot, or a symptom of the general decline in confidence in the possibilities of achieving complete objectivity or unbiased "truth"'.[56] The unfortunate effect of the contested and controversial nature of counterfactual thinking is that counterfactualism is used implicitly and without sufficient methodological rigour. As with the tension between camps in Legal History, the answer is to recognise the value of both perspectives and to reach a position which builds upon both. Counterfactual history should neither be dismissed outright nor universally adopted. Rather, there is a need to examine what counterfactual

53 Ibid 18.

54 Allan Megill, *Historical Knowledge, Historical Error: A Contemporary Guide to Practice* (University of Chicago Press, 2007) xiii.

55 Jeremy Black, *What If? Counterfactualism and the Problem of History* (Social Affairs Unit, 1998) 175.

56 Catherine Gallagher, *Telling It Like It Wasn't: The Counterfactual Imagination in History and Fiction* (University of Chicago Press, 2018) 9.

history is and should be. A key question that needs to be explored as a precursor to this is to ask why counterfactual history is controversial.

Counterfactual history is controversial in academic history because it is suspected that it lacks the rigour usually expected in the academic discipline. Christopher Prendergast commented that 'polemic' was 'the name of a further large country in the geography of the counterfactual'.[57] Historians speculating what might have happened have less evidence to rely upon than those who account for what did happen.[58] Richard J Evans has noted that ironically counterfactuals 'always cast more light on the present than on the past'.[59] This is because 'detached from the need to back arguments with actual, concrete evidence, it allows historians to rewrite history according to their present-day political purposes and prejudices'.[60] This is reflected even in the choice of the counterfactual variable, a choice which 'is the outcome of the historian's intention, political orientation, factual knowledge and contemporary context'.[61] For Evans, counterfactual history has 'been more or less a monopoly of the Right'.[62] He noted that not only are counterfactual accounts invariably nostalgic but that also 'counterfactualists routinely stress their belief in contingency and chance as a collary of their championing of the rights of the individual'. This can often lead to unimaginative counterfactuals that seek to cement the status quo. As Philip E Tetlock, Richard N Lebow and Geoffrey Parker pointed out, many counterfactualists 'who lean toward the political Right are more likely to maintain that things had to work out roughly as they did and that Western dominance has been in the historical cards for a long time' and their counterfactuals invariably 'bring history back on track in fairly short order'.[63] However, this does not mean that Right-wing counterfactuals are not critical. Jeremy Black has pointed out that both the Left and the Right have an interest in critiquing the present and both can draw on counterfactualism to critique the past.[64] Tetlock, Lebow and Parker described two warring tribes who are 'quick to mock the other': 'the gloating "it had to be" counterfactuals from the triumphalist Right have crossed swords with bad loser "could have been a contender" counterfactuals from the multiculturalist Left'.[65]

57 Christopher Prendergast, *Counterfactuals: Paths of the Might Have Been* (Bloomsbury, 2019) 3.
58 Ibid 57.
59 Richard J Evans, *Altered Pasts: Counterfactuals in History* (Abacus, 2016) 176–177.
60 Ibid 88.
61 Ibid 175.
62 Ibid 51.
63 Philip E Tetlock, Richard N Lebow and Geoffrey Parker, 'Preface: Unmaking the Middle Kingdom' in Philip E Tetlock, Richard N Lebow and Geoffrey Parker (eds) *Unmaking the West: 'What-If' Scenarios That Rewrite World History* (University of Michigan Press, 2006) 1, 8.
64 Jeremy Black, *What If? Counterfactualism and the Problem of History* (Social Affairs Unit, 1998) 8.
65 Philip E Tetlock, Richard N Lebow and Geoffrey Parker, 'Preface: Unmaking the Middle Kingdom' in Philip E Tetlock, Richard N Lebow and Geoffrey Parker (eds) *Unmaking the West: 'What-If' Scenarios That Rewrite World History* (University of Michigan Press, 2006) 1, 9.

However, the reason for Evans' statement that counterfactualism tends to be associated with the Right points to a deeper characteristic of counterfactual history: the way in which it serves as a critique of determinism; that is, 'the belief that events are, of can be, caused by forces external to human will'.[66] Counterfactual history rejects the idea that the narrative thrust of history should be largely fixed as a story of improvement, of 'evolution towards perfection'.[67] This means, as Andrew Roberts put it, 'this line of thought infuriates the Whigs, Marxists and Determinists and anyone who believes that some kind of preordained Destiny or Fate or Providence determines human existence'.[68] The reason why counterfactual history has been associated with the Right is therefore due to the historical context in which such work has taken place. As Evans pointed out, 'the principal target of the counterfactualists was clearly Marxism, or what they imagined to be Marxism'.[69] Yet, these political traditions do not have a monopoly on determinism. Rather, determinism understood in the sense that outcomes are largely fixed is also subscribed to by those who see social systems such as law as being autonomous. A deterministic position is adopted by those for whom evolutionary functionalism is the norm. As the previous chapters have argued, such dependence is common within Law Schools generally.

Proponents of counterfactual history invariably view it as a remedy to determinism.[70] As Tetlock and Parker noted, 'the best antidote to excessively deterministic thinking is granting greater academic license to explore counterfactual possibilities'.[71] Although there is some debate as to the meaning of determinism in this context,[72] Simon T Kaye has argued that counterfactual

66 Richard J Evans, *Altered Pasts: Counterfactuals in History* (Abacus, 2016) 57.

67 Niall Ferguson 'Introduction – Virtual History: Towards a "Chaotic" Theory of the Past' in Niall Ferguson (ed) *Virtual History: Alternatives and Counterfactuals* (Papermac, 1998) 1, 43.

68 Andrew Roberts, 'Introduction' in Andrew Roberts (ed) *What Might Have Been* (Phoenix, 2004) 1, 2.

69 Richard J Evans, *Altered Pasts: Counterfactuals in History* (Abacus, 2016) 52.

70 Simon T Kaye, 'Challenging Certainty: The Utility and History of Counter factualism' (2010) 49 *History and Theory* 38, 49–50. Kaye cites the example of Winston Churchill's 'If Lee Had Not Won the Battle of Gettysburg', originally published in J C Squire, *If it had Happened Otherwise* (Longmans, 1931), but later included as part of what Kaye dubs 'Churchill's history-as-progress canon' (his *History of the English Speaking Peoples* series). Churchill's essay is written about the absurdity of our history from the perspective of someone within a world where Lee had swept aside the Union armies in 1863 and shortly thereafter won the American Civil War.

71 Philip E Tetlock and Geoffrey Parker, 'Counterfactual History: Its Advocates Its Critics & Its Uses' in Philip E Tetlock, Richard N Lebow and Geoffrey Parker (eds) *Unmaking the West: 'What-If' Scenarios That Rewrite World History* (University of Michigan Press, 2006) 363, 366.

72 Richard J Evans suggested that the use of the term by Niall Ferguson contested four main ideas: first, 'teleology, the writing of history in terms of how it moved toward a given end'; second, the claim that 'political events are determined by social and economic forces'; third, the idea that history is determined by general laws of development; and fourth, that the way history is written – as tragic or as comic, for example, 'presumes a specific outcome by virtue of historic style rather than historic content'. However, Evans doubted whether counterfactual work can overcome all of these problems. He argued that a 'counterfactual might be used to cast doubt on a teleology at some point along its trajectory but cannot undermine it as a whole'. He was

thought experiments if utilised correctly could undermine, avoid and solve three problematical historical assumptions.[73] The first is the 'assumption of indispensability' that 'the real world, as it exists, is both "inevitable" and "the best of all possible worlds"' which takes 'an overly simplistic understanding of human progress'.[74] The second is the 'assumption of causality' in that 'by removing elements, factor by factor, in a series of educated thought experiments, historians can begin to test a causal hypothesis quasi-scientifically'.[75] The third, and for Kaye probably the most important, is the 'assumption of inevitability' whereby 'events that were very much in doubt in their own time may be presented by a historian as being ultimately inevitable'. This means that 'the understanding of the preceding period is often coloured by the assumption and awareness of what was to come next'. As Kaye put it, 'Counterfactualism is a useful process for historians as a thought experiment because it offers grounds to challenge an unfortunate contemporary historical mindset of assumed, deterministic certainty'.[76]

Counterfactual history can therefore be regarded as the antidote to what Tetlock and Parker call 'retrospective determinism'.[77] They warned:

> of the dangers of hindsight bias: the powerful tendency of human beings to start forgetting, as soon as we learn what happened, how unpredictable the world looked beforehand and to dedicate ourselves to forging chains of reasons that make what happened appear to be the inevitable outcome of prior causes.

Counterfactual history, then, can be understood as a 'shattering hindsight complacency', highlighting 'how uncertain everything seemed before everyone became contaminated by outcome knowledge'. Writing with Lebow, they regarded the primary value of counterfactual thinking as an exercise in humility, appreciating that 'the world we inhabit is but one of a vast array of possible worlds that

---

critical of the way in which Fergusson uses the label of determinism to provide an attack 'not only on any notion of wider forces and deeper currents in history, but on any concept of causation at all' and concluded that counterfactuals 'do not do the job of undermining determinism in any of its possible meaning as well as simple factual evidence does': Richard J Evans, *Altered Pasts: Counterfactuals in History* (Abacus, 2016) 57–58, 62, 63, 58, 65, 66.

73 He noted that these 'may be solved or avoided by use of other than counterfactual methods, but alternative histories are an efficient and instructive way of doing so (perhaps *the* most efficient and instructive of such methods)': Simon T Kaye, 'Challenging Certainty: The Utility and History of Counter factualism' (2010) 49 *History and Theory* 38, 40.

74 For Kaye, 'This is distinct from the assumption of indispensability (above) in that it does not necessarily imply an assumed hierarchy between perceived causal links among events': ibid 40–41.

75 Ibid 41.

76 Ibid 38.

77 Philip E Tetlock and Geoffrey Parker, 'Counterfactual Thought Experiments: Why We Can't Live without Them & How We Must Learn to Live with Them' in Philip E Tetlock, Richard N Lebow and Geoffrey Parker (eds) *Unmaking the West: 'What-If' Scenarios that Rewrite World History* (University of Michigan Press, 2006) 14, 17.

might have been'.[78] It offers questions and possible answers rather than giving 'the answer'.[79] As Kaye puts it:

> Counterfactualism is a powerful corrective tool that undoes the tendency of "History" to hide the fact of plausible alternative outcomes and the reflexive importance of uncertainty in human affairs as they occur. Counterfactualism is the handmaiden of agency and its crucial role in human life.[80]

This can be linked to the concept of entropic complexity, as discussed in the previous chapter. By underscoring contingency and agency, counterfactualism underlines that order and progress are not the default. Counterfactual history is potentially of value as a thought experiment that provides a methodology to challenge evolutionary functionalism. As Tetlock, Lebow and Parker noted, such experiments provide an 'indispensable tool for drawing thoughtful lessons from the past, above all giving us a nuanced sense of the degree of inevitability in what occurred'.[81] It therefore has the potential to be part of the Subversive Legal History toolkit, especially since it is a method that is underappreciated in history (and, as we will see, in law) and which then may disturb the orthodox perspective. However, as with any experiment or method, counterfactual history needs to be undertaken in a rigorous way. As John Lewis Gaddis noted, 'the use of counterfactuals in history has got to be highly disciplined':[82]

> Counterfactual reasoning does have to proceed, to be sure, by certain rules. You wouldn't, in a chemistry laboratory, attempt to identify a critical compound by throwing in everything available – eye of newt, say, or toe of frog – into a giant bubbling cauldron to see what happens. You'd instead change only a single variable at a time while keeping the others constant. It's much the same with counterfactual history.[83]

Tetlock and Parker pointed out that: 'If counterfactual probing of the past can be done rigorously we could evaluate the contingency of the developments that led up to today's world and thus understand more fully why events unfolded as

78 Philip E Tetlock, Richard N Lebow and Geoffrey Parker, 'Preface: Unmaking the Middle Kingdom' in Philip E Tetlock, Richard N Lebow and Geoffrey Parker (eds) *Unmaking the West: 'What-If' Scenarios That Rewrite World History* (University of Michigan Press, 2006) 1, 3.

79 Jeremy Black, *What If? Counterfactualism and the Problem of History* (Social Affairs Unit, 1998) 14.

80 Simon T Kaye, 'Challenging Certainty: The Utility and History of Counter factualism' (2010) 49 *History and Theory* 38, 57.

81 Philip E Tetlock, Richard N Lebow and Geoffrey Parker, 'Preface: Unmaking the Middle Kingdom' in Philip E Tetlock, Richard N Lebow and Geoffrey Parker (eds) *Unmaking the West: 'What-If' Scenarios That Rewrite World History* (University of Michigan Press, 2006) 1, 4.

82 John Lewis Gaddis, *The Landscape of History* (Oxford University Press, 2002) 102.

83 Ibid 101.

they did'.[84] The next section of this chapter will explore that 'if'. Drawing upon the literature on counterfactual history, and in particular the methodological discussion which often comes in the introduction to edited collections on the topic, it will distil the main rules of how counterfactual-historical analysis should operate if it is to be rigorous enough for academic purposes.

The Eight Rules of Counterfactual History

A variety of different labels have been used to distinguish good counterfactual history, which can be the basis of academic analysis, from bad counterfactual history, which is the basis of science fiction.

Allan Megill distinguished between 'restrained' counterfactual history which 'involves an explicit canvassing of alternative possibilities that existed in the real past' and 'exuberant' counterfactual history 'which deals in past historical outcomes that never in fact came to be' and where 'counterfactual history diverges radically from normal historical research and writing'.[85] While exuberant counterfactual historians move further into the imaginary, restrained counterfactualists 'are pinned down by what actually did happen in the end' in that 'in imagining how things might have been different, the restrained counterfactualist moves from known effect to hypothesized cause'.[86] Catherine Gallagher made a similar distinction but for her such exuberant work is not counterfactual history at all but is alternative history.[87] For Gallagher, counterfactual histories explore 'sudden, unexpected changes in the status quo' but tend to 'indicate the multiple possibilities that went unrealized rather than to trace out single historical alternative trajectories in detail'. This can be contrasted with alternate histories, 'that describe one continuous sequence of departures from the historical record, thereby inventing a long counterfactual narrative with a correspondingly divergent fictional world, while drawing the dramatis personae exclusively from the actual historical record'. Richard J Evans made a similar distinction:

> Counterfactual history foregrounds the effects of a single change in an existing causal chain, leading to a whole series of consequent changes in the course of history. Alternative history simply poses a world parallel to our own without enquiring too closely into how it came into being. Investigative medical or journalistic alternate history focuses on establishing that one single fact in history changed, devoting hundreds of pages of "proving" that

84 Philip E Tetlock, Richard N Lebow and Geoffrey Parker, 'Preface: Unmaking the Middle Kingdom' in Philip E Tetlock, Richard N Lebow and Geoffrey Parker (eds) *Unmaking the West: 'What-If' Scenarios That Rewrite World History* (University of Michigan Press, 2006) 1, 2.

85 Allan Megill, *Historical Knowledge, Historical Error: A Contemporary Guide to Practice* (University of Chicago Press, 2007) 151.

86 Ibid 153.

87 Catherine Gallagher, *Telling It Like It Wasn't: The Counterfactual Imagination in History and Fiction* (University of Chicago Press. 2018) 3.

> Hitler survived in Argentina after the war..., but is not really interested in suggesting what difference these discoveries make to the course of history in a wider sense.[88]

This is similar to Jon Elster's distinction between 'ontological' counterfactuals, which are about alternative worlds, and 'meta-linguistic' counterfactuals, which focus on the causal ramifications of specific changes'.[89] As Simon T Kaye noted, only works that 'accommodate an emphasis on the causal relationships among the events that led to a specific point of divergence from the actual course of history should be considered as a subset of academic history, rather than a branch of science fiction'.[90] The diversity of labels used by these authors masks a common distinction: what these authors are invariably distinguishing is their perception of good counterfactual history from their perception of bad counterfactual history. These different authors, and others who have examined or practised counterfactual history, all have different ideas of what makes counterfactual history good or bad; where the line is drawn between academic history and science fiction. The following will explore how counterfactual history has policed this border by drawing upon the approach of editors of four influential edited volumes. It will explore the rules and standards of counterfactual history as laid out by Daniel Snowman in 1979,[91] Niall Ferguson in 1998,[92] Andrew Roberts in 2004[93] and Philip E Tetlock, Richard N Lebow and Geoffrey Parker in 2006.[94] Given that each editor takes a different approach and deals with different aspects of and objections to counterfactual history, the four volumes will be looked at in turn. Following this, eight rules of counterfactual history will be expounded.

Snowman's volume and approach is important because it set a standard for counterfactual histories. In his introduction, he stated that 'the "ifs" of this book occur within a framework carefully circumscribed by historical facts'.[95] He set out to achieve this by asking his contributors to 'concentrate upon a genuine moment in the past and upon the decision-making that took place at the time: speculation about what might or might not have happened subsequently was to be only a secondary consideration'. Moreover, the contributors were asked:

> to evoke a strictly authentically historical setting and to recreate as accurately as possible the situation facing the personality around whom their essay revolved. There was to be no *deus ex machina*, no invented assassination,

88 Richard J Evans, *Altered Pasts: Counterfactuals in History* (Abacus, 2016) 128.

89 Jon Elster, *Logic and Society: Contradictions and Possible Worlds* (Wiley & Sons, 1978) 181.

90 Simon T Kaye, 'Challenging Certainty: The Utility and History of Counter factualism' (2010) 49 *History and Theory* 38, 43.

91 Daniel Snowman (ed) *If I Had Been ... Ten Historical Fantasies* (Harper Collins, 1979).

92 Niall Ferguson (ed) *Virtual History: Alternatives and Counterfactuals* (Papermac, 1998).

93 Andrew Roberts (ed) *What Might Have Been* (Phoenix, 2004).

94 Philip E Tetlock, Richard N Lebow and Geoffrey Parker (eds) *Unmaking the West: 'What-If' Scenarios That Rewrite World History* (University of Michigan Press, 2006).

95 Daniel Snowman (ed) *If I Had Been ... Ten Historical Fantasies* (Harper Collins, 1979) 2.

> no melodramatic intervention of the fates to give artificial wings to the imagination.

Snowman was adamant that all that would be 'changed is that the central character of each piece is deemed to have decided upon a slightly different, but entirely plausible course of action from that actually adopted'. Richard J Evans has noted that this procedure 'introduced major constraining factors here, which limited the degree of speculation in an effective way' and that this gave Snowman's 'collection a unity found in few others'.[96] It underscored that significant care needs to be taken with the choice of the counterfactual variable. As Catherine Gallagher noted, counterfactual histories must be 'hinged onto the actual historical record, usually at a juncture that is widely recognized to have been both crucial and underdetermined'.[97]

However, Evans also noted that 'by choosing "great men" (and they are indeed all men)' Snowman had:

> given credence to the discredited idea that history is made by great men and little or nothing else, where most historians would point to the role of more impersonal factors in addition or even in place of the impact of the individual.[98]

Evans pointed out that such a focus is flawed in that:

> no historian, asked how he would have behaved had he been in the shoes of a major historical person, is going to say that he would not have been able to match up to that person's acumen, brilliance of boldness. The whole point of the exercise is that he is going to do better; he is going to avoid the mistakes of his avatar and succeed where his avatar failed.[99]

Moreover, this approach stressing how individuals can change the course of history is problematic.[100] This approach has been popularised by science fiction such as *Back to the Future* and is common in popular counterfactuals.[101]

96 Richard J Evans, *Altered Pasts: Counterfactuals in History* (Abacus, 2016) 28.
97 Catherine Gallagher, *Telling It Like It Wasn't: The Counterfactual Imagination in History and Fiction* (University of Chicago Press. 2018) 2.
98 Richard J Evans, *Altered Pasts: Counterfactuals in History* (Abacus, 2016) 28.
99 Ibid 29.
100 See Richard J Evans, *Altered Pasts: Counterfactuals in History* (Abacus, 2016) 173 for the criticism that counterfactuals 'frequently tackle historical topics of enormous complexity ... by simply asserting the power of the individual actor to change things'.
101 Simon T Kaye, 'Challenging Certainty: The Utility and History of Counter factualism' (2010) 49 *History and Theory* 38, 47. Kaye states that this science fiction trope was first recorded in the French author Rene Barjavel's 1943 book *Le Voyageur Imprudent*, which featured an unwary time-traveller who, while exploring the past, unwittingly alters some tiny factor, perhaps squashing an insect, and then returns to his own period only to find that everything has altered

As Simon T Kaye noted, 'the concept of plastic, malleable history is now the generally accepted fictional paradigm'.[102] Yet, this is controversial in academic history. As Kaye noted, 'we cannot assume that an arrow launched seconds later in a battle is any more or less important than a person sitting down to his breakfast an hour earlier than usual'.[103] He asserted that 'this mentality is responsible for some of the most unreasonable and unrealistic counterfactual explorations of all'. However, some of this criticism of Snowman seems misguided. It is correct that Snowman's focus on 'great figures' is more appropriate for entertainment rather than historical purposes.[104] However, as noted in the previous chapter, the idea that significant effects can arise from trivial causes is a key part of chaos theory.

Niall Ferguson's edited collection is perhaps the most widely cited work on counterfactual history, which he refers to as 'virtual history'.[105] Ferguson's approach continued to place emphasis upon the choice of counterfactual variable. His introduction stated that the crucial matter is 'the form the counterfactual question takes'.[106] He gave Patrick Gardiner's example of the counterfactual question, 'were shots on the boulevards the cause of the 1848 Revolution in France?' Gardiner asked:

> Does this mean: "Would the Revolution have broken out at the precise time at which it did break out had they not occurred?" or does it mean: "Would the Revolution have broken out sooner or later even if there had been no shots?" And if, after receiving an affirmative answer to the latter question, we ask: "What then was the real cause of the Revolution?" further specification is again required.[107]

For Ferguson, the limitless number of different alternate questions that can be considered is one of the strongest arguments against counterfactual history and means that there is a 'need for plausibility in the formulation of counterfactual

irrevocably: ibid 52–53. This idea is now most commonly associated with the *Back to the Future* series of films (1985, 1989 and 1990). This interpretation of time travel is not always followed in popular culture, however. It was distinguished and critiqued in the Marvel superhero film *Avengers Endgame* (2019) where it was suggested that in time travel you do not change the future if you visit your past since that past becomes your future in your own individual timeline.

102 Simon T Kaye, 'Challenging Certainty: The Utility and History of Counter factualism' (2010) 49 *History and Theory* 38, 47.

103 Ibid 52–53.

104 As shown in the 'celebrity historical' episodes in time travel programmes such as *Doctor Who*.

105 Niall Ferguson (ed) *Virtual History: Alternatives and Counterfactuals* (Papermac, 1998). Although counterfactualism is used in his other works, most controversially in Niall Ferguson, *The Pity of War* (New ed, Penguin, 2009).

106 Niall Ferguson 'Introduction – Virtual History: Towards a "Chaotic" Theory of the Past' in Niall Ferguson (ed) *Virtual History: Alternatives and Counterfactuals* (Papermac, 1998) 1, 82.

107 Patrick Gardiner, *The Nature of Historical Explanation* (Oxford University Press, 1952) 107.

questions'.[108] This means that the 'distinction between what did happen and what could plausibly have happened is of critical importance'.[109] For Ferguson, the counterfactual historian is only 'concerned with possibilities which seemed probable in the past'. At any given point in history there are always alternatives and an historian can only explain what happened and why 'if we live for a moment, as the men of the time lived, in [the past's] still fluid context and among its still unresolved problems'.[110] Ferguson insisted that the only counterfactual variables that should be considered are 'those alternatives which we can show on the basis of contemporary evidence that contemporaries actually considered'.[111] For Ferguson, 'by replacing the enigma of chance with the calculation of probabilities – we solve the dilemma of choosing between a single deterministic past and an unmanageably infinite number of possible pasts'.[112] He called this approach 'virtual history' since the counterfactual scenarios constructed 'are not mere fantasy: they are simulations based on calculations about the relative probability of plausible outcomes in a chaotic world'. Ferguson regarded this as providing 'the manifesto for a new 'chaosty' – a chaotic approach to history', though he considered that 'in many ways they simply make explicit what many historians have been doing for years in the privacy of their own imaginations'.[113] In other words, it recognises the implicit counterfactual history that all historians employ when examining causation.

As Richard J Evans has noted, Ferguson's focus on 'possible alternatives that contemporaries actually considered and wrote about (for if they did not write about them there is no evidence that they considered them)... seems a perfectly reasonable way of proceeding' but closer thought highlights a number of short-comings.[114] Ferguson is correct to say that the counterfactual variable needs to be a position that could have been taken and as Evans noted, 'by carefully scrutinising the positions confronting decision-makers... we can come to understand better the decisions they actually took'. However, Ferguson's concession that the number of possibilities is finite seems to go against chaos theory. As Evans pointed out, it rules out 'factors such as impulsive behaviours, human

108 Niall Ferguson 'Introduction – Virtual History: Towards a "Chaotic" Theory of the Past' in Niall Ferguson (ed) *Virtual History: Alternatives and Counterfactuals* (Papermac, 1998) 1, 83.
109 Ibid 84.
110 Hugh Trevor-Roper, *History and Imagination* (Gerald Duckworth and Co, 1981) 363.
111 Niall Ferguson 'Introduction – Virtual History: Towards a "Chaotic" Theory of the Past' in Niall Ferguson (ed) *Virtual History: Alternatives and Counterfactuals* (Papermac, 1998) 1, 86. For Ferguson, this mandates the use of counterfactual history on the basis that 'if all history is the history of (recorded) thought, surely we must attach equal significance to *all* the outcomes thought about. The historian who allows his knowledge as to which of these outcomes subsequently happened to obliterate the other outcomes people regarded as possible cannot hope to recapture the past "as it actually was": ibid 86–87.
112 Ibid 85.
113 Ibid 89.
114 Richard J Evans, *Altered Pasts: Counterfactuals in History* (Abacus, 2016) 67.

accident, unanticipated errors and the like'. Ironically, it means that Ferguson's approach is itself deterministic.

Moreover, while Ferguson's inherent conservatism is too constraining, his subsequent construction of a virtual reality suffers from being too bold. As Alan Megill put it, 'virtual history starts out from a moment in the real past where things might have worked out differently, and then moves forward in time, getting even further from a world that existed'.[115] Evans pointed out that by 'positing long term consequences from changing a single event' then 'far from liberating history from an imaginary straightjacket of Marxist determinism' virtual history confines it in a 'far more constricting' way:

> This is because the counterfactual proposes an alternative future... then assumes or posits a whole series of other events that would have inevitably happened. ... But of course a thousand other things might, or would, have intervened to make this alternative course of events in practice completely unpredictable.[116]

This means that, for Megill, Ferguson's kind of counterfactual history falls outside the academic discipline of history.[117] He noted that virtual history is therefore an appropriate label for what Ferguson sets out to achieve since it is not grounded but evokes 'virtual reality' and 'the world of historically based game-playing. ... It is a game, dressed up with certain features of a real past'.[118]

The next counterfactual book to be examined, Andrew Roberts' popular book,[119] is much lighter on the theory of counterfactuals but is actually more restrained than Ferguson. Roberts stated that 'the rule is to keep it short'.[120] The fact that he went on to say that 'the genre lends itself naturally to the essay rather than to the book', correct as that assertion is, does suggest that he might have been referring to the length of the counterfactual piece rather than the time period after the counterfactual change that is to be explored. Roberts did, however, stress that what if 'history-writing should be to keep it as believable as possible'.[121] As he put it, 'we can untune one string, but not the whole violin'.

115 Allan Megill, *Historical Knowledge, Historical Error: A Contemporary Guide to Practice* (University of Chicago Press, 2007) 152–153.

116 Richard J Evans, *Altered Pasts: Counterfactuals in History* (Abacus, 2016) 81–82.

117 Allan Megill, *Historical Knowledge, Historical Error: A Contemporary Guide to Practice* (University of Chicago Press, 2007) 151.

118 Megill went as far as to assert that: 'When professional historians write virtual history, we ought to treat their claims concerning "what might have been" with the same distanced scepticism with which we would treat the playing out of World War II by a group of fifteen year olds' (ibid 152).

119 Andrew Roberts (ed) *What Might Have Been* (Phoenix, 2004).

120 Andrew Roberts, 'Introduction' in Andrew Roberts (ed) *What Might Have Been* (Phoenix, 2004) 1, 8.

121 Ibid 7.

He also cautioned that sometimes changing a variable will not necessarily change the end result. He wrote of the 'counter-counterfactual, whereby the most likely alternative outcome is much the same as the one that actually took place'. He gives the example that:

> we can speculate what might have happened if Hitler's parents had never met, but must be prepared for the possibility that someone almost equally cynical and fanatical would have become Chancellor of Germany in the early 1930s, there being no shortage of ambitious fascist politicians around at the time.

The most sophisticated account of the rules of counterfactual history can be found, however, in the volume edited by Philip E Tetlock, Richard N Lebow and Geoffrey Parker.[122] Their objective was to 'demonstrate the utility – indeed, the necessity – of using properly constructed counterfactual tools to study history'.[123] In their view, counterfactual history is needed to balance factual history.[124] They pointed out that 'history looks different when our initial question is factual (why did *x* occur?) as opposed to "counterfactual" (why did alternatives to *x* fail to occur?)'[125] and that both of these questions need answering: 'it is essential to balance any inquiry which begins with the factual query "why did the observed outcome occur?" with the complementary counterfactual query "why did the many possible alternatives to the observed outcome fail to occur?"'.[126] They also argued that the 'quality control' needed for counterfactual history is not dissimilar to that required for factual history.[127] Importantly, Tetlock,

122 Philip E Tetlock, Richard N Lebow and Geoffrey Parker (eds) *Unmaking the West: 'What-If' Scenarios That Rewrite World History* (University of Michigan Press, 2006).

123 Philip E Tetlock, Richard N Lebow and Geoffrey Parker, 'Preface: Unmaking the Middle Kingdom' in Philip E Tetlock, Richard N Lebow and Geoffrey Parker (eds) *Unmaking the West: 'What-If' Scenarios That Rewrite World History* (University of Michigan Press, 2006) 1, 11.

124 As Tetlock and Parker put it in one of their methodological chapters in the collection, 'a balanced appraisal of history requires striking what philosophers call a "reflective equilibrium" between factual and counterfactual methods of framing our questions about what had to be and what could have been': Philip E Tetlock and Geoffrey Parker, 'Counterfactual Thought Experiments: Why We Can't Live without Them & How We Must Learn to Live with Them' in Philip E Tetlock, Richard N Lebow and Geoffrey Parker (eds) *Unmaking the West: 'What-If' Scenarios that Rewrite World History* (University of Michigan Press, 2006) 14, 17.

125 Philip E Tetlock, Richard N Lebow and Geoffrey Parker, 'Preface: Unmaking the Middle Kingdom' in Philip E Tetlock, Richard N Lebow and Geoffrey Parker (eds) *Unmaking the West: 'What-If' Scenarios That Rewrite World History* (University of Michigan Press, 2006) 1, 5.

126 Philip E Tetlock and Geoffrey Parker, 'Counterfactual Thought Experiments: Why We Can't Live without Them & How We Must Learn to Live with Them' in Philip E Tetlock, Richard N Lebow and Geoffrey Parker (eds) *Unmaking the West: 'What-If' Scenarios That Rewrite World History* (University of Michigan Press, 2006) 14, 17–18.

127 As they note, 'such experiments must be conducted in a careful manner, must make rigorous use of evidence in support of their claims, and must not differ in fundamental ways from so-called factual history': Philip E Tetlock, Richard N Lebow and Geoffrey Parker, 'Preface: Unmaking the Middle Kingdom' in Philip E Tetlock, Richard N Lebow and Geoffrey Parker (eds) *Unmaking the West: 'What-If' Scenarios That Rewrite World History* (University of Michigan Press, 2006) 1, 9.

Lebow and Parker also argued that counterfactual analysis can be applied just as much to macro-history as micro-history.[128] For them, counterfactual history is a means of problematising complacency:

> We see enormous intellectual value – perhaps, indeed, the greatest service counterfactual historians can render – in unearthing the labyrinthine logical complexity of "what-if" assumptions underpinning the often all too confident claims about why the West, and not one of the rest, rose to global hegemony. We all need to be reminded that the greater the number of probabilistic "if-then" linkages in our arguments the more the sources of uncertainty add up and so the more vulnerable our conclusions become.[129]

Tetlock, Lebow and Parker insisted upon 'three exacting quality-control questions' which were designed to neutralise the 'three principal objections advanced by critics who feel that counterfactual history is beyond methodological redemption'.[130] The first criticism is that counterfactual history is 'hopelessly arbitrary... because it offers no principles for winnowing out which of the infinity of possible what-ifs warrant our attention'. To answer this charge, Tetlock and Parker suggested focusing on the question of 'what criteria –aside from hindsight – can scholars use in choosing which events, forces or agents to place in the narrative foreground and which to relegate to the background'.[131] They asked contributors: 'How they chose the antecedents for their thought experiments (those things that, if different, might have put us – at least temporarily – on a different historical path)'.[132] They asked them 'to be explicit about how they selected, from the vast universe of possibilities, the pivotal junctures at which they believe history could have been redirected'.[133] This involved respecting the 'minimal-rewrite rule',[134] which favours counterfactuals that require little tampering with

128 Compare: 'Micro-history can be regarded as not lending itself to counterfactualism because causation is largely dropped in favour of small-scale reconstruction': Jeremy Black, *What If? Counterfactualism and the Problem of History* (Social Affairs Unit, 1998) 45.

129 Philip E Tetlock, Richard N Lebow and Geoffrey Parker, 'Preface: Unmaking the Middle Kingdom' in Philip E Tetlock, Richard N Lebow and Geoffrey Parker (eds) *Unmaking the West: 'What-If' Scenarios That Rewrite World History* (University of Michigan Press, 2006) 1, 9.

130 Ibid; Philip E Tetlock and Geoffrey Parker, 'Counterfactual Thought Experiments: Why We Can't Live without Them & How We Must Learn to Live with Them' in Philip E Tetlock, Richard N Lebow and Geoffrey Parker (eds) *Unmaking the West: 'What-If' Scenarios That Rewrite World History* (University of Michigan Press, 2006) 14, 16.

131 Ibid 30.

132 Philip E Tetlock and Geoffrey Parker, 'Counterfactual History: Its Advocates Its Critics & Its Uses' in Philip E Tetlock, Richard N Lebow and Geoffrey Parker (eds) *Unmaking the West: 'What-If' Scenarios That Rewrite World History* (University of Michigan Press, 2006) 363, 368.

133 Philip E Tetlock and Geoffrey Parker, 'Counterfactual Thought Experiments: Why We Can't Live without Them & How We Must Learn to Live with Them' in Philip E Tetlock, Richard N Lebow and Geoffrey Parker (eds) *Unmaking the West: 'What-If' Scenarios That Rewrite World History* (University of Michigan Press, 2006) 14, 33–34.

134 The term was coined in Phillip Tetlock and Aaron Belkin (eds) *Counterfactual Thought Experiments in World Politics* (Princeton University Press, 1996) 21.

the actual historical record.[135] Under this approach, only 'tiny changes that might have forestalled these developments or led to different outcomes at key turning points' are examined'.[136] Contributors were asked to ensure that they 'launched their inquiries from plausible premises that require tweaking as little of the actual historical record as possible'.[137]

The second criticism addressed by Tetlock, Lebow and Parker is that counterfactuals are 'hopelessly speculative...because it gives us no way of determining who was right'.[138] Tetlock and Parker stated that this raised the question of 'what criteria can scholars use to winnow out such frivolous scenarios and to stop speculation from running riot'?[139] They asked contributors: 'How they forged the connecting principles between their antecedents' starting points and the projected consequences of those starting points'.[140] They were instructed 'to be explicit about the connecting principles they used to draw conclusions about what would have happened if their hypothesized antecedents had taken other forms'.[141] They noted that:

> Most contributions adopted three criteria for justifying the connecting principles in their counterfactual scenarios: consistency with well-established historical facts and regularities, consistency with well-established statistical generalizations that transcend what is true at that particular time and place and consistency with well-established theoretical laws of cause and effect.

This runs the risk, however, of being too conservative and of reintroducing assumptions imbued with evolutionary functionalism. It also raises the issue of where a counterfactual alteration is made, then 'how strong a case can be made as to the directions that subsequent events would have taken' and 'how far "down the road" is it prudent to try to project what would have happened'.[142]

135 Philip E Tetlock, Richard N Lebow and Geoffrey Parker, 'Preface: Unmaking the Middle Kingdom' in Philip E Tetlock, Richard N Lebow and Geoffrey Parker (eds) *Unmaking the West: 'What-If' Scenarios That Rewrite World History* (University of Michigan Press, 2006) 1, 9–10.

136 Ibid, 2.

137 Philip E Tetlock and Geoffrey Parker, 'Counterfactual Thought Experiments: Why We Can't Live without Them & How We Must Learn to Live with Them' in Philip E Tetlock, Richard N Lebow and Geoffrey Parker (eds) *Unmaking the West: 'What-If' Scenarios That Rewrite World History* (University of Michigan Press, 2006) 14, 34.

138 Ibid 16.

139 Ibid 31.

140 Philip E Tetlock and Geoffrey Parker, 'Counterfactual History: Its Advocates Its Critics & Its Uses' in Philip E Tetlock, Richard N Lebow and Geoffrey Parker (eds) *Unmaking the West: 'What-If' Scenarios That Rewrite World History* (University of Michigan Press, 2006) 363, 368.

141 Philip E Tetlock and Geoffrey Parker, 'Counterfactual Thought Experiments: Why We Can't Live without Them & How We Must Learn to Live with Them' in Philip E Tetlock, Richard N Lebow and Geoffrey Parker (eds) *Unmaking the West: 'What-If' Scenarios That Rewrite World History* (University of Michigan Press, 2006) 14, 34.

142 Philip E Tetlock, Richard N Lebow and Geoffrey Parker, 'Preface: Unmaking the Middle Kingdom' in Philip E Tetlock, Richard N Lebow and Geoffrey Parker (eds) *Unmaking the West: 'What-If' Scenarios That Rewrite World History* (University of Michigan Press, 2006) 1, 10.

Other commentators have addressed this by ruling out long-range counterfactual histories because, in the words of Richard J Evans, 'they elide too many links in the proposed causative chain after the initial altered event'.[143] Tetlock and Parker agreed that 'as scenarios grow increasingly elaborate the connecting principles linking antecedent and consequences become increasingly vulnerable to challenge' and that the 'deeper authors try to see into the futures of their counterfactual worlds the frailer their connecting principles become'.[144] However, they see this as being necessary because it would be ludicrous for historians to 'suppose that, once they enter their hypothetical world and make their first change (even if it is a minimal rewrite) everything else will remain the same as actual history'.[145] Rather, even the most minimal of rewrites will create a different world.[146] Implicitly reflecting chaos theory, they noted that history 'is a path-dependent system with positive feedback. It resembles a vortex in which what has already happened quickly accentuates the probability of certain events and reduces that of others, making escape from the new path difficult'.[147]

The third criticism of counterfactual history addressed by Tetlock, Lebow and Parker is that it is 'hopelessly self-serving... because, in the absence of reality checks, it leaves us free to invent whatever what-if scenarios we wish to prop up

143 He argued that the longer away a counterfactual analysis 'gets from the starting point the less useful it becomes, and the more it enters the worlds of alternative reality to which increasing numbers of people are turning in search of spaces for their imagination to roam free, unfettered by facts': Richard J Evans, *Altered Pasts: Counterfactuals in History* (Abacus, 2016) 175. See also Jeremy Black, *What If? Counterfactualism and the Problem of History* (Social Affairs Unit, 1998) 135–136.

144 Philip E Tetlock and Geoffrey Parker, 'Counterfactual Thought Experiments: Why We Can't Live without Them & How We Must Learn to Live with Them' in Philip E Tetlock, Richard N Lebow and Geoffrey Parker (eds) *Unmaking the West: 'What-If' Scenarios That Rewrite World History* (University of Michigan Press, 2006) 14, 34, 35

145 Philip E Tetlock and Geoffrey Parker, 'Counterfactual History: Its Advocates Its Critics & Its Uses' in Philip E Tetlock, Richard N Lebow and Geoffrey Parker (eds) *Unmaking the West: 'What-If' Scenarios That Rewrite World History* (University of Michigan Press, 2006) 363, 371.

146 This follows the 'Many Worlds' interpretation of quantum physics, pioneered by Hugh Everett which suggests that 'every possibility or outcome in history that does not take place in our world does in fact take place in a separate reality or universe. Points of divergence generate these new realities constantly and infinitely, as ever rippling outcomes even on the molecular level are each played out in their entirety in another part of a "multiverse"': Simon T Kaye, 'Challenging Certainty: The Utility and History of Counter factualism' (2010) 49 *History and Theory* 38, 53.

147 Philip E Tetlock and Geoffrey Parker, 'Counterfactual History: Its Advocates Its Critics & Its Uses' in Philip E Tetlock, Richard N Lebow and Geoffrey Parker (eds) *Unmaking the West: 'What-If' Scenarios That Rewrite World History* (University of Michigan Press, 2006) 363, 372. Indeed, 'once things start moving in any particular direction, they pick up momentum, increasing the odds of further movement in the same direction and rapidly transforming the improbable into the inevitable': Philip E Tetlock and Geoffrey Parker, 'Counterfactual Thought Experiments: Why We Can't Live without Them & How We Must Learn to Live with Them' in Philip E Tetlock, Richard N Lebow and Geoffrey Parker (eds) *Unmaking the West: 'What-If' Scenarios That Rewrite World History* (University of Michigan Press, 2006) 14, 20.

our prejudices'.[148] For Tetlock, Lebow and Parker, the answer to this was to require the contributors to self-reflect upon the exercise and to 'identify ways in which the exercise either undermines or reinforces the particular interpretations of history one held at the outset?'[149] They instructed them:

> to be explicit about the distinctive benefits of framing historical questions in counterfactual forms, about which schools of thought are most likely to take umbrage at the conclusions they reached, about what surprised them in working through their thought experiments.[150]

However, Tetlock and Parker noted that 'surprising oneself – self-subversion– is a high standard, implying a reversal of an author's prior opinion' and so 'we should not expect to observe it often'.[151] The test is not so much what goes on in the mind of the author but rather whether their counterfactual analysis serves to 'sensitize us, the readers, to aspect of reality that we otherwise would have overlooked'. Tetlock and Parker regarded this third criticism as 'the toughest of all the objections to counterfactual history'.[152] Yet, as with the other two criticisms, they noted that although 'there are many examples of past counterfactual studies to which each indictment fairly applies; such 'indictments do not address flaws in the enterprise but rather the flaws inherent in any carelessly executed historical endeavour'.[153]

Although as Tetlock and Parker noted, their three quality control questions do not 'provide the final word on how to do counterfactual history – clearing up all possible reservations that reasonable people might have toward this form of scholarship',[154] they do present a major step forward. Taken together, the

148 Ibid 16. Jeremy Black agrees that there needs to be an 'explicit awareness of the role of scholar as interpreter': Jeremy Black, *What If? Counterfactualism and the Problem of History* (Social Affairs Unit, 1998) 13.

149 Philip E Tetlock, Richard N Lebow and Geoffrey Parker, 'Preface: Unmaking the Middle Kingdom' in Philip E Tetlock, Richard N Lebow and Geoffrey Parker (eds) *Unmaking the West: 'What-If' Scenarios That Rewrite World History* (University of Michigan Press, 2006) 1, 10.

150 Philip E Tetlock and Geoffrey Parker, 'Counterfactual Thought Experiments: Why We Can't Live without Them & How We Must Learn to Live with Them' in Philip E Tetlock, Richard N Lebow and Geoffrey Parker (eds) *Unmaking the West: 'What-If' Scenarios That Rewrite World History* (University of Michigan Press, 2006) 14, 35.

151 Philip E Tetlock and Geoffrey Parker, 'Counterfactual History: Its Advocates Its Critics & Its Uses' in Philip E Tetlock, Richard N Lebow and Geoffrey Parker (eds) *Unmaking the West: 'What-If' Scenarios That Rewrite World History* (University of Michigan Press, 2006) 363, 366.

152 Philip E Tetlock and Geoffrey Parker, 'Counterfactual Thought Experiments: Why We Can't Live without Them & How We Must Learn to Live with Them' in Philip E Tetlock, Richard N Lebow and Geoffrey Parker (eds) *Unmaking the West: 'What-If' Scenarios That Rewrite World History* (University of Michigan Press, 2006) 14, 35–36.

153 Ibid 14, 29.

154 Philip E Tetlock and Geoffrey Parker, 'Counterfactual History: Its Advocates Its Critics & Its Uses' in Philip E Tetlock, Richard N Lebow and Geoffrey Parker (eds) *Unmaking the West: 'What-If' Scenarios That Rewrite World History* (University of Michigan Press, 2006) 363, 367.

instructions by Daniel Snowman,[155] Niall Fergusson,[156] Andrew Roberts[157] and Philip E Tetlock, Richard N Lebow and Geoffrey Parker[158] provide a guide on how a restrained[159] or meta-linguistic[160] counterfactual history can be achieved that does not become a work of science fiction creating an alternative world.[161]

Eight rules of counterfactual history can be distilled from this discussion. The first is that counterfactual history should be subject to the same standard and the same level of care as factual history. The second is that the counterfactual variation that is chosen needs to be at a turning point or key juncture in the historical record, a point of decision-making or a moment of other crucial importance. The counterfactual variable should not normally be an individual achievement that changes the course of history because a person is born or dies or is otherwise present or not present at a particular time and place. The third rule is that the counterfactual variation needs to be the only change made. The fourth is that counterfactual variation needs to be a plausible one – and this means that it needs to have been plausible at the time. The fifth is the minimal re-write rule that the least tampering that there is with the historical record the better. The sixth rule is that the reason for the choice of the counterfactual variation needs to be explicitly explained. The seventh rule is that the counterfactual account should focus on the short-term or alternatively needs to defend every projected consequence it identifies. The eighth and final rule is that all counterfactual histories should conclude with a self-reflection as to the benefit of the thought experiment and the challenges it makes to conventional thinking – in other words, how subversive it is.

Counterfactual history is a way of highlighting, challenging and superseding conventional and complacent deterministic accounts of history – evolutionary functionalist accounts. It therefore has the potential to be part of a subversive approach provided it is suitably rigorous and the eight rules are designed to safeguard this. Having explored the benefits of counterfactual history and how its rigour can be ensured, the final section of this chapter will suggest how this

155 Daniel Snowman (ed) *If I Had Been … Ten Historical Fantasies* (Harper Collins, 1979).

156 Niall Ferguson 'Introduction – Virtual History: Towards a "Chaotic" Theory of the Past' in Niall Ferguson (ed) *Virtual History: Alternatives and Counterfactuals* (Papermac, 1998).

157 Andrew Roberts, 'Introduction' in Andrew Roberts (ed) *What Might Have Been* (Phoenix, 2004).

158 Philip E Tetlock, Richard N Lebow and Geoffrey Parker (eds) *Unmaking the West: 'What-If' Scenarios That Rewrite World History* (University of Michigan Press, 2006).

159 Allan Megill, *Historical Knowledge, Historical Error: A Contemporary Guide to Practice* (University of Chicago Press, 2007) 151.

160 Jon Elster, *Logic and Society: Contradictions and Possible Worlds* (Wiley & Sons, 1978) 181.

161 Catherine Gallagher, *Telling It Like It Wasn't: The Counterfactual Imagination in History and Fiction* (University of Chicago Press. 2018) 3. Though as Richard J Evans has observed, 'counterfactualists who propose sensible limitations to their thought experiments too often forget them altogether in the heady excitement of speculative imagining': Richard J Evans, *Altered Pasts: Counterfactuals in History* (Abacus, 2016) 174.

historical method can be used in relation to law – how a Counterfactual Legal History can operate as part of a Subversive Legal History.

Counterfactual Legal History

In Law Schools, counterfactual thinking is paradoxically both nowhere and everywhere.

There is no tradition of Counterfactual Legal History in England and Wales.[162] Even the most creative work on the historical study of law – such as the work on legal archaeology – is concerned with what did happen rather than what did not happen. At most, counterfactualism exists implicitly in discussion about causation. In the rare instance where a legal historian has undertaken an explicitly counterfactual analysis – R C Van Caenegem's study of the origins of the First World War[163] – this work is not an example of *legal* history. Yet, counterfactual thinking is actually endemic in Legal History and in law generally. Although it is seldom acknowledged, let alone framed as such, counterfactual questions are prevalent in the Law School, both in teaching and in research. Lawyers need to prove what happened and this often requires them to prove that other things did not happen. This opens the door to counterfactual speculation. As Amy Knight Burns has noted:

> The law is full of exercises in counterfactual speculation. At the most basic level, the causation inquiry at the heart of any action for negligence involves counterfactual thinking. Similarly, remedies doctrine often involves considering the position in which a plaintiff *would have* been in *if* she had not been injured. Courts must also engage in counterfactual evaluation when interpreting wills that cannot be implemented exactly as written under the cy-pres doctrine. … These are commonplace legal questions without which adjudication as we know it would not be possible. Courts do this day in and day out. The point is not to catalogue the full list of substantive areas in which courts routinely use counterfactual reasoning – there are plenty

162 It has been noted that 'the US legal context is the legal tradition in which the debate around the use of counterfactual reasoning in legal interpretation has made most headway': Antonio Estella de Noriega, 'Rationality and Counterfactual Legal Analysis' (2016) 2(1) *The Italian Law Journal* 105, 110. The US historian Catherine Gallagher noted that 'the 'explicit use of past counterfactual hypotheses in the field of law began shortly after their appearance in military history, and they have become an indispensible tool of legal reasoning': Catherine Gallagher, *Telling It Like It Wasn't: The Counterfactual Imagination in History and Fiction* (University of Chicago Press. 2018) 5–6.

163 R C Van Caenegem, 'Counterfactual History and the First World War' (2017) 25 (3) *European Review* 494. See Dirk Heirbaut, 'The Life and Work of Raoul Charles van Caenegem (1927–2018)' (2019) 87 *Tijdschrift voor Rechtsgeschiedenis* 309 and Dirk Heirbaut, A Source of Inspiration for Legal Historians: Raoul van Caenegem's Views on Legal History' (2020) 88 *Tijdschrift voor Rechtsgeschiedenis* 24.

more – but rather to observe that the practice sweeps across divergent areas of the law.[164]

As Robert N Strassfeld has noted, 'legal decision makers cannot avoid counterfactual questions'.[165] However, even when legal actors deal with causation, they often do not adopt a straightforward counterfactual analysis.[166] For instance, in criminal law, certain criminal offences (often called 'result' crimes), require proof of causation. This necessitates proof beyond reasonable doubt that it was the defendant's actions that caused the wrong and there is a counterfactual element to this in that it needs to be proven that there was no alternative explanation. However, this straightforward counterfactual test is just the first of two considerations. This first test, known as factual causation, involves a straightforward counterfactual test, often summarised as the 'but for test': but for the actions of the defendant would the criminal consequence have taken place.[167] But the second test, one of legal causation also needs to be proved which requires the defendant's actions to have been a substantial cause[168] and requires that there is no break in the chain of causation.[169] This requirement for legal causation excludes the defendant's responsibility for some acts, where although they factually caused them, their actions are not considered to be legally significant enough. Glanville Williams, arguably the most eminent criminal law scholar of the twentieth century, regarded legal causation as being 'not a test of causation but a moral reaction'.[170] This example, familiar to all law students, shows how counterfactual analysis occurs within legal reasoning but is not understood as such and is therefore neither properly theorised nor rigorously pursued. Understanding this, and the plethora of other examples of which the list by Amy Knight Burns gives merely a taste, as a counterfactual analysis would have the benefit of ensuring consistency and thoroughness. Indeed, as Ingo Venzke has

164 Amy Knight Burns, 'Counterfactual Contradictions: Interpretive Error in the Analysis of AEDPA' (2013) 65 *Stanford Law Review* 205, 210–211.

165 Robert N Strassfeld, 'If. . .: Counterfactuals in the Law' [1992] *Faculty Publications* 339, 344. <https://scholarlycommons.law.case.edu/faculty_publications/373>.

166 See H L A Hart and Tony Honore, *Causation in the Law* (2nd ed, Oxford University Press, 1985).

167 *R v White* [1910] 2 KB 124; *R v Mitchell* [1983] 2 All ER 427.

168 *R v Cato* [1976] 1 All ER 260.

169 While foreseeable actions by the victim, such as jumping from a moving car to avoid assault, will not break the chain of causation (*R v Roberts* (1971) 56 Cr App R 95), free, deliberate and informed actions such as the self-injection of a drug provided will break the chain where the victim is an informed adult of sound mind (*R v Kennedy (No 2)* [2007] UKHL 38). Actions by a third party, such as medical negligence treatment, will break the chain of causation where they are unforeseeable (*R v Paggett* (1983) 76 Cr App R 279) or so potent that they render the contribution made by the defendant as insignificant (*R v Cheshire* [1991] 3 All ER 670).

170 He wrote that 'the question is whether the result can fairly be said to be imputable to the defendant. ... if the term "cause" must be used, it can best be distinguished in this meaning as the "imputable" or "responsible" or "blameable" cause, to indicate the value-judgement involved': Glanville Williams, *Textbook of Criminal Law* (2nd ed, Stevens, 1983) 381.

noted, 'moral assessments typically involve implicit assumptions about alternatives that counterfactual thinking makes explicit'.[171] This is not just an issue for Law Schools. Counterfactual thinking tends to be most often applied to questions of fact rather than to law which are dealt with in courts.[172] As Robert N Strassfeld has noted:

> Courts often fail to recognize that they are dealing with counterfactuals. When they do recognize the counterfactual nature of their inquiry, they fail to relate it to other counterfactual inquiries in the law. Lacking a general understanding of counterfactuals and their place in legal decision making, courts' treatment of legal counterfactuals is ad hoc, localized, and inconsistent.[173]

Overall, although counterfactual considerations occur implicitly, the field of counterfactual history has had little influence on law.[174] Yet, a Counterfactual Legal History is likely to benefit both lawyers and historians.[175] Legal change provides clear turning points which a counterfactual analysis could probe. In law, there are binary outcomes: a case is either upheld or dismissed; a statute (or a provision therein) is either passed or not. A counterfactual analysis could explore what would have been the implications had the law gone the other way and this is likely to shed light upon the importance of the legal development. Indeed, it may also question the emphasis and weight we place on particular developments by indicating that legal change would have still happened but taken longer. This could cast attention on which cases should be used as vehicles of reform; whether legal change is better predicated on some factual scenarios than others. This could underscore the randomness – the chaos even – of the common law: the way in which a myriad of variables determine which cases go as far as the appellate courts and have the potential to result in a judgment which could be legally significant. A counterfactual analysis could also enable analysis as to the effect of statutes and indeed of individual statutory provisions. Here the analysis could be more ambitious than simply speculating how the law might have continued

171 Ingo Venzke, 'What If? Counterfactual (Hi)Stories of International Law' (2018) 8 *Asian Journal of International Law* 403, 406.

172 Amy Knight Burns, 'Counterfactual Contradictions: Interpretive Error in the Analysis of AEDPA' (2013) 65 *Stanford Law Review* 205, 211.

173 Robert N Strassfeld, 'If . . .: Counterfactuals in the Law' [1992] *Faculty Publications* 339, 348. <https://scholarlycommons.law.case.edu/faculty_publications/373>.

174 There have been few calls for such an approach. Exceptionally, Robert N Strassfeld argued that 'legal fact finders should and do reconstruct the past and construct alternative counterfactual pasts' and that 'the most promising discipline to turn to is history: ibid 345.

175 As Ingo Venzke has noted in relation to international law: 'While it is a vibrant practice in historiography, counterfactual thinking has yet to be attuned to international law's distinct premises and sensibilities. But here, too, it can help in freeing legal thinking from false beliefs in the necessity of outcomes and developments': Ingo Venzke, 'What If? Counterfactual (Hi)Stories of International Law' (2018) 8 *Asian Journal of International Law* 403, 405.

without the statutory change; it would be possible to also analyse what the effect could have been had the reform been different.[176]

However, considerable care would be needed in pursuing this analysis. Although legal decisions are binary, a myriad of possibilities can still occur: there may be several means that reach the particular end. For instance, a case might be unsuccessful for several reasons. There is an even larger range of variables when determining the effect or use of the law. In a rare discussion of Legal History in the counterfactual history debate, Jeremy Black noted that:

> in the case of legal history, there may appear to be the simple choice posed by questions such as "What if this judgment had not been made or piece of legislation passed?", but the choices can be most profitably discussed by considering them in relation to the nature of society, not least the willingness to implement particular laws. To propose a "what if" in terms of the implications, especially in case-law systems, of an individual judgment or law, requires also considering whether it could have been enforced. Thus, the assessment involves two different types of counterfactuals, and appreciating the complex relationship between them entails scholarly understanding.[177]

This underscores the importance of consolidating Counterfactual Legal History within Legal History work in both the intellectual history and the social history traditions. As with counterfactual studies in academic history, counterfactual analysis in law needs to be done properly.[178] An excellent example of such work – though not framed as being counterfactual – can be found in the Feminist judgments projects, which raises the question of what would the decision and reasoning have been in particular cases had the judge been informed by feminism.[179]

176 Amy Knight Burns proposes distinguishing between 'what we might call a "hard counterfactual" – regarding things that definitely did not happen – and a "soft counterfactual" – regarding things that may or may not have happened, though we cannot know whether they did or not: Amy Knight Burns, 'Counterfactual Contradictions: Interpretive Error in the Analysis of AEDPA' (2013) 65 *Stanford Law Review* 205, 208.

177 Jeremy Black, *What If? Counterfactualism and the Problem of History* (Social Affairs Unit, 1998) 190.

178 This is the conclusion reached by Amy Knight Burns who in her critique of the US Supreme Court concludes that 'we are left to wonder what the Court might have done had it fully considered its holdings in the context of counterfactual analysis': Amy Knight Burns, 'Counterfactual Contradictions: Interpretive Error in the Analysis of AEDPA' (2013) 65 *Stanford Law Review* 205, 239.

179 Rosemary Hunter, Clare McGlynn and Erika Rackley (eds) *Feminist Judgments: From Theory to Practice* (Hart, 2010) has spawned a growing literature including books dedicated to particular areas of law (e.g. Loveday Hodson and Troy Lavers (eds) *Feminist Judgments in International Law* (Hart, 2019) and specific jurisdictions (e.g., Sharon Cowan, Chloe Kennedy and Vanessa Munro (eds) *Scottish Feminist Judgments: (Re)creating Law from the Outside In* (Hart, 2019)). Other approaches have also been used: for instance, the contributors to Stephen W Smith *et al.*

The ubiquity of implicit counterfactual thinking in Law Schools suggests that there is a need to take counterfactual methodology seriously. A counterfactual analysis has the potential to enrich understandings of the legacy of particular legal turning points. It can reappraise the importance of the change but this must be within the context in which it occurred as. As Ingo Venzke has noted in relation to international law, a counterfactual approach, can be used to 'improve our understanding of how and why international law has assumed its present shape'.[180] Crucially this recognises the contingency of law. As Venzke put it, 'counterfactual thinking helps to expose contingencies and to counteract the bias of hindsight – the bias, namely, that makes us think that outcomes were more likely once we knew about them'. Counterfactual thinking can be used to question deterministic accounts of legal change. In the words of Ingo Venzke, 'the practice of writing counterfactual (hi)stories unravels and shakes the paths on which the development of... law seems to depend'.[181] It can be used to question and to challenge the stories that are taken for granted and which have become foundational. It can also question any assumption that the current shape of the law was inevitable or is natural. Counterfactuals provide a means of highlighting, questioning and superseding evolutionary functionalist assumptions by providing an alternative which presents entropic complexity as the default. Counterfactual thinking, then, has a similar potential in relation to history and law. In both disciplines, it is currently endemic but in an implicit, under-theorised way. This can and should change by adopting the eight rules outlined above. Used carefully, there is a great potential for counterfactual work in both disciplines and for both to learn from one another.[182] Counterfactualism can be used as part of a subversive approach. It is one way of shifting the lens and writing in a different perspective. However, Counterfactual Legal History should not be seen as a specialism or even the preserve of legal historians. The prevalence of counterfactual thinking and the potential role of properly theorised subversive counterfactual analysis suggest that such counterfactual analysis should be part of the general methodological toolkit for academic lawyers and law students. This underscores how legal historians should not have a monopoly on thinking about law historically. This is what a Subversive Legal History seeks

(eds) *Ethical Judgments: Re-Writing Medical Law* (Hart, 2017) rewrote judgments on the basis that the decisions have to be ethically as well as legally valid.

180 Ingo Venzke, 'What If? Counterfactual (Hi)Stories of International Law' (2018)8 *Asian Journal of International Law* 403, 405.

181 Ibid 403, 431.

182 Robert N Strassfeld's conclusion is that we need to 'make our use of legal counterfactuals more consistent and sensible by recognizing them for what they are and examining their use in law and in history. Only then can we make reasoned decisions about when and how to use them. That examination should encompass the broad sweep of legal doctrines and subspecialties, and it therefore must emerge dialogically': Robert N Strassfeld, 'If ...: Counterfactuals in the Law' [1992] *Faculty Publications* 339, 416: <https://scholarlycommons.law.case.edu/faculty_publications/373>.

to provide – and counterfactual analysis should form a part of that.[183] Counterfactualism is a way to highlight, question, challenge and revise conventional narratives imbued by evolutionary functionalist assumptions of progress. It underscores the contingency, chaos and interconnectedness of the phenomenon we call law. E P Thompson was wrong. Counterfactual thinking is not '*Geschichtenscheissenschlopff*, unhistorical shit'.[184] It is, rather, a necessary tool to call out the *Geschichtenscheissenschlopff* that clogs up our understanding of law.

183 Other approaches are also needed. There is also a need to examine how legal actors deliberately re-write history, a phenomenon that has been described as a 'judicial retcon': Russell Sandberg, 'The Employment Status of Ministers: A Judicial Retcon?' (2018) 13(1) *Religion and Human Rights* 27. Recent years have witnessed a growth on literature on 'memory laws' the way in which 'laws enshrine state-approved interpretation of crucial historical events': Uladzislau Belavusua and Alexandra Gliszczynska-Grabais, 'Memory Laws: Mapping a New Subject in Comparative Law and Transitional Justice' in Uladzislau Belavusua and Alexandra Gliszczynska-Grabais (eds) *Law and Memory: Towards Legal Governance of History* (Cambridge University Press, 2017) 1. (See also Uladzislau Belavusua and Alexandra Gliszczynska-Grabais, 'The Remarkable Rise of "Law and Historical Memory" in Europe: Theorizing Trends and Prospects in the Recent Literature' (2020) 47(2) *Journal of Law and Society* 326.) As Richard J Evans noted, 'retrospective historical falsification … is not really counterfactual … because it is merely concerned with rewriting the entire factual record, not with positing an alternative to it deriving from one small change to it': Richard J Evans, *Altered Pasts: Counterfactuals in History* (Abacus, 2016) 134. Yet, analysing the judicial rewriting of history is important in showing how the law's historical narrative is authored and contested.

184 Cf. E P Thompson, *The Poverty of Theory and Other Essays* (Merlin Press, 1978) 100.

7 The Parallel World of Legal Geography

Space: the final frontier.

Numerous academic commentators have criticised how the scholarly focus has been on time (and history) rather than on space (and geography). This can be shown by looking at the arguments put forward by three such commentators: Michel Foucault, Edward Soja and Nicholas Blomley.

The French philosopher Michel Foucault commented on the 'devaluation of space that has prevailed for generations'.[1] Foucault continued that 'Space was treated as the dead, the unfixed, the undialectical, the immobile. Time, on the contrary, was richness, fecundity, life and dialectic'. For Foucault, history was 'the great obsession of the nineteenth century… with its themes of development and of suspension, of crisis, and cycle, themes of the ever-accumulating past, with its great preponderance of dead men and the menacing glaciation of the world'.[2] Indeed, for Foucault, the influence of history and its confusion with 'old schemas of evolution' led to space not only being ignored but it also being seen to be in opposition to time.[3] As he put it, 'the use of spatial terms seems to have the air of an anti-history. If one started to talk in terms of space that meant that one was hostile to time. It meant, as the fools say, that one "denied history"'. This entrenched difference between time and space furthered a conflict between 'the pious descendants of time and the determined inhabitants of space'.[4] Yet, Foucault insisted that time and space were actually interwoven: 'space itself has a history in Western experience, and it is not possible to disregard the fatal intersection of time with space'. Indeed, he predicted that 'the present epoch will perhaps be above all the epoch of space. We are in the epoch of simultaneity: we

1 Michel Foucault, *Power/Knowledge: Selected Interviews & Other Writings 1972–1977* (Harvester Press, 1980) 70.

2 Michel Foucault, 'Of Other Spaces: Utopias and Heterotopias' (1986) 16 *Diacritics* 22. He noted that the 'nineteenth century found its essential mythological resources in the second principle of thermodynamics'.

3 Michel Foucault, *Power/Knowledge: Selected Interviews & Other Writings 1972–1977* (Harvester Press, 1980) 70.

4 Michel Foucault, 'Of Other Spaces: Utopias and Heterotopias' (1986) 16 *Diacritics* 22.

are in the epoch of juxtaposition, the epoch of the near and far, of the side-by-side, of the dispersed'.

The American political geographer and urban theorist Edward Soja echoed these concerns that time had been prioritised in academic research and that this had meant that little attention had been afforded to space. He complained that the 'prevailing temporal din' of the late nineteenth century had continued throughout the twentieth century.[5] This was particularly so in relation to modern social theory where there still existed 'a privileged place for "the historical imagination" in defining the very nature of critical insight and interpretation'.[6] The influence of Marx and the determination 'to understand the development of capitalism as a historical, but only incidentally geographical, process' had a profound impact upon the development of the new social sciences.[7] Though 'little eddies of a lively geographical imagination survived',[8] these were marginalised. Like Foucault, Soja noted that things had begun to change. For Soja, this occurred from the 1960s onwards, when 'Western Marxism and critical social science appeared to explode into more heterogeneous fragments, losing much of their separate cohesiveness and centralities'.[9] A 'new animating polemic' had appeared on the theoretical and political agenda: a 'distinctively postmodern and critical human geography... brashly reasserting the interpretive significance of space in the historically privileged confines of contemporary critical thought'.[10] While geography had 'not yet ... displaced history at the heart of contemporary theory and criticism' and 'confrontational polemics' continue to divide the two,[11] this was slowly giving way to 'a more flexible and balanced critical theory that re-entwines the making of history with the social production of space, with the construction and configuration of human geographies'. Soja asserted

5 Soja dates this pervasiveness to the last decades of the nineteenth century. He noted that, by contrast, the middle half of the century was 'a period in which historicity and spatiality were in approximate balance as sources of emancipatory consciousness' but 'the explicitly spatial critiques, radical and liberal, began to recede behind the more powerful Eurocentric assertions of the revolutionary subjectivity of time and history': Edward W Soja, *Postmodern Geographies: The Reassertion of Space in Critical Social Theory* (Verso, 1989) 13, 11, 10, 4.

6 Ibid 10.

7 Ibid 4, 13. This was reflected in 'the sociological imagination' espoused by C Wright Mills which 'enables us to grasp history and biography and the relations between the two in society'. One of the three key questions for sociology is 'where does this society stand in human history?' and this includes determining what are the essential features of this period: C Wright Mills, *The Sociological Imagination* (Fortieth Anniversary Edition Oxford University Press, 2000) 6, 7.

8 Edward W Soja, *Postmodern Geographies: The Reassertion of Space in Critical Social Theory* (Verso, 1989) 4.

9 Ibid 4–5.

10 Ibid 11.

11 'It remains all too easy for even the best of the "pious descendants of time" to respond to these pesky postmodern intrusions with an antidisestablishmentarian wave of a still confident upper hand or with the presumptive yawns of a seen-it-all-before complacency. In response, the determined intruders often tend to overstate their case, creating the unproductive aura of an anti-history, inflexibly exaggerating the critical privilege of contemporary spatiality in isolation from an increasingly silenced embrace of time': ibid.

that now 'it may be space more than time that hides consequences from us, the "making of geography" more than the "making of history" that provides the most revealing tactical and theoretical world'.[12] Yet, he conceded for the work done so far, 'the interpretation of postmodern geographies can be no more than a beginning'.[13] There remains a need:

> to tamper with the familiar modalities of time, to shake up the flow of the linear text to allow other, more "lateral" connections to be made. The discipline imprinted in a sequentially unfolding narrative predisposes the reader to think historically, making it difficult to see the text as a map, a geography of simultaneous relations and meanings that are tied together by a spatial rather than temporal logic.[14]

In short, there remains a need to 'to spatialize the historical narrative'.

The British-Canadian geographer Nicholas Blomley observed a similar trend specifically in relation to law. For Blomley, legal theory too reflected 'the *centrality* of the historical, and the implicit exclusion of the geographical'.[15] He bemoaned that a 'geographically informed critical legal analysis' continued to cut 'against the grain, given the centrality of historical imagination within law'. Blomley noted that this was true of both 'internal' attacks by critical legal scholars which provide 'an attempt at unravelling and contesting legal discourse on its own terms' and 'external' attacks which challenge the autonomy of law 'by exploring and challenging its claims concerning law in society' and which therefore make unintelligible the very boundaries that separate law from "society"' and any 'distinction between "internal" and "external" critique'.[16] Echoing Soja, Blomley noted that the use of history in critical legal scholarship was 'powerful, provocative and political' but not surprising 'given its prevalence within modern social theory'.[17] He argued that 'in deploying history to argue against the closure of the legal system,[18] legal scholars failed to recognise the profound importance of space in the regulation of social life and the subversive potential of what might be called a geographical critique'.[19] Blomley saw 'the centrality of an historical analysis within critical legal inquiry' as being 'at once a problem and a solution'.[20] He wrote that geographers had 'spent too much time bemoaning the historical imagination as an obstacle to the development of a geographically

12 Ibid 1.
13 Ibid 2.
14 Ibid 1.
15 Nicholas Blomley, *Law, Space and Geographies of Power* (Guilford Press, 1994) 8.
16 Ibid 15.
17 Ibid 8, 15.
18 That is, the presentation of law as an autonomous phenomenon.
19 Ibid 25. For Blomley, in addition to '"vertical differences" revealed by legal history, the multiple and heterogeneous ways in which law is understood "horizontally," in the diverse spatial settings of social life could also prove critically potent': ibid 26.
20 Ibid 56, fn 23.

informed critical theory' and that there was a need to spatialise the historical in understanding law.[21]

Foucault, Soja and Blomley all argued that more attention should be afforded to questions of space than time. On the face of it, they seem to argue against a historical approach and in favour of a geographical approach. It might therefore be considered that their arguments and proposed approach would not be of interest to legal historians. This chapter, however, argues that this is not the case. Rather, there are three reasons why those interested in developing a Subversive Legal History need to follow the lead of Foucault, Soja and Blomley and pay attention to geography.

The first reason why attention needs to be paid to geography is that the criticisms of Foucault, Soja and Blomley against time highlight the particular problem of a particular historical approach. They are not actually arguing against history *per se*. Despite what they say, the enemy is not history itself. Rather, what all three writers were criticising was the pervasiveness of 'bad' history. They are arguing against the dominance of a particular kind of historical approach. They were critical of the dominance of a particular historical narrative: the progress myth derived from the Enlightenment that Robert Gordon called evolutionary functionalism.[22] As Blomley rightly noted, it is 'impossible to disentangle the language of social theory from the Enlightenment project and the processes of modernization' and this has resulted in 'the creation of a specific understanding of space and of time' whereby modernity 'is a historical not a geographic project'.[23] Further, modernity is a historical project in a specific sense: it is seen within an evolutionary framework whereby reason has come to replace irrationality in a way that constitutes progress. This explains the paradox at the heart of legal education: how history can be both everywhere and nowhere. It is not history that is everywhere but rather the progress narrative of evolutionary functionalism which is dressed up as history. It is not history itself but the use of history; or to be more precise, the misuse of history.[24] History is twisted and made subservient to law, whereby in the words of Blomley, 'the effect is to subjugate the flux of historical contingency to the imperious logic of the law'. This is the way in which history is currently prevalent in Law Schools: this everyday history is not history at all.

This everyday history of evolutionary functionalism is prevalent not only in academia but throughout the legal system. Blomley noted that 'judges and legal scholars… spend a lot of time coming up with such legal histories that serve, ultimately, to undergird closure'.[25] History is misused in order to cement and

21 Ibid 8.

22 Robert W Gordon, 'Critical Legal Histories' (1984) 36 *Stanford Law Review* 57.

23 Nicholas Blomley, *Law, Space and Geographies of Power* (Guilford Press, 1994) 15, fn 5.

24 Blomley recognised this in his criticism of the way in which legal histories are 'both ideological and partial, shoehorning a multiplicity of historical possibilities and legal voices into a univocal and self-serving narrative': ibid 17.

25 Ibid 16–17.

stabilise the status quo. The progress narrative of evolutionary functionalism is used to ensure that radical change is not an option since the precedent of the past must be followed. We must continue on our journey of progress. As Blomley noted, 'by rooting contemporary law in the determinate values of "our forefathers", whether inscribed in Magna Carta or the Constitution, law acquires profound stability'.[26] A undirectional model of uniform evolution is assumed.[27] Blomley was critical of how history was used to provide a progressive vision of the law whereby law 'evolves teleologically, furthering the advancement of humanity'.[28] He argued that there is a need to ask what legal histories are being evoked by judges and scholars and with what effect.[29] A critical approach could recover 'alternative histories' to threaten 'the telos of law (from good to better)'.[30] He asked: 'What if legal history reveals that the law of the past was underlain not by the impartial rule of law, but by "social" and "political" forces, such as class rule, cynicism, selective enforcement, and corruption, that again intersect with the present?' For Blomley, legal histories in this critical sense become 'histories of difference, reminding us of the contingency of our own legal culture (reminding us that it is, indeed, a culture)'.[31] They are 'social and political histories, imbued with contingency and struggle'.[32] He noted that: 'If legal categories are shown to have not always been "out there" but are the product of past historical contingencies, the critics hope that they become "unfrozen" and the possibility for opposition can emerge'.[33]

As previous chapters have discussed, this is precisely what Subversive Legal History seeks to achieve. Rather than using history to stabilise and entrench the law as it is, a subversive approach seeks to challenge, to disturb, to subvert. History in this subversive sense uses historical method to expose the misuse of history. Looking at the geographical criticism of the focus on time therefore reveals the precise problem, namely the prevalent evolutionary functionalist mindset which is not history at all. Looking at the matter from a different disciplinary vantage point helps to distinguish the everyday 'bad' history infused with evolutionary functionalism from what the previous chapters have identified as the subversive history where entropic complexity is understood as the default.

The second reason for looking at a geographical approach is that it can show additional dimensions of the subversive critique of law. Blomley was adamant

26 Ibid 17.

27 Blomley suggested in a footnote that such an approach was even endemic in specialist Legal History writings. He commented that 'we might understand the nineteenth century "historical" school of legal thought – associated with … Maitland in Britain – in these terms': ibid, fn 8.

28 Ibid 17.

29 Ibid 16. The 'judicial retcon' device may be useful here: see Russell Sandberg, 'The Employment Status of Ministers: A Judicial Retcon?' (2018) 13(1) *Religion and Human Rights* 27.

30 Nicholas Blomley, *Law, Space and Geographies of Power* (Guilford Press, 1994) 17. Counterfactual Legal History, as discussed in the previous chapter, is likely to be helpful here.

31 Ibid 22.

32 Ibid 68.

33 Ibid 23.

that 'legal histories are also legal geographies'.[34] He insisted that 'a close reading of this historical moment reveals the profound significance of a range of interlocking geographic representations and structures'. This point has been forcibly made by Gareth A Jones in the context of land law reform.[35] He noted that paradoxically while 'we mostly think of land rights as inherently spatial... we usually think of land law reform with an historical framework'.[36] This is used to legitimise an evolutionary narrative which ignores the spatiality of land rights and masks 'their diversity, instability under apparently similar legal conditions, and the range of extra-legal influences on outcomes'.[37] For Jones, 'the drive to find an undefined set of "commonalities" seems to be an attempt to remove geography through administration'.[38] This is achieved 'through building a very persuasive argument that organizes a historical view of the world. This device comes very naturally to law (makers) accustomed to a discipline which is built on precedent and a vast professional machinery to reform laws that did not work in the past'.[39] The resulting framework imposed is too neat and makes the status quo appear natural.[40] Jones called for a geographical approach which 'destabilizes the normativity and objectivity of law' by opening up law 'to scrutiny as a narrative reflective of ideologies that people either share, or relate to and may accept or not'.[41] This call is compelling.[42] Geographical approaches as well as historical ones have a part to play in challenging and overcoming the narrative of evolutionary functionalism dressed up as history. A subversive approach requires both historical and geographical approaches.

The third reason why Subversive Legal History needs to pay attention to geography is that legal historians have much to learn from how legal geography has developed. Indeed, Luke Bennett and Antonia Layard have commented that it is now temporality which 'is under-researched in socio-legal scholarship'.[43] Legal geography has become better regarded as an interdisciplinary way of contextualising and critiquing law than Legal History. As Mariana Valverde has noted:

> The fact that sessions on "law and space" or legal geography draw large numbers of people at Law and Society Association meetings, whereas legal

34 Ibid 68.

35 Gareth A Jones, 'Camels, Chameleons and Coyotes: Problematizing the "Histories" of Land Law Reform' in Jane Holder and Carolyn Harrison (eds) *Law and Geography* (Oxford University Press, 2003) 169.

36 Ibid 170.

37 Ibid 171. However, he does note that 'it would be wrong to present the study of land law reform as completely ignorant of geography, or that adopting a history of laws framework is in opposition to a spatially sensitive understanding of reform' (ibid 173).

38 Ibid 174.

39 Ibid 171.

40 Ibid 185.

41 Ibid 186, 187.

42 The chronological narrative of improvement is so prevalent in legal writings that its use in this introduction has probably escaped your attention.

43 Luke Bennett and Antonia Layard, 'Legal Geography: Becoming Spatial Detectives' (2015) 9(7) *Geography Compass* 406, 416.

> history is not seen as fashionable or theoretical (even though law schools, institutionally resistant to change, generally employ legal historians not legal geographers), appears to be a fashion trend whose driving forces are mysterious or simply invisible to the very people caught up on it.[44]

It is this third reason for looking at legal geography that this chapter mostly focuses upon. This chapter seeks to deduce what the mysterious driving forces mentioned by Valverde have been to explore how legal geography has developed and what Legal History can learn from this. Although legal geography remains a dynamic field in development and therefore a work in progress,[45] it is possible to extrapolate how it has developed and its character from accounts of how legal geography has come to exist as a rich and diverse critical interdisciplinary project. This chapter, therefore, explores the legal geography project by reference to how it presents itself. It falls into three sections mapping three phases of legal geographic scholarship. The first will explore the trajectory of the legal geography movement and how it took on a critical character, paying special attention to Nicholas Blomley's 1994 monograph.[46] The second section will explore how today the legal geography project seeks to go further, exploring the post-disciplinary project epitomised by David Delaney's 2010 monograph.[47] The third section will explore how recent legal geographical work stresses the need to study both law and time, examining Mariana Valverde's 2015 monograph on chronotopes that subjects time to the same critical scrutiny as space.[48]

Phase One: Towards a Critical Legal Geography

Unlike Legal History, legal geography has not developed as a disciplinary specialism in Law Schools with its own institutional apparatus.

The geographical study of law has developed in a number of different ways. Irus Braverman, Nicholas Blomley, David Delaney and Alexandre Kedar suggested that there are 'three modes of legal geography research':

> The first mode of legal geography includes disciplinary work in law or in geography that is modelled on the conventional image of import and

44 Mariana Valverde, *Chronotopes of Law: Jurisdiction, Scale and Governance* (Routledge, 2015) 37.

45 Soja's warning remains valid that it is too early 'to give a comprehensive and confident epistemological account' of the field of legal geography since that would be 'a premature totalization of a still shifting discourse': Edward W Soja, *Postmodern Geographies: The Reassertion of Space in Critical Social Theory* (Verso, 1989) 12.

46 Nicholas Blomley, *Law, Space and Geographies of Power* (Guilford Press, 1994).

47 David Delaney, *The Spatial. The Legal and the Pragmatics of World Making: Nomospheric Investigations* (Routledge, 2010).

48 Mariana Valverde, *Chronotopes of Law: Jurisdiction, Scale and Governance* (Routledge, 2015).

> export. The second is an interdisciplinary pursuit in which scholars in law and geography draw on the work of another and seek to contribute to the development of a common project. The third mode moves beyond the interdisciplinary to transdisciplinary, or perhaps postdisciplinary, modes of scholarship. Although these three modes exist concurrently, the general trajectory over time has been from disciplinary to interdisciplinary and, finally, to postdisciplinary orientations.[49]

As Braverman *et al.* concede, this classification is contestable in two respects. First, explorations of the relationship between space and law predated their 1980s starting point. The term 'legal geography' was first used by German scholars in the 1920s and work on intertwining of the spatial and the legal has existed for generations,[50] albeit typically taking other forms and labels such as comparative law.[51] Second, Braverman *et al.* concede that 'the linear depiction of these modes as progressing in time – namely of subsequent modes that supersede what preceded them – is not fully accurate'.[52] They point out that 'antecedents of post-disciplinary work were discernible' at the start of the period and 'much excellent and necessary discipline-specific work continues to be done today'. There is a further weakness in the articulation of these three modes: Braverman *et al.*'s schema suggests that legal geography is a homogenous body of scholarship when

49 Irus Braverman, Nicholas Blomley, David Delaney and Alexandre Kedar, 'Introduction: Expanding the Spaces of Law' in Irus Braverman, Nicholas Blomley, David Delaney and Alexandre Kedar (eds) *The Expanding Spaces of Law: A Timely Legal Geography* (Stanford University Press, 2014) 1, 2.

50 Alexandre Kedar, 'On the Legal Geography of Ethnographic Settler States: Notes Towards a Research Agenda' in Jane Holder and Carolyn Harrison (eds) *Law and Geography* (Oxford University Press, 2003) 402, 405. David Delaney has suggested that the 'intertwining of the spatial and the legal with modalities of social power can be traced back to Eden' and that 'learning to recognize and reproduce these practical intertwinings is a basic point of competent socialization': David Delaney, *The Spatial, the Legal and the Pragmatics of World-Making: Nomospheric Investigations* (Routledge, 2010) 8.

51 See Nicholas Blomley, *Law, Space and Geographies of Power* (Guilford Press, 1994) 28–29. As early as the sixteenth century, Jean Bodin provided 'an exhaustive comparison of European legal systems, with a classification of the specific characteristics to which they were adapted'. This developed into a comparative law literature which regarded 'space (or the regional-geographic environment) as a vital structuring agent of law'. This is perhaps epitomised in the work of John Wigmore, which mapped the regional diversity of law (John Wigmore, *A Panorama of the World's Legal Systems* (Washington Law Book Co, 1928); John Wigmore 'A Map of the World's Law' (1929) 19(1) *Geographical Review* 114; John Wigmore, *A Kaleidoscope of Justice* (Fred B Rothman, 1940). There were also examples of work which did the reverse: 'theorizing law as an external variable that affects spatial configurations'. Blomley gives the example of the work of Derwent Whittlesey which explored the effect of central authority upon the landscape. (Derwent Whittlesey, 'The Impress of Central Authority upon the Landscape' (1935) 25 *Annals of the Association of American Geographers* 85).

52 Irus Braverman, Nicholas Blomley, David Delaney and Alexandre Kedar, 'Introduction: Expanding the Spaces of Law' in Irus Braverman, Nicholas Blomley, David Delaney and Alexandre Kedar (eds) *The Expanding Spaces of Law: A Timely Legal Geography* (Stanford University Press, 2014) 1, 2.

it is not. Much work on what we might call legal geography is not 'conducted self-consciously' under the banner of legal geography.[53] And even where a label is applied to such work, a number of different banners are used including 'law and geography' and 'law and space'. Braverman *et al.*'s modes should, therefore, be treated as ideal types. Their three modes need to be understood as showing not a linear story of progression but three forms of legal geography work: academic isolationism, critical legal geography and the post-disciplinary project. This section will explore the move from the first to the second form.

The study of the relationship between law and geography was previously characterised by academic isolationism. The relationship was 'both poorly documented and inadequately theorized'.[54] Space was frequently taken as a given.[55] Legal writers were 'indifferent to space' and precious few 'consciously concerned themselves with the geographies of social and political life'.[56] This was reciprocated: geographers appeared blasé about law and very few afforded it attention. For Blomley, before the late 1980s, any conversation between the two 'tended not only to be muted, but to replicate a view of the world that treats time and space as analytically quite distinct, related in circumscribed ways'.[57] Powerful institutional and intellectual barriers perpetuated this academic silence.[58] Although both legal scholarship and human geography had strong interdisciplinary traditions,[59] their institutional and disciplinary nature seemed 'antithetical to mutual exchange'.[60] As Blomley put it, 'geography – as a formal social science – and law – as a professionalized vocation – seem to lack a common theoretical and analytic vocabulary'. This was even so in the United States where the 'robust tradition of "law ands" (law and economics, law and sociology, law and politics, legal history, legal anthropology, law and psychology)' dating back to at least the 1920s 'did not recognize the value of geographical scholarship for exploring legal questions'.[61]

The first steps of what was to become the law and geography movement were extremely tentative. Lawyers studying geographical topics did not problematise geography whilst geographers studying legal topics did not problematise

53 Jane Holder and Carolyn Harrison, 'Connecting Law and Geography' in Jane Holder and Carolyn Harrison (eds) *Law and Geography* (Oxford University Press, 2003) 3.

54 Nicholas Blomley, *Law, Space and Geographies of Power* (Guilford Press, 1994) vii.

55 David Delaney, Richard T Ford and Nicholas Blomley, 'Preface: Where is Law?' in Nicholas Blomley, David Delaney and Richard T Ford (eds) *The Legal Geographies Reader* (Blackwell, 2001) xiii, xvi.

56 Nicholas Blomley, *Law, Space and Geographies of Power* (Guilford Press, 1994) viii, 27.

57 Nicholas Blomley, 'From "What?" to "So What?": Law and Geography in Retrospect' in Jane Holder and Carolyn Harrison (eds) *Law and Geography* (Oxford University Press, 2003) 13, 22.

58 Nicholas Blomley, *Law, Space and Geographies of Power* (Guilford Press, 1994) vii.

59 David Delaney, *The Spatial, the Legal and the Pragmatics of World-Making: Nomospheric Investigations* (Routledge, 2010) 9.

60 Nicholas Blomley, *Law, Space and Geographies of Power* (Guilford Press, 1994) 4.

61 David Delaney, *The Spatial, the Legal and the Pragmatics of World-Making: Nomospheric Investigations* (Routledge, 2010) 9.

law. Occasional articles in legal journals by the likes of Gerald Neuman,[62] John Calmore[63] and Gerald Frug[64] explored geographical topics but only from the perspective of law. As Braverman *et al.* put it, such authors were not interested in engaging 'with the problematic, complex, and fluid nature of social space; nor were they usually interested in the range of unconventional and intellectual resources for thinking through the spacialities that critical human geographers were developing at this time'.[65] Similarly, on the geography side, the few human geographers who began writing about legal topics did so exclusively from the perspective of their home discipline. They took 'law as a given and were not concerned with debates about law within legal scholarship'.[66] The development of legal geography was 'sparse and unsystematized'.[67] However, this was to be to its advantage.

The vast social changes of the 1960s transformed the perceived tasks for scholarship ushering in a new critical approach.[68] The undeveloped state of legal geography meant that it responded to this critical turn differently than established fields like Legal History did. Legal geography arose after and as a result of the rise of postmodernism and the critical approach.[69] It was infused not only by the Critical Legal Studies movement but also by the critical geography movement, which saw scholars in both disciplines holding up for 'scrutiny the central, organizing apparatus of their disciplines – the rule of law, and space'. The relationship between the two movements and their convergence into the legal geography project is a matter of debate. Braverman *et al.* suggested that the shift towards a 'strong and explicit commitment to interdisciplinary research and programmatic bridge building' was 'triggered' by the Critical Legal Studies movement.[70] However, David Delaney noted that, although Critical Legal Studies was of

62 Gerald Neuman, 'Territorial Discrimination, Equal Protection and Self-Determination' (1987) 135 *University of Pennsylvania Law Review* 261.

63 John Calmore, 'Racialized Space and the Culture of Segregation: Hewing a Stone of Hope from a Mountain of Despair' (1995) 143 *University of Pennsylvania Law Review* 1233.

64 Gerald Frug, 'The Geography of Community' (1996) 48 *Stanford Law Review* 1047.

65 Irus Braverman, Nicholas Blomley, David Delaney and Alexandre Kedar, 'Introduction: Expanding the Spaces of Law' in Irus Braverman, Nicholas Blomley, David Delaney and Alexandre Kedar (eds) *The Expanding Spaces of Law: A Timely Legal Geography* (Stanford University Press, 2014) 1, 3.

66 Ibid 4.

67 Nicholas Blomley, *Law, Space and Geographies of Power* (Guilford Press, 1994) 28.

68 David Delaney, *The Spatial, the Legal and the Pragmatics of World-Making: Nomospheric Investigations* (Routledge, 2010) 9.

69 As Jane Holder and Carolyn Harrison noted, 'the critical dimension of this area of scholarship was waiting to happen': Jane Holder and Carolyn Harrison, 'Connecting Law and Geography' in Jane Holder and Carolyn Harrison (eds) *Law and Geography* (Oxford University Press, 2003) 3, 4.

70 Irus Braverman, Nicholas Blomley, David Delaney and Alexandre Kedar, 'Introduction: Expanding the Spaces of Law' in Irus Braverman, Nicholas Blomley, David Delaney and Alexandre Kedar (eds) *The Expanding Spaces of Law: A Timely Legal Geography* (Stanford University Press, 2014) 1, 4.

great significance, that movement 'took sustenance from the widening pool of critical social theorization and philosophy, including Marxism and post-structuralism'.[71] Nicholas Blomley suggested that, although both drew on wider theoretical debates, critical geographical inquiry ran parallel to but independent from Critical Legal Studies.[72] He saw a 'critical legal geography' developing 'as part of a much broader shift in theoretical human geography'.[73] Indeed, Franz von Benda-Beckmann, Keebet von Benda-Beckmann and Anne Griffiths suggested that the 'spatialization of social theory has been prompted by a critical social geography and a heightened interests in the effects of globalization'.[74] Establishing a neat line of cause and effect is therefore problematic and actually foolhardy. A two way process of borrowing took place within a wider context where, as Gordon L Clark put it, 'we have all learnt the lessons of the interpretative turn, and postmodernism'.[75] The important thing is not who influenced who but rather that, as Braverman *et al.* noted, 'legal scholars and human geographers were suddenly reading the same theorists, asking similar questions, and talking account of one another's scholarship'.[76]

The result of this critical turn was that from the beginning legal geography problematised orthodox notions of both law and space. Legal geographers saw the legal and the spatial as being 'conjoined and co-constituted'; 'law is always "worlded" in some way. Likewise, social spaces, lived spaces, and landscapes are inscribed with legal significance'.[77] Braverman *et al.* defined legal geography as 'a stream of scholarship that makes the interconnections between law and spatiality, and especially their reciprocal construction, into core objects of inquiry'. Likewise, Luke Bennett and Antonia Layard called for legal scholars and geographers to become 'spatial detectives', 'learning, Sherlock Holmes-like, to

71 David Delaney, *The Spatial, the Legal and the Pragmatics of World-Making: Nomospheric Investigations* (Routledge, 2010) 10. For Mariana Valverde, the tradition by which socio-legal studies has kept abreast and borrowed general theoretical developments has meant that socio-legal studies 'has witnessed much enthusiasm, in recent years, for theoretical exploration of space and spatial governance': Mariana Valverde, *Chronotopes of Law: Jurisdiction, Scale and Governance* (Routledge, 2015) 37.

72 Nicholas Blomley, *Law, Space and Geographies of Power* (Guilford Press, 1994) 44–45.

73 Ibid 28. Edward Soja regarded this as the postmodern turn which 'led to an exploration of a multiplicity of alternatives to the more rigid structures that have tended to evolve within': Edward Soja, 'Afterword' (1996) 48 *Stanford Law Review* 1421, 1422.

74 Franz von Benda-Beckmann, Keebet von Benda-Beckmann and Anne Griffiths, 'Space and Legal Pluralism: An Introduction' in Franz von Benda-Beckmann, Keebet von Benda-Beckmann and Anne Griffiths (eds) *Spatializing Law: An Anthropological Geography of Law in Society* (Routledge, 2009) 1.

75 Gordon L Clark, 'Foreword' in Nicholas Blomley, David Delaney and Richard T Ford (eds) *The Legal Geographies Reader* (Blackwell, 2001) x.

76 Irus Braverman, Nicholas Blomley, David Delaney and Alexandre Kedar, 'Introduction: Expanding the Spaces of Law' in Irus Braverman, Nicholas Blomley, David Delaney and Alexandre Kedar (eds) *The Expanding Spaces of Law: A Timely Legal Geography* (Stanford University Press, 2014) 1, 4.

77 Ibid 1.

search out the presence and absence of spatialities in legal practice and of law's traces and effects embedded within places'.[78] Legal geography provided not just another context in which to place law but also a way of challenging and revisiting the nature of law itself. Jane Holder and Carolyn Harrison asserted that legal geography 'has the capacity to release law from its imposed (and self-imposed) confinement as "word" (interpretation, meaning, discourse) and to show the legal at work in the world'.[79] Legal geography provided more than an external critique of law understanding its place and relationship to other social systems, it also provided a new way to explore and challenge the internal workings of law.

Alexandre Kedar has distinguished between 'geography in law', that is, 'how geography and social space affect law and legal development' and 'law in geography', 'how law contributes to the social production of space, what is the role of law in constructing, organising and legitimating social spatiality'.[80] As well as echoing the distinction found in the Law and Literature movement between 'law in literature' (the examination of 'the possible relevance of literary texts... as texts appropriate for legal scholars') and 'law as literature' (which 'seeks to apply the techniques of literary criticism to legal texts'),[81] Kedar's distinction drew upon the work of Edward W Soja.[82] While Nicholas Blomley has criticised such approaches on the basis that they 'not only [impoverish] inquiry into what is a complex and profoundly subtle relation, but also implicitly [constrict] two

78 Luke Bennett and Antonia Layard, 'Legal Geography: Becoming Spatial Detectives' (2015) 9(7) *Geography Compass* 406.

79 Jane Holder and Carolyn Harrison, 'Connecting Law and Geography' in Jane Holder and Carolyn Harrison (eds) *Law and Geography* (Oxford University Press, 2003) 3, 5.

80 Alexandre Kedar, 'On the Legal Geography of Ethnographic Settler States: Notes Towards a Research Agenda' in Jane Holder and Carolyn Harrison (eds) *Law and Geography* (Oxford University Press, 2003) 402, 406–407.

81 Ian Ward, *Law and Literature: Possibilities and Perspectives* (Cambridge University Press, 1995) 3. A similar distinction has been employed in law and religion between study of the religious dimensions of law, the legal dimensions of religion and the interaction of legal and religious ideas and institutions, norms and practices: John Witte, Jr., 'The Study of Law and Religion in the United States: An Interim Report' (2012) 14 *Ecclesiastical Law Journal* 327.

82 Soja distinguished two ways of looking at the relationship between law and geography: the first 'focuses on how geography or more broadly social space, social spatiality, affects law and legal development' examining how 'the law has always involved itself with the location of things, with disputes over turf, territories, boundaries, borders, jurisdictions'; the second deals with the reverse, 'how law shapes geographies', exploring how 'legal understandings and knowledge of law are applied to help in understanding the social production of space, how social spatiality is constructed and organized and expressed': Edward W Soja, 'Afterword' (1996) 48 *Stanford Law Review* 1421, 1425, 1426. David Delaney has made the distinction between 'Law in Space', the way in which 'situated legal practices, for example, legislation or formal legal judgment, contribute to the shaping and reshaping of the spacialities of social life', and 'Space in Law', 'the analysis and/or critique of the work that spatial representations perform in legal discourse I will call Space-In Law': David Delaney, 'Beyond the Word: Law as a Thing of this World' in Jane Holder and Carolyn Harrison (eds) *Law and Geography* (Oxford University Press, 2003) 67, 68–69.

self-contained categories of discrete objects',[83] the point of making the distinction is to stress how 'the legal and the spatial, the discursive and the material, are inextricable'.[84] Indeed, one of the hallmarks of the law and geography movement has been the way in which it has transcended the two disciplines of law and geography. As Jane Holder and Carolyn Harrison put it, many contributors to the legal geography project:

> offer not just a geographical dimension to law – or a view of law in its geographical context. Instead, an attempt is made to identify how law and geography bear upon each other, and draw out the points of contrast, support, complicity, especially with respect of taken-for-granted distinctions between the social and the material, the human and non-human, and what constitutes people and things.[85]

Crucially, although the legal geography project is sometimes seen as arising from the intersection of the disciplines of law and geography, noticing and filling gap between the two,[86] it is not commonly understood to be a distinct sub-discipline of either discipline.[87] This is despite how both the disciplines of law and geography are commonly divided into sub-disciplines.[88] This is in stark contrast to Legal History which is largely seen as a sub-discipline of law (with similarly focused work in history departments not commonly being included within the Legal History canon). The difference between Legal History and legal geography is that the legal geography project is interdisciplinary and not institutionalised.[89]

83 Nicholas Blomley, *Law, Space and Geographies of Power* (Guilford Press, 1994) xiii.

84 David Delaney, 'Beyond the Word: Law as a Thing of this World' in Jane Holder and Carolyn Harrison (eds) *Law and Geography* (Oxford University Press, 2003) 67, 71.

85 Jane Holder and Carolyn Harrison, 'Connecting Law and Geography' in Jane Holder and Carolyn Harrison (eds) *Law and Geography* (Oxford University Press, 2003) 3.

86 David Delaney, 'Beyond the Word: Law as a Thing of This World' in Jane Holder and Carolyn Harrison (eds) *Law and Geography* (Oxford University Press, 2003) 67; Luke Bennett and Antonia Layard, 'Legal Geography: Becoming Spatial Detectives' (2015) 9(7) *Geography Compass* 406, 407.

87 'Legal geography is not a sub-discipline of human geography, nor does it name an area of specialized legal scholarship': Irus Braverman, Nicholas Blomley, David Delaney and Alexandre Kedar, 'Introduction: Expanding the Spaces of Law' in Irus Braverman, Nicholas Blomley, David Delaney and Alexandre Kedar (eds) *The Expanding Spaces of Law: A Timely Legal Geography* (Stanford University Press, 2014) 1.

88 'Geography has long been hyphenated into specialities – the geographies of health, the economy, culture, politics or sociality, for example – to say nothing of the divide into "human" and "physical" domains': Nicholas Blomley, *Law, Space and Geographies of Power* (Guilford Press, 1994) 27.

89 Braverman *et al.* note that although legal geography 'shares important conceptual similarities with other interdisciplinary and subdisciplinary endeavours' such as law and society and Legal History, in that it foregrounds space rather than the social or time, the difference that allows it to be interdisciplinary is that law and geography 'occupies little institutional presence': Irus Braverman, Nicholas Blomley, David Delaney and Alexandre Kedar, 'Introduction: Expanding the Spaces of Law' in Irus Braverman, Nicholas Blomley, David Delaney and Alexandre Kedar (eds) *The Expanding Spaces of Law: A Timely Legal Geography* (Stanford University Press, 2014) 1, 1–2.

It is not a sub-discipline found within Law Schools with its own specialist journals, book series and professional associations. It is also rarely taught as a specialist module in Law Schools. This has meant that legal geography is not yoked to one discipline and rather can become in the words of Braverman *et al.*, 'a truly interdisciplinary intellectual project': 'It is less a "field" than braided lines of inquiry that have emerged out of the confluence of various intellectual interests'.[90]

This was the consequence of legal geography developing in the heat of the critical turn. This also meant that from the start 'the law and geography project became not merely contextual, but profoundly critical'.[91] It developed as 'a "critical" geographic scholarship that professes a sensitivity to power and politics'.[92] By contrast, Legal History was already well established within Law Schools and so the impact of Critical Legal Studies was more limited and faded as that movement declined as a distinct force. This is one respect in which Legal History has much to learn from legal geography; though, as earlier chapters have shown, the contaminated nature of the word 'critical' means that the term 'subversive' is to be preferred. Previous chapters have shown how Subversive Legal History can disturb, de-construct and re-construct both the internal and external dimensions of law. Legal geography can provide an inspiration in this regard. A critical geographical approach, like a subversive historical one, underscores the contingency of law and the pragmatic nature of legal change. As Gareth A Jones pointed out, paying attention to the spatiality of law can 'show up important influences on the positivism of law, including informal social institutions and practices such as community, custom, and citizenship'.[93] This has the effect of 'destabilising the normativity and objectivity of law'.

Although a range of lawyers[94] and geographers[95] contributed to this critical geography project, this inherently critical approach was epitomised by Nicholas

90 Ibid 1.

91 Jane Holder and Carolyn Harrison, 'Connecting Law and Geography' in Jane Holder and Carolyn Harrison (eds) *Law and Geography* (Oxford University Press, 2003) 3, 4.

92 Nicholas Blomley, *Law, Space and Geographies of Power* (Guilford Press, 1994) 27.

93 Gareth A Jones, 'Camels, Chameleons and Coyotes: Problematizing the "Histories" of Land Law Reform' in Jane Holder and Carolyn Harrison (eds) *Law and Geography* (Oxford University Press, 2003) 169, 186.

94 Braverman *et al.* mention the work of Davina Cooper (Davina Cooper, *Governing Out of Order: Space, Law and the Politics of Belonging* (Rivers Oram Press, 1998)) and Eve Darian Smith (Eve Darian Smith, *Bridging Divides: The Channel Tunnel and English Legal Identity in the New Europe* (University of California Press, 1999)) as well as special issues of journals such as the 'Surveying Law and Border' issue of *Stanford Law Review* in 1996 which included an afterword from Edward Soja: Irus Braverman, Nicholas Blomley, David Delaney and Alexandre Kedar, 'Introduction: Expanding the Spaces of Law' in Irus Braverman, Nicholas Blomley, David Delaney and Alexandre Kedar (eds) *The Expanding Spaces of Law: A Timely Legal Geography* (Stanford University Press, 2014) 1, 6.

95 Commentators often hail Gordon L Clark, *Judges and the Cities: Interpreting Local Autonomy* (University of Chicago Press, 1985) as one of the two pivotal texts alongside Blomley's 1994 book. See ibid 4–5 and David Delaney, *The Spatial, the Legal and the Pragmatics of World-Making: Nomospheric Investigations* (Routledge, 2010) 11. Clark as a geographer drew upon sophisticated legal philosophical resources to argue how 'our institutions make and remake

Blomley's 1994 monograph *Law, Space and Geographies of Power*.[96] This work will therefore be discussed in some detail as an exemplar of the critical approach. *Law, Space and Geographies of Power* provided 'an exploration and a tentative map of the intriguing and politically significant territory between law and geography' and argued the need for multidisciplinary interaction between lawyers and geographers who both 'have a lot to learn from each other and a lot to teach each other'.[97] Blomley set out 'to convince critical geographers of the political and geographic significance of law, whilst also trying to persuade leftist legal scholars of the critical power of the "geographical imagination"'. He argued that the geographies and spatial understandings were always present and that 'concealed within legal thought and legal practice are a number of representations – or "geographies" – of the spaces of political, social and economic life'. This meant that 'in much the same way that law relies in various ways on claims concerning history, so it both defines and draws upon a complex range of geographies and spatial understandings'. Blomley argued that these 'geographies of law are not passive backdrops in the legal process, or of random import, but, in combination with their implied claims concerning social life, can be powerful, even oppressive'.[98] The study of legal geography was then 'from the start, explicitly and normatively critical' with a 'radical normative commitment'.[99] This entailed an insistence that 'a critical legal geography can not only *document* the relation between law, space, and power but also can begin to *challenge* the orthodox linkage'.[100] For Blomley:

> The very spatiality of legal knowledge… is potentially subversive of imperial claims to legal objectivity, totality, and stability. The orthodox legal representation of space, in other words, is only one plausible map of the spaces of social life.

This sounds similar to Subversive Legal History as developed in previous chapters. It challenges the orthodox approach that presents law and space as being 'objective, asocial and "innocent"'.[101] It contests the representation that their analysis is a closed activity, 'a technical art, conducted respectively by technical

society through their interpretative and determinant actions': Gordon Clark, *Judges and the Cities: Interpreting Local Autonomy* (University of Chicago Press, 1985) xi.

96 Nicholas Blomley, *Law, Space and Geographies of Power* (Guilford Press, 1994).

97 Ibid xi.

98 Ibid xii.

99 Braverman *et al.* suggest that such a 'designation refers not only to avowed leftist or radical political commitments but also to a broad scepticism toward the state and the pieties of many rule-of-law claims': Irus Braverman, Nicholas Blomley, David Delaney and Alexandre Kedar, 'Introduction: Expanding the Spaces of Law' in Irus Braverman, Nicholas Blomley, David Delaney and Alexandre Kedar (eds) *The Expanding Spaces of Law: A Timely Legal Geography* (Stanford University Press, 2014) 1, 6.

100 Ibid xii.

101 Nicholas Blomley, *Law, Space and Geographies of Power* (Guilford Press, 1994) xiii.

experts, such as judges and cartographers'. A critical approach questioned the autonomy of law, the way in which 'legal interpretation is understood as distinct, structured by its own logic and rationality'.[102] For Blomley, 'the very existence of a critical law and geography is nothing short of revolutionary'.[103] This revolution has two effects: first, it affects the object of study and second it affects the nature and purpose of study. A critical approach underscores how 'law and space are entangled in important ways, being mutually constitutive and deeply implicated in power relations'. Blomley argued that 'in interweaving law and space, rather than treating them in terms of the "effect" of one upon another, we challenge the theoretical and political terrain in suggestive and provocative ways'.[104] This brings to the fore power relations and makes a 'normative commitment to a radical vision of social justice'.[105]A critical legal geography treats 'the legal places of "everyday life" as politically significant'.[106] As Blomley put it, under a critical approach 'law and space are thus cast as relational, acquiring meaning through social action, rather than objective categories that operate prior to social life'.[107] For Blomley, this means that:

> Both critical lawyers and critical geographers have rejected legal science and spatial science, respectively, concentrating on the political significance of law and space, both within their disciplines and within wider social life. As a result, the gap between law and geography becomes less tenable.

102 Nicholas Blomley, 'From "What?" to "So What?": Law and Geography in Retrospect' in Jane Holder and Carolyn Harrison (eds) *Law and Geography* (Oxford University Press, 2003) 13, 20. However, it is important not to simplify here. Luke Bennett and Antonia Layard have argued that law 'should not be understood as a "straw man" in these endeavours, berated for its aspatiality when all is perhaps not quite as it seems'. They maintain that their spatial detective work reveals that 'the law actually approaches spatiality selectively – sometimes ignoring it, while at other times embracing it'. And so, 'it is insufficient to regard law as spatially blind or to assert that embracing locational differentiation would always be progressive. Instead, what needs to be teased out of any encounter between law and spatiality is whether, and if so how and for what purpose (and what period of time), spatiality is being invoked or ignored, for an apparent absence of space is also doing spatial and legal work: Luke Bennett and Antonia Layard, 'Legal Geography: Becoming Spatial Detectives' (2015) 9(7) *Geography Compass* 406, 418.

103 Nicholas Blomley, 'From "What?" to "So What?": Law and Geography in Retrospect' in Jane Holder and Carolyn Harrison (eds) *Law and Geography* (Oxford University Press, 2003) 24.

104 Nicholas Blomley, *Law, Space and Geographies of Power* (Guilford Press, 1994) 51–52.

105 Irus Braverman, Nicholas Blomley, David Delaney and Alexandre Kedar, 'Introduction: Expanding the Spaces of Law' in Irus Braverman, Nicholas Blomley, David Delaney and Alexandre Kedar (eds) *The Expanding Spaces of Law: A Timely Legal Geography* (Stanford University Press, 2014) 1, 5.

106 Nicholas Blomley, *Law, Space and Geographies of Power* (Guilford Press, 1994) 48.

107 'The spatially defined environments we move in – the homes, workplaces, streets, neighbourhood, shops, and so on – can serve to reflect and reinforce social relations of power, through complex and layered spatial processes and practices that code, exclude, enable, stage, locate and so on': Nicholas Blomley, 'From "What?" to "So What?": Law and Geography in Retrospect' in Jane Holder and Carolyn Harrison (eds) *Law and Geography* (Oxford University Press, 2003) 13, 22.

This is the second revolutionary effect: the transformation of how law and space is studied. Blomley's talk of the rejection of legal and spatial science in favour of focusing on politics is certainly bold. He noted that it 'would seem a self-destructive, even suicidal, act'.[108] However, he argued that it is actually a re-constructive act that may 'provide the basis for a fuller and richer account of both law and space'. He was not arguing for the dominance of political science, rather he was maintaining that the way in which the legal and the spatial fuse is political. Blomley's entanglement thesis means that legal geography cannot be seen as the bridge between law and space because 'the argument here is that there is no gap to bridge'.[109] Rather the 'perceived divide is merely a function of an institutional categorization' which needs itself to be supplanted. A critical approach highlights questions of power and how they are perpetuated through discourse.[110] It also crucially reveals the power relations between disciplines.[111] The solution for Blomley is not to reject disciplinary specialism but to abandon 'disciplinary myopia'.[112] He noted that such critical perspectives begin to lay the groundwork for a more nuanced – and necessarily transdisciplinary – account of law, space and power'. This is reminiscent of the work of Roger Cotterrell discussed previously which saw a sociological approach as a transdisciplinary critique which seeks to transgress the boundaries of the science system.[113] This was to become a key characteristic of the legal geography project – and is an insight that the disciplinary-based and institutionalised field of Legal History can learn from. The next section will explore how legal geography has developed and can develop further as a post-disciplinary project.

Phase Two: The Post-Disciplinary Project

Foucault's prediction of an 'epoch of space' has to some extent become true.[114]

By the twenty-first century, legal geography scholarship had become a recognised project.[115] The 'spatial turn' both escalated and stabilised but in the

108 Nicholas Blomley, *Law, Space and Geographies of Power* (Guilford Press, 1994) 5.

109 Ibid 37.

110 Delaney, Ford and Blomley wryly note that 'critical social theory in the last generation has highlighted – perhaps to the point of obsession – the connections between discourse and power'. David Delaney, Richard T Ford and Nicholas Blomley, 'Preface: Where is Law?' in Nicholas Blomley, David Delaney and Richard T Ford (eds) *The Legal Geographies Reader* (Blackwell, 2001) xiii, xix.

111 Blomley identifies a hierarchy at work whereby 'law vigorously places knowledge, with a suspicion of that deemed to lie outside its boundaries. External influences, such as geography, are thus admitted – if they are admitted at all on law's terms': Nicholas Blomley, 'From "What?" to "So What?": Law and Geography in Retrospect' in Jane Holder and Carolyn Harrison (eds) *Law and Geography* (Oxford University Press, 2003) 13, 20, 21.

112 Nicholas Blomley, *Law, Space and Geographies of Power* (Guilford Press, 1994) 5.

113 Roger Cotterrell, *Law, Culture and Society* (Ashgate, 2006) 54–55.

114 Michel Foucault, 'Of Other Spaces: Utopias and Heterotopias' (1986) 16 *Diacritics* 22.

115 Irus Braverman, Nicholas Blomley, David Delaney and Alexandre Kedar, 'Introduction: Expanding the Spaces of Law' in Irus Braverman, Nicholas Blomley, David Delaney and Alexandre

forms of occasional collaborations such as journal special editions and edited volumes,[116] rather than in institutional or disciplinary-based forms. A key characteristic of the project remained how it has become neither a legal nor geographical sub-discipline.[117] As Luke Bennett and Antonia Layard point out, a 'co-constitutive approach became a leitmotif of legal geography';[118] legal geography work became characterised as being a co-production of scholars. The term 'legal geography' itself reflected a bygone attachment to disciplinary labels and identities.

This led some proponents to devote energy to questions of naming. Soja raised not the question of what the project is to be called and how it is to be defined and understood, but rather what he saw as 'the interesting little problem of what to call those scholars who are developing this transdisciplinary spatial perspective'.[119] 'Critical human geographers' was dismissed as being 'probably still too narrowly confined' while the labels 'spatio-analyst', 'spatiologist' and 'geosopher' were all mooted. Others have focused on what to call the object of the inquiry. Delaney offered the term 'nomosphericity';[120] Kedar preferred 'jurispacedence';[121] and, perhaps most influentially, Blomley advocated that 'in thinking about the relation of space and law' we should 'literally run the words together, and refer to the conjunction as a "splice".[122] This terminology, he argued, casts critical fire on 'the active, constructed way in which splices are made', which he refers to as 'splicing'.[123] He contended that the independent orthodox

Kedar (eds) *The Expanding Spaces of Law: A Timely Legal Geography* (Stanford University Press, 2014) 1, 7.

116 E.g., Nicholas Blomley, David Delaney and Richard T Ford (eds) The *Legal Geographies Reader* (Blackwell, 2001); Jane Holder and Carolyn Harrison (eds) *Law and Geography* (Oxford University Press, 2003) and Austin Sarat, Lawrence Douglas and Martha Umphrey (eds) *The Place of Law* (University of Michigan Press, 2003).

117 The geographical turn has, however, been more closely embraced by the adherents of some legal sub-disciplines. Braverman *et al.* note how 'in international law, for example, scholars ... have emphasized that a contingent way of imagining space is foundational for international law as a discourse and that reimagining and investigating the difference space makes may severely problematize the practices carried out under the auspices of the conventionally imagined "international community"': Irus Braverman, Nicholas Blomley, David Delaney and Alexandre Kedar, 'Introduction: Expanding the Spaces of Law' in Irus Braverman, Nicholas Blomley, David Delaney and Alexandre Kedar (eds) *The Expanding Spaces of Law: A Timely Legal Geography* (Stanford University Press, 2014) 1, 7.

118 Luke Bennett and Antonia Layard, 'Legal Geography: Becoming Spatial Detectives' (2015) 9(7) *Geography Compass* 406, 408.

119 Edward Soja, 'Afterword' (1996) 48 *Stanford Law Review* 1421, 1423.

120 David Delaney, *The Spatial, the Legal and the Pragmatics of World-Making: Nomospheric Investigations* (Routledge, 2010) 24, 8.

121 Alexandre Kedar, 'On the Legal Geography of Ethnographic Settler States: Notes towards a Research Agenda' in Jane Holder and Carolyn Harrison (eds) *Law and Geography* (Oxford University Press, 2003) 402, 407.

122 Nicholas Blomley, 'From "What?" to "So What?": Law and Geography in Retrospect' in Jane Holder and Carolyn Harrison (eds) *Law and Geography* (Oxford University Press, 2003) 13, 30.

123 Ibid 31.

representations of both law and space 'have an air of neutrality and objectivity' which means that splices 'can appear simply part of the order of things and thus non-negotiable'.[124] By contrast, focusing on splicing reveals how splices 'tend to construct the world in ways that systemically favour the powerful: employers, men, white, property owners and so on. But the apparent neutrality of splices can neutralize or obscure the differential treatment of legal subjects'. For Blomley, 'the complex geographies of law can be made to reveal their culpability, their construction and their contingency'.[125] This terminological discussion underscored that a new language is needed because talk of 'legal geography' or 'law and space' imposes a disciplinary mindset.[126]

Proponents of legal geography have referred to the field as being transdisciplinary[127] or post-disciplinary.[128] Although a number of different definitions and understandings of these terms exist,[129] the term 'transdisciplinary' is typically defined as an advanced form of critical[130] interdisciplinarity where disciplinary approaches and structures are transgressed and transformed,[131] while the closely linked concept of post-disciplinary is often understood to include a critique of and a break away from disciplinary approaches. This can be seen in some respect as a return to the predisciplinary intellectual tradition of polymaths answering large questions and surveying several fields. It is a rejection of the distinctions of modernity, 'the discursive and organisational construction (and worse, the

124 Ibid 30.

125 Nicholas Blomley, *Law, Space and Geographies of Power* (Guilford Press, 1994) 227.

126 Luke Bennett and Antonia Layard contend that the project's 'goal of developing common conceptual frameworks that both lawyers and geographers can use, which connect meaningfully into the concerns and conventions of each discipline' has to date 'reflected the project's beginnings in critical geography, and these concepts may require re-thinking and expanding today': Luke Bennett and Antonia Layard, 'Legal Geography: Becoming Spatial Detectives' (2015) 9(7) *Geography Compass* 406, 408.

127 Nicholas Blomley, *Law, Space and Geographies of Power* (Guilford Press, 1994) 5; David Delaney, *The Spatial, the Legal and the Pragmatics of World-Making: Nomospheric Investigations* (Routledge, 2010) 11.

128 Irus Braverman, Nicholas Blomley, David Delaney and Alexandre Kedar, 'Introduction: Expanding the Spaces of Law' in Irus Braverman, Nicholas Blomley, David Delaney and Alexandre Kedar (eds) *The Expanding Spaces of Law: A Timely Legal Geography* (Stanford University Press, 2014) 1, 10.

129 Multidisciplinary work is understood as the juxtapositioning of materials from different disciplines, while interdisciplinary work requires the integration of material from different disciplines. See Russell Sandberg, *Religion, Law and Society* (Cambridge University Press, 2014) 233 *et seq.* and Allen F Repko, *Interdisciplinary Research: Process and Theory* (3rd ed, Sage, 2016).

130 Within interdisciplinary work, 'instrumental' forms which regard themselves as growing from the foundations provided by the disciplines and regard their function as furthering the needs of the disciplines amidst wider social changes can be contrasted with 'critical' forms which seek to de-construct disciplinary distinctions, paying particular attention to the implicit values and purposes hidden within such approaches.

131 The transdisciplinary vision is not the erecting of a new discipline or super discipline but rather the 'elaboration of new language, logics and concepts to permit genuine dialogue': Julie Thompson Klein, 'Prospects for Transdisciplinarity' (2004) 36 *Futures* 515, 516.

fetishisation) of disciplinary boundaries' which underpins not only the modern university but the education system as a whole.[132] The post-disciplinary vision entails 'the breakdown of these established disciplinary boundaries as well as the rediscovery of space and time as socially constructed, socially constitutive relations'.[133] For Braverman *et al.*, this required 'a 'move beyond legal geography in a way that both draws on and contributes to broader social and humanities studies'.[134] Although they noted that there are several examples of post-disciplinary legal geography work,[135] Braverman *et al.* singled out David Delaney's 2010 monograph *The Spatial. The Legal and the Pragmatics of World Making: Nomospheric Investigations*[136] as having 'a distinctively post-disciplinary orientation to legal geography throughout'.[137] It is to that work, therefore, that we now turn.

Delaney developed a seven step plan to move beyond 'law and geography'.[138] The first step was 'twisting the split' by 'repositioning materiality and discursivity in terms of each other– not as opposite but as mutually constitutive'; in other words, seeing worlds and words as shaping one another. The second step involved 'foregrounding performativity' by assuming 'that discourses take on a worldly presence through how they are performed or put into practice, or through how cultural performative repertoires are improvised or reiterated'.[139] This involved stressing that discourses have social effect through their performance. The third and fourth steps applied this to geographical and legal discourses respectively. The third step entailed 'rotating the spatial' by 'seeing space as imagined and

132 Bob Jessop and Ngai-Ling Sum, 'Pre-Disciplinary and Post-Disciplinary Perspectives' (2001) 6(1) *New Political Economy* 89.

133 Ibid 91.

134 Irus Braverman, Nicholas Blomley, David Delaney and Alexandre Kedar, 'Introduction: Expanding the Spaces of Law' in Irus Braverman, Nicholas Blomley, David Delaney and Alexandre Kedar (eds) *The Expanding Spaces of Law: A Timely Legal Geography* (Stanford University Press, 2014) 1, 10.

135 Braverman *et al.* (ibid 11, 3) mentioned the work of Irus Braverman herself and Andreas Philippopoulos-Mihalopoulos 'in his conceptualization of a genuinely "spatial justice" – and in contract with conventional *aspatial* notions of spatial justice' (Andreas Philippopoulos-Mihalopoulos, *Spatial Justice: Body, Lawscape, Atmosphere* (Routledge, 2015)). They also noted that Boaventura Santos' 1987 article 'Law: A Map of Misreading – Toward a Postmodern Conception of Law' (Boaventura Santos, 'Law: A Map of Misreading – Toward a Postmodern Conception of Law' (1987) 14 *Journal of Law and Society* 279, 286) provided a very early example of such work. See also the work of Edward W Soja, which is explicitly transdisciplinary cutting 'across all perspectives and all modes of thought': Edward W Soja *Thirdspace* (Blackwell, 1996) 3; Edward W Soja, *Seeking Spatial Justice* (University of Minnesota Press, 2010).

136 David Delaney, *The Spatial. The Legal and the Pragmatics of World Making: Nomospheric Investigations* (Routledge, 2010).

137 Irus Braverman, Nicholas Blomley, David Delaney and Alexandre Kedar, 'Introduction: Expanding the Spaces of Law' in Irus Braverman, Nicholas Blomley, David Delaney and Alexandre Kedar (eds) *The Expanding Spaces of Law: A Timely Legal Geography* (Stanford University Press, 2014) 1, 10.

138 David Delaney, *The Spatial, the Legal and the Pragmatics of World-Making: Nomospheric Investigations* (Routledge, 2010) 12, 14.

139 Ibid 14–15.

discursively organized', 'seeing space as performed' and 'rethinking the materiality of space in light of these other critical operations'. Correspondingly, the fourth step rotated the legal by stressing how that too is continuously performed and 'creatively done and redone' not only by legal actors but 'by everyone who acts in accordance with (or with transgressive references to) understandings of rules, authority, rights, permissions, prohibitions, duties and so on'.[140]

The fifth step – arguably the most important – involved 'braiding' these 'strands of unconventional (and unconventional*izing*) thinking about the spatial and the legal' together 'in a way that highlights the worldly, pragmatic processes of their mutual constitutivity'.[141] Delaney noted that 'braiding' was similar to Blomley's concept of 'splicing' and that this represented a move 'beyond the domain of law and geography' whereby 'we can begin to investigate *how* traces of the spatial imaginary variously condition legal performances... or *how* legal materialities condition spatial imaginaries or *how* spatial performances affect the playing out of legal imaginaries'. The fifth step, therefore, stresses that legal and geographical discourses interweave and create one another. The sixth and seventh steps then are to politicise and historicise the investigation. This would highlight 'the always political (normatively contested) and historical (dynamic, transformational) character of the pragmatics of world-making and the simultaneously durable and malleable character of the worlds so made'. For Delaney, these seven steps were intended to ensure that:

> The foci of these inquires would not be on what "the spatial" and "the legal" are, nor merely on how the legal and the spatial are "related" but on how they happen – and so, on the pragmatics of world-making.

Given the title of Delaney's book, it is easy to focus on the end of this quote; however, it is the middle part which is crucial. The task of post-disciplinary legal geographers is to look beyond how the legal and the spatial are related and how this is achieved and re-achieved. The focus is no longer on the legal and the spatial as two separate entities. This was stressed by Luke Bennett and Antonia Layard who regarded Delaney's idea of 'braiding' and Blomley's notion of 'splicing' as being more or less identical and as 'the foundational conceptual device in legal geography'.[142] They understood splices or braids as being 'locally enacted encodings, which weave together spatial and legal meanings'. For Bennett and

140 Ibid 19. 'If we restrict our understanding of the legal to the conventional we will think more or less conventional thoughts. If we provisionally try out less conventional ways of thinking we might think thoughts that had been unthinkable and ask questions that it had not occurred to us to ask. This is the pragmatic attraction of looking at the legal in new ways. However, thinking about the legal in these ways might be asking too much. Maybe a better strategy is to simply call this something else altogether': ibid 20.

141 Ibid 23.

142 Luke Bennett and Antonia Layard, 'Legal Geography: Becoming Spatial Detectives' (2015) 9(7) *Geography Compass* 406, 409–410.

Layard, the task 'for legal geographers – for spatial detectives – is to identify each of the braids, to tease them apart and to attempt to identify what work law and spatiality are doing at any particular place and time'.[143] This is a practical act, 'reflecting legal geography's locating of itself in the field' and 'its commitment to social justice', meaning that 'in most legal geographic studies, investigation has been 'from the site up', focusing on explicating historical, social and spatial specificity'.[144] This recognises, in the words of Doreen Massey, that space is 'created out of the vast intricacies, the incredible complexities of the interlocking and the noninterlocking and the networks of relations at every scale from local to global'.[145] This is a dynamic process and 'space is by its nature full of power and symbolism, a complex web of relations of domination and subordination, or solidarity and co-operation'. And this 'means that the spatial has both an element of order and an element of chaos'.

This is reminiscent of the discussion in previous chapters about how a subversive approach to Legal History can develop by accepting entropic complexity as the norm. It is also evocative of the relational approach which has not only 'long constituted a key component of geographical work',[146] but is also playing an increasingly important role in legal theory.[147] As noted above, Blomley contended that under a critical approach law and space are 'cast as relational, acquiring meaning through social action'.[148] As he put it, under this 'fundamentally contextual' approach 'people do not understand themselves as fully autonomous individuals, but as relationally structured by diverse social and economic roles'.[149] In short, 'our sense of who we are is constituted by our relations with others. And, of course, our sense of who we are changes according to the social (and, of course, legal) context within which find ourselves'. Braverman *et al.* hail relational thinking as a possible future direction for legal geography, arguing that such an approach 'eschews essentialism by insisting that all social entities are to

143 Ibid 409.

144 Fieldwork, often with an ethnographic dimension, 'seeks to investigate precisely how (and why) sites are framed, managed or used in the way that they are': ibid 410, 411.

145 Doreen Massey, *Space, Place and Gender* (Polity, 1994) 265.

146 Though 'the sub-disciplinary division between human and physical geography has often prevented the discipline from entering fully into a relational mode of thinking': Jonathan Murdoch, *Post-Structuralist Geography: A Guide to Relational Space* (Sage, 2006) 3, 19.

147 See, generally, Jonathan Herring, *Law and the Relational Self* (Cambridge University Press, 2020). Most notably, Relational Contract Theory (RCT), as primarily developed by Ian Macneil, has criticised orthodox contract for its focus on agreements as discrete one-off transactions, and for failing to recognise the relationships between the parties, as he argued that these relationships significantly influence the ways in which decisions are made. See, e.g., Ian R Macneil, 'Relational Contract: What We Do and Do Not Know' (1985) *Wisconsin Law Review* 484; Ian R Macneil, 'The New Social Contract: An Inquiry into Modern Contractual Relations' (1996) 15(1) *Journal of Public Policy & Marketing* 157 and the essays in David Campbell (ed) *The Relational Theory of Contract: Selected Works of Ian Macneil* (Sweet & Maxwell, 2001).

148 Nicholas Blomley, 'From "What?" to "So What?": Law and Geography in Retrospect' in Jane Holder and Carolyn Harrison (eds) *Law and Geography* (Oxford University Press, 2003) 13, 22.

149 Nicholas Blomley, *Law, Space and Geographies of Power* (Guilford Press, 1994) 219–220.

be understood and explained according to their interactions, avoiding a view of internally stable concepts and entities'.[150] A relational approach allows the questioning of the architecture of law and regards spaces not as 'territorial units but dynamic compositions':

> Such a shift would allow us to begin to transform our analysis from legally consequential spaces such as to the state border, to more creative explorations of the process of bordering, where bodies are understood not as inert, fixed sites, but as fluid, nonlinear, and experimental practices produced by law.

This too reflects the subversive approach advocated in previous chapters. The need for a practical rational grounded approach was also highlighted in the chapter on Feminist Legal History.[151] Indeed, as with Legal History, a feminist approach has begun to develop as 'a new and distinctive "stream" within legal geography'.[152] Though in its infancy, engagement and relationship-building is beginning to take place between feminist geography, the legal geography project and Feminist Legal Studies.[153] This has been led by two agenda-setting articles and a special issue curated by Dana Cuomo and Katherine Brickell.[154] They advocated the need for feminist legal geographies or 'feminist geolegality' (so called because it 'integrates the intellectual terrains of legal geography and feminist geopolitics').[155] As Cynthia S Gorman has pointed out, such work makes 'visible the discursive tactics and legal manoeuvres involved in the struggle to delineate… juridical borders'.[156] An explicitly geographic analysis brings to the fore not only 'how laws are constituted through contested socio-spatial ideas, but also the dynamic ways in which discourse is constituted through interactions within the legal process that are always spatially and territorially embedded'.[157] A feminist approach adds to this a focus on 'how the law is sustained by a

150 Irus Braverman, Nicholas Blomley, David Delaney and Alexandre Kedar, 'Introduction: Expanding the Spaces of Law' in Irus Braverman, Nicholas Blomley, David Delaney and Alexandre Kedar (eds) *The Expanding Spaces of Law: A Timely Legal Geography* (Stanford University Press, 2014) 1, 17.

151 For an example of the use of relationality in the feminist legal literature see Sharon Thompson's Feminist Relational Contract Theory (FRCT): Sharon Thompson, *Prenuptial Agreements and the Presumption of Free Choice: Issues of Power in Theory and Practice* (Hart, 2015); Sharon Thompson, 'Feminist Relational Contract Theory: A New Model for Family Property Agreements' (2018) 45(4) *Journal of Law and Society* 617.

152 Dana Cuomo and Katherine Brickell, 'Feminist Legal Geographies' (2019) 51(5) *EPA: Economy and Space* 1043.

153 Ibid 1047.

154 Ibid and Katherine Brickell and Dana Cuomo, 'Feminist Geolegality' (2019) 43 (1) *Progress in Human Geography* 104.

155 Ibid 105.

156 Cynthia S Gorman, 'Feminist Legal Archaeology, Domestic violence and the Raced-gendered juridical Boundaries of U.S. Asylum Law' (2019) 51(5) *EPA: Economy and Space* 1050, 1052.

157 Ibid 1054.

variety of power dynamics that structure women's lives including analysis of the varied hierarchies that subordinate and denigrate women'.[158] Both Gorman and Cuomo and Brickell stress that such a feminist orientation 'necessarily involves the theory and methodology of intersectionality, which emphasizes the constitutive relationship between gender and other social vectors of power such as race, class, age, nationality and sexual orientation'.[159]

Post-disciplinary work on legal geography also provides an inspiration for Subversive Legal History in that it presents its approach as a methodology that can be adopted by all rather than being the preserve of specialists. Luke Bennett and Antonia Layard argued that 'the practice of law itself involves such spatial detective work'.[160] Although they noted that legal geographers often have a different starting point from other academic lawyers, beginning with 'an interest in mundane sites' rather than starting with the text, they maintained that the spatial detective 'expands doctrinal legal analysis' exploring the understanding of 'space-talk' or a lack of 'space-talk' in judgments:[161]

> Legal geographers tend to take the analysis wider, considering a wider range of stakeholder and situational influences. This more legal geographically infused doctrinal method echoes the intellectual traditions of the interpretivist turn, which looked to discursive analyses of legal provisions and practice.[162]

Bennett and Layard therefore present the legal geography project as a widely required methodological supplement. The non-institutionalised state of the project as well as its interdisciplinary nature and post-disciplinary ambitions enables it to be used as a tool to further legal doctrinal work. This contrasts with Legal History whose institutionalised nature as a sub-discipline often frustrates such a potential. Reference to legal geography is therefore instructive as an analogy of how approaches to law can develop (comparing the buoyant legal geography with the comatosed institutionalised and disciplinary-based Legal History). Indeed, some recent legal geography work develops the argument that attention should be afforded to time as well as to space. The epitome of such an approach can be found in Mariana Valverde's identification and discussion of 'chronotopes',[163] which the third and final section of this chapter will now discuss.

158 Ibid 1053.

159 Ibid; Katherine Brickell and Dana Cuomo, 'Feminist Geolegality' (2019) 43 (1) *Progress in Human Geography* 104, 107.

160 Luke Bennett and Antonia Layard, 'Legal Geography: Becoming Spatial Detectives' (2015) 9(7) *Geography Compass* 406, 409.

161 Ibid 413.

162 Ibid 412.

163 Mariana Valverde, *Chronotopes of Law: Jurisdiction, Scale and Governance* (Routledge, 2015).

Phase Three: Interweaving Space and Time

Ironically, while the early proponents of legal geography were critical of the ubiquity of history, recent advocates of legal geography have lamented that the focus on space means that now it is time that is neglected.

Doreen Massey has observed that 'if once it was "time" that framed the privileged angle of vision, today, so it is often said, that role has been taken over by space'.[164] Indeed, Braverman *et al.* have criticised legal geography as being 'guilty of privileging space over time', noting that 'deep engagements with history or historiography are relatively infrequent in contemporary legal geography'.[165] And Bennett and Layard have called for greater inquisitiveness about the past as well as other 'multiple aspects of temporality' and the dynamics of 'space-time'.[166] Although there are a few other examples of work that seek to do this,[167] the most thorough examination of the development of 'space-time' has been the work of Canadian academic Mariana Valverde, which has drawn upon the Russian philosopher Mikhail Bakhtin to develop the concept of 'chronotopes'.[168] Mariana Valverde pointed out that:

> the argument – and by now, often just the assumption – that space is more important than other categories of analysis has had the intended effect of reviving an old metaphysical fallacy: namely, treating space and time as abstract and separate entities, Newton-fashion.[169]

This has meant that 'sociolegal work on space tends to neglect or subordinate temporality, as geography generally does'.[170] Valverde talked of a 'one-sided

164 Doreen Massey, *For Space* (Sage, 2005) 62.

165 Irus Braverman, Nicholas Blomley, David Delaney and Alexandre Kedar, 'Introduction: Expanding the Spaces of Law' in Irus Braverman, Nicholas Blomley, David Delaney and Alexandre Kedar (eds) *The Expanding Spaces of Law: A Timely Legal Geography* (Stanford University Press, 2014) 1, 14. For discussion about the interaction between history and geography generally see Alan R H Baker, *Geography and History: Bridging the Divide* (Cambridge University Press, 2003).

166 Luke Bennett and Antonia Layard, 'Legal Geography: Becoming Spatial Detectives' (2015) 9(7) *Geography Compass* 406, 415.

167 Bennett and Layard (ibid) note that 'concern with the playing out of the spatio-legal across time (and amidst socio-economic relations) has always been evident in historical legal geographies, for example, E.P. Thompson's analysis of the Black Act which criminalised poaching at a time of mass land enclosure and agro-industrial change – thus figuring deer, rabbits and fish within class antagonism over access to land and its produce'.

168 Bakhtin defines chronotope as the name given 'to the intrinsic connectedness of temporal and spatial relationships that are artistically expressed in literature': Mikhail M Bakhtin, *The Dialogic Imagination: Four Essays* (University of Texas Press, 1981) 84. The concept of timespace has also been discussed for some time generally within the field of geography. See, e.g., John May and Nigel Thrift (eds) *Timespace: Geographies of Temporality* (Routledge, 2001).

169 Mariana Valverde, *Chronotopes of Law: Jurisdiction, Scale and Governance* (Routledge, 2015) 31.

170 Though Valverde opined that neglecting one dimension of social and legal life altogether (at least, a dimension that is being explored by other scholars, albeit not as numerous or

battle between advocates of space and time': geographers have 'impoverished their analysis' by acting imperially, regarding time as falling within geography; while 'historians have not been rushing to defend time as such as a category of analysis, perhaps because few of them are theoretically inclined, and those that are so inclined are more likely to read philosophy or anthropology rather than geography'.[171] For Valverde, the solution to this impasse comes from the work of Mikhail Bakhtin and his notion of the 'chronotope' as developed in his literary theory.[172] Bakhtin applied a 'relational approach' exploring how 'text and speech acts are always in constitutive relationships with one another, and, simultaneously, with their producers and with their changing audiences'.[173] He used analytical terms like chronotope not as 'precious conceptual jewels to be polished and displayed, but rather tools whose purpose is to help us understand how works of literature (and works of everyday embodied speech) are put together, and with what effects'.[174] Such an approach fits well with the focus of law as communication found in the elucidation of entropic complexity in the previous chapters, drawing on complexity and social systems theory. This is because, although the term chronotope 'synthesizes spatial and temporal scales',[175] it does not provide a theory of time and space or space-time but rather provides 'at most, a theory of communication that can be adapted for a variety of uses, including for legal studies purposes'.[176] For Valverde, the notion of the chronotope has 'the precise purpose of analyzing how the temporal and the spatial dimensions of life and governance affect each other'.[177] It is the equivalent of Blomley's concept of splicing and Delaney's talk of braiding applied to the interaction between space/geography and the law but here the context is the interaction between space/geography and time/history. It focuses on how the interaction occurs and its effect (in a similar manner to how Cotterrell highlighted the constant interpenetration and therefore the lack of separation between the legal and the social).

---

influential) is not nearly as problematic as the reification of the central category: "space"': ibid 31–32.

171 Ibid 38. This is somewhat reminiscent of the relationship between practitioners of old and new Legal History.

172 The key text quoted by Valverde is Mikhail M Bakhtin, *The Dialogic Imagination: Four Essays* (University of Texas Press, 1981) especially his essay 'Forms of Time and of the Chronotope in the Novel' in ibid 84.

173 Mariana Valverde, *Chronotopes of Law: Jurisdiction, Scale and Governance* (Routledge, 2015) 5.

174 Ibid 2.

175 The term "chronotope" was apparently inspired by early twentieth century relativity theory, which broke with the 'Newtonian habit of regarding time and space as separate and objectively real dimensions of the world in favour of a dynamic and indeed "relativistic" model of "space-time"': ibid 9, citing Mikhail M Bakhtin, *The Dialogic Imagination: Four Essays* (University of Texas Press, 1981) 84.

176 Mariana Valverde, *Chronotopes of Law: Jurisdiction, Scale and Governance* (Routledge, 2015) 7. Law is briefly mentioned by Bakhtin as a file that is particularly intertextual: ibid 5, citing Tzvetan Todorov, *Mikhail Bakhtin: The Dialogical Principle* (Manchester University Press, 1986) 63.

177 Mariana Valverde, *Chronotopes of Law: Jurisdiction, Scale and Governance* (Routledge, 2015) 9.

Bakhtin's work showed that 'each genre constructs time and space in characteristic ways' and that 'particular spatiotemporal modes constitute the "essence" of each genre, each major mode of cultural expression'.[178] For Valverde, this means that 'like literary genres, different legal processes are shaped and given meanings by particular spacetimes'.[179] She gave the example of the penal code, noting that if the code is seen as a genre then:

> We see that penal codes are written in a manner that homogenizes the spacetime of the state – or more accurately, a manner that tends towards homogenizing political spacetime and in so doing boosting the unity of the state. Modern penal codes create crimes that are absolute prohibitions applying to all persons, or at least non-insane adults, at all times, without considering the social status of the person or the time, space, and context of the event. This logic is in sharp contrast with earlier, highly status differentiated forms of law.[180]

She noted that the specificity of the chronotope of the modern penal code is shown by contrasting it to the way in which 'most non-criminal systems of legal rules apply only to people in particular relationships (e.g. employers, landlords, parents, spouses, vehicle drivers)'. Paying attention to chronotopes therefore 'encourages us to explore how different legal times create or shape spaces and vice versa: how the spatial location and spatial dynamics of legal processes in turn shape law's times – how spatial dynamics thickens time'.[181] Like Blomley, Delaney and Cotterrell, Valverde was adamant that lines of separation cannot be drawn.[182] Moreover, as Valverde put it, 'chronotopic analysis demands not only that we consider how temporalization affects spatialisation and vice versa, but also how heterogeneous and even contradictory chronotopes exist not only in a single literary (or legal) text but even within a single utterance'. This requires paying attention to the tensions between chronotopes and it is this that ensures that chronotope analysis is inherently critical. Valverde noted that 'there can be multiple mini-chronotopes, as it were, within a particular work'.[183] Bakhtin's work showed that it was dangerous to regard each work of literature as being internally cohesive; rather, 'elements can be inserted that carry in their wake logics that are quite at odds with that of the main plot'.[184] For Valverde, this point 'has great significance for any adaption of Bakhtin's work for legal studies': 'legal

178 Ibid 10.
179 Ibid 11.
180 Ibid 11–12.
181 Ibid 17–18.
182 'temporality cannot be measured or analyzed as if it were independent of spatial considerations, and vice versa': ibid 22.
183 Ibid 23, citing Mikhail M Bakhtin, *The Dialogic Imagination: Four Essays* (University of Texas Press, 1981) 158–159.
184 Mariana Valverde, *Chronotopes of Law: Jurisdiction, Scale and Governance* (Routledge, 2015) 23.

chronotopes are also often shot through and even undermined by eruptions, as it were, of conflicting chronotopes'. Valverde noted that feminist legal analysis can often provide an example of an eruption process, giving the example of the criminalisation of marital rape as 'an example of the eruption of one kind of legal chronotope (centred on the free autonomous person whose consent is formally required for all transactions) in the middle of a different chronotope'.[185]

In his essay 'Discourse in the Novel'[186] Bakhtin discussed how this use of multiple chronotopes exists not only at the scale of the work but also at the scale of the individual "utterance" or speech act'.[187] He introduced the concept of 'hybridization' to describe the 'mixture of two social languages within the arena of an utterance, between two different social consciousnesses, separated from one another by an epoch, by a social differentiation or by some other fact'.[188] Hybridization can be both intentional and unintentional and both 'are important features of legal discourse' for Valverde.[189] An example of intentional hybridization is the incorporation of international law terms into domestic law or the mixing of legal French with common law terminology while examples of unintentional hybridization can be found in the unthinking use of foreign language terms 'such as "junta", "coup d'état", "jihad", etc.' and 'the most famous example perhaps being the emergence of "three-strikes" laws in the USA, laws that relied not on social science evidence but rather on the powerful chronotope of baseball as their underpinning'. This underscores how law like any other discourse is contingent. As Valverde put it, 'each chronotope, while analytically distinct, does not function as a unified entity with solid borders'. This means that we 'always have opportunities to re-assemble existing chronotopes in novel ways'.[190] It also shows, however, that law is pragmatic given that:

> the vast majority of the hybridization processes that one can discern in various legal complexes are not produced by the creative efforts of individual authors or autonomous ethical subjects but rather by the mostly collective and largely unplanned workings of legal processes.

A chronotopic analysis therefore seems to sit well with Subversive Legal History, providing a vocabulary to identify and explain the needed disturbances in the field (as rival chronotopes) while stressing how law is relational and performed: a pragmatic construct which is contingent and therefore malleable. Valverde noted

185 Ibid 24.

186 Mikhail M Bakhtin, *The Dialogic Imagination: Four Essays* (University of Texas Press, 1981) 259

187 Mariana Valverde, *Chronotopes of Law: Jurisdiction, Scale and Governance* (Routledge, 2015) 24.

188 Mikhail M Bakhtin, *The Dialogic Imagination: Four Essays* (University of Texas Press, 1981) 358.

189 Mariana Valverde, *Chronotopes of Law: Jurisdiction, Scale and Governance* (Routledge, 2015) 24.

190 Ibid 26.

this 'not only enables new insights about governance, but also, at the reflexive level, challenges taken-for-granted divisions of intellectual labour that are produced by the kind of normalization of academic work that goes on not only through "disciplinarization" but also in interdisciplinary fields such as legal anthropology and legal geography'.[191] This furthers the post-disciplinary approach discussed above. A chronotopic analysis underscores that 'our first commitment is not promoting the prestige or the theoretical rigour of our chosen disciplines or fields – much less our chosen neologisms – but rather understanding the world we live in'. This reminder is important for Subversive Legal History and questions the term's capitalisation and use of the word history. Talk of Subversive Legal History is likely to exclude or subordinate space (which in reality is invariably inseparable from time) and risk perpetuating the institutionalised disciplinary ghettos that the post-disciplinary legal geography project has transcended. This raises the question of whether it is appropriate to talk about a Subversive Legal History at all. Perhaps we should be thinking instead of a wider approach not limited to any one interaction/discipline such as a 'law and humanities' approach, for instance.

Clearly thinking of scholars such as Foucault, Soja and Blomley, Valverde commented that the new focus on space 'has allowed some promoters of the new spatial analyses to slide from the very plausible remark that the nineteenth century's historicist arguments are inadequate for today to what amounts to a metaphysical claim that temporality as such is old-fashioned and perhaps irrelevant – at least theoretically irrelevant'.[192] A chronotopic analysis does not suffer from this shortcoming. For Valverde, 'chronotopic analysis does not privilege either space or time, but focuses on their interaction'. Yet, Valverde followed the approach of Foucault, Soja and Blomley in expressing concern about the dominance of history.[193] She wrote of the need to develop approaches that open 'the door to ways of thinking about temporality that are not reducible to "history"'.[194] Like the others, Valverde was not so much criticising history as a field or an approach but was rather concerned about the use of a particular form of history. She noted that 'the way in which legal spaces are constituted historically is an important and indeed central element in many studies by legal geographers; but the temporal dimension of human experience is all too often reduced to a rather atheoretical notion of history'.[195] Valverde's concern was that this 'by now routine invocation of historical specificity serves to conceal from view all manner

191 Ibid 26–27.

192 Ibid 39. See also Doreen Massey, *Space, Place and Gender* (Polity, 1994) 250.

193 However, unlike the others, Valverde regarded the undeveloped theoretical investigation of time as resulting in space becoming a 'privileged inquiry' and saw this as being dangerous: Mariana Valverde, *Chronotopes of Law: Jurisdiction, Scale and Governance* (Routledge, 2015) 39.

194 Ibid 34.

195 Ibid 39.

of other complex relations between modes of power/knowledge and modes of temporalization'.[196] The concern, then, was with evolutionary functionalism.

Moreover, Valverde insisted that this issue could not be resolved simply by revisiting Critical Legal Studies, which was, in her view 'a mature, if not frankly elderly, literature' with the term 'critical' being 'now wholly devoid of meaning'.[197] She noted that 'some legal historians have begun to go beyond the identification of "historical" with "critical" found in critical socio-legal studies generally':[198]

> Whether attentive to the constant return of the temporally unstable spectres that western positive law represses, or mining the common law's own internal legal-temporal pluralism... contemporary philosophically orientated legal historians are radically questioning the taken-for-granted identification of time as such with history – the intellectual move that grounds the common assumption that outlining the historical "context" of law amounts to and suffices for critical legal studies.

Valverde lamented that such 'recent historiographical work has not been taken up in any serious way by sociolegal scholars primarily interested in spatial logics'. She wrote that this was 'due to the institutional boundaries that continue to separate legal geography from legal history (and legal anthropology), even as individual scholars are increasingly free to roam across fields'. It is institutional boundaries that hampered the development of Legal History and have stopped interactions with and knowledge exchange with legal geography. As Valverde put it, 'Why legal history should appear as antiquated and empiricist while legal geography appears as youthful, theoretical, and trendy, is not a question that our current academic arrangements encourage us to ask'.[199] Yet, this is the question that this chapter has sought to address.

For Valverde, the solution is 'for scholars, even those fully located, institutionally, in a traditional discipline, to disavow the disciplinary standpoint altogether'.[200] Crucially this is not about making institutional change but moving beyond that. As she waspishly noted: 'I think it would be better to spend less time debating actual or potential changes in the shape and layout of the ivory tower's various rooms (which is what the tedious discussions of "interdisciplinary" amount to)'. Noting that the term post-disciplinary has an even 'fuzzier meaning than interdisciplinary' and that all scholars 'have particular intellectual habit and preferences' she nevertheless maintained that 'it is possible to put in

196 Ibid 45.

197 Ibid 47, 31.

198 Ibid 47.

199 Mariana Valverde, '"Time Thickens, Takes on Flesh": Spatiotemporal Dynamics in Law' in Irus Braverman, Nicholas Blomley, David Delaney and Alexandre Kedar (eds) *The Expanding Spaces of Law: A Timely Legal Geography* (Stanford University Press, 2014) 53, 54.

200 Mariana Valverde, *Chronotopes of Law: Jurisdiction, Scale and Governance* (Routledge, 2015) 42.

question and to try to undermine these habits and preferences that do nothing but reinscribe the quite arbitrary organization of the disciplines that emerged in twentieth-century universities'.[201] This is in line with the post-disciplinary ambitions of legal geography, though Valverde underlined that the focus on space in that literature betrays a disciplinary bias. As Valverde conceded, 'attacks on the academy's institutional and intellectual dividing practices and scholarly habits are by no means unusual'.[202] Yet, her adaptation of Bakhtin's concept of the chronotope applied in a legal setting provides a step forward: Valverde provided not just critique and de-construction; she also provided a means of re-construction, stressing the constant performative fusion of time, space and law at various levels of social interaction.[203]

The literature discussed in this chapter supports and refines the call for a Subversive Legal History which has been made in the previous chapters. What is needed is not a reintroduction of Critical Legal Studies but rather an informed move beyond it. A critical and post-disciplinary approach is needed; a subversive approach. This would be subversive in the sense that it functions as a critique, de-constructing but also – and this is where the use of the word subversive becomes key – re-constructing by shifting the viewpoint and the centre of gravity. Such an approach is relational and performative, subverting expectation of social entities as being fixed, objective and eternal. Moreover, and vitally, this approach is also subversive in terms of actively disturbing and transcending existing disciplinary borders, expectations, norms and traditions. The legal geography project shows how a subversive approach can be taken. Ironically (given their critique of the perceived dominance of history), it is the legal geography project that points to a way forward for legal historians. Reference to legal geography is important, however, not just as an analogy of how approaches to law can develop by comparing Legal History and legal geography. It is also important in that it demonstrates that a subversive approach should include space alongside time. A subversive approach recognises but questions, attacks and scrutinises both the temporal and the spatial stressing their interpenetration as well as the interpenetration of the legal and the social. It is sceptical of all binary distinctions and seeks to remove comfort blankets that have the effect of closing off academic discourses from one another and of making the legal appear to be separate, autonomous and closed. Ironically a Subversive Legal History casts critical fire at what we mean by the legal and what we mean by Legal History.

Nicholas Blomley's 1994 book *Law, Space and Geographies of Power* began with two quotes: Lawrence Friedman's assertion that law 'is too important to be left to the lawyers' and David Harvey's declaration that 'geography is too important to be left to geographers'.[204] Both statements are correct but a third

201 Ibid 42–43.

202 Ibid 178.

203 This develops the emphasis upon performativity found in Delaney's work, discussed above.

204 Lawrence M Friedman, 'The Law and Society Movement' (1986) 38 *Stanford Law Review* 763, 780; David Harvey, 'On the History and Present Condition of Geography: An Historical

and fourth need to be added: history is too important to be left to the historians and Legal History is too important to be left to the legal historians. In the same way that neither lawyers nor geographers should have a monopoly over legal geography, neither lawyers nor historians should have a monopoly over Legal History. Like legal geography, the historical study of law should become less institutionalised. It should be a post-disciplinary phenomenon. At the very least, it is time to get rid of the capital letters: Legal History needs to become legal history, not a specialist sub-discipline of law but a post-disciplinary approach; one could say, a method.

The continuing journey of legal geography, which itself is contested and non-linear, reveals the scope of this challenge. It questions whether the focus on subversive legal history remains too timid (even with the lower case lettering) given that it betrays its origins and fidelity with the discipline of law and with historical method. The post-disciplinary drive clearly informs the on-going battle between the camps of legal historians. Those who are placed in the new camp despite their own subjective eschewing of the label of legal historian are clearly driven by at least some of the values of the post-disciplinary project. But this is no mere battle over the identity and usefulness of legal history. There is a much larger on-going war. It is a war for the soul of Law Schools, both in terms of their identity and also their worth. It is a war about the values that Law Schools teach, what law students are indoctrinated into as they are moulded into thinking like lawyers; it is a war about those chants from the monastic Law School that rebound outside the university campus. As Nicholas Blomley noted:

> If the liberal-legal imagination is, indeed, constitutive of social life, the critical challenge cannot be confined to the law school. A challenge to the legal orthodoxy constitutes a contest over the terms of social and political life, and the language and logic by which social relations are to be structured.[205]

This raises the question of whether subversive legal history is capable of fighting the battles ahead, transforming the nature, purpose and worth of legal education. It is to that question that the next and final chapter turns.

Materialist Method' (1984) 36 *The Professional Geographer* 1, 7: quoted in Nicholas Blomley, *Law, Space and Geographies of Power* (Guilford Press, 1994).

205 Ibid 24.

8 We Are all Legal Historians Now

The creator of time travel regarded the legal mind to be retrospective, interpreting the present entirely in relation to the past.

In a lecture delivered to the Royal Institution in 1902, H G Wells (1866–1946), the author who invented (or at least popularised) the notion of time travel in his novel, *The Time Machine*,[1] distinguished between 'two divergent types of mind'.[2] The first and predominant type of mind 'seems scarcely to think of the future at all'; it regards it 'as a sort of blank canvas upon which the advancing present will presently write events'. This state of mind 'is retrospective in habit, and interprets the things of the present, and gives value of this and denies it to that, entirely with relation to the past'. The second, 'a more modern and much less abundant state of mind, thinks constantly and by preference of things to come, and of present things mainly in relation to the results that must arise from them'. This second state of mind 'is constructive in habit, it interprets the things of the present and gives value to this or that, entirely in relation to things designed or foreseen'. The first state of mind, then, understands the present through the lens of the past while the second does so by reference to the future.[3]

1 The book was first published in 1895 by Heinemann but had been previously serialised in *New Review* from 1894 to 1895 and in an earlier form a decade earlier in *The School Science Journal*: Gwyneth Jones, 'Introduction' in H G Wells, *The Time Machine* (Gollancz, 2017) vii. Although there were some precursors, the term time travel first appeared in the Oxford English Dictionary in 1914 and 'one way or another, the inventions of H G Wells color every time-travel story that followed. When you write about time-travel, you either pay homage to *The Time Machine* or dodge its shadows': James Gleick, *Time Travel: A History* (4th Estate, 2017) 23, 25. Though compare: 'The theme of time travel was not new but in Wells' hand it became accessible and gripping; more than this it was a metaphor and a warning': Michael Coren, *The Invisible Man: The Life and Liberties of H G Wells* (Bloomsbury, 1993) 50.

2 These are presented as ideal types: H G Wells, *The Discovery of the Future* (Independently published, 2018) 5. This was originally delivered as a lecture to the Royal Institution in 1902.

3 Ibid 6. The distinction broadly corresponds to Edward Soja's definition of the border between modernism and postmodernism, which he noted 'relates to how much weight one gives to continuities versus what is new and different in the contemporary moment. The modernist in my argument is someone who would give greater emphasis to the power and importance of historical continuity, not to ignore all changes but rather with the view that there is a powerful persistence of the past in the present and that strategically at least the best way to understand

It is striking that in explaining these two types of mind, Wells made reference to law. He referred to the first as the 'legal or submissive type of mind' and the second as 'the legislative, creative, organizing or masterful type':

> The former type one might speak of as the legal or submissive type of mind, because the business, the practice, and the training of a lawyer dispose him toward it; he of all men must constantly refer to the law made, the right established, the precedent set, and consistently ignore or condemn the thing that is only seeking to establish itself. The later type of mind I might for contrast call the legislative, creative, organizing or masterful type, because it is perpetually attacking and altering the established order of things, perpetually falling away from respect for what the past has given us.[4]

This highlights a contrast that is hidden but is at the heart of studying law. Although the study of Legal History itself is seen as unfashionable, legal education is inherently dominated by the past. Law Schools indoctrinate law students into the first state of mind identified by Wells: 'thinking as a lawyer' in Law School develops what Wells described as the 'legal or submissive type of mind': it entails understanding the law within its own context and analysing it only within that context. The process is backwards looking, searching for the precedent, mapping the evolution of the case law.[5] The scope of legal change, as a result, is very narrow. In contrast, law in practice is actually always forward-looking.[6] 'Thinking as a lawyer' in practice entails seeking to develop, depart or alter the law – or seeking to prevent such a departure from happening. One side in every court dispute, after all, is seeking not to be bound by the understanding of the precedent. Wells, by calling the second type of mind 'legislative', seems to recognise this. This embraces a wider understanding of the scope of legal change, often by reference to non-legal evidence and factors. Wells' discussion of the two types

the contemporary world critically and pragmatically is to emphasize the historical continuities. The postmodernist switches the weighting. Without denying the importance of continuities, the postmodernist argues that what's new and different is of such significance understanding it becomes the core of any kind of strategic form of critical thinking and practice': Edward Soja, 'Afterword' (1996) 48 *Stanford Law Review* 1421, 1422–1423.

4 H G Wells, *The Discovery of the Future* (Independently published, 2018) 6.

5 As Peter Goodrich put it, 'the burden of history weighs heavily upon the study of common law'. Law students are 'frequently forced to return to ancient cases, to interpret archaic Latin maxims or to confront doctrinal principles which are simply asserted to be part of the immemorial wisdom or "timeless reason" of the English legal tradition': Peter Goodrich, 'Poor Illiterate Reason: History, Nationalism and Common Law' (1992) 1 *Social and Legal Studies* 7.

6 Although the profession, constrained by their education, is often conservative. As Richard A Posner put it: 'Law is the most historically orientated – more bluntly, the most backward-looking, the most "past dependent" – of the professions. It venerates tradition, precedent, pedigree, ritual, customs, ancient practices, ancient texts, archaic terminology, ritual, custom, seniority, gerontocracy and interpretation conceived of as a method of recovering history. It is suspicious of innovation, discontinuities, "paradigm shifts", and the energy and brashness of youth': Richard A Posner, *Frontiers of Legal Theory* (Harvard University Press, 2001) 145.

of mind shows the tension of how law is torn between being both shaped by the past and focused on the future. Both mindsets are required but law students are socialised into only one mindset, the very mindset which frustrates the potential of law. As Wells put it, 'The legal mind becomes glorified and transfigured in the form of hopeless loyalty, the creative mind inspires revolutions and reconstructions'.[7] Law Schools indoctrinate students, and therefore the practitioners and citizens of tomorrow, to think as lawyers rather than legislators (in Wells' terms). And in so doing, they curtail the likelihood and scope of legal change. Legal change is presented as a game of chess;[8] with law students forced to follow the rules of the game and to stay on the board rather than questioning those rules, what game moves can be taken and whether that game ought to be played at all.

The past is seen as stabilising and restraining law. As Ronald Dworkin put it, it is history which provides law's integrity.[9] Past precedent provides authority for today's decision and practice. This is an example of presentism, the privileging of the present.[10] As Dworkin noted, the enquiry 'begins in the present and pursues the past only so far as and in the way its contemporary focus dictates'. History, or to be more precise oldness, is used to cloak and justify the operation of law. It hides the fingerprints that are found on the law. As Peter Goodrich put it, it promotes the 'belief in the rule of law as the governance of rules and not of men'.[11] It also lowers expectations and slows change. In the words of Goodrich: 'Time honoured, venerable and slow to change, the reason of common law is conventionally expressed as an inheritance of established customs, long observed conventions and inveterate usage'.[12] This is likely to lead to fatigue. Law students, especially those who are naturally progressive, come to resent history (or perhaps even the law itself – it is noticeable how many undergraduate law students do not end up in practice). This perhaps goes some way to explain the comatose state of Legal History.[13] History is seen as the enemy.

The way in which the common law uses history (or to be more precise, misuses history) means that historical analysis has little place in the Law School. This creates a paradox at the heart of legal education: how history can be both everywhere and nowhere. Goodrich noted that despite the 'obviousness of the historical character of English law, jurisprudence has seldom sought to understand the law as either history or tradition'.[14] This is because the role of the common law judge or scholar is to construct an account which shows legal change as

7 H G Wells, *The Discovery of the Future* (ad fontes, 2018) 12.

8 Cf. David Ibbetson, *A Historical Introduction to the Law of Obligations* (Oxford University Press, 1999) 11.

9 Ronald Dworkin, *Law's Empire* (Belknap Press, 1986) 227.

10 Cf. Jonathan Clark, *Our Shadowed Present* (Atlantic Books, 2003) 2, 7.

11 Peter Goodrich, 'Poor Illiterate Reason: History, Nationalism and Common Law' (1992) 1 *Social and Legal Studies* 7, 8.

12 Ibid 7.

13 Cf. Daniel Siemens, 'Towards a New Cultural History of Law' (2012) 2 *InterDisciplines* 18, 19.

14 'With the exception of the historical jurisprudence of Sir Henry Maine, modern legal theory has only very recently come to acknowledge a historical dimension to the study of positive

being ordered, which invariably shows a move towards progress and that does not appear to be constructed at all. As Goodrich put it, the notion of jurisprudence:

> as a system of norms or rules or doctrinal principles, is predicated on the exclusion of history in favour of the continuous present and coherence of a system [and] to suggest otherwise would be dispiriting for the student and demoralizing for the public.[15]

The problem, therefore, is not history itself but rather its misuse. As discussed in the previous chapter in relation to the concerns expressed by some legal geographers about the obsession with time and history, it is not history that is ubiquitous but rather 'bad' history. This everyday history is not history at all but is rather the progress narrative, what Robert Gordon called evolutionary functionalism.[16] This progress myth is not only entrenched in Law Schools but is also ingrained in society at large. Indeed, despite his call for the future orientated state of mind, H G Wells' own nonfiction work was clearly informed by the progress narrative.[17] The existence of the progress narrative in law (in judgments and in works on the law) is more subtle than this but is therefore even more dangerous. It is so endemic that it is hidden. It masks how law is contingent, authored and contestable. It results in legal conservatism. Legal change is constrained within narrow parameters. Presenting the past not only as a foreign country[18] but also as a primitive and barbarous one and hiding the historical fact that different and often still feasible approaches have been available means that it is not realised that different options and realities are possible and may be desirable. This is the conspiracy of the common law, the lie at the heart of legal education. It is difficult

---

law': Peter Goodrich, 'Poor Illiterate Reason: History, Nationalism and Common Law' (1992) 1 *Social and Legal Studies* 7, 7–8.

15 Ibid 8.

16 Robert W Gordon, 'Critical Legal Histories' (1984) 36 *Stanford Law Review* 57.

17 This can be found not only in his political and sociological work (see, for instance, H G Wells, *Anticipations* (Dover, 1999), H G Wells, *The Open Conspiracy and Other Writings* (Waterlow and Sons, 1933), H G Wells, *The Rights of Man* (Penguin, 2015) and H G Wells, *Mind at the End of Its Tether* (Heinemann, 1945) as well as his two volumes of autobiography: H G Wells, *Experiment in Autobiography: Discoveries and Conclusions of a Very Ordinary Brain* (H G Wells Library, 2016) and H G Wells, *HG Wells in Love: Postscript to an Experiment in Autobiography* (Faber and Faber, 2009)) but also notably in his historical work (H G Wells, *The Outline of History* (Cassell and Company, 1930) and H G Wells, *A Short History of the World* (Penguin, 2006)). Wells' history was 'designed to popularise the ideology appropriate to the task of creating a World State', presenting this as the next step in the evolution of human society (H G Wells, *A History of Mr Polly* (Pan Books, 1910) 9. See H G Wells, *A Short History of the World* (Penguin, 2006) chapter 67 and H G Wells, *The Outline of History* (Cassell and Company, 1930) chapter 39). It is also worth noting that much of his work has been subject to criticism for his questionable political views: see Michael Coren, *The Invisible Man: The Life and Liberties of H G Wells* (Bloomsbury, 1993) and Michael Seabourne, *H G Wells: Another King of Life* (Peter Owens, 2010).

18 Cf. L P Hartley, *The Go-Between* (Penguin, 2004) 5.

even now to completely rebut a statement made in a 1951 publication prepared by members of the Haldane Society of socialist lawyers and edited by Glanville Williams that stated that:

> The reform of the teaching of law is vital to the reform of the law itself. At present, the drive of law teaching is towards protecting the dead practices of the past against the imperative needs of the present. It is hostile to the analysis of law in action. It is largely ignorant of important foreign experience – it suffers from complacency. It does not properly utilise the material it has, either of persons or facts. It fails to criticise with the appropriate penetration. It gives us legal habit without legal philosophy.[19]

Law students are socialised into an ahistorical understanding of law which presents the object of their study as being separate, autonomous and natural. They are indoctrinated into expecting neat categories, order and progress. No one quite believes but everyone still tip toes around what E P Thompson called the 'greatest of all legal fictions': 'the claim that the law itself evolves, from case by case, by its own impartial logic, true to its own integrity, unswayed by expedient concerns'.[20] Of course, there is talk of 'law and society' and there is mention of context, but most of the time the law is presented to students in a particular way, through the lens of evolutionary functionalism. To re-visit the colourful phrase of E P Thompson, it is evolutionary functionalism which could be described as '*Geschichtenscheissenschlopff*, unhistorical shit'.[21] Legal education is based on and perpetrates a perversion of history which distorts how law actually exists and operates. Everything law students think is true is a lie. They think they are receiving an education into the common law but they are actually being indoctrinated into the common lore.

The Common Lore

Ronald Dworkin once compared judges to authors of chain novels:

> In this enterprise a group of novelists writes a novel *seriatim*; each novelist in the chain interprets the chapters he has been given to write a new chapter, which is then added to what the next novelist receives, and so on. Each has the job of writing his chapter so as to make the novel being constructed the best it can be, and the complexity of this tasks models the complexity of deciding a hard case under law.[22]

19 Glanville Williams (ed) *The Reform of the Law* (Victor Gollancz, 1951) 215.
20 E P Thompson, *Whigs and Hunters: The Origins of the Black Act* (Allen Lane, 1975) 300.
21 E P Thompson, *The Poverty of Theory and Other Essays* (Merlin Press, 1978) 100.
22 Ronald Dworkin, *Law's Empire* (Belknap Press, 1986) 229.

Judges, he reasoned, could be compared to literary critics in that their role is to interrogate texts, 'teasing out the various dimensions of value'.[23] However, judges 'are authors as well as critics' because the judge 'adds to the tradition he interprets'.[24] For judges, 'the distinction between author and interpreter' is more 'a matter of different aspects of the same process'. This is why the 'more fruitful comparison' is between judges and authors of chain novels. Such authors interpret the text they receive and then author the text going forward based on that. For Dworkin, the complexity of this task models the complexity of deciding a hard case under law. He conceded that few chain novels have actually been written but that parlour games played on 'rainy weekends in English country houses have something of the same structure' as do television soap operas which 'span decades with the same characters and some minimal continuity of personality and plot'. However, he pointed out that in his analogy 'the novelists are expected to take their responsibilities of continuity more seriously; they aim jointly to create, so far as they can, a single unified novel that is the best it can be'. Comparing judges to chain novelists underscores how the common law is both authored and is a narrative. It also underlines that this is concealed. As Dworkin put it:

> Each novelist aims to make a single novel of the material he has been given, what he adds to it, and (so far as he can control this) what his successors will want or be able to add. He must try to make this the best novel it can be construed as the work of a single author rather than, as is the fact, the product of many different hands.

The chain novel analogy is interesting and useful in that it raises the question of the extent to which judges are bound by the past. The chain novelist does not have 'total creative freedom or mechanical textual constraint' but rather has to walk a balancing line between those two extremes.[25] Dworkin identified two dimensions.[26] The first was the 'the dimension of fit' whereby the interpretation taken must 'flow throughout the text; it must have general explanatory power, and it is flawed if it leaves unexplained some major structural aspect of the text, a subplot treated as having a great dramatic importance or a dominant and repeated metaphor'. The second was the aesthetic dimension which requires the novelist 'to judge which of these eligible readings makes the work in progress best, all things considered'.[27] He noted that: 'Judgments about textual coherence and integrity, reflecting different formal literary values, are interwoven with more substantive aesthetic judgments that themselves assume different literary

23 Ibid 228.
24 Ibid 229.
25 Ibid 234.
26 Ibid 230.
27 Ibid 231.

aims'.[28] The same is true of judges: the judgments they write need to fit within the existing case law while at the same time dealing with the issue in the instant case and doing justice. The fact that the second dimension for chain novelist and judge alike requires a value judgment means that there is an inbuilt expectation of progress. The progress narrative is embedded as the norm in both literature and the law: this is a challenge in terms of avoiding simplified linearity and the appeal of a firm conclusion if not a happy ending.

Dworkin's reference to soap opera writing may perhaps be a stronger analogy than the chain novel since it is an on-going phenomenon. He comments that chain novelists and judges need to lower their 'sights (as conscientious writers who join the team of an interminable soap opera might do) by trying to construct an interpretation that takes the bulk of what you take to be artistically most fundamental in the text'.[29] The role of judges as interpreters and hidden authors of the common law, largely maintaining but also updating and revising the text, can be compared to the operation of the 'writers' room' set up to run long-running television serials. This raises the question, however, of who the lead writer is. Although the hierarchal court structure might point towards a nominal 'showrunner', individual judges, however senior, rarely shape the law as a whole. Judges are more like those in the writers' room, largely focusing on keeping things running and concentrating very much on today's episode. They seldom focus on the series as a whole, as it were. They do not write the 'series bible', describing what the original 'pitch' was and the overall understanding of the fictional universe of the programme. There is no legal equivalent of the original creator of the drama serial or current executive producer making macro decisions, concerning the enterprise as a whole and its 'canon'. In relation to drama serials, where the creator/showrunner voice is silent then the questions of interpretation, of 'fit', of change or continuity, of 'canon' are left to the viewer: the fans. Fans may produce, formally or informally, guides to the series which fill in the gaps, deal with inconsistencies and provide a framework. In law, where judges are not creators or showrunners, this activity is left to the textbook writers. It is they who deal with the question of 'fit'.

Indeed, in creating these 'fan' productions, textbook writers themselves then take on the mantle of lead writers. There is an important hierarchy at play in terms of textbook writers which can be compared with the roles played by the original series creator and the current showrunner. The original series creator made the original decisions, a lot of which stick. The current showrunner inherits this and although they can make departures from it these are conscious departures; the parameters are set for them. The original series creators can be compared with the original textbook writers. The current showrunners in this analogy are the present day textbook writers whether they are writing an updated version of a classic textbook or their own textbook on the field.

28 Ibid 230.
29 Ibid 237.

The decisions of their predecessors continue to exert influence. They do not bind their successors but they do set the terms of the canon, which their successors can mould or even reject but this is a deliberate and controversial choice. The canon remains undisturbed most of the time. Although there is now a plethora of legal textbooks with dozens being published regularly for each area of law, it is noticeable that their contents pages, major classifications and much of the substantive content is similar if not identical. Most textbooks follow the same approach as others in their sub-discipline (or make a selling point of the few usually minor changes they do make). Today's textbook writers tend to follow (often instinctively and uncritically) previous decisions about the canon of their field. It is those original textbook writers who established the canon who are the true creators; it is they who established the common lore.

In the mid-twentieth century, a generation of scholars (mostly male and Oxbridge based) wrote what would become the definitive textbook accounts of their areas of law.[30] Many of these books remain in print today, now curated and updated by modern scholars, and are seen as the leading academic works in their fields.[31] These included works on established areas of the common law such as John Smith and Brian Hogan[32] on criminal law; Guenter Treitel[33] and Geoffrey Cheshire and C HS Fifoot[34] on contract law; Percy Winfield[35] on tort; Robert Megarry and William Wade[36] on land law; and Harold Hanbury[37] on equity. Some works became the foundation for new legal sub-disciplines such as Peter Bromley[38] and Stephen Cretney[39] on family law. The decisions that these authors made about what topics were to be included and excluded, how topics

30 There was also what David Sugarman has referred to as a 'classical' period of jurists from c1850 to 1907: David Sugarman, 'Legal Theory, the Common Law Mind and the Making of the Textbook Tradition' in William Twining (ed) *Legal Theory and the Common Law* (Blackwell, 1986) 26, 28. But these works tend no longer to be used as accounts of the current law in the same way as the more recent textbooks are.

31 There are also leading practitioner works in most areas of law, organised around areas of practice which sometimes correspond to academic sub-disciplines in Law Schools.

32 First published in 1965. The most recent edition is: David Ormerod and Karl Laid, *Smith, Hogan and Ormerod's Criminal Law* (16th ed, Oxford University Press, 2021).

33 First published in 1962. The most recent edition is Edwin Peel, *Treitel on the Law of Contract* (14th ed, Sweet and Maxwell, 2020).

34 First published in 1945. The most recent edition is: Michael Furmston, *Cheshire, Fifoot, and Furmston's Law of Contract* (17th ed, Oxford University Press, 2017).

35 First published in 1937. The most recent edition is: James Goudkamp and Donal Nolan, *Winfield and Jolowicz on Tort* (20th ed, Sweet and Maxwell, 2020).

36 First published in 1957. The most recent edition is: Stuart Bridge, Elizabeth Cooke and Martin Dixon, *Megarry and Wade the Law of Real Property* (9th ed, Sweet and Maxwell, 2019).

37 First published in 1935. The most recent edition is: James Glister and James Lee, *Hanbury & Martin: Modern Equity* (21st ed, Sweet and Maxwell, 2018).

38 First published in 1957. The most recent edition is: Nigel Lowe, Gillian Douglas, Emma Hitchings and Rachel Taylor, *Bromley's Family Law* (12th ed, Oxford University Press, 2021).

39 His *Principles of Family Law* was first published in 1974 while his *Elements of Family Law* was first published in 1987. The most recent editions are: Judith Masson, Rebecca Bailey-Harris and Rebecca Probert, *Cretney's Principles of Family Law* (8th ed, Sweet &Maxwell, 2008) and

were presented and discussed, what principles of law were to be elucidated and how and the materials that were to be cited continue to exert influence today. In each legal area, there are now a significant number of student textbooks reflecting various pedagogical styles but all mirror – or in a few cases, consciously reject – the decisions as to content made by the original leading work. Their classifications and distinctions have become entrenched. These authors were the high priests of the common lore.

While the most obvious members of this priesthood are the textbook writers whose work continues to be produced in new editions, there have been other sacred texts which have been influential despite not leading to numerous editions.[40] For instance, in criminal law, although Smith and Hogan is the leading textbook, Glanville Williams has been described as the foremost twentieth century authority on English criminal law.[41] It was Williams who developed the now entrenched distinction between the general and the special part of the criminal law.[42] His work established 'a centre and organisation and logic' and set 'the liberal orthodoxy of criminal law and its analytical framework'.[43] Yet, although his overall schema of criminal law is most clearly articulated in the textbooks he authored,[44] one of which was revived relatively recently,[45] the influence of Glanville Williams comes from his corpus of writings as a whole, which often influenced reform and were discussed by the higher judiciary. This underscores the need to place and understand the high priests within the intellectual history of their respective areas of law. They are not objective oracles from which we can read the 'story'; they are rather part of the story.[46] This is almost always

Rebecca Probert and Maebh Harding, *Cretney and Probert's Family Law* (10th ed, Sweet & Maxwell, 2018).

40 The language of priesthood is also used by Thomas J McSweeney in his monograph exploring the first legal writers. He noted that: 'Through their writing, the authors of *Bracton* transformed themselves from servants of the king to priests of the law' (Thomas J McSweeney, *Priests of the Common Law: Roman Law and the Making of the Common Law's First Professionals* (Oxford University Press, 2019) 32). By contrast, conventionally, law and religion – lawyers and priests – are regarded in opposition. Law is often seen as the successor of religion as a, if not the, main agency of socialisation as in Philip R Wood, *The Fall of the Priests and the Rise of the Lawyers* (Hart, 2017).

41 E.g., Eric Pace, 'Glanville Williams, 86, Teacher and Authority on Criminal Law' *New York Times* (21 April 1997).

42 As Ngaire Naffine has put it, Williams 'organised and shaped' the criminal law: 'He helped to identify and develop what came to be known as the general part of the criminal law, with its idea of a centre or a core of principles and a special part (particular offences) which were meant to reflect these principles': Ngaire Naffine, *Criminal Law and the Man Problem* (Hart, 2019) 94.

43 Ibid 95.

44 Glanville Williams, *Criminal Law: The General Part* (Steven & Sons, 1953). A second edition was published in 1961.

45 Dennis J Baker, *Glanville Williams: Textbook of Criminal Law* (4th ed, Sweet & Maxwell, 2015). The first edition was published in 1978 with Williams authoring a second edition in 1983. The third edition was published in 2012 by Dennis J Baker.

46 For an example, see Catharine Macmillan, 'Rogues, Swindlers and Cheats: The Development of Mistake of Identity in English Contract Law' 64(3) (2005) *Cambridge Law Journal* 711,

forgotten as their classifications, distinctions and inventions have become taken for granted.[47]

The high priests of the common lore were the formative writers on areas of the common law who put to paper the classifications, distinctions and fundamental ideas which underpin their respective areas of law. Much of what is taught in Law Schools – the monastic chanting that takes place – either repeats or, much less often, challenges the common lore. It was the priestly class that decided the canon: what is taught and who is read. Subsequent legal developments are, of course, studied but are placed within their framework, only very occasionally resulting in the rejection and rewriting of that framework. This can mean that what Law Schools teach can sometimes seems to be irrelevant or outmoded. Their focus on senior appellate courts removes the law student from the reality of how law operates. The law degree basically trains students to be appellate court judges. In criminal law, when the focus shifts from general principles that seemingly exist in abstract and in eternity, law students are then typically introduced to a small number of serious crimes rather than the dozens of offences that are much more frequently prosecuted.[48] The same is true in other fields: nineteenth century concepts propounded in contract law classes do not correspond to commercial agreements in an electronic age, for instance.[49] The conspiracy of the common law whereby the common lore is presented as an objective ahistorical

741, in which she showed that the law on 'mistake of identity is introduced and "explained" by ... treatise writers. Judges were not initially concerned with the development of a doctrine as such'. She noted that this 'accords a much more powerful role to treatises than the common law generally likes to admit'.

47 The same is true of earlier works. For instance, as the work of Robin Chapman Stacey has argued, the medieval Welsh law books need to be seen as examples of law as literature. She noted that they were 'composed by and for lawyers' and so reflect their values. Her work argues that 'they are literary compositions rather than legislation or objective accounts, a fact that has interesting implications for how they need to be read': Robin Chapman Stacey, 'Law and Lawbooks in Mediaeval Wales' (2010) 8(10) *History Compass* 1180, 1182; Robin Chapman Stacey, Law *and the Imagination in Medieval Wales* (University of Pennsylvania Press, 2018).

48 As Celia Wells has noted: 'Public order offences were usually taught as part of constitutional law but in fact in terms of everyday policing and frequency of prosecution they are far more significant than the headline offences of assault, rape and murder'. For Wells, 'the way criminal law was expounded by the doctrinal leaders of the late-twentieth century' was problematic not only given 'the invisibility of women in law;' but also because of the pervasive distinction 'between regulatory law (not really criminal) and "real" criminal law, and the individualism in the rhetoric of the criminal law'. Her 'main gripe was the way criminal law was taught in a way that assumed that convicted offenders were "them" and ignored the "us" of white collar and corporate offending': Celia Wells, *A Woman in Law: Reflections on Gender, Class and Politics* (Waterside Press, 2019) 101, 100.

49 'In short, contract formation in the commercial sector is complex and messy: behaviour and express intentions are often indeterminate. Agreements commonly arise from an extensive and tangled trail of correspondence and negotiation involving conduct, written documents and discussions in which ... fresh consideration play little part': Linda Mulcahy and Sally Wheeler, 'Contract Law: Socio-Legal Accounts of the Lived World of Contract' in Caroline Hunter (ed) *Integrating Socio-Legal Studies Into the Law Curriculum* (Palgrave, 2012) 104, 113.

truth means that law students are taught about and socialised into a fictional world. The Law School does not fully prepare students for the world of legal practice and for their role as informed citizens. They instead partake in intellectual parlour games that resemble only the work of appellate court judges.

It is time for a reformation of legal education. The role of legal education is more than the learning of a body of knowledge that we reify as 'the law'. That would be insufficient even if the law degree was purely vocational in nature and ambition. A degree level subject requires more than this. It requires students to question, to highlight and to challenge. Students entering the workplace and indeed society at large as graduates need to be able to de-construct and re-construct meanings. As Terry Eagleton noted, the practice of de-construction:

> is to reinscribe and resituate meanings, events and objects within broader movements and structures; it is, so to speak, to reverse the imposing tapestry in order to expose in all its unglamorously dishevelled tangle the threads constituting the well heeled image it presents to the world.[50]

It is, then, a critical act and as the previous chapters have argued, this can be referred to as a subversive approach where this de-construction also involves re-construction, where the lens is changed, and where the orthodox account is seen as precisely that: an authored construction.

The message of this book is that Legal History – long dismissed as being quaint, constraining, and of limited importance in the Law School – can ironically play a key part in this subversion. A historical approach highlights the contingency and constructed nature of law: it slaughters sacred cows by revealing that nothing is universal, ever-lasting or mandated. As Maitland notably put it, history provides the 'lesson that each generation has an enormous power of shaping its own law'; it shows law students that they 'have free hands'.[51] Yet, as the last chapter showed, the historical imagination alone is not sufficient. History has a part to play in the subversion but so too must geography. Legal geography shows that the problem is the sub-disciplinary institutional mindset that Legal History has found itself in. There is a need to ditch the capital letters and all that comes with them. Comparison with legal geography also shows how Legal History – or to be more precise, the Legal History canon – has been the construction and plaything of lawyers. By contrast, legal geography has been the result of work by lawyers, geographers and others. Reference to geography can show why the subversive nature of history has not been realised and can contribute to remedying this, not only by showing by contrast how a geographical approach to law has flowered but also by insisting upon the importance of geographical analysis: the need to subvert law by reference to both time and space

50 Terry Eagleton, *Against the Grain: Essays 1975–1985* (Verso, 1986) 80.

51 Frederic W Maitland, 'Maitland to AV Dicey, c. July 1896' quoted in C H S Fifoot, *Frederic William Maitland* (Harvard University Press, 1971) 143.

(and how a distinction between time and space, like between law and society, cannot be made).

Legal History has been hampered by its development within the disciplinary confines of law as a sub-discipline of law. This has meant that the critical turn has not affected the mainstream of the Legal History canon; rather, the critical turn has led to an abundance of historical work on law but outside the Legal History canon. There are many academic lawyers doing historical work who would not consider themselves legal historians and whose work tends not to interact with the Legal History canon. This has meant that a scholarly community has not developed. Rather, Legal History remains unchanged and risks becoming obsolete while new generations of scholarship exist in isolation from one another. And this is not to mention the work done on the history of law outside of Law Schools. There is another book to be written about how historians have written about and analysed the law and the extent to which they have used legal materials and the Legal History canon. Legal materials are of interest to the historian notwithstanding the shift in academic history away from the 'top down' Kings and Queens version of history to a 'bottom up' social history of lived experiences. As E P Thompson once remarked, law is 'at every bloody level'.[52] Law provides a concrete marker of social change. Legal records are already frequently used by historians (alongside other records) and there is clearly the potential for them being even more widely used by historians. There is room for much greater interaction, knowledge exchange and collaboration between those who happen to find themselves employed in Law Schools and those who happen to find themselves employed in history departments. In many respects, experts in each discipline can provide the perspective that the other is missing.

As noted in the previous chapter, the revolution in legal geography has two effects. The same will be true in legal history. The first effect will be upon the object of study and second effect will be upon the nature and purpose of study. First, as we have noted, a subversive approach is needed. Grounded analysis is required to hold up for scrutiny the central, organising framework of law.[53] As Nicholas Blomley noted, a critical approach is needed to both document and to challenge: It is 'subversive of imperial claims to legal objectivity, totality, and stability'.[54] Such an approach highlights questions of power and how they are perpetuated through discourse and performance. It shows how law, time and space are 'mutually constitutive and deeply implicated in power relations' (and the same is true of law and society *pace* Cotterrell). As Blomley put it, this sees law 'cast as relational, acquiring meaning through social action, rather than objective categories that operate prior to social life'. Second, a post-disciplinary

52 E P Thompson, *The Poverty of Theory and Other Essays* (Monthly Review Press, 1978) 96.

53 Cf. Jane Holder and Carolyn Harrison, 'Connecting Law and Geography' in Jane Holder and Carolyn Harrison (eds) *Law and Geography* (Oxford University Press, 2003) 3, 4.

54 Nicholas Blomley, 'From "What?" to "So What?": Law and Geography in Retrospect' in Jane Holder and Carolyn Harrison (eds) *Law and Geography* (Oxford University Press, 2003) 13, 24, 22.

approach is required. This requires a 'co-constitutive approach',[55] which moves away from seeing law and history as two disciplines and which extends to a suspicion about the label 'Legal History' itself with or without the capital letters. This transdisciplinary or post-disciplinary approach does not require the establishment of a new sub-discipline, discipline or super-discipline or indeed any of the institutional clutter that leads to segregation. Rather, this approach requires not just the move away from but also the critique of disciplinary approaches, frameworks, norms, habits and expectations. The focus is not on disciplinary concepts such as law, time, space, society or how they relate to each other; rather, in the words of David Delaney, the focus is on 'how they happen'.[56] As Braverman *et al.* put it in the context of legal geography, there is a need to move beyond the disciplines and indeed the interdisciplinary offspring of such disciplines 'in a way that both draws on and contributes to broader social and humanities studies'.[57] In short, legal history needs to be a sub-discipline no more. It needs to become a method.[58]

Legal History as a Method

In English and Welsh Law Schools, talk of method is paradoxically both nowhere and everywhere.

On the one hand, talk of method is absent from the Law School curriculum when compared to other subjects.[59] As Laura Cahillane and Jennifer Schweppe noted:

> While in other disciplines, students are taught at the earliest stages in their University education *how* research is conducted within that discipline, in

55 Cf. Luke Bennett and Antonia Layard, 'Legal Geography: Becoming Spatial Detectives' (2015) 9(7) *Geography Compass* 406, 408.

56 David Delaney, *The Spatial, the Legal and the Pragmatics of World-Making: Nomospheric Investigations* (Routledge, 2010) 123.

57 Irus Braverman, Nicholas Blomley, David Delaney and Alexandre Kedar, 'Introduction: Expanding the Spaces of Law' in Irus Braverman, Nicholas Blomley, David Delaney and Alexandre Kedar (eds) *The Expanding Spaces of Law: A Timely Legal Geography* (Stanford University Press, 2014) 1, 10.

58 Markus D Dubber has also made the argument that legal history needs to be understood 'as one mode of critical analysis of law along with other modes of "interdisciplinary" analysis' but he sees history as 'a mode of jurisprudence (in fact, we might call it New Historical Jurisprudence) rather than a subspecialty of law or a form of applied history': Markus D Dubber, 'Legal History as Legal Scholarship: Doctrinalism, Interdisciplinary and Critical Analysis of Law' in Markus D Dubber and Christopher Tomlins (eds) *The Oxford Handbook of Legal History* (Oxford University Press, 2018) 99, 99–100.

59 'In sociology textbooks one is struck by the fact that much of what counts as knowledge is, to a greater or lesser extent, about methodology': Geoffrey Samuel, 'Is Law Really a Social Science? A View from Comparative Law' (2008) 67 (2) *Cambridge Law Journal* 288, 289.

law schools, we prefer to discuss the *why*, *what* and *when* of research; indeed, anything other than the *how*.[60]

Unlike their peers, law students are not really inducted into a scholarly community. They are not treated so much like trainee academics as students who study other subjects are. The role of academics in writing about the law (and therefore constructing the law) is hidden from them. They are introduced to 'the mechanics of research' but this is usually pitched as learning how to act as lawyers: how to find and how to read legal materials. This is not presented as being training in an academic method and typically there is not even a reference to the existence of any other methods. This means that law graduates seeking to do postgraduate research 'are rarely if ever conversant in the method and methodologies of legal research'. Indeed, until recently, this was even true of PhD students where 'discussing methodology was dismissed at as not really something that lawyers did and was dealt with in a rather cursory manner at the early stages of a thesis'. Although this has now changed for doctoral students and for academics who are seeking research funding,[61] it remains seen as a formality and as the acquisition of a skill from outside the Law School, usually to satisfy the expectations of the interdisciplinary funding bodies. Questions of method remain alien in Law Schools, especially in terms of undergraduate teaching.

Yet, method is also everywhere. Every piece of legal writing and every presentation of the law operates within and perpetuates a particular legal method. As Robert Cryer, Tamara Hervey and Bal Sokhi-Bulley noted, every 'project begins from a theoretical basis or bases whether such bases are articulated or not' and 'the theoretical basis of a project will inform how law is conceptualised in the project, which in turn will determine what kinds of research questions are deemed meaningful or useful, what data is examined and how it is analysed (the method)'.[62] They pointed out that these choices are often 'arrived at unconsciously' where it would be 'better to be open about the bases of research and to think about them rather than to leave them unaddressed and uncritically accepted'. Law students do receive training in and are expected to develop skills in method but it is often not explicitly styled as such. The method of the undergraduate law degree is the method of doctrinal research, the elucidation, explanation and evaluation of legal sources.[63] Learning to 'think like a lawyer' entails privileging the descriptive question of 'how does law read?' followed by

60 Laura Cahillane and Jennifer Schweppe, 'Legal Research Methodologies: Framing the Context' in Laura Cahillane and Jennifer Schweppe (eds) *Legal Research Methods: Principles and Practicalities* (Clarus Press, 2016) 1.

61 Now 'a description and discussion of the methodology employed in the research is seen as one of its core elements': Ibid 2.

62 Robert Cryer, Tamara Hervey and Bal Sokhi-Bulley, *Research Methodologies in EU and International Law* (Hart, 2011) 5.

63 For a staunch defence see Terry Hutchinson, 'Doctrinal Research: Researching the Jury' in Dawn Watkins and Mandy Burton (eds) *Research Methods in Law* (2nd ed, Routledge, 2018) 8.

the normative question of 'how ought the law to read?'[64] Doctrinal legal method is not limited to description or the systemisation of knowledge. It involves the evaluation of existing and proposed laws.[65] However, even these normative and evaluative aspects of doctrinal study remain within the parameters set by law. As Shane Kilcommins put it, 'law is technocratic, employing rigorous analytical processes, emphasising precision and inductive-deductive logic, but also fidelity to complex institutional practices'.[66] The issue, therefore, is not whether doctrinal legal study is important or useful (it is) but that it is not typically regarded as *a* method (rather than *the* method). The danger is that, in the words of Kilcommins: 'For the most part, doctrinal legal methodology is something which is acted upon by us lawyers but rarely articulated in a systematised way'.

Doctrinal legal scholarship is the necessary foundation upon which further questions and approaches can be developed. It provides a vital 'internal' textual analysis of law. Any analysis concerning law that does not build upon the insights gleaned by doctrinal methods is likely to run the risk of being like a house built on sand. Such 'law-lite' accounts are likely to be simplifications and can even be premised upon errors given that the initial impressions of the legal problems can be opened to question by the meticulous analysis of case law and statute.[67] Yet, there is also a risk that doctrinal legal scholarship alone is insufficient. As Anthony Bradney has noted, 'in seeking to understand and explain even the narrowest of legal rules doctrinal scholars have constantly felt it necessary to ask questions which, because they were political, ethical or sociological, could not be answered by their own chosen method' and this runs the risk of answers being provided by reference to 'mere anecdote, hearsay, and assertion'.[68] Doctrinal legal study alone cannot explain the context that the law is placed in and so that gap could be easily filled by 'man in pub' philosophising: impressionistic and impulsive explanations not grounded in research and much like the conversation that would be had at a bar after a few drinks.[69]

Doctrinal legal scholarship needs to be seen as one of the methods used in Law Schools; the foundational method perhaps but not the only method. Other methods need to be seen as being integral to legal education rather than being

64 These questions may be followed by the question 'what are the consequences of applying a certain legal rule?' which examines the effect of law in society and the question 'what is law?' which concerns law's relationship with other normative systems and 'usually tries to explain the law from an external perspective': J M Smits, *The Mind and Method of the Legal Academic* (Edward Elgar, 2012) 9.

65 Douglas Vick, 'Interdisciplinarity and the Discipline of Law' (2004) 31(2) *Journal of Law and Society* 163, 179.

66 Shane Kilcommins, 'Doctrinal Legal Method (Black-Letterism): Assumptions, Commitments and Shortcomings' in Laura Cahillane and Jennifer Schweppe (eds) *Legal Research Methods: Principles and Practicalities* (Clarus Press, 2016) 7, 8.

67 Russell Sandberg, *Religion, Law and Society* (Cambridge University Press, 2014) 257–258.

68 Anthony Bradney, 'Law as a Parasitic Discipline' (1998) 25(1) *Journal of Law and Society* 71, 72.

69 Russell Sandberg, *Religion, Law and Society* (Cambridge University Press, 2014) 259.

regarded as at best borrowed from other disciplines. Regarding non-doctrinal methods as sub-disciplines within law, with their own distinct modules on the Law School curriculum, frustrates this by furthering their 'otherness'. Instead, legal history (and indeed, other non-doctrinal legal subjects like the sociology of law)[70] is better regarded, not as a sub-discipline, but as a method. Legal history, like the sociology of law, should not be regarded as a separate sub-discipline but rather as an integral part of the study of law (and therefore every legal sub-discipline) alongside the doctrinal study of the current legal position. This is not to say that every legal question demands a historical (or sociological) approach to its answer. Whether it does, and if so which method is suitable, will depend upon the research question. But legal history needs to be part of the toolkit available to all who study law and so needs to be part of the toolkit that law students are trained to use.

It is true, of course, that students rarely (if ever) get an exclusively doctrinal legal education. Most (if not all) will take optional modules on other approaches to law or will experience a legal module that is not taught completely in the conventional doctrinal manner. Yet, doctrinal study alone remains reified as the norm. The literatures, skills and distinctive questions of (say) legal historical analysis are usually limited only to specialists and do not tend to become part of the general toolkit of those researching and studying law. Seeing legal history and other non-doctrinal approaches as methods which complement and build upon doctrinal approaches throughout the curriculum would allow this to occur. This is especially important given that these historical and other approaches serve as a subversive critique, highlighting the constructed nature of the law and stressing its contingency. It follows that it is also vital that firm distinctions are not made between parts of the toolkit. A subversive approach shows labels, classifications, distinctions up as being constructed and arbitrary. Neatly distinguishing between (say) historical or geographical approaches to law is foolhardy given that law, time and space (like law and society) constantly constitute and re-constitute one another. The same is true of the often made internal/external distinction, though it should be remembered that doctrinal legal analysis provides only an internal perspective on the law and so needs complementing by external perspectives. History is particularly helpful in this regard given that it has both an internal and external dimension. The same is true of other non-doctrinal approaches and, importantly, a subversive approach highlights how the internal and the external interpenetrate each other. This underlines the need for all law students to have access to an array of tools to build upon and to question the results of doctrinal legal analysis.

The discussion about the need to go beyond doctrinal legal analysis is typically presented with 'socio-legal studies' being offered as the solution. Fiona Cownie and Anthony Bradney present the usual story that the major growth of universities and the fact that 'law schools began to employ young lecturers who were full

70 See ibid 262.

time academics' rather than part-time practitioners led to an interest in socio-legal studies which was furthered by the rise of alternative approaches to studying law such as Critical Legal Studies and Feminist Legal Studies.[71] Yet, the diffuse nature of socio-legal studies has meant that it has not supplanted the doctrinal orthodoxy, especially in relation to the undergraduate legal curriculum. Moreover, the effect of alternative approaches upon the mainstream has been muted. It is also concerning that the 'socio-legal' label reflects an entrenched preference for regarding law as a social science. One response to this is to adopt an ever-expansive definition of the term 'socio-legal' but this hides a tension that exists in terms of the disciplinary directions the interdisciplinary Law School can go in. As we have seen, Mathias Siems and Daithi Mac Sithigh spoke of a choice as to 'whether to "go American" in moving closer to social sciences, or "go German" in remaining closer to the humanities'.[72] The ubiquitous usage of the 'socio-legal' label suggests that this choice in England and Wales has been made in favour of social science. This has received some resistance. David Nelken has written of the emergence of 'a much more complex picture of law' where 'analogies are more likely to be drawn between law and theology or law and literary theory than between law and the social and policy sciences'.[73] Sionaidh Douglas-Scott has written that 'law is as much a matter of culture as it is a system of rules' and has maintained that law 'has its own aesthetic and may be envisioned as a creative art form as much as a science'.[74] Without denying the importance of a social scientific approach to law, there is the additional need to also place law within the humanities.

Placing law within the humanities is difficult, however, given the lack of definition of what the humanities is. Costas Douzinas noted that the humanities 'are a consummately modern and decidedly American invention'.[75] Steven Cammiss and Dawn Watkins have stated that the humanities label refers to 'the branch of learning concerned with human culture' and reflects the 'cultural turn'.[76] Austin Sarat, Matthew Anderson and Cathrine O Frank, referring to the 'field of law and the humanities', have noted that 'neither institutional attempts to define it (merely as a group of disciplines not found in the social and natural sciences), nor efforts to identify a common methodological foundation (for

71 Fiona Cownie and Anthony Bradney, 'Socio-Legal Studies: A Challenge to the Doctrinal Approach' in Dawn Watkins and Mandy Burton (eds) *Research Methods in Law* (2nd ed, Routledge, 2018) 40–41.

72 Mathias M Siems and Daithi Mac Sithigh, 'Mapping Legal Research' [2012] *Cambridge Law Journal* 651, 673.

73 David Nelken, 'Can Law Learn from Social Science?' (2001) 35 *Israel Law Review* 205, 211.

74 Sionaidh Douglas-Scott, *Law after Modernity* (Hart, 2013) 253.

75 Costas Douzinas, 'A Humanities of Resistance: Fragments for a Legal History of Humanity' in Austin Sarat, Matthew Anderson and Cathrine O Frank (eds) *Law and Humanities: An Introduction* (Cambridge University Press, 2010) 49. But compare: Rens Bod, *A New History of the Humanities* (Oxford University Press, 2013).

76 Steven Cammiss and Dawn Watkins, 'Legal Research in the Humanities' in Dawn Watkins and Mandy Burton (eds) *Research Methods in Law* (2nd ed, Routledge, 2018) 86, 87.

example, in interpretation) could succeed because they were either too restrictive or too broad'.[77] Yet, this idea of a heterogeneous cluster of subjects which are not scientific (or perhaps wholly scientific) in outlook is useful in that it provides a loose understanding of what the humanities are; and this looseness is apt given that this also reflects the nature of the grouping itself. Sara Ramshaw has argued that law and humanities exists 'not as a "canon" per se, but as a "field without a canon" or a canon that resists canonization'.[78] For Ramshaw, by its very nature law and humanities needs to 'leap ahead fearlessly to properly defy disciplinary boundaries and move the field beyond siloed thinking'. This 'is one of the preliminary aims of law and humanities scholarship and pedagogy'. This requires using the rigour found within humanities disciplines,[79] without insisting upon disciplinary distinctions. Situating law as part of the humanities, then, encourages subversive thinking about boundaries, disciplines and methods. Perhaps the label given to the field needs revising to reflect this: from 'law and humanities' to 'law as humanities'. This would see law as part of the humanities and also would normalise the interaction between law and other humanities disciplines, ideas and methods. A humanities understanding of law emphasises that a rich methodological toolkit is needed to understand the various dimensions of law and that this extends beyond seeing law as a social science.

This can be further developed by looking at Sarat *et al.*'s exploration of how the 'law and humanities field' has developed. They posit the origins of law and humanities in the US in the law and literature movement and in particular, James Boyd White's seminal book *The Legal Imagination*.[80] This led to a focus on the language of law and on law as a language. As Sarat *et al.* put it:

> If this point of view could be reduced to a maxim, it might be this: Law is a language and language matters. Another way to put it would be to say that the education of lawyers should include the cultivation of a meaningful appreciation of law as rhetoric practice – not just in the sense of an art of persuasion, but of a disciplined, textual self-directed habit of reading, speaking,

77 Austin Sarat, Matthew Anderson and Cathrine O Frank, 'Introduction: On the Origins and Prospects of the Humanistic Study of Law' in Austin Sarat, Matthew Anderson and Cathrine O Frank (eds) *Law and Humanities: An Introduction* (Cambridge University Press, 2010) 1, 9. Compare: 'Since the nineteenth century the humanities have generally been defined as the disciplines that investigate the expressions of the human mind' (Rens Bod, *A New History of the Humanities* (Oxford University Press, 2013) 1).

78 Sara Ramshaw, 'Law and Humanities: A Field without a Canon' (2019) *Law, Culture and the Humanities* (Online First Access) 1, 3.

79 The risk is otherwise that 'Law and Humanities courses end up entertaining and lightening the heavy load of law students as well as giving them a useful cultural gloss': Costas Douzinas, 'A Humanities of Resistance: Fragments for a Legal History of Humanity' in Austin Sarat, Matthew Anderson and Cathrine O Frank (eds) *Law and Humanities: An Introduction* (Cambridge University Press, 2010) 49, 56.

80 James Boyd White, *The Legal Imagination* (University of Chicago Press, 1973).

> and above all, writing, that has at its root critical understanding of the links among language, consciousness, and power.[81]

The subversive approach to legal history which has been expounded in previous chapters shares this focus on language and narrative. One of the main contributions a subversive approach provides is to reveal the authored nature of the law and the prevalent narratives, most notably the progress narrative of evolutionary functionalism. A subversive approach regarding entropic complexity as the norm regards law as a system of communication. As Peter Goodrich has written: 'To study the common law historically is to study it as tradition, as a plural set of practices which developed over long periods of time… as a mixture of image and myth, oral memory and written text, custom and judicial legislation'.[82] This approach sees an obvious overlap between law and literature and legal history since for Goodrich:

> Traditions are not simply accounts of the past but are rather narratives or, more technically, genealogies of human groupings, they are fictions to which we belong, stories by reference to which we are told from where we come and are given an identity and place within nature or the order of things.[83]

A subversive approach to legal education embraces this in highlighting how narratives often embrace fictions, muddying the line between fact and fiction. By focusing upon the authored and constructed nature of law and lore, a subversive approach brings methods, concepts and analysis often employed in literature and applies them in relation to law. The strong literary focus in the law and humanities movement has been countered, however, most notably by Robin West,[84] on the grounds that such an approach would 'leave out much that is nontextual in our interaction with actual people'.[85] There has been a call for a perspective which 'pushes beyond the literary' and raises the question of 'how would a study of the way in which law constitutes persons proceed'.[86] Simon Stern, Maksymilian Del Mar and Bernadette Meyler have argued that 'to practice the humanities is to approach, with certain attitudes and sensitivities, a multitude of practices of making (of making things, making meaning, making senses) including relations

81 Austin Sarat, Matthew Anderson and Cathrine O Frank, 'Introduction: On the Origins and Prospects of the Humanistic Study of Law' in Austin Sarat, Matthew Anderson and Cathrine O Frank (eds) *Law and Humanities: An Introduction* (Cambridge University Press, 2010) 1, 4.

82 Peter Goodrich, 'Poor Illiterate Reason: History, Nationalism and Common Law' (1992) 1 *Social and Legal Studies* 7, 8.

83 Ibid 9.

84 Robin West, 'Communities, Texts and Law: Reflections on the Law and Literature Movement' (1988) 1 *Yale Journal of Law and Humanities* 154.

85 Austin Sarat, Matthew Anderson and Cathrine O Frank, 'Introduction: On the Origins and Prospects of the Humanistic Study of Law' in Austin Sarat, Matthew Anderson and Cathrine O Frank (eds) *Law and Humanities: An Introduction* (Cambridge University Press, 2010) 1, 7.

86 Ibid 7–8.

between those practices of making and the values that may be at stake in such practices and their relations to each other'.[87] Crucially they note that these 'attitudes and sensitivities' include 'sensitivity not so much (and certainly not only) to the regular and patterned, but instead to the irregular and unpatterned' paying attention to 'the unpredictability of human behavior'; 'sensitivity to the blind spots in our abilities to sense who is in anger, suffering or vulnerable'; and 'sensitivity to the apparently superficial, superfluous, unnecessary, insufficient, marginal, or-by-the-by'.[88] Put another way, 'the humanities look, with delicacy and care through the garbage bins of history'. A historical approach, suitably grounded and relational, can help to provide this. A subversive approach critically engages with both text and context, employing a range of methods without being troubled as to the disciplinary origins. This is why placing a subversive law within the humanities is important: it stresses the need for subversive legal education to expand beyond historical method and to be a post-disciplinary phenomenon. As Stern *et al.* note:

> Discussions of the law's deep roots in the humanities, and its need for the humanities, have most often associated law with legal doctrines and rhetoric, in particular, and have looked to the humanities for representations of legal actors and dilemmas, and for ethical resources that can shed light on legal problems. Work that investigates those issues remains vitally important; however, we take the humanities to encompass not only history, literature, art, and philosophy but the whole range of fields that use interpretative methods to study creativity, expression, and the imagination. These include many fields – such as architecture, geography, book history, cognitive studies, science and technology studies, and performance studies – that influence, and are influenced by legal concepts and methods, but that appear only sporadically, if at all, in law journals.[89]

Law and humanities has grown as a field, not only in the US where the *Yale Journal of Law and the Humanities* was the first scholarly journal devoted exclusively to the field, but also subsequently on this side of the pond.[90] Law and humanities naturally continues to defy categorisation but as the introduction to the first issue of the *Yale Journal of Law and the Humanities* put it, the general

87 Simon Stern, Maksymilian Del Mar and Bernadette Meyler, 'Introduction' in Simon Stern, Maksymilian Del Mar and Bernadette Meyler (eds) *The Oxford Handbook of Law and Humanities* (Oxford University Press, 2020) xxi, xxii.

88 Ibid xxiii.

89 Ibid xxiv. The previous chapter questions, however, the extent to which this is true in relation to legal geography.

90 Research centres or clusters titled 'Law and Humanities' exist at Birkbeck, Warwick and Northumbria Universities, being parts of Law Schools and including experts in legal history. Journals include *Law and Humanities* and *Law, Culture and the Humanities.*

aim is 'to restore to legal studies a proper place for the question of values'.[91] For Austin Sarat *et al.*, in the law and humanities:

> critical impulses abound, not looking to save or humanize law or lawyers, but to expose their hidden assumptions that structure their work, the values that privilege some views and silence others, the identities that law privileges and those it pushes to the margins and, in doing so, to call law and lawyers to account.[92]

This impulse clearly animates a subversive approach which questions the predominance of evolutionary functionalism and the values that underpin it. This, however, needs to amount to more than critique. The purpose of subversive legal history – as one of the humanities tools available to all who study law – is to re-construct as well as to de-construct. There is a need to build a new conception of the purpose and nature of legal education.

The Chaotic Law School

H G Wells was right.

Time travel is possible. We constantly time travel in our dreams, our thoughts and our memories. Historical analysis is time travel not only in terms of going back into the past and trying to study it in its own terms but also in terms of what it tells us about the present and about the future. Time travel shows us the contingency of the past, present and the future. It debunks linear understandings of change and troubles further the relationship between change and continuity. It questions the accounts that we have of the past. Such insights are not fixed but are forever changing.[93]

Time travel disturbs and subverts our understandings. Wells' Time Traveller warns his guests that what he is about to tell them will 'have to controvert one or two ideas that are almost universally accepted'.[94] The message of this book has been that legal history does the same. A historical analysis of law is necessary to controvert the foundational ideas that law students are socialised into: the common lore. Indeed, many of the lessons espoused by the Time Traveller are also gained through subversive legal history. The last chapter came to the same

91 Owen M Fiss, 'The Challenge Ahead' (1988) 1 *Yale Journal of Law and Humanities* viii, x.

92 Austin Sarat, Matthew Anderson and Cathrine O Frank, 'Introduction: On the Origins and Prospects of the Humanistic Study of Law' in Austin Sarat, Matthew Anderson and Cathrine O Frank (eds) *Law and Humanities: An Introduction* (Cambridge University Press, 2010) 1, 11.

93 Every time you access a memory, you transform it. Every time you reactivate a memory, you re-encode it and the next time you go to access that memory what you actually access is the re-encoded version: see Michael A Yassa and Zachariah M Reagh, 'Competitive Trace Theory: A Role for the Hippocampus in Contextual Interference during Retrieval' (2013) 7(107) *Frontiers in Behavioural Neuroscience* 1.

94 H G Wells, *The Time Machine* (Gollancz, 2017) 1.

conclusion as the Time Traveller that 'Time is only a kind of Space'.[95] The two cannot be separated: there is a need for both historical and geographical analysis; a law and humanities approach. Moreover, Wells was right in identifying that the future does not necessarily bring with it improvement or progress. Wells showed that the Time Traveller had assumed that this was so: he had 'always anticipated that the people of the year Eight Hundred and Two Thousand odd would be incredibly in front of us in knowledge, art, everything'.[96] However, his first journey in time was enough to question what he now considered to be 'the absurd assumption that the men of the Future would certainly be infinitely ahead of ourselves in all their appliances'.[97] The Time Traveller, like the subversive history-informed law student or scholar, comes to question the prevalent myth of evolutionary functionalism and what they see in its place is the same thing: entropic complexity. As James Gleick has noted, the future illustrated in *The Time Machine* was that of 'maximum entropy, the condition of ultimate disorder from which there is no return'.[98]

Entropic complexity can be used to provide an alternative and a corrective to the progress myth of evolutionary functionalism. Social entropy theory, chaos theory and complexity theory underline the randomness of change, debunking any linear understanding of cause and effect and stressing that the default is increasing complexity and chaos. Such an understanding highlights the accidental, pragmatic and political nature of legal change as well as emphasising the role of human agency and challenging binary understandings of 'law and society'. It also crucially recognises that the role of jurists – those following the high priests of the common lore – has been to impose order where there is no such order. Seeing chaos as the default highlights law's authored and constructed nature and makes this the object of scrutiny and questioning. A move from accepting evolutionary functionalism to acknowledging entropic complexity transforms the role of law students from chanting the common lore to questioning that lore and subjecting the secondary sources of law to the same textual and contextual scrutiny as doctrinal study subjects primary legal sources to.

Law Schools are strange and dangerous places. Law Schools need to embrace this chaos and be critical of the role that they and others play in authoring the common lore. This necessitates not only highlighting and questioning the constructed nature of the law but also embracing different perspectives that change the lens by which law students see and understand not only law but how law operates within, is constitutive of and is constantly re-constituting what we might for lack of a better term refer to as its context. Intersectional analyses are likely to be usefully transformative given the gender, race, class, background and assumptions of many of the high priests of the common lore. Grounded approaches that take a relational approach can not only place emphasis upon agency but can also

95 Ibid 4.

96 Ibid 31–32.

97 Ibid 73.

98 James Gleick, *Time Travel: A History* (4th Estate, 2017) 120.

critique neo-liberal assumptions of equality that underpin legal fictions and assumptions concerning individual autonomy.[99] A subversive approach – of which a subversive historical analysis is a key part but not itself entirely sufficient – does not prevent law students from developing the traditional doctrinal skills that are needed for legal practice. However, it supplements this with a much wider skill-set and a much more questioning mindset that not only better prepares law students for legal practice but also for contributing to social, political, cultural and economic life. A subversive legal education developing a critical, questioning approach which sees law as contingent, which questions assumptions of linear progress and that subjects all materials – both primary and secondary – to sustained textual and contextual analysis provides a far better academic and vocational training than the current approach. More importantly, a subversive legal education provides what a university level education ought to provide: preparing students to contribute to society at large both as graduates and as citizens.

This raises the questions of how a subversive legal education would operate and what it would look like. These questions can and should be asked both at a degree level and at a module level. At degree level, the notion of legal subdisciplines needs to be questioned. The modules that populate law degrees are a heterogeneous bunch: some correspond to legal actions (contract, tort, trusts, criminal law, for instance); others relate to legal relationships (family law, education law, discrimination law and so on), while others still to particular methods or approaches to law (sociology of law, jurisprudence/legal theory, law and literature). The Law School curriculum tries to embrace and make sense of all of these classifications, treating all of them the same as standalone modules. This needs to stop. One way of rethinking law modules would be to distinguish between vertical and horizontal focuses. The study of particular legal actions and legal relationships could be seen as a vertical focus with each studied in their own module (with some awareness and analysis of the overlap). By contrast, particular methods or approaches to law could be seen as horizontal in focus in that they cut across and are part of every legal action and relationship (and therefore very module). These horizontal topics would not be reserved only to 'law and' subjects but would encompass other analyses that cut across traditional legal areas. This could include the study of non-domestic law: for instance, public international law including European Union and human rights laws could benefit from being taught across the curriculum rather than as a specialism.[100] It could

99 See, further, Maks Del Mar, 'On the Hinges of History: For a Relational Legal Historiography' in Justin Desautels-Stein and Christopher Tomlins (eds) *Searching for Contemporary Legal Thought* (Cambridge University Press, 2017) 61, 63 who has argued that 'relational historiography treats pastness as a kind of sea in which we are all submerged, and in which our travels are mostly a matter of accident, what we bump into, what we swallow as we go along without realising it. Thus, what interests the relational historian are … "the hinges of history" – the little, often unconsciously used and seemingly invisible (because used so often, or said by-the-by), modes and devices through which persons, practices and texts relate with and influence each other'.

100 As could, in Wales, the law resulting from devolution.

and should also include the study of perspectives upon the law: Feminist Legal Studies, for instance, should not be in a specialist box but should cut across and challenge the curriculum. A subversive legal education should highlight, critique and analyse gender, race, class and other inequalities. This should not be an optional part of the curriculum but an integral part of its mainstream.

This also applies at a modular level: modules devoted to legal actions or relationships should introduce students to the doctrinal study of those actions or relationships but only as one method amongst many. In Chapter 3, it was noted that subversive legal history needs to develop both an intellectual history and a social history dimension.[101] This can be applied to all legal modules: in addition to teaching doctrinal legal analysis, they also need to cover the intellectual development of the law and its development within a social context. In other words, there always needs to be both an intellectual history and a social history of the law being studied. Law modules need to include the study of the intellectual history of those particular areas of law.[102] They need to include not just the analysis of the primary legal sources but also the secondary sources of legal commentary and how they have shaped the way in which that area of law is seen and what are considered to be the pressing issues.[103] The work of high priests of the textbook tradition need to be treated not as authoritative tomes but as attempts to rationalise and make sense of that particular legal area. The names of the high priests need to be more than merely cited; they should be studied as the people they were, with reference to their backgrounds, assumptions, contributions and legacy in the areas of law. Some legal academics in recent years have paid attention to the genealogy of their sub-disciplines[104] but this work remains at the margins of the subject and outside the scope of the undergraduate law curriculum.

101 This highlighted that legal history provides both an internal and external perspective on law not least because the two cannot be demarcated.

102 David Sugarman has referred to 'the lack of an adequate intellectual history of modern legal education and thought in England': David Sugarman, 'Legal Theory, the Common Law Mind and the Making of the Textbook Tradition' in William Twining (ed) *Legal Theory and the Common Law* (Blackwell, 1986) 26, 28. In her discussion of property law, Rosemary Auchmuty has called on law teachers to cover what she calls 'the historiography of property law (that is, the ways different historians have approaches writing its history)': Rosemary Auchmuty, 'Land Law and Equity and Trusts' in Caroline Hunter (ed) *Integrating Socio-Legal Studies into the Law Curriculum* (Palgrave, 2012) 69, 77. The problem with this language, however, is that many of the authors whose work needs to be analysed would see themselves as providing an exposition of the law rather than its history.

103 On which see Susan Bartie, 'Histories of Legal Scholars: The Power of Possibility' (2014) 32(2) *Legal Studies* 305.

104 See, e.g., Janet Halley, 'What Is Family Law?: A Genealogy Part I' (2011) 23 *Yale Journal of Law and the Humanities* 1 and Janet Halley, 'What Is Family Law?: A Genealogy Part II (2011) 23 *Yale Journal of Law and the Humanities* 189; James Goudkamp and Donal Nolan (eds) *Scholars of Tort Law* (Hart, 2019). See also the Analysing Leading Works in Law series published by Routledge. This approach is perhaps best established in jurisprudence: see, e.g., Richard A Cosgrove, *Scholars of the Law: English Jurisprudence from Blackstone to Hart* (New York University Press, 1996).

This needs to change. A critical and subversive approach is required to the intellectual history of each area of law, seeing them as bundles of stories and challenging the rhetoric about them in legal discourse as well as the constructed and artificial nature of boundaries between and within areas of law.[105] This would stress a much larger scope of opportunities for reform. Moreover, in addition to teaching the intellectual history of areas of law, there is a need to teach their social history too. When studying doctrinal development, the importance of social change and extra-legal pressures needs to be more than an afterthought. Rather than speaking about what 'the law' did, there is a need to trace developments further and to look beyond the pomp of Parliament to see how the need for reform began at grass roots level. There is a need to look further than the case law of the appellate courts to determine the efficiency and the effect of legal reforms. As with intellectual history, social history will shift the focus onto people and their varied experiences. Placing a social understanding of law at the mainstream of legal education will underscore that, although legal materials are important, law is neither autonomous nor objective.

There clearly needs to be a stronger historical orientation in the Law School curriculum. However, where and how this is taught is another question. A subversive legal education regards legal history as an important method but questions whether it ought to be a separate module. And a subversive legal education would completely reject the notion that historical analysis should be specialist. Law Schools need to teach the history of the common law.[106] This may or may not be best served by legal history being a module in its own right; it may be preferable to regard it as a horizontal focus, a method.[107] The focus needs to be on ensuring that all law students are introduced to the conventional histories of

105 As Ian Ward has pointed out, if we wanted to 'trace the evolution of English constitutional law during the twentieth century, we could do worse than plot our path through successive editorial introductions to Dicey's *Law of the Constitution*': Ian Ward, *Writing the Victorian Constitution* (Palgrave, 2018) 17.

106 Rosemary Auchmuty has argued that 'the challenge for a feminist legal curriculum is to *keep* the black-letter approach of learning cases and statutes and applying the law to the facts, but to go *beyond it*'. She added: 'Paradoxically, the traditional "black-letter" legal education which still dominates UK law schools is not a bad education for a feminist, or anyone else with political awareness and experience. … [The]feminist law student needs to read the cases, the textbooks, the "great" male legal philosophers and jurists of history. You need to know the law of rape, the rules of co-ownership, the history of divorce; you need to understand the way judges reason, and how statutes come into being – because only when you grasp all these can you develop an informed feminist critique of the law' (Rosemary Auchmuty, 'Agenda for a Feminist Legal Curriculum' (2003) 23(3) *Legal Studies* 377, 394, 388–389).

107 One way of doing this would be to place historical study within an introductory law module, to then develop it though each or most other modules through the focus on the intellectual and social history of each module, and then perhaps to have a history focused module that brings this together and which enables students to highlight and critique the artificial distinctions between the modules they have studied and to carry out detailed historical analyses.

the common law. These stories and the resulting characteristics of the common law need to be explicitly presented as being authored, as constructed stories of the common law. Law students need to be aware of these stories in order to question them, in order to be subversive. It follows that in the same way that legal history should not be always taught separately, works on legal history should not always exist separately. Legal history needs to be written and presented in an accessible way. Legal history should not be written only for legal historians. Indeed, it should be written not only for lawyers. And there is a need for texts that introduce the conventional stories and the authors of those stories, enabling students to understand these before they question them. There is a need for a different kind of textbook – across the board not just on legal history but for each area of law – which introduces the law alongside its intellectual and social history and which itself is more self-aware, more explicitly authored.

In the end, the institutional questions of how the Law School curriculum and timetable are drawn up matter significantly less than the question of how Law Schools teach law. Regardless of whether legal history is seen as a vertical or horizontal subject, whether it is infused through the core curriculum or relegated to an optional module, what matters is that history is taught as a method. Law Schools need to introduce students to a range of methods. Doctrinal legal study should be explicitly introduced as a method together with the assertion that other methods are also important and are complementary. There is a need to reflect this in the learning outcomes and questions we ask of law students. The questions asked need to be rephrased and re-constructed so as not to centralise the legal issue and to encourage students to question the framing of the legal issue, asking why this has become a legal problem, why it is expressed in such a way and assessing alternatives. This last question involves comparative law playing a larger and different role. A subversive legal education draws upon comparative law not only in respect of space but also in respect of time, highlighting the contingency of law and the scope of reform. This is not reserved only to comparing other jurisdictions geographically and historically, it also involves the realisation that time and space interact and are inseparable. This means that other legal arrangements from another time and/or another space cannot be simply transplanted into the present. Rather, it underscores the complex, non-linear and knotty nature of each time and each space. This, again, underscores the importance of human agency.

A subversive legal education, as the name suggests, requires a radical reappraisal and re-design of the legal curriculum. It develops from and extends from a subversive legal history which transforms our understanding of law. It subverts what we thought we knew, questioning and critiquing the common lore. It changes the lens, shifts the focus and alters the questions we ask in order to re-construct something that, though still imperfect and constantly a work in progress, is more fit for purpose. Such an approach moves history from being relegated as a niche specialism in Law Schools to being at the beating heart of the legal curriculum. This is needed not only to rehabilitate legal history. This is needed because it is not only legal history that has been 'slowly and inevitably dying – or that… has been in a coma for the last 30 years, at least'.[108] This has also been true of Law Schools. This might appear to be an absurd claim given the increase in student numbers and the public successes of Law Schools. Yet, it is no overstatement to fear that an identity crisis grips them. Law Schools continue to be pulled between the vocational needs of the profession and the academic needs of the University as a whole and invariably fail to satisfy either master. The way ahead is for Law Schools to have the confidence to assert their distinctive mission. Not only are Law Schools in general and the undergraduate law degree in particular, both academic and vocational but also there is no line between the two. The skills developed through a subversive legal education, including and building upon doctrinal legal analysis, are the very skills that law students of today need in order to be the graduates, professionals and citizens of tomorrow.

Theodore Plucknett once observed that 'the real question is not whether we should teach legal history, but whether we can give to students law, and nothing but law, and still call it a liberal education'.[109] The message of this book is that these two questions are related. Teaching legal history is a way of ensuring that law students not only receive more than law but also develop the ability to truly critique the law and to subvert and question its institutional and scholarly apparatus. Doctrinal legal analysis is a vital part of the law student's toolkit but is only one part of it. Historical understanding and analysis is another crucial tool. For too long, this tool has been the preserve of specialists with many legal academics carrying out historical research resisting the label of legal historian. Legal history is too important to be left just to legal historians. History has the ability to subvert, de-construct and re-construct everything that we think we know about the law. It provides a subversive corrective to legal and social orthodoxies. History is therefore an essential tool for all those studying and understanding law. We are all legal historians now.

108 Daniel Siemens, 'Towards a New Cultural History of Law' (2012) 2 *InterDisciplines* 18, 19.
109 Theodore F T Plucknett, *Early English Legal Literature* (Cambridge University Press, 1958) 17.

Afterword

This book develops an argument that is the exact opposite to that developed in my previous two sole-authored books.

In those two books I explored and argued for the development of Law and Religion as a sub-discipline in its own right.[1] I wrote against a backdrop of a new legal framework regulating religion coming into effect in England and Wales: religion became seen as a human right, religious discrimination and hatred became unlawful and there were high profile cases about the right to wear religious dress and discriminate on grounds of sexual orientation. My first book, *Law and Religion*, argued that these developments and the resulting academic attention now meant that Law and Religion could be spoken of and formalised in the same way as family law, sports law and other legal areas that focus on relationships. I followed this up by developing institutional forms that nurtured the development of this sub-discipline: learned organisations, specialist conferences, book series and the like. My second book, *Religion, Law and Society*, developed this theme further, showing why Law and Religion academics should talk with and learn from sociologists of religion.

However, the seeds of doubt were planted in the final chapter of that book. There, I looked at the sociology of law and explored how it could serve as a bridge between academic lawyers and sociologists. In so doing, I found myself lamenting the way in which the sociology of law had become a specialism – a legal sub-discipline in its own right – and how this meant that its methods and theories were not part of the toolkit of all academic lawyers. I mentioned in passing that the same was true of legal history. This book has returned to that suggestion and made an argument that is the exact opposite to that developed in the previous two books: here I have argued against the development of legal history as a sub-discipline in its own right. Indeed, this book applies this not only to legal history but also calls for a re-construction of legal education generally. The argument developed here is that legal history is more important than it is commonly assumed to be. This book contends that a historical approach should

1 Russell Sandberg, *Law and Religion* (Cambridge University Press, 2011); Russell Sandberg, *Religion, Law and Society* (Cambridge University Press, 2014).

be at the beating heart of the Law School but that in order to be so the historical approach needs to be subversive. In making that argument, the call for subversion is not made lightly. My critique has focused on ideal types. There is much excellent work done in the field of legal history and in Law Schools generally. I continue to passionately believe that both are important. There is no subject I would rather teach and it is a pleasure to see how the law degree can engage students and develop the skills needed in the twenty-first century: the ability to focus and interrogate the details while simultaneously paying attention to the wider context and the real world setting. My critique here comes from a position of frustration. I am frustrated that the potential of legal history and of law as an academic discipline is not being fully realised.

My argument in this book has been that the fates of legal history and law as an academic discipline are connected. A historical approach provides the subversive critique that Law Schools need and this means that legal history ceases to be a specialism relegated at the margins of Law School life. My critique is meant to be constructive. I hope that this book is about highlighting and grabbing opportunities rather than conducting post-mortems. It seeks to set an agenda. This book seeks to do one of the main things that, in my mind, a subversive approach can provide: it shows an alternative; it shows that different ways of thinking and doing law are possible.

I also know that I am not alone in the regret of the current marginalisation of legal history. There are several works that are critical of the development of legal history and most, if not all, legal historians call for a more historical approach to law (indeed, it would be odd if they did not). It is also important to note that it is written from the perspective of a Law School in England and Wales. Although it is hoped that the book will appeal to others from different disciplines and jurisdictions, the arguments here are coloured by my experiences and the norms of where I work. It is written from my perspective.

Indeed, this is true of all books. This is one of the main themes of this book: how a subversive approach is needed to uncover the lie at the heart of legal education that law is universal, natural and autonomous. As we have seen, rather, law is contingent, constructed and authored. And we also need to treat authors of legal works not just as authorities to cite but as contributors to the intellectual development of law. We also need to note the lie common to most books: the lie on the spine of this book. My name on the spine of the book suggests that this book is created by me. However, this is a lie: the book that you are holding in your hand is not entirely my own work. No book ever is the work of one person. Rather, it shaped by a range of influences and the author's experiences. Much of this has happened unwittingly and in ways that I cannot articulate but there are some influences that I would like to highlight:

The roots of this book can be dated back even further than that mention in *Religion, Law and Society*, back to my own undergraduate degree and the second year module on English legal history that I studied under Professor Thomas Watkin. That module made my Law degree make sense. It was from knowing from what and how they had developed that contract, tort and land law made sense to me. In recent years, after I had written that passage in *Religion, Law and Society* and became intrigued about the importance and contribution of a historical approach to law, it has been a pleasure to reinstate the legal history module to the curriculum at Cardiff and to see it have the same effect upon my students. And so in addition to the debt I owe to Professor Thomas Watkin whose undergraduate lectures on the topic many years ago first stimulated my interest in Legal History, I am also indebted to those who have taught the legal history course with me, Professor Norman Doe and Dr Sharon Thompson, from whom I have learnt a great deal and who have both inspired my work in this area through their dazzling scholarship and outstanding friendship. I have also gained a great deal from the students who have studied the module over the years. Their questions, puzzled looks and general indulgence have helped shape many of the ideas expressed here (and the omission of several other ideas!).

I have also benefitted from presenting aspects of this book at various conferences, workshops and guest lectures over the last few years. Nods and raised eyebrows have all been very helpful in respectively solidifying convictions or sending me back to the drawing board. I am immensely grateful to all who attended, questioned and encouraged. Some of the ideas in this book have been previously published in embryonic form. I am indebted to peer reviewers, editors and readers for their feedback. My particular debts are as follows:

- Some of the ideas here developed as Chapters 1–3 originally took the form of the introductory chapter to a four volume collection of previously published articles and book chapters on legal history.[2] They were also presented as part of a staff seminar at the School of Law and Politics at Cardiff University in September 2016.[3] They have also been the basis of guest lectures to successive cohorts of postgraduate students on the Themes in Empirical Studies in Law module at Cardiff.
- Chapter 4 was first developed in a presentation at the 'Doing Women's Legal History' conference at the Institute of Advanced Legal Studies conference in London in October 2016 and then refined in a presentation to the legal history stream of the Society of Legal Scholars Conference at Queen Mary's University London in September 2018. The chapter also draws upon publications on feminist legal theory which I have co-written with Dr Sharon Thompson.[4]

2 Russell Sandberg and Norman Doe, 'Textual and Contextual Legal History' in Norman Doe and Russell Sandberg (eds) *Law and History – Critical Concepts in Law* (Routledge, 2017) 1.

3 An extremely abridged version of some of the arguments was published as Russell Sandberg, 'The Time for Legal History: Some Reflections on Maitland and Milsom Fifty Years On' (2018) 180 *Law & Justice* 21.

4 Most notably, Sharon Thompson and Russell Sandberg, 'Multicultural Jurisdictions: The Need for a Feminist Approach to Law and Religion' in Russell Sandberg (ed) *Leading Works in Law and Religion* (Routledge, 2019) 179.

- Chapter 5 has its origins in a paper presented at 'The Law and Politics of Temporality and Periodization' conference held in Cardiff University in May 2017 and elements of it were also presented as the keynote address at the 'Multidisciplinary Approaches to Contemporary Issues in Religion and Society' workshop at the University of Westminster in October 2019.

In addition, this book and the arguments developed in it have also benefitted from more informal feedback and indeed often from conversations and interactions on other things entirely. Almost every work conversation over the last few years has fed into this book in some way and so I cannot thank or acknowledge every one. However, as is customary I would like to conclude by mentioning my largest debts, excluding my mortgage.

This is the first book in Routledge's Transforming Legal Histories series. I am very grateful to my co-editors on the series, Dr Sharon Thompson, Professor Lydia Hayes and Dr Katie Richards for their support and encouragement. Although this book seeks to set an agenda for the series and more generally, it does not seek to prescribe the content or approach of the series as it develops. I am also thankful to Alison Kirk and her team at Routledge for all that they have done to support the series in general and this book in particular. During the writing process, I have been indebted to Dr Sharon Thompson for her comments on draft ideas, daft ideas and chapters in draft. As ever, many of my best ideas have been formed in conversations with her (and usually when I am not the one speaking). Her own research into the history of Family Law reform and the role of activism provides a dazzling example not only of Feminist Legal History and of the subversive legal history that I have argued for in this book but also of the very best that legal scholarship has to offer.

I owe the most, of course, to my family and especially to my partner Emma. We are all stories in the end. And it is thanks to them that my story is a good one.

Russell Sandberg
Neath, South Wales
January 2021

Index

Note: Page numbers followed by "n" denote notes.

For Product Safety Concerns and Information please contact our EU
representative GPSR@taylorandfrancis.com
Taylor & Francis Verlag GmbH, Kaufingerstraße 24, 80331 München, Germany

www.ingramcontent.com/pod-product-compliance
Lightning Source LLC
LaVergne TN
LVHW011126300926
849160LV00008B/532
9781032044415